Reversing Industrial Decline?

Industrial Structure and Policy in Britain and Her Competitors

Reversing Industrial Decline?

Industrial Structure and Policy in Britain and Her Competitors

Edited by
Paul Hirst *and*
Jonathan Zeitlin

Learning Resources
Centre

BERG
Oxford/New York/Hamburg
Distributed exclusively in the US and Canada by
St. Martin's Press, New York

1111721/4

First published in 1989 by
Berg Publishers Limited
77 Morrell Avenue, Oxford OX4 1NQ, UK
175 Fifth Avenue/Room 400, New York, NY 10010, USA
Nordalbingerweg 14, 2000 Hamburg 61, FRG

British Library Cataloguing in Publication Data

Reversing industrial decline: industrial
    structure and policy in Britain and her
    competitors.
    1. Industrial development
    I. Hirst, Paul Q. (Paul Quentin), 1946–
    II. Zeitlin, Jonathan
    338

    ISBN 0-85496-029-5

Library of Congress Cataloging-in-Publication Data
CIP data applied for.

Printed in Great Britain by Billings of Worcester

Contents

Contributors   vi

Introduction *Paul Hirst and Jonathan Zeitlin*   1

1 Flexible Specialisation and the Re-emergence of Regional
   Economies *Charles F. Sabel*   17

2 Facing up to Manufacturing Failure *Karel Williams, John
   Williams, Colin Haslam and Andrew Wardlow*   71

3 Flexible Automation and Factory Politics: The United
   Kingdom in Comparative Perspective *Bryn Jones*   95

4 The Search for Flexibility: Subcontracting Networks in
   French and British Engineering *Edward H. Lorenz*   122

5 Innovation, Skills and Training: Micro-electronics and
   Manpower in the United Kingdom and West Germany
   Adrian Campbell, Wendy Currie and Malcolm Warner   133

6 Markets, Technology and Local Intervention: The Case of
   Clothing *Jonathan Zeitlin and Peter Totterdill*   155

7 Sector Strategies and Industrial Policy: The Furniture
   Industry and the Greater London Enterprise
   Board *Michael H. Best*   191

8 Sector Strategy in the West Midlands *David Elliott and
   Michael Marshall*   223

9 Macro-economic Management and Industrial
   Policy *Jim Tomlinson*   248

10 The Politics of Industrial Policy *Paul Hirst*   269

Index

Contributors

Paul Hirst is Professor of Social Theory at Birkbeck College, University of London.

Jonathan Zeitlin is Lecturer in Modern Social and Economic History at Birkbeck College, University of London. He has worked as a consultant on industrial policy for the Greater London Council and the United Nations Industrial Development Organisation.

Charles F. Sabel is Professor of Social Science at the Massachusetts Institute of Technology. He has worked as an adviser on industrial policy to trade unions in Austria and Italy, the Green Party in West Germany and local economic development agencies in the United States.

Karel and John Williams are, respectively, Senior Lecturer in and Professor of Economic History at the University College of Wales at Aberystwyth. **Colin Haslam** is Lecturer in Sociology at North East London Polytechnic, and **Andrew Wardlow** is a research student at The University College of Wales at Aberystwyth. Karel Williams, John Williams and Colin Haslam are the authors of **The Breakdown of Austin Rover** (Berg Publishers, 1987), have submitted evidence to the House of Commons Select Committee on Motor Vehicle Components, and together with Anthony Cutler, produced the **Aberystwyth Report on Coal** (1985).

Bryn Jones is Lecturer in Industrial Sociology at the University of Bath.

Edward H. Lorenz is Associate Professor of Economics at Notre Dame University.

Adrian Campbell is a Research Fellow at the Institute of Design and Operations Management in the University of Aston. **Malcolm Warner** is Professor of Sociology and Research Co-ordinator at Henley, the Management College and Brunel University. **Wendy Currie** is a Research Associate at Henley, the Management College.

Peter Totterdill is Director of Research at the Employment and Economic Development Unit of Sheffield City Council. He has also worked as an Economic Development Officer for Nottingham City Council and is a member of the steering committee of Local Action for Textiles and Clothing.

Michael H. Best is Professor of Economics at the University of Massachusetts at Amherst. He has worked as an industrial strategist for the Greater London Enterprise Board and is currently a board member of the Massachusetts Product Development Corporation.

David Elliott and **Michael Marshall** are Principal Economists with the West Midlands Enterprise Board.

Jim Tomlinson is Senior Lecturer in Economics at Brunel University.

Tables and Figures

Tables

2.1.	The UK's share in the volume of manufactured exports	72
2.2.	Britain's balance of trade in manufactures	73
2.3.	Net output and employment in the advanced countries	76
2.4.	British trade in manufactures with West Germany and Japan, 1986	87
6.1.	The market share of major clothing and textile outlets, 1977	158
6.2.	The structure of the European clothing industry, 1971	159
6.3.	British clothing industry enterprises by size of total employment, 1982	160
6.4.	UK imports and exports of made-up clothing	161
6.5.	UK trade balance in clothing	168
6.6.	Clothing imports by main trading area	169
7.1.	World export of furniture by major furniture exporters	197
7.2.	Furniture consumption and imports in various European countries	198
7.3.	Furniture trade balance, 1980 and 1984	199
7.4.	Losers and survivors in the North London furniture industry	200
7.5.	Macro-economic data for Italian furniture firms with over 20 employees, 1967–81	206
7.6.	Consumption of Italian furniture and wood furnishing business units by numbers of employees, 1961–81	207
7.7.	Composition of the work-force in Italian furniture firms, 1961–81	208
9.1.	Levels of import penetration	249
9.2.	Fixed investment in manufacturing in the UK, 1965–85	262
9.3.	Gross fixed capital formation	263
9.4.	Share of investment in government expenditure on goods and services	264

Figures

8.1.	Unemployment rates in the West Midlands and UK	225
8.2.	Employment structure in the West Midlands and the UK, 1981	226

Introduction

Paul Hirst and Jonathan Zeitlin

Policies for industrial renewal are now an important feature of political debate in advanced industrial countries such as the United Kingdom and the United States, where they have been proposed as a response to fundamental failure in the performance of the manufacturing sector. The one-time economic leaders are now faced with the need to understand the economic success of countries such as West Germany, Italy and Japan and to try to achieve by means of public policy initiatives what they have failed to do in the marketplace. There are those, generally on the right of the political spectrum, who deny this failure. They see the UK and USA as 'mature economies' moving towards concentration on financial and marketed services. These views encounter two basic difficulties: first, that standards of living in UK and USA are declining in comparison with the successful manufacturing nations; and second, that it is the allegedly 'mature' economies that face the greatest and growing problems of macro-economic regulation. Industrial policies are proposed by those committed to maintaining the highest possible levels of employment and preserving a high average standard of living, but these policies are no longer tied to traditional Keynesian or state socialist recipes for intervention. Indeed, what is distinctive about the industrial policy debate is the attempt to devise new patterns of economic regulation that break out of the opposition between the free market and state provision.

This book is concerned both to diagnose the sources of industrial failure of nations such as the UK and USA in the prevailing patterns of international competition, and to prescribe new policy instruments in order to respond to these patterns. Four major themes are considered: the emergence of new patterns of international competition centred on market fragmentation and productive flexibility; the British economy's response to international pressures and explanations for the competitive failure of its manufacturing sector; the evaluation of strategies for the regeneration of regional and local economies; and the macroeconomic and political requirements for industrial renewal at the national level. The book, therefore, combines analysis and policy pre-

1

scription, and, in line with this combination, it is written both by social
scientific analysts and policy practitioners.

International Competition and the Rise of Flexible Specialisation

The 1970s and 1980s have seen far-reaching dislocations of the international economic environment which had sustained the long post-war
boom. Unstable exchange rates and raw material prices; slowly growing national markets, intensified international competition and fragmentation of demand for manufactured products; restrictive macro-
economic policies and the growth of protectionism: each of these
interrelated tendencies has dramatically increased the uncertainty surrounding economic decision-making and investment strategies. The
persistent volatility of international markets has given rise in turn to
marked changes in perceptions of the basis for competitive success in
manufacturing, which a growing number of observers now see in terms
of a shift away from mass production to flexible specialisation (Piore
and Sabel 1984; Sabel and Zeitlin 1985; Tolliday and Zeitlin 1987).

At the most basic level, flexible specialisation can be defined as a
technological paradigm or ideal-typical model of industrial efficiency:
the manufacture of specialised goods using flexible machinery and
skilled labour in contrast to the mass production of standardised goods
using special-purpose equipment and unskilled workers. But, as Piore
and Sabel (1984) were at pains to emphasise, both flexible specialisation
and mass production also depend for their success on a contingent and
variable framework of institutional regulation at the micro level of the
firm or region and the macro level of the national and international
economy. Hence the technological dynamism of each model and its
potentialities for future development cannot be evaluated outside of a
definite institutional and environmental context.

In his chapter in this book, Charles F. Sabel outlines the major
features of the shift towards flexible specialisation observable in the
advanced industrial countries under conditions of continued economic
turbulence. First and most striking is the emergence of highly successful regional economies or industrial districts composed of interdependent networks of small firms in parts of Italy, West Germany,
Scandinavia, the USA and Japan. These districts stand out not only for
their flexible and innovative response to the demands of changing
markets but also for the complex balance of co-operation and competition between individual firms which makes possible the constant recombination of resources. Equally important is the decentralisation of
large multinational corporations into looser federations of operating
units and their pursuit of more specialised products and more flexible
production methods. These developments, Sabel argues, are produc-

ing a convergence of large and small-firm structures as small firms in the industrial districts build wider forms of common services often inspired by large-firm models, while the large firms themselves increasingly seek to recreate among their subsidiaries and subcontractors the collaborative relationships characteristic of the industrial districts. This convergence in turn permits a useful redefinition of flexible specialisation as a system of network production 'in which firms know that they do not know precisely what they will have to produce, and further that they must count on the collaboration of workers and subcontractors in meeting the market's eventual demand'.

This interpretation of recent shifts in manufacturing practice as a movement from mass production towards flexible specialisation is far from uncontroversial, and it would not be accepted by some of the contributors to this volume (see also Wiliams *et al.* 1987). As Sabel himself observes, mass production was never so dominant as the consensus about its technological superiority might have led one to suppose, and considerable ambiguity surrounds the future significance of current experiments in industrial organisation. But, as we shall see in the next section, there is evidence to support two further observations. In those regions and companies which have responded most successfully to changing patterns of international competition, elements of flexible specialisation can be discerned not only in day-to-day practice, but also in the expectations of key economic and political decision-makers. Conversely, flexible specialisation strategies are also least present, or least effectively applied, in those regional and national economies experiencing the greatest difficulty in the current phase of industrial restructuring — notably the UK.

British Decline and its Causes

The second main purpose of this volume is to describe the place and fortunes of the British economy in this new regime of international competition and to consider explanations for the rapid decline of the UK's manufacturing base in the 1970s and 1980s. The British manufacturing sector failed to adapt to the pattern of the internationalisation of trade in manufactures between the advanced industrial countries that has developed on an increasing scale since the late 1960s. British firms suffered particularly from the new regime of internationalised competition, fragmented markets and slow and uncertain growth in world trade.

The UK has suffered accelerating industrial decline since 1973, summed up in the concept of 'deindustrialisation'. British firms have lost domestic market shares and British industry has suffered a marked decline in both employment and output. This crisis in British manufacturing is often seen by commentators as just another stage in the long process of economic decline going back at east to the last quarter of the nineteenth century. This perspective tends to obscure the specificity of what has happened since the early 1970s. The UK has operated under a number of quite distinct regimes of international trade and competition in this century. In the open and internationalised economy of the pre-1914 era the UK was suffering from foreign import penetration, particularly in new and advanced sectors like chemical products and electrical goods, and was failing to innovate and adapt in order to respond to the superior production methods and products of foreign competitors, notably Germany, in established sectors such as iron and steel. Between the First World War and the 1960s the regimes of international trade allowed for a relatively 'sheltered' national manufacturing sector, with secure home markets. During the First World War significant sectors of British industry were modernised in order to substitute for German imports. During the 1930s industry was protected by tariffs. During the Second World War it was protected by a state monopoly on foreign trade and a non-competitive regime of war production. In the immediate post-war period British manufacturing enjoyed both sheltered internal markets and a weak competitive environment with strong demand for its exports because of the large-scale destruction of industrial capacity in key competitor nations during the war.

In the late 1960s and early 1970s Britain was again exposed to strong competition in an open international economy. Competitors' industries had not only been rebuilt, but West Germany, Italy and France had enjoyed faster post-war rates of growth than the UK. In this period the combined effects of GATT and joining the EEC opened British markets to foreign competitors as never before. Until the late 1970s British economic decline was perceived as a relative decline in the UK's share of world trade and as slower economic growth than in key competitor nations like France, West Germany and Japan. The UK may have been declining, but output was growing and the economy was at near full-employment levels. In the late 1970s the phenomenon of 'deindustrialisation' was first recognised and with it evidence of absolute decline in output and employment in sector after sector.

Certainly, it is necessary to look for the long-run causes of the UK's economic decline, but in respect of manufacturing it is misleading to present decline as a single and continuous process stretching back into the nineteenth century. In the twentieth century the UK has suffered different conjunctures of decline and different types of decline, punctuated by periods of industrial revitalisation and recovery. These periods of renewal generally coincided with a weakening of the regime of international competition and the deliberate or *de facto* protection of domestic production.

How can we explain this failure to meet the prevailing standards of international competition in sector after sector of manufacturing? The chapter by Karel Williams *et al.* addresses this issue, trying to refine and develop the analysis of their earlier book (Williams *et al* 1983). They make four essential points.

The first of these is the failure of firm-level management decision-making in relation to the character of the product, the nature of the market and appropriate marketing strategy. Firms in many different industries, from motor cycles to machine-tools, have suffered a simultaneous failure to design and produce the right product ranges and to market them effectively, with adequate investment in sales and service networks. These failures are so widespread that they cannot be due to mere happenstance, but must be due to basic features of British management's approach and to the environment of the firm.

Second, strategic failure is coupled with failure effectively to utilise forms of production technique that have proved successful elsewhere. Often machinery is imported but not the forms of organisation and working needed to make it fully efficient. In Chapter 3, Jones gives a good example of the rigid and inflexible use of potentially flexible automation equipment by British and American companies compared to the use made by the Japanese and the Italians. Jones's discussion of the flexible use of automation shows that the potential of computerised technologies for the manufacture of a wide and changing array of products is possible only if accompanied by appropriate management practices and the flexible utilisation of skilled labour. In Japan and Emilia-Romagna equipment is integrated into already flexible systems of work organisation whereas in the UK and USA narrow job definitions, an obsession with hierarchical control and managerial pressures for short-term cost savings inhibit the pursuit of flexibility. The failure to organise production properly, the inefficient use of technology as compared with the practices of competitors, therefore, leads to a failure to exploit investment to the full, to enjoy comparable productivity gains and profit margins comparable to those enjoyed by competitors.

Third, Williams, *et al.* stress the importance of non-price factors in foreign competitive advantage. Superior design, production quality and service often allow foreign firms to succeed even with a price premium. British managements and government policy-makers are frequently obsessed with price and particularly with unit labour costs as factors in competition. Labour is often blamed for productivity failures that are predominantly within management's sphere of responsibility.

Fourth, they also stress that a crucial determinant of manufacturing performance is the utilisation of investment and not just the overall level of investment. Those on the left and right of the political spectrum often simplify this issue. Apologists for British industry often argue that, expressed in terms of percentage of GNP, British rates of invest-ment are not so different from those of major competitors, while critics on the left often imply that British failure in manufacturing is mainly a question of underinvestment because there are more profitable non-industrial alternatives. British failure is more complex. Similar percen-tages hide smaller amounts of investment in absolute terms because British GNP is significantly less than that of major competitors like West Germany. Failure to utilise investments effectively means that they earn less and are less profitable because they are unable to retain or capture a satisfactory domestic market share. Hence non-industrial investments *do* tend to be more profitable, but to a significant degree because of the failure of the manufacturing sector itself.

How can we explain this poor quality of management decision-making which Williams *et al.* contend is central to British industrial decline? The issue is a complex one and it would be naive to wish it away with references to 'national culture' or even 'management atti-tudes'. These words are merely a cover for a vacuity of analysis. Many industrial managers do desperately want to succeed, and know enough about the successes of competitors to try to copy them. Why do they so often get it wrong? Explanations which centre on the decline of the 'entrepreneurial spirit' in the 1880s are hard pressed to explain why in the 1980s, obsessed with 'enterprise' culture', mistake after mistake is still being made.

One argument can be offered on the basis of Sabel's chapter and is echoed by a number of contributors, that is, that British firms have been generally unwilling to adopt a strategy of flexible specialisation. Furthermore, even when they have tried to do so, they have seen it in terms of specific manufacturing techniques rather than as a complex ensemble of practices at firm level combined with relationships with subcontractors, with other firms, and with the sectoral and district institutions which support and sustain this system of production. Williams *et al.* disagree with this view and see British failure as essen-tially due to the reinforcing effects of the inability to retain or capture market share on already sub-optimal organisations of volume produc-tion. A limited market reinforces the poor quality of production organi-sation by denying the firm economies of scale comparable to those of competitors.

The chapter by Adrian Campbell, Malcolm Warner and Wendy Currie emphasises the education and training policies for both manage-ment and labour which form the context of poor decision-making and poor utilisation of production technique. What they emphasise is the limited character of industrial training at *all* levels compared to that in West Germany. British practice tends to make the division between management and other levels very rigid, to separate conception and execution, and to try to minimise autonomous skill and responsibility at lower levels in the hierarchy. British industry could be characterised as a narrow band of rather rigidly trained specialist industrial managers, sandwiched between a financially orientated senior management and workers expected to execute given orders, with little use for generalised skills since the initiative they make possible is minimised by the overall management system. Flexible patterns of working rely on less rigid hierarchy, upon the skill base for initiative, and on the ability of workers at all levels to upgrade their specific skills from a sound base of education in general principles.

Edward Lorenz's chapter uses a comparative study of subcontracting relationships in Lyons and the West Midlands to point to another source of weakness in British industry, the isolation of the firm and the lack of a supportive industrial environment. This may seen irrelevant to very large firms like Austin Rover, for example, but, on the contrary, even with such giants it shows up in a failure to build an ongoing and two-sided relationship with components manufacturers and subcontractors. The British climate of political debate and management thinking stresses the efficiency gains from competition virtually to the complete exclusion of comprehension of the value of collaboration and mutual assistance between firms. A supportive 'industrial environment' means not only patterns of public support for firms, but also that firms themselves contribute to building the 'public sphere' for a specific industry or industrial region. The stress on cut-throat competition between firms and the virtual isolation of the firm except for market relations with others inevitably inhibit the building of patterns of collaboration based on trust between firms. Such patterns can benefit the majority of firms and help to protect and upgrade the whole industry or industrial district.

Emphasising the saliency of price competition leads neighbour firms into mutually destructive and divisive strategies, the primacy of price-cutting forces firms into a downward spiral of cutting back on 'overheads' such as research and development and taking product ranges down-market. In such a climate there is an inevitable failure to create an inter-firm culture that values and strives for quality design and which upgrades the skills of the labour force too match rising product quality. The result of intense competition between manufacturers, reinforced by ruthless price policies on the part of major retailers, is to drive an industry towards poor-quality products, static production techniques, and the given skills of a labour force whose wages and conditions are driven down to maintain price competitiveness. At the end of this cycle the firm is dependent on the low-price segment of the market and, therefore, open to competition from even cheaper newly industrialising countries (NICs).

Lest this be thought an exaggeration, one has only to turn to the chapters by Jonathan Zeitlin and Peter Totterdill on clothing, and by

Michael H. Best on furniture, to see graphic examples of this process. Best shows the destructive nature of ruthless price competition in the North London furniture industry and the impossibility, on this antagonistic basis, of any strategy of upgrading design and product quality to match the Italians. As in furniture, so in clothing; competitive pressures led British firms to concentrate on long runs of cheap garments and paved the way for large-scale import penetration from low-wage producers, whilst other high-wage countries, such as Italy, creamed off the quality end of the market.

Is such co-operation possible? Lorenz's discussion of the Lyons metal working industry indicates that it is and that it is mutually beneficial to the participating firms. He identifies three forms of such co-operation: sharing knowledge about markets, industrial processes, and so on, through inter-firm contacts and through local 'public' institution; aiding, upgrading and investing in subcontractors as a strategy for raising overall product quality and for ensuring reliable and prompt supplies of parts; and sharing market opportunities, where firms with an excess of orders subcontract to or use the facilities of less successful firms.

The 'public sphere' of British industry at both local and national level is limited in extent and functions. In particular, British firms are unwilling to contribute, to co-operate, or to invest in industrial training as a 'public resource' and they fear the diffusion of basic skills that make workers more capable and more mobile. As Campbell, Warner and Currie show, West Germany is much more effective at creating a co-operative climate among industry, labour and the state for industrial training.

The upshot is that an emphasis on price competition and the absence of a supportive inter-firm culture encourages the openness to foreign competition at the upper end of the market on the basis of superior design and quality and at the lower end from low-cost products form NICs. British consumers have not generally shared British manufacturers' and policy-makers' attitudes about the saliency of price and prefer superior foreign goods. British manufacturers have failed to work to create a climate in which best practice in product design, production organisation and labour skills is generalised, and in which upgrading within the whole industry and region is seen as a valuable goal by the industrial firms themselves.

Regenerating Local Economies

The third main purpose of this book is to assess local and regional strategies of industrial renewal. Across a wide range of advanced countries, as Sabel describes, the devolution of industrial policy to local authorities has formed a major feature of the political response to the upheavals in the international economy. In part, this trend reflects the re-emergence of regions as meaningful economic units, as discussed earlier; but even more it reflects the political disintegration of the welfare state and the declining support for macro-economic policies aimed at promoting employment and growth at a national level. The resurgence of local industrial intervention initially represented little more in most cases than *ad hoc* responses to the retreat of the national state, but increasingly, as Sabel argues, such policies have given rise to more conscious strategies of endogenous development aimed at increasing the coherence of the local economy and its adaptability in the face of a changing external environment.

Undoubtedly the best publicised example of local industrial policy in Britain has been the Greater London Council (GLC), abolished by the Conservative government in the spring of 1986. In assessing the experience of the GLC, a careful balance sheet is required, since it has become a political shibboleth whose record is either defended or denigrated *in toto* depending on one's ideological standpoint.[1] The GLC's activities ranged in any case from grand declarations of principle derived from abstract tenets of Marxist theory to a plurality of initiatives at the firm and sectoral levels often inspired by countervailing assumptions.

In the sphere of industrial policy, there were three major limitations to the GLC's approach. First, through the Greater London Enterprise Board (GLEB), it emphasised direct investment in firms as the central instrument of industrial intervention. As Best's chapter shows, the GLEB's emphasis on direct investment was based on the assumption that taking an equity stake in a firm brought control over the activities of its management, an assumption which largely proves illusory in practice. Second, as part of its strategy of 'restructuring for labour', the GLC tended to treat investment as a means of tipping the balance of power within the enterprise towards the work-force, pursuing social and political objectives unrelated or explicitly counterposed to economic success. These commitments in turn led the GLC explicitly to avoid working with smaller firms, since the costs of investment assessment were higher for these firms while they were also believed to offer less favourable conditions for worker organisation; the Council thus cut itself off from large sections of the metropolitan industrial structure such as the clothing industry.[2]

But these failures at the strategic level were counterbalanced by a variety of more pragmatic interventions, such as the establishment of a Computer-Aided Design bureau for the East End clothing industry or the financing of a collaborative network of small furniture producers, as well as by the accumulation of detailed knowledge and expertise in a number of key industrial sectors. As Best's chapter itself illustrates, these experiences were giving rise to considerable rethinking of overall policies within the GLC, and its industrial interventions can thus be regarded as a collective learning process with wider implications which was prematurely cut short by abolition.

The West Midland County Council (WMCC) was a regional authority comparable in scale to the GLC and abolished at the same time by Mrs Thatcher. But there were also important differences in its access to capital and severity of industrial decline, since the GLC by contrast could draw on lucrative business rates while deindustrialisation in London was more localised and counterbalanced by the bouyancy of the financial and service sectors. Hence, the chapter by David Elliot and Michael Marshall shows, the balance between ideological principles and pragmatic intervention was drawn rather differently in the West Midlands than in London. The WMCC and the West Midland Enterprise Board also favoured direct investment and sought to improve the position of labour in the region. But where direct investment seemed inappropriate, as in the case of clothing, they were also prepared to support the establishment of agencies for the provision of collective service and to work together with private employers in an effort to improve the market position of local firms and thus upgrade employment conditions.

These characteristics of pragmatic experimentation are even more pronounced in the lower tier of local authorities such as Nottingham City Council which have survived the current phase of abolition. Their lower political profile and more limited financial base have necessarily meant less pretence at grand strategic capacity and more emphasis on the accumulation of detailed knowledge of local industry and on cheap and effective forms of intervention through the provision of collective services, as in the case of the clothing centres discussed by Zeitlin and Totterdill. These smaller councils have also felt the need to pool their expertise, resources and political clout among themselves, and hence are pioneering the development of new structures of inter-authority collaboration, from Local Action for Textiles and Clothing (LATC), described in this volume, to the Motor Industry Local Authority Network (MILAN) and the South East Economic Development Strategy (SEEDS).[3] But, however promising these initiatives may appear, there will be stark limits to what they can accomplish if the central state in Britain continues its efforts — against the grain of developments in other advanced economies — to destroy the financial and political autonomy of local government.

National Policies and Industrial Renewal

As these efforts at inter-authority collaboration show, there are clear limits to what can be achieved by public policy at the local level alone. The very scale of British national decline and the continuing failure of

British firms to reverse it by their own efforts point to the need for national policies; examining these policies is the final main purpose of this volume. Combatting large-scale deindustrialisation presents politicians and economic policy-makers with an entirely novel problem. It is all too evident that neither an adequate analysis of the problem nor policy instruments to solve it have been developed. Those seeking to frame positive policies for renewal are faced with a very difficult and unstable economic environment. The internationalisation of trade in manufactures among the advanced industrial countries means that a national strategy for industrial renewal has to be geared to meeting the prevailing conditions of international competition. But since failure to meet these conditions is the main source of national industrial decline this is hardly a very helpful specification of the policy goal. At the same time there is a great deal of unresolved argument about why major competitors are successful and the nature of the prevailing trends in competition. The result is that both investment planning by large firms and central government industrial policies are bedevilled by uncertainty. The Conservative government in the UK has explicitly avoided an activist policy of industrial recovery, leaving the task to the efforts of firms. The Labour opposition has made much of the need for an industrial policy, but there is little evidence that the Party has matched rhetoric with effective policy content.

Most of the contributors to this volume accept that flexible specialisation strategies have enabled firms to minimise the effects of uncertainty stemming from fragmented markets and slow growth in world trade. Those national economies and regions that have weathered the crisis of the 1970s and 1980s best seem to be those whose firms have gone furthest down the route of flexible specialisation or have managed to introduce elements of flexibility into mass production. The countries that have failed so to adapt, including the UK now face the complex problem of trying to achieve by public policy what the national firms have failed to achieve by their own strategies.

This is difficult because traditional tools of economic management and intervention are simply inappropriate for the problem. Keynesian strategies of stimulating output by demand management assume industrial crisis is the by-product of a deficiency of effective demand. A policy that depends on the adjustment of macro-economic aggregates presupposes an effective industrial sector and managements that make appropriate investment and production decisions. Keynesianism has nothing to say about an open economy in which too many domestic managements get these decisions wrong or where stimulating effective demand may simply offer a bonus to foreign competitors. State planning of production and the central direction of investment are unlikely to lead to high-quality decision-making about particular sectors. There is no reason to suppose that public officials will have better information about products, production processes and marketing strategies than the managers of firms, and if the firms fail to make the correct decisions why assume that officials will succeed in doing so? Planning works best in a stable and predictable economic environment, not in a world of uncertainty and unpredictable change, and it also works best when setting overall goals rather than substituting for detailed management decisions.

The failure of these traditional Keynesian and state socialist 'solutions' is in-built, they are answers to other economic problems and cannot address problems of modern industrial decline at their own level. *Laissez-faire* policies are not an answer either, since their proponents are happy to accept whatever outcomes weakly regulated markets dictate and do not wish to set substantive goals for the economy, such as the maintenance of a successful manufacturing sector. Public policy needs to be reorientated towards stimulating firms to revitalise industry, rather than trying to substitute itself for their decisions or supposing that it can structure their decisions by the adjustment of macro-economic aggregates alone. Public policy needs to be interventionist but not to usurp the decision-making capacities of firms. An effective policy would aim to aid firms in identifying best practice abroad and then help them match it with investments at home.

Difficult as it may be to devise such an industrial policy, the consequences of not doing so are extremely serious and alternative economic policies will then have to be followed to cope with those consequences. There are two main alternative policy programmes. Both seek to cope with the major consequence of industrial decline, a chronic tendency towards balance-of-payments crisis due to an unfavourable underlying balance of trade in manufactures. The first consists in deflationary policies to cope with this effect of industrial decline, the damping down of domestic demand to choke off imports, on the one hand, and the maintenance of high interest rates to sustain the exchange rate and encourage a positive inward flow of foreign funds, on the other. The problem is that this strategy reinforces decline whilst 'meeting' it by macro-economic policies. Depressed domestic demand and high interest rates are hardly a propitious climate for new industrial investment. The other strategy would be reflationary policies behind exclusionary tariff walls or other protectionist measures. Such a strategy is perilous for a country such as the UK, which has an open economy and is dependent on exports to pay for vital imports of food, raw materials, components and machine-tools. It means breaking with GATT and the EEC if protection is to be tight enough to work.

Williams *et al.* are pessimistic, both in their chapter in this book and in their other writings, about the policy of Britain meeting international competition without some form of protectionism. They are well aware of the political and economic difficulties in instituting a 'siege economy'. They propose instead a sectoral protectionism based on key industries like cars and video-cassette recorders and suggest import-substituting investment through local content regulations. The assumption is that in certain key industries British management simply cannot meet foreign competition and that it may be necessary to import best practice in the form of foreign assembly plants, buyouts of British firms or co-production deals. It would be foolish to be optimistic about the prospects for an industrial policy, but even limited local content regulation would be resisted by the EEC and, given the extent of import penetration, other sectors would rapidly follow cars and VCRs in demanding similar protection by local content regulation. A limited quasi-protectionist strategy tends to assume we can restrict deindus-trialisation to certain industrial sectors; but even if that were true it does nothing to address the wider problem of lost employment and output. It is less a strategy for industrial renewal than for containing decline.

Jim Tomlinson's chapter demonstrates the failure of the British economy to maintain an adequate share of national income devoted to manufacturing and infrastructure investment. He argues that if the wider problems of lost employment and output are to be addressed then there must be a significant shift in the balance of national income from consumption to investment. Without this macro-economic change and without appropriate means of channelling capital to manufacturing industry an industrial policy will simply be starved of funds. Such a shift in national income. implies taxation and incomes policies that establish an appropriate structure of incentives and constraints. It would be politically unpopular since it implies at least a short-term fall in households' disposable income.

No macro policy can work on its own, for the reasons given in our discussion above on the British decline and its causes; it must be complemented by adequate institutions and practices at the level of industry, region and firms which ensure investment is both effectively channelled and utilised. This indicates that a successful industrial policy is a very tall order, for macro, regional and sectoral, and micro policies must all be co-ordinated and must all work if the policy is to succeed. If the macro climate remains hostile, as it does with current Conservative policies, then local and sectoral strategies like those discussed in the previous section are severely constrained. Without such local and sectoral strategies, without the building of a collabora-tive inter-firm culture, without research and information directed to product upgrading and new marketing strategies, a radical shift from consumption to investment at national level will not mesh with corres-ponding transformations at the level of the firm.

As several contributors to this volume point out, and Hirst emphasises, an industrial policy can only succeed in a severely deindustrialised country like the UK if it is sufficiently catholic and avoids over-deterministic assumptions about the industrial sectors where success is to be expected. Traditional sectors like furniture and textiles should not be written off; countries like Italy have managed to make them major success stories both for export earnings and for employment. Building capital-funding institutions, sectoral and regional policy and assistance networks between firms and public bodies, and providing collective services to industries in particular localities needs to be done on a broad front if it is to succeed. Industrial revitalisation may have to come from the medium and small-firms sector where managements can take a lead in enhancing flexibility and where the capital needed for any given project is of modest scale. Major industrial firms' managements are generally more rigid and more dependent for capital on their City-orientated group headquarters. *If* flexible specialisation is the most effective response to prevailing market conditions then the aim of industrial policy should be to build the institutions that sustain it: regional industrial environments, patterns of inter-firm co-operation and not just competition, and the building of a 'public sphere' of common services for industry to which industry, labour and the state contribute.

This implies very different patterns of political and public action from the essentially limited and firm-neutral instruments of traditional Keynesian and from the *dirigisme* of the state planning of industry. An industrial policy of this kind involves local and national state agencies, not only providing specific collective services to industry, but also helping to orchestrate institutions of co-ordination and collaboration. It implies a constructive partnership between the state and the major social interests at local and national level. This is something particularly missing in the UK but very evident in those small industrial states that have adapted well to an open international economy, such as Austria or Sweden, or those states where regional governments and identities have remained strong, such as Italy or West Germany. The UK is a highly centralised state with weak institutions of corporatist collaboration both at peak and regional levels.

This weakness of the British state institutions and political culture also has serious implications for the possibility of macro policies to complement the sort of industrial policy outlined above. A macro policy that puts industrial investment before the household sector's consumption must have widespread political support and be followed over some time if it is to succeed. It must be sustained by policies to control wages in the industrial sectors receiving investment to keep them in line with productivity growth. It also needs policies to insulate investments in key sectors through short-term economic fluctuations until they mature. Controls on incomes and subsidies to investment inevitably appear to hit at the pocket of the worker and consumer in the short-term whatever the long-run benefits. A policy that takes time to succeed, that involves sacrifices, and is for the overall public good rather than immediate and tangible individual benefits is very problematic in a democracy. An unpopular policy will be voted down before it can succeed. Therefore, such a macro policy needs to be sustained by a political coalition strong enough that it cannot be unseated by voters' revolts at the margin and a coalition cemented by the recognition of the dire consequences if such a policy is not followed. Such a policy needs to be complemented by corporate bargaining to obtain widespread consent from organised social interests who then collaborate in legitimating the policy and imposing it on their members. Other countries faced with economic calamity have managed to forge such conditions, for example, Sweden in the 1930s. The question now is whether British industrial decline will impose its necessities of collaboration on an unpropitious political culture, or whether the centralised state, in collaboration with those who still enjoy prosperity, will seek to marginalise and to repress the victims of industrial decline. The prospects for industrial renewal in the UK depend primarily on political changes. The question still open is whether the parties and organised interests are capable of breaking out of their present political culture of antagonism and immobilism.

Notes

1. For the GLC's own view of itself, see GLC (1985a); and for a sympathetic but critical account by its former staffers, see McIntosh and Wainwright (1987).
2. For a fuller discussion of these issues, see GLC (1985b) and Gough (1986).
3. For a recent survey of inter-authority collaboration, see Murray (1988).

References

Gough, J. (1986), 'Industrial Policy and Socialist Strategy: Restructuring and the Unity of the Working Class', *Capital and Class*, 29

Greater London Council (1985a), *The London Industrial Strategy*, London: GLC

Greater London Council (1985b), *The London Clothing Strategy: A Debate*, Economic Policy Group Strategy Document no, 39, London: GLC

Mackintosh, M. and H. Wainwright, eds. (1987), *A Taste of Power: The Politics of Local Economics*, London: Verso

Murray, R., ed. (1988), *Technology Strategies and Local Economic Development*, Nottingham: Spokesman Books, forthcoming

Piore, M. and C. Sabel (1984), *The Second Industrial Divide: Possibilities for Prosperity*, New York: Basic Books

Sabel, C. and J. Zeitlin (1985), 'Historical Alternatives to Mass Production', *Past and Present*, 108

Tolliday, S. and J. Zeitlin, eds. (1987), *The Automobile Industry and Its Workers: Between Fordism and Flexibility*, Oxford: Polity Press

Williams, K., T. Cutler, J. Williams, and C. Haslam (1987), 'The End of Mass Production?', *Economy and Society*, 16.3

Williams, K., J. Williams, and D. Thomas (1983), *Why are the British Bad at Manufacturing?*, London: Routledge and Kegan Paul

1 Flexible Specialisation and the Re-emergence of Regional Economies

Charles F. Sabel

Introduction

Until at least the mid-nineteenth century, the region was a natural unit of economic activity and analysis. Lyons produced silks, Sheffield and Solingen cutlery, Birmingham and St Etienne guns and hardware. These regions were both flexible and specialised. They constantly varied their products to satisfy changing tastes and extend their markets by defining new wants. They developed general-purpose technologies and a highly skilled work-force to cut production costs without inhibiting flexibility. To discourage price competition, they created insitutions to police working conditions, set minimum wages and detect the use of inferior materials. To encourage competition in new products and processes, they created co-operative banks willing to give failing firms credit for reorganisation and vocational schools to ensure the supply of skilled labour. Even the strongest firms in these systems of flexible specialisation depended on extensive co-operation with their competitors either directly through complex, rapidly changing subcontracting relations or indirectly through joint participation in the institutions regulating the municipal economy.[1]

The success of each agglomeration depended almost exclusively on its ability to respond to the rapidly changing international markets which absorbed much of its output. The national economy was a category in the thought of the mercantilists and their heirs, the political economists. But in fact, the nation's economy was the sum of its parts. National economic development was only marginally controlled by central political authorities. Even as late as the 1920s, Alfred Marshall, a founder of neo-classical economics, was fascinated by the regional character of much industrial production. He spoke of Sheffield and South-East Lancashire for example, as 'industrial districts' to emphasise that the matrix of production there was an area, not a firm.[2]

By the 1960s, the region had become at most a derivative category of analysis and a secondary locus of economic activity. Despite continuing differences in national industrial structure, there was widespread agreement that the most effective productive unit was the giant corporation, which at the limit integrated in one physical structure the activities of independent firms in the industrial districts. A system of mass production incorporated as subcontractors the pieces of the older regional economies which it had not already swept aside. Products were standardised, production routinised and decomposed into simple operations performed by product-specific or dedicated machines tended and supplemented by semi-skilled workers. Nationally, states increasingly used their fiscal and monetary powers to stabilise the long-term growth of demand. The aim was to induce firms to expand by ensuring markets for their increased output. National social welfare and unemployment-insurance programmes protected individuals against personal disasters and further stabilised demand by guaranteeing minimum levels of purchasing power for persons with no income. The drive for Keynesian macro-economic control and social welfare insurance was, like the drive for mass production, as much programme as reality. National differences in the speed and mode of implementation persisted here too. But even allowing for the wide gap separating aim and actuality, between the microcosm of independent firms and individuals and the macrocosm of the self-sufficient national economy, there was a near vacuum in theory and a jumble of confused activities in practice.[3] Regional and local governments increasingly became subordinate agencies in the national social welfare administrations.

But in the early 1970s, as international competition increased and world markets fragmented, firms became more and more wary of long-term investments in product-specific machinery. The product's market often disappeared before the machinery's costs were recovered. The more volatile markets became, the more firms experimented with flexible forms of organisation which permitted rapid shifts in output. As they did, they encouraged the reconsolidation of the region as an integrated unit of production.[4]

Five developments, each expediting the others and influenced by them, contribute to this result. The first is the emergence of conspicuously successful, twentieth-century variants of industrial districts in Italy, West Germany, Japan, Denmark, Austria, France, and the United States. The second is the reorganisation of large, multinational firms. Product lines are being concentrated in single operating units which have increased authority to organise their own sales, subcontracting, and even research.

The next development, the double convergence of large- and small-firm structures, is a clear extension of the preceding two. As large firms reorganise, they try to recreate among their specialised units the collaboration characteristic of relations among firms in the flexible-specialisation economies. As these latter expand, they create centralised laboratories, marketing agencies and technology consultancies inspired by large-firm models. And as this reciprocal borrowing proceeds, flexible large firms and their smaller counterparts enter direct alliances. One form such alliances take is a long-term subcontracting relation between the newly consolidated operating unit of multinational and a nearby network of flexible subcontractors. Another is the formation within one or several areas of flexible specialisation of an industrial group composed of a large firm (where large is defined by local standards) with expertise in marketing and finance and smaller firms with expertise in production. Either way, the fabric of the local economy is reinforced at the same time as local firms are more directly tied in international markets.

A fourth sign of the re-emergence of the region as an economic unit is the slow transformation of local governments from welfare dispensaries to job-creation agencies. This transformation is a response to the pressure for new services imposed by the growing networks of large and small firms and the pressure for increased social insurance outlays imposed by failing businesses. In extreme cases, these reorganised authorities resemble the nuclei of local welfare states loosely tied to the national political centre.

The fifth development can be viewed as circumstantial evidence of the pervasiveness of the preceding four. It is that plant- or regional-level officials of American, West German and Italian trade unions are co-operating — often under duress — in the industrial reorganisation just described. As they do they are coming to defend labour's interests through agreements in which the work-force accepts constant reorganisation of the work-place in return for the right to participate in and review the results of local strategic decisions affecting its fate. Willy nilly, labour is reshaped by its association with the newly autonomous local management.

It is unclear what will come of these changes. Not all firms in the advanced industrial countries will tie their future to specialisation and regional co-operation. There are, we shall see, forces driving many in a contrary direction. Nor will the complex, closely connected structures of local and national government automatically adjust to the needs of firms that do regroup regionally. National political responses to the crisis have often obstructed such adjustment; and where local institutions have accommodated company reorganisation, their reaction has been more a reflex of prior institutional developments than a strategic choice. Similarly, national unions have often blocked plant-level adjustment even where local circumstance favoured it.

Finally, even if numerous regional economies do emerge, it is unlikely that they will survive without the help of still undefined national institutions. Flexibly specialised production systems seem better able to survive the current economic turbulence than the mass-production systems they are displacing. Yet that hardly means that each of the new territorial systems can resist all shifts in demand or production technology. To adjust, crisis regions will have to depend on assistance from flourishing ones; and this could well require the creation of a new national system of resource allocation. No one has a clear idea of how such a system would work, still less of how to integrate it with the institutions of parliamentary democracy. To make matters worse, the *de facto* devolution of responsibility for national economic policy to firms and local unions and governments weakens just those institutions — national employers associations and trade unions, and the state agencies with whom they treat — which might well play a central role in reconstructing the machinery of co-ordination.

But these considerations do not alter the fact that the relation between the economy and its territory is changing. In the late 1960s and early 1970s, almost all the advanced industrial societies responded to the first disruptions of the post-war boom by trying to reinforce the existing system of macro-economic control and mass production. Governments, umbrella associations of employers, and trade union confederations created or augmented the authority of tripartite, neo-corporatist institutions to co-ordinate national wage and price levels.[5] Firms pursued the logic of mass production and tried to cut costs by increasing economies of scale: Products intended for domestic sale were further standardised for sale in world markets, as in the introduction of 'world cars' by Ford and General Motors. Production was reorganised to allow decentralisation of labour-intensive processes to low-wage areas.[6]

Neither strategy was successful. In some cases the comprehensive efforts at macro-economic control were stillborn because of opposition within the labour movement (the USA) or from key state institutions (the Bundesbank in West Germany). In others, ongoing programmes were wrecked by labour's dissatisfaction with the results (the British 'winter of discontent' in 1978–9), or by capital's (the Italian employers' opposition in the late 1970s to wage indexation formulae agreed on only a few years earlier). In the remaining cases, aggressive policies for reducing unemployment through reflation, subsidisation of state industry, and vocational training were abandoned when they threatened to bankrupt the national treasury. This was the story in Austria, France and Sweden. Treatment of the unemployed and youth entering the labour market was better in these three countries than in the United States or the United Kingdom, for there the failure of Keynesianism was often accompanied by a brutal attack on the social welfare rights of the poor.[7] But the idea that improvements in institutional design — more comprehensive trade unions with correspondingly greater interest in the general level of employment, for example — would make it possible to pursue the old macro-economic strategy was almost everywhere discredited.

The firms' world-car strategy of market stabilisation was no more successful than state-co-ordinated, macro-economic efforts. Fluctuations in oil prices and differences in national tastes make it extremely difficult to develop models with universal appeal. Long-distance decentralisation hindered the timely detection of defective parts, and raised the costs of remedying the defects. Maintenance of large buffer stocks to hedge against the disruption of long supply lines became prohibitively expensive as interest rates rose with inflation. Workers in low-wage areas demanded pay increases much sooner than expected.[8] By the late 1980s, executives at Ford and General Motors often attributed the idea for the world car in conversation to their competitors.

The almost complete defeat of neo-corporatist efforts to relaunch growth is, of course, proof that promising strategies are not self-executing. But it would be foolhardy to dismiss the change as a mere change of fashion. A novel strategy commands attention as a sign that those with the most to lose think the conditions of their survival have changed.

This chapter considers the possible consequences of this strategic reorientation for relations among the state, the economy, and the organisations connecting the two. It leaves aside discussion of the decay of the nineteenth-century regional economies and the rise and decline of the mass-production system. Rather, the core of the essay concerns the reaction of firms and local authorities to the continuing, current economic turbulence. The focus is on industrial firms, but the argument applies to important segments of the service sector and banking and insurance as well.[9] The chapter begins with a look at developments from the vantage point of small and medium-sized firms. It treats cases where such firms have formed or revitalised internationally competitive, technologically sophisticated regional economies. It then moves on to consider the way multinationals have adjusted as new products are introduced more rapidly and development costs soar. Together these sections argue that an emergent corporate form which blurs familiar distinctions between large and small firms, is spreading — in different variants and speeds in every country — through the advanced capitalist world. The next section focuses on coordinate changes in the job-creation strategies of local authorities, whose past failures lead them to dream of new regional economies, just as the luckiest among them discover that such things are already flourishing in their own countries.

The final sections address the future of these inchoate economic forms. The question for section five is this: Assuming that regional economies enjoy competitive advantages under conditions of continuing economic uncertainty, can political intervention encourage their formation where tradition has not? The conclusion discusses the role the state, trade unions, and employers' associations could play if the advanced economies did become confederations of flexible regional economies, and the problems that arise in constructing such a confederal state from the institutional fragments of the mass-production system.

A Renaissance of Regional Economies

Perhaps the most dramatic response to the continuing instability of international markets has been the formation or revitalisation of regional economies that strongly resemble the nineteenth-century centres of flexible specialisation. These districts escape ruinous price competition with low-wage mass producers by using flexible machines and skilled workers to make semi-custom goods that command an affordable premium in the market. Their technological dynamism distinguishes them from the small firms that emerged during the Great Depression of the 1930s. Whereas the firms of that volatile epoch used traditional tools and skills to maintain existing goods, the new industrial districts constantly renew their products and production methods.

The first conspicuous case was the Third Italy, identified — in contrast to the impoverished South and the old industrial triangle of Genoa, Turin, and Milan — by Bagnasco.[10] It is a string of industrial districts stretching from the Venetian provinces in the North through Bologna and Florence to Ancona in the South, and producing everything from knitted goods (Carpi), to special machines (Parma, Bologna), ceramic tiles (Sassuolo), textiles (Como, Prato) agricultural implements (Reggio Emilia), hydraulic devices (Modena), shoes, white goods, plastic tableware, and electronic musical instruments (Ancona). But the example of the Third Italy is conquering the first two as the organisational practices of the industrial districts spread to Turin (factory automation)[11] and the Canavese (software and computer equipment) in Piedmont,[12] the Milanese provinces (furniture, machine tools) in Lombardy[13] and Bari in the South.[14]

And besides the many Italies there is a 'Second Denmark': Jutland, the traditionally poor agricultural West of the country is now a patchwork of textile, garment, furniture, machine-tool, and shipbuilding districts that are outgrowing the established centres of industry surrounding Copenhagen in the East.[15] The Swedish metalworking producers in Småland are another Scandinavian case in point.[16] In West Germany, industrial districts in the *Land* of Baden-Württemberg are flourishing in textiles, garments, textile machinery, machine tools, and automobile components.[17] The metalworking firms there are doing substantially better than similar firms in northern *Länder* that dominated the national economy during the heyday of mass production.

The United States is known for two high-technology industrial districts: the center of semiconductor production in Silicon Valley, southeast of San Francisco, and the concentration of mini-computer producers along Route 128 circling Boston.[18] But in Los Angeles, too, there are growing, often technologically advanced agglomerations of firms specialising in processes required in the closely related motion-picture, television, video-game, and music-recording industries — as well as in injection moulding, garments, and (in neighbouring Orange County) aerospace products.[19] Geographers are beginning to see these assemblies of industrial districts as a new model of urban reindustrialisation, and to speak of Los Angeles as the 'capital of the late twentieth century'.[20] Officials in the Port Authority of New York City, which has traditionally operated as a kind of economic development agency for that city, are having similar thoughts regarding the garment, printing, publishing and financial industries. In Japan the remote mountain village of Sakaki — to take one of many possible examples — has 0.02 per cent of the national population, but 0.2 per cent of the entire national stock of numerically-controlled (NC) machine-tools. Almost every household has at least one machine, and the village sets its prices collectively.[21] In France, studies of industry in the Lyons area have brought to light a town (Oyonnax) of injection moulders that is indistinguishable from equivalent areas of the Third Italy,[22] as well as substantial metalworking sectors that use NC machine-tools on the lines of the flexible specialisation model.[23] Researchers studying the eastern Valles near Barcelona explicitly liken the cotton textile, wooden furniture, and metalworking complex situated there to the Italian industrial districts.[24]

A proverb has it that 'for example is not a proof'. A list of modern industrial districts much longer than the preceding one would still not warrant general conclusions about the expansionary potential of the small-firm systems. Systematic efforts to assess the weight of such productive systems in the advanced economies are in their infancy.[25] But evidentiary problems aside, there is something arresting about the proliferation in such different industries and locations of an industrial system, novel for this century, and able to hold its own against the world's most powerful enterprises.

One indirect indication of the transformative potential of the new industrial districts is that during the last decade their development has repeatedly redefined managers' and researchers' understanding of competitive efficiency. Almost no one expected rapidly growing clusters of new firms to emerge where they did. Many of the first researchers to notice these developments found the new factories almost literally before their front doors. Brusco was living in Modena when he began writing about the Third Italy; Saglio, who studied the plastic firms of Oyonnax, heads a research team in Lyons; the geographers who proclaim Los Angeles the 'capital of the late twentieth century' are talking about their home city; Hull Kristensen, who writes about the transformation of Danish industry, is a native of Jutland; among the first insightful reports about Baden-Württemberg was a book of political self-advertisement by the governor of the *Land*, Lothar Spaeth.[26]

Other researchers happened on industrial districts while evaluating statistical anomalies only loosely connected with questions of industrial structure. Bagnasco found the Third Italy while sorting through industrial census data. Borken, a township in the North-west of the Federal Republic of Germany which converted textile mills to the production of speciality fabrics, attracted attention because of its low unemployment rates.[27] Baden-Württemberg appeared as a unified entity in a study of the spatial preconditions for the diffusion of new metalworking technologies in West Germany.[28]

Precisely because the discoveries were so unexpected, it was almost inevitable that the first reports of the industrial districts reduced them to something familiar, be it malignant or benign. To many Western Europeans, and particularly the Italians, the development of a huge informal or underground economy seemed a return to turn-of-century sweatshop conditions; to many Americans, the growth of the high-technology areas looked like a return to pristine *laissez-faire*. There was substantial truth in both views. Many of the new firms in the Third Italy were founded in the early 1970s expressly to avoid the unions' growing control of the large factories. Many of the new firms evaded taxes, refused to pay social welfare benefits, imposed long hours, used toxic materials hazardously, and paid substandard wages.[29] Conversely, many of the new, high-technology firms in the USA were created by real-life entrepreneurs possessed by new ideas and in revolt against the existing corporate structures — including the corporations, compromises with trade unions and the state.[30]

During the last decade, however, views on both sides have been substantially modified. The lesser part of this change resulted from a better understanding of how these industrial systems worked. In Italy, for instance, much of what first seemed child labour proved to be the carefully monitored initiation of children in their parents' work-day world. In Japan, the gap between high-wage large firms and low-wage small firms in some sectors of the metalworking industry is substantially reduced once *lifetime* earnings of cohorts in the two different sized firms are compared: In some Japanese industrial districts, as many as one-third of the workers in small firms go into business for themselves; but their high earnings are recorded as profits or salaries, while the less successful members of their age group report wages below those of comparable workers in large firms.[31] In the United States it became clear that, in addition to all their Schumpeterian attributes, the new entrepreneurs depended on ties with one another, universities and local government for their success.

The greater part in the change in perception of the industrial districts reflected successive changes in the organisation of the new regional economies. From the early 1970s to the early 1980s the small and medium-sized firms learned to make efficiently flexible use of the new microprocessor-based technologies and elaborated extensive but generally informal co-operative practices. From the early 1980s to the present they have begun to formalise relations among themselves by entering explicit but loose business alliances while also collectively expanding the range of services provided to the district as a whole.

In many parts of the Third Italy, for example, by the late 1970s wages and investment per capita approached or exceeded those in the traditionally advanced areas of the country.[32] Prato and Carpi became two of the largest concentrations of modern looms in the world, as well as centres for the development of many specialised pieces of textile machinery.[33] In Japan, Sakaki was only one of many industrial districts which turned to the massive use of NC equipment.[34] Baden-Württemberg was one of the first areas of West Germany to make massive use of computer-controlled equipment.[35]

Equally important, during this period the new regional economies began to elaborate or revitalise systems for regulating co-operation between firms and workers that recalled the earlier controls on competition in the nineteenth-century industrial districts. Bagnasco's[36] and Contarino's[37] accounts of the elaborate combination of conflict and consensus at the root of wage determination in the Third Italy are clearly echoed in Hildebrandt's[38] reports from Baden-Württemberg and Saglio's from Lyons. The general practice became that minimum pay scales and acceptable working conditions are set through collective bargaining. Subsequent, frequently informal, negotiations regarding wages or other matters exclude demands that imperil the flexible use of labour or capital equipment. This did not mean that labour relations in the industrial districts became harmonious, let alone joyously communal. Bagnasco and Trigilia note that the strike rate in the Third Italy is among the highest in the country.[39] But it did mean that conflicts were conducted and concluded with respect for the preconditions for continuous redisposition of resources. Strikes in the Third Italy thus tend to be shorter than in other areas of Italy, and to eventuate in agreements in principle rather than detailed rules. Similarly, metalworkers in Baden-Württemberg supported what became, at the national level, a bitter strike in 1984; but the conflict had by all accounts no repercussions on labour relations in the small shops, where workers quickly recouped production losses by putting in overtime once labour peace was restored.[40]

Nineteenth-century notions of partially formalised but still flexible relations among firms with overlapping interests have also been reinvented or reaffirmed in the new industrial districts. In Italy, firms formed consortia to secure cheap credit, buy raw materials, bid on public projects, commercialise their products and conduct research;[41] in Lyons firms began to exchange information in a way that would have been 'unthinkable' thirty years ago.[42]

Trade associations in Baden-Württemberg, continuing practices well established by the 1920s, did the same things more formally. They policed co-operation within each industry by seeing to it that firms kept to their specialities. These specialisation cartels or finishing associations have made the firms more dependent on their neighbours' complementary products, and hence more willing to exchange information with them and to support the vocational schools, research institutes and marketing agencies that serve the industry as a whole. This co-operation is facilitated by the entrepreneurs' frequent meetings as members of the supervisory boards of local co-operative banks, a common occurrence in Italy as well.[43]

The changes characteristic of the second period — from roughly 1980 to the present — amount to a more conscious elaboration of the traditions and spontaneous experiments which proved themselves in the turbulence of the preceding decade. As managers and workers came to a more systematic understanding of their success, they became more decisive in judging what the industrial districts required or excluded. The cumulative effect of those decisions is to create structures which resemble and sometimes mesh with those we will see emerging in large firms.

In the region of Emilia-Romagna, for instance, provinces such as Modena substantially expanded the technical consulting services provided to the small and medium-sized firms.[44] In Baden-Württemberg, the already excellent public technical consulting services and vocational and technical education system have been substantially improved. Vocational high schools (*Berufsschulen*) once gave elementary instruction to apprentices. Now they are teaching the skills formerly taught to technicians and engineering students in community colleges or polytechnics (*Fachhochschulen*). Meanwhile, the latter are beginning to do the kind of research and teaching once reserved for technical universities.[45] On the other hand, when the Christian Democratic *Land* government tried to gain control over the co-operative banks and create agencies with omnibus powers for industrial policy similar to those supposedly concentrated in the Japanese Ministry of International Trade and Industry, industrialists, local bankers and bureaucrats blocked the reorganisation as a threat to the region's system decentralised decision-making.[46]

Such changes have been accompanied by less conspicuous ones in relations among firms. To gain access to technical expertise and sometimes the capital necessary to apply it, small- and medium-sized firms in the industrial districts appear to be seeking long-term, collaborative relations with larger partners inside or outside the industrial district. Sometimes these relations take the form of long-term subcontracting arrangements; sometimes the larger firm purchases equity in the smaller. Benetton, a huge clothing company, is a frequently cited example here. The firm orchestrates relations among a vast network of subcontractors in the Italian industrial districts — whence it itself came — and a second network of franchisees who retail the finished goods in Western Europe and the United States.[47] It is even harder to assess the growth of these networks within the industrial districts than to weigh the role of the latter in national economies. But scanty as it is, the evidence suggests that they are numerous and rapidly multiplying. In Prato, for instance, there are about 800 'industrial' firms with an average of 25 employees and 7,000 'artisan' firms with on average 2.5 employees. Trigilia reports that these roughly 8,000 firms are formed in some 400 groups.[48] My own discussions with entrepreneurs in many parts of Italy, Baden-Württemberg and Western Massachusetts suggest that the specialist firms are seeking and often finding allies who will teach them new production technologies, not abandon them during downturns, and yet not try to reduce their autonomy.[49] Sometimes these alliances are contractual, but more often they are informal matters of fact. The logic of these relations is a topic for the next section.

Of course not all the established regional economies have institutionalised co-operation among specialists as extensively as Baden-Württemberg or Modena. The textile producers in Prato have been unable to agree on how to introduce a telecommunication system which would in theory lead to more efficient capacity utilisation: the *impannatori* — brokers who collect orders from final customers and then assemble networks of small firms to fill them — fear that such a system would ultimately make their vast knowedge of the area's productive capacity superfluous.[50] In Los Angeles, the trade unions formed inside the vertically integrated movie studios are having difficulty incorporating the workers employed in the highly specialised shops dispersed throughout the city.[51] In the absence of strong trade associations like those in Baden-Württemberg or even traditions of long-term collaboration, large firms in Silicon Valley and Route 128 pursue contradictory subcontracting policies. At times they promise to co-operate with their small suppliers, at times they try to crush them through direct competition.[52]

And there are, furthermore, emergent regional economies which seem unlikely to proceed even as far down the path to flexible specialisation as Los Angeles, Silicon Valley, or Route 128. For example, Benton found shoe firms in Madrid more interested in the advantages of tax evasion, low wages and bankruptcy laws than in investment in more productive equipment. (Small firms in the electronics sector of the same city, however, showed signs of consolidating into a technologically dynamic industrial district.)[53]

Yet, despite these qualifications, the view that the decentralisation of production and technological innovation resulted from a capitalist strategy to subdue an unruly work-force or a renaissance of untrammelled entrepreneurship is wide of the mark. Christopherson, Morales, Scott, and Storper thought their studies of Los Angeles would vindicate the first hypothesis. Instead of finding capital in flight, they found the disintegration of vertically integrated manufacturing systems, and their reconstruction as regional economies. Hildebrandt and his colleagues expected managers in the machine-tool industry in Baden-Württemberg to use the introduction of flexible manufacturing systems to control a highly skilled work-force. They found instead that managers and workers had consciously agreed to a complex informal 'social pact'; and their use of the technology was subordinated to the maintenance of that agreement. And, as we shall see, even conservative Republican governors in the USA now admit 'entrepreneurship' cannot flourish without complementary state support.

But what is to replace these discredited views? What, exactly, are the general principles governing the relations among firms, and between firms, workers and government in the new industrial districts? It has proved much easier to exemplify and typologise the flexibly specialised regional economies than rigorously to explain them. Many observers, myself included, have relied on what anthropologists delicately call the ethnographer's privilege — the right to ask the reader to believe in what the author has seen — in asserting the distinctiveness of this form of production; and the most diverse efforts at rigorous explanation, despite indubitable advances, seem for the moment stalemated.

Thus attempts to arrive at even a rough characterisation of the logic of the industrial districts by following the writings and practices of late eighteenth- and early nineteenth-century artisan-radicals like Paine, Proudhon, or the French societies of *compagnons* produce only a fuzzy picture of an artisan republic in which the exercise of property rights is subordinated to principles of social equity, particularly prohibitions against using accumulated property to deprive others of their independence.[54] Monographic descriptions of nineteenth-century industrial districts add institutional detail to this picture without framing it analytically.

Nor do ethnographies of the new industrial districts based on interviews or survey questionnaires produce uniform, analytically precise self-explications. Efforts to solicit such self-characterisation are, except in areas (such as parts of the Third Italy) with strong mutualist or co-operative traditions, almost always disastrous. Businesses, especially small businesses, prize their autonomy. Asking proprietors who *do* co-operate whether they in fact do is like asking members of a loving family whether they commit incest. They are so offended by the question that it is almost impossible to discern amidst the expostulations their offhand references to collaboration — which they take as self-evidently compatible with complete autonomy. Friedman, for example, reports that the small-shop owners in Sakaki vehemently denied that they co-operated in any way — the customary right of each shop-owner to run parts-cutting programmes on the idle machines of the others for free and the *de facto* existence of a municipal price list for products (justified by reference to the quasi-collective utilisation of the machine park) notwithstanding.[55] Herrigel and I found machine-tool firms in Baden-Württemberg insisting on their autonomy — despite the fact that they frequently sit on the same boards of directors of local co-operative banks, grant one another loans, and thus become in effect stockholders in a joint enterprise.

Not surprisingly, then, analytic efforts by historians, sociologists, political scientists or industrial economists that begin with ethnographic interrogation and direct observation have produced inconclusive results. Certainly, markets in the new industrial districts are 'socially constructed'[56] in that they form 'productive communities'[57] which limit competition to encourage innovation by means of 'social pacts'.[58] But should these regional economies be considered a negotiated alliance of fundamentally distinct groups, or integral communities with a fluid but discernable division of labour? If the latter, does the community operate according to a single logic — the logic of permanent innovation — expressed in a vocabulary of solidarity provided indifferently by religious, political, or local tradition? In that case it might approximate Rousseau's ideal republic, in which the young (following the pedagogy of *Émile*) are socialised to see the constraints on individual behaviour required for the innovative good of all as a condition of personal freedom. Or does the community depend on the fusion of more fundamental, distinct principles — for example, the principles of self-regarding market exchanges and familial solidarity? Each conceptualisation suggests different potential fault lines in the industrial districts — class against class, individuals or factions against the whole, families against one another or against merchants — and different principles for remediating conflict. All are plausible, none wholly persuasive.[59]

Sociologists studying organisational behaviour and economists studying industrial structures as instruments for minimising the costs of transaction among production units or as solutions to the related problems faced by principals in controlling their agents have also detected something significantly novel in the kinds of arrangements associated with the new industrial districts. But their analyses seem no more trenchant than the preceding ones. For example, Williamson once held that, depending on circumstances, transaction costs could be minimised by markets or hierarchies.[60] The argument was that frequent, product-specific exchanges — sales of, say, components for a certain make of automobile as against bushels of wheat or boxes of standard screws — led to the integration of the suppliers into the hierarchies of their large customers. This eliminated the dependence of the latter on the former (a problem that always arises when the number of potential parties to a bargain is small) and reduced the customers' costs of monitoring performance (which are high so long as the supplier has exclusive knowledge of production costs and hence the ability to act on an allegedly fundamental propensity for selfish opportunism. Now, influenced by Ouchi, he allows that *networks* of firms or managers, perhaps bound together by a 'clan culture', may sometimes be the more competitive form of organisation. Why do current conditions favour the latter to the detriment of the former?[61]

Drawing on work in population biology, organisational theorists provide models supporting the equally broad conclusion that 'generalist' organisations have advantages over 'specialist' ones under various combinations of environmental instability and institutional flexibility: for example, when the period required to specialise resources is long relative to the frequency of environmental change.[62] But we already know that industrial districts adopt generalist organisations because they know that by the time they have dedicated resources to meet one situation, they will face another. The question is, how do the generalist organisations work?

Information economists such as Grossman and Hart[63] explain the creation of networks of firms linked through exchange of equity as a collective strategy of risk reduction. They argue that boundaries among firms will depend on the costs or gains associated with events that cannot be anticipated in contractual provisions. The greater the uncovered risk in its dealings with is partners, the greater will be the company's interest in purchasing the residual contract rights — the rights to decide matters not governed by the formal agreement. Acquisition of these rights is tantamount to purchase of a property right in the partner. On this view, as uncertainty increases, novel forms of property — such as those observed in the industrial districts — will distribute residual rights so as to spread risk among the relevant parties without reducing their flexibility. But the precise forms of property will depend on the sources and nature of the uncertainty. The mass-production corporation was often formed through the fusion of smaller firms in an effort to accomodate fluctuations in the level of demand for standard items. What precisely in the current environment leads to an exchange of property rights short of fusion? On this question the theory is silent. Thus, like ethnographic accounts, the economic models are more descriptive and suggestive than predictive. They, too, seem as much an expression of the new developments as an explanation of them.

A more promising line of attack regards the learning advantages of network systems as industrial organisation. Johanson and Mattson[64] argue that firms which have stable but not exclusive relations adjust most rapidly to each others' needs and hence to market demand. Familiarity facilitates co-operation; autonomy allows each to benefit from the novel experiences of the other. Long-term development costs are reduced because an important by-product of current production is knowledge about potential new products and processes. The argument suggests that the spreading of risks and the minimisation of transaction costs are not the causes of network formation but rather the consequences of the networks' superior learning capacity. But Johanson and Mattson also do not provide a precise enough account of the relation between the structure of the network and its environment. How is learning organised? Why do firms increasingly think they need to learn this way? To answer these questions it is necessary to look at the lessons large firms have drawn from their experience since 1973, and to see why they are imitating and allying with the industrial districts.

The Reorganisation of the Multinationals

In the last fifteen years, many of the largest multinationals have shifted strategy. Often without explicitly repudiating the mass-production model, they have begun to organise production on the lines of flexible specialisation.[65] They have been moved to do this by their previous failures, by the exemplary successes of the new industrial districts, and by their fear of Japanese competitors — who are themselves perfecting systems of flexible production. West German, Italian and Japanese firms have moved most quickly in this direction because they never fully switched to mass production, and, where they did, they institutionalised it in a way which did not impede subsequent reorganisation. American corporations have moved most slowly because they had profited longest from mass production of a kind which proves particularly recalcitrant to piecemeal reform. The world-car strategy was an emblem of their traditional attachments, and its costly failure a further impediment to reorganisation. It is all the more significant, then, that the American firms — and the French companies such as Renault which most faithfully imitated them — are now pursuing flexible strategies as well.

To grasp the reorientation of strategy it will be helpful to add some detail to the notion of the separation of conception and execution which defines the mass-production corporation. In the textbook case, an elite corps of strategic planners at company headquarters allocated investments among current businesses, research into new products, and stabilising revenues — through the acquisition of firms whose profits rose and fell during phases of the business cycle when the new parent company's did the opposite. A central research laboratory made 'break-through discoveries' leading to 'blockbuster industries'. One hierarchy of engineers applied the breakthroughs in the design of new products — Nylon and transistors were favourite examples.[66] A second, subordinate hierarchy of engineers translated the designs into instructions; the company's own relatively unskilled work-force or outside contractors then executed the directives.

This division of labour had to be elaborately policed. Supervisors made sure that workers followed the rules; a quality-control division monitored the supervisors' success. Purchasing agents played subcontractors off against each other to assure they met elaborate specifications at the agreed price. An industrial relations department managed disputes between managers and workers arising over the interpretation of the rules. Unions defended workers in these disputes, using selected cases to advance their members' common interests and incidentally making the rules still more complex.

Because tasks changed slowly and their definition was tied to the manufacture of particular products, most learning by workers and managers was done on the job, regardless of their formal education. Workers advanced up a hierarchy of semiskilled jobs, each requiring familiarity with the preceding one. Managers progressed up the ranks of their operating units as they became more adept at applying standard operating procedures in varying circumstances.

This division of conception and execution made sense only if the huge costs of building such organisations could be amortised over huge production runs. But the more markets fragmented in the 1970s, the more difficult this became. Here, too, the failure of the world-car strategy is emblematic. Firms learned to expect the unexpected from the market. Once they assumed that they could not foresee which products would succeed, they introduced more new items to increase the chances of finding a winner. To speed up the development of new products and assure that winners selected by the market could be manufactured in time to meet the demand, the firms then had to learn to cut the costs of reorganising production. In a word — their word — they had to become more flexible. To do that, they had to reintegrate conception and execution, thereby blurring the distinction between planning and production at all but the highest levels of the corporation, and reducing costs and time required for both.

In the textbook case this has meant reconcentration of strategic power in the hands of senior managers. All but truly strategic decision-making authority is decentralised to operating units. Specialised bureaucracies within the operating units are reintegrated into normal chain of command. The workers and subcontractors are treated not as programmable automata but as (junior) partners in production with some capacity to reshape the product or the production process.

Headquarters therefore shrink dramatically. Strategic planners go as senior managers regain control of planning. Many of the officers who oversaw the finances or purchases of the operating units are eliminated as final authority for most of these matters is pushed down to the units themselves. Central research facilities either cease to grow or are dismantled as operating units build their own local laboratories and wholly new technologies are introduced into the corporation through joint ventures or participation in new firms.

The operating units, meanwhile, come to resemble autonomous small- or medium-sized firms. The parent corporation often transforms itself into a holding company, and treats its subsidiaries as quasi-independent companies whose profits and losses are obscured by intra-firm transfers of goods or funds. Ideally, each operating unit is the corporation's unique representative in a distinct market. To meet the changing needs of that market, production is reorganised to permit continuous reorganisation of production.

Products must be designed rapidly, and so that they can be efficiently produced. Design engineering and production engineering are therefore combined in a process — integrated or simultaneous engineering, of course — which accelerates product development and requires fewer engineers because the designers help the production experts, and vice versa. Similarly, supervisors and workers no longer respectively enforce and obey rules. Rather, like the merged groups of engineers, they co-operate in solving common problems. The supervisors who policed the old system are either eliminated or made part of work teams which define their members' jobs as they perfect their work. Flexible capital goods often replace product-specific machines. Or the costs and time required to produce dedicated equipment are so reduced that it can be scrapped without compunction when the market shifts: the higher the scrapping rate, the more a succession of product-specific machines resembles a single piece of flexible equipment.

These changes entail broader training of workers and collaborative industrial relations. Workers are encouraged to learn many tasks so that they can move quickly from job to job as reorganisation requires. They are given some fundamental instruction in the theoretical background of their work — metallurgy, chemistry, electronics — to facilitate this more applied training. In unionised firms the unions negotiate general standards which reflect the demands of local circumstance and periodically verify that continuous reorganisation of work respects those standards. To do this they must be so fully informed of business decisions and so empowered to veto or amend them that they assume some limited but undeniable responsibility for management. In non-union firms the company establishes an employee participation system to elaborate the standards.

The decentralisation of the corporation and the blurring of hierarchical distinctions also require a reorientation of management training. Because the operating units are so autonomous, it is important that their managers' responses to change be motivated by such similar concerns that local strategies are mutually reinforcing. To cultivate this spontaneous co-ordination, corporate headquarters insists that managers not only encourage co-operation within their own operating unit, but also learn enough about the others to anticipate corporate needs in their separate decisions. The rotation of managers through different units thus becomes an administrative instrument for guaranteeing corporate unity.

The transformation of the operating units extends, finally, to their relations with subcontractors. As product cycles shorten, development costs of new products and production processes go up. The operating units have to share those costs with outsiders, without, however, assuming ultimate responsibility for the latter's survival. The large corporations concentrate their expertise in co-ordinating the design and assembly of the final product, and in advancing a few key technologies. They develop complementary parts, products and processes in collaboration with selected subcontractors. In the paradigmatic case, the product is redesigned so that it is constructed of a set of modules, each available in a number of variants, which can be recombined into many versions of the basic item. Principal subcontractors then become responsible for whatever modules the large corporation does not reserve itself.

This strategy requires the creation of inter-industry production networks. When a subcontractor works for, say, five large firms in as many industries, a customer need not fear that information passed to its supplier will circulate to its competitors. At the same time, the customers profit from the subcontractor's experience in other industries. The diversified subcontractor is hedged against slumps in any one line of business.

Subcontractors in the new flexible system are thus expected to become both more and less closely integrated with their large-firm customer. They become more integrated in the sense that major subcontractors are expected to enter long-term conracts with their customers, share the burden of designing parts and components and guarantee delivery of defect-free products as they are needed — the just-in-time system which reduce the customer's inventory costs and facilitates rapid detection of defects. They become less integrated in that the corporations oblige subcontractors to seek outside customers and, in effect, demonstrate the capacity to survive without their most important client. Customers and subcontractors therefore share information much more freely than before, but the former impose ceilings on the percentage of the latter's output they will buy. Major subcontractors in turn apply these rules to *their* subcontractors, and so on down the chain of production.

The cumulative result of these changes is the twofold convergence of large- and small-firm structures I spoke of earlier. The quasi-independent operating units have the agility, dedication to circumscribed markets, and informal operating procedures usually associated with small firms, whatever their exact size as measured by turnover or number of employees. Moreover, the operating units are inserted into and dependent upon a network of still smaller firms whose procedures are increasingly similar to their own.

This account of the strategic reorientation of the large corporation supports and extends the tentative conclusion that network production is best viewed as a learning system. Not volatility *per se* but the fragmentation of markets, overwhelmed the adaptive capacities of the hierarchical corporation. In particular, the drive to spread development costs among subcontractors strongly suggests that even the largest firms no longer know exactly what to produce or how. To track changes in the market, the corporations or the managers in each operating unit must learn from their subordinates (respectively the subcontractors or workers); and they must teach the subordinates how to teach them what they need to know.[67] The optimal learning system also diversifies the participants' risk: One example is the inter-industry subcontracting network which cross-pollinates technologies while hedging both suppliers and their customers against the risk of excessive mutual dependence; analogous cases are the use of broadly skilled workers and flexible or easily scrapped special machines.

This same learning system also minimises transaction costs by fostering high-trust relations typical of clans, socially constructed markets, and productive communities. The premise that all economic exchanges must also be occasions for reciprocal learning implies that the parties anticipate problems, and that the problems will be solved jointly. This is the definition of a high-trust relation, and in the current economic environment it minimises transaction costs by freeing the parties from the impossible task of precisely specifying their respective rights and responsibilities through elaborate contracts (as in markets) or bureaucratic rules (as in hierarchy).

But here the argument is moving too fast. In drawing theoretical conclusions from a textbook picture I have proceeded as though the possibility of diversified learning systems assured their realisation. The trope is familiar from the ontological proof of the existence of God. The proof asserts that God exists because we can conceive of an omnipotent being, and such a being will inevitably exercise the power to exist which omnipotence implies. But on this earth theories are not self-realising, and it is therefore necessary to assess the correspondence between the textbook picture of corporate reorganisation and a composite picture of actual practice. In the absence of comprehensive evidence it is helpful to establish two polar reference points — cases where corporate reorganisation matches the foregoing description, and cases where the goal is a clear alternative — and then scrutinise intermediate developments for clues about the viability and potential diffusion of the extremes.

First, as in the case of the industrial districts, it is significant that many companies look like a stylised picture no one could have drawn a decade ago. Take the example of Montedison at Ferrara studied by Bordogna.[68] Here the firm — itself recently reconstituted as a holding company — divided a single chemical complex into five companies. Four (of which one was ceded to the public-sector chemical corporation, Enichem) manufacture well-defined product lines. The fifth provides services to the others. These services range from the technical — maintenance of equipment, planning of new facilities, testing of feed stocks and final products — to the administrative — collective bargaining with unions, management of layoffs (workers dismissed from the production plants pass through the service firm before being expelled onto the external labour market). Production work is organised by teams; skill levels are rising; wherever possible capital goods are designed to facilitate changes in the product and product mix. In one case — Himont — a new polypropylene technology developed at Ferrara is both more flexible and cheaper to build and operate than its competitors. Senior managers are trained (according to a model developed by the American firm Johnson and Johnson, and carefully adapted to local conditions) reflexively to coordinate the goals of the operating units and the corporation. The whole system looks, in fact, like one of the small-firm districts described earlier, with the difference that the service company rather than the municipality and employers' associations provides the production units with whatever they cannot provide themselves.

Among the large American firms, Xerox comes closest to the ideal picture.[69] There is a regional reconcentration of production at Rochester, NY; product lines are grouped by geographic area (the Japanese subsidiary specialises in small copiers, the Rochester complex in large ones); production work is organised in teams that include engineers; subcontractors are being taught to innovate, and so on. The Ford Motor Company is moving in this direction as well. Magna, the Canadian automobile parts supplier described by Herzenberg, is an extreme case in point. Each of its seventy-two plants (with an average of 100 employees) has full responsibility for its business plan, capital budgeting, profitability and recruiting. Each plant makes one product, family of products, or works with one customer. The aim is to meet shifting demands through continuous specialisation. The corporation maintains research facilities and raises capital for the operating units.[70] In the American computer industry, large circuit board manufacturers and assemblers such as Flextronics are building regional production facilities to serve clusters of customers in the same way.[71]

In West Germany, Robert Bosch, the largest West German manufacturer of automobile parts, has consciously pursued many elements of the textbook strategy since the early 1970s. Indeed, the preceding account of a diversified subcontractor network is an elaboration of company policy as described in conversation with the firm's director of purchasing; I will refer to such systems as the Bosch model.[72]

But second, many corporations have adopted elements of the decentralised model without breaking fully with the organisational principles of the mass-production firm. Here, as with many of the newer industrial districts, it is hard to decide whether the firms are progressing towards flexible specialisation, have been obstructed in their efforts to move in that direction, or are successfully pursuing a long-term strategy which amounts to a modification — and not a repudiation — of past practice.

Many American firms, for example, appear to be pursuing what might be called a Japanese (as opposed to world-car) variant of this strategy of flexible mass production. The aim is to increase the variants of production without abandoning the distinction between conception and execution. The corporation still assumes that it can anticipate demand. Rather than expecting the unexpected and learning to organise permanent reorganisation, it simply tries to accomodate larger market fluctuations than before. Product development is still centralised, but development time is reduced through the use of computer-aided design. Some supervisory levels are eliminated at corporate headquarters. But operating units — even if consolidated according to product line — are still regarded as divisions of the parent company, not independent firms. Programmable automation is used to reap the benefits of dedicated equipment in the manufacture of a few closely related variants of a part or product instead of one. Workers are taught to operate the full range of new equipment so that they can shift jobs easily; but because the range of products is already well defined and the machines programmed accordingly, there is little incentive to teach them the fundamentals of the new technology. The emphasis instead is on giving workers the knowledge and autonomy necessary to operate just-in-time delivery systems, which includes teaching them to detect defects and help identify and eliminate their source.

Subcontractors are treated analogously. They are no longer pitted against one another in brutal price wars; they can expect advice from their customers on how to use new technologies, maintain quality control and organise just-in-time delivery. But they are still regarded as executors with little capacity to take the initiative in the design of products or production processes. At most they are seen as possessing a single innovation which the corporate customer will appropriate through collaboration.

Managerial training, finally, is also a hybrid of old and new. Low and middle-level managers progress up narrow hierarchies within their operating units as in the mass production system. Only a small number of potential high-flyers are selected by corporate headquarters for a programme of rotation through various divisions which prepares them for one of the reduced number of supervisory positions at the top of the company later in their careers.

The American power-tool manufacturer Black and Decker comes closest to embodying this model. But firms such as General Motors, Kodak and the appliance division of General Electric might be cited as instances as well. However traumatic the introduction of this understanding of Japanese manufacturing methods may be for such American firms, it is surely more a matter of perfecting the mass-production system than of abandoning it.[73]

But this second model appears unable to accommodate the currently necessary pace of product development. Firms which once applied it successfully — first and foremost the large Japanese manufacturers of automobiles and integrated circuits — are increasingly adopting the organisational forms of the more decentralised large corporation. These piecemeal changes are hardly proof of an inevitable rejection of mass production, but they are the best guide to the drift of current developments.

A conspicuous sign of change in the Japanese model of mass production is the redefinition of subcontracting relations. As the pace of new-product introduction increased, the large corporations began radically to extend and thereby change the terms of their collaboration with their subcontractors in two ways. First, Nishiguchi has shown that they are delegating complete assembly of small-lot products to leading suppliers, a practice called *itaku seisan* or contract assembly. Thus while Toyota produces high-volume cars in its own plants, the Kanto Auto Works, once an autobody supplier to the firm, now alternately produces a sports car, luxury saloon, and middle-class passenger car on the same extremely flexible assembly line in its Higashifuji factory.[74] Ikeda reports similar examples from the automobile industry and in consumer electronics as well.[75] Contract assembly also leads to contract development, with the supplier elaborating the customer's initial idea and producing the eventual product. Second, the large corporations ask subcontractors to manufacture prototypes of end-products under extremely tight deadlines.

In both cases these subcontractors must be substantially more independent than before; and when the existing suppliers do not seem able to assume the greater responsibility — perhaps because of their loyalty to their chief customer makes it hard to conceive of themselves as operating in more open markets — new ones are created which can.

Aoki reports many large corporations laying off their own managers and encouraging them to form legally autonomous firms with the capacity for innovative production. He calls this process, which recalls the corporate drive for cost reduction and increased flexibility which contributed importantly to the rise of the Third Italy, 'quasi-disintegration'.[76] One prototype manufacturer of small appliances, for another example, has established an 'educational factory' where skilled workers from the firm learn to use a variety of machines while taking their first steps as independent producers. Their lessons consist of turning out parts on machinery purchased with a loan from their employer. Fully thirty of the prototype manufacturer's subcontractors were firms established by former employees who had attended this school.[77]

A natural result of the increased design capacity, flexible production facilities, and more versatile supplier network is that the subcontractors begin to diversify into new industries. The prototype manufacturer supplies many segments of the electrical equipment industry, and it is not unusual for second- or third-tier suppliers in the automobile industry to work for computer manufacturers. Aoki's new subcontractors frequently worked for clients outside their parent's group. In short, the Japanese subcontracting system as understood in Western managerial circles is beginning to look like the Bosch model, and this shift is indicative of a general redirection of the Japanese manufacturing sector toward more specialised and flexible production.

Evidence regarding several large metalworking firms in the North of the Federal Republic of Germany gives a further indication of the strength of the forces driving firms to adopt more flexible production set-ups. Firms such as Demag (construction equipment) and Krupp (steel, special machines) have always been speciality producers, collaborating closely with their customers in the design of capital goods. But unlike the Baden-Württemberg firms, with their ever more extensive subcontracting networks, these large combines have traditionally pursued a policy of corporate autarky. The vast majority of necessary parts were produced in the firms' semi-independent workshops. Workshops with slack capacity acted as subcontractors, preferentially for other units in the company. Flexibility was thus compatible with insulation from the local economy. Recently, however, the firms have for the familiar reasons begun to decentralise whenever they could make use of qualified suppliers without jeopardising relations with their skilled workers. Krupp for example, does not integrate newly acquired companies into the existing network of workshops, allowing them instead to choose suppliers freely among local firms. Demag has begun to delegate more and more responsibility to its subcontractors; Gildermeister, a leading machine-tool maker, has decentralised operations in Bielefeld along South-West German lines. Thus the Bosch model and the drive for maximum flexibility and integration into the regional economy with which it is associated appear attractive to firms that were already highly flexible by American standards. Moreover, distressed companies which do not adopt the model themselves may be forced to by others. There are signs that the southerners are toying with the idea of purchasing pieces of wrecked firms in Bremen and Hamburg and integrating them into their own production network.[78]

If the experience of these Japanese and West German companies indicates a trend, then the shift towards the textbook picture will be self-reinforcing. The more the Toyotas of the world pin their strategies to flexibility and diversity through decentralisation, the more they undercut the economies of scale in production and design of the neo-Fordists — the 'Japanese' corporations of much current debate — by fragmenting the latter's markets. The more the neo-Fordists try to meet the new competition, the more they are driven to use their equipment and work-force in new, flexible ways — or the more likely they are to fall victim to competitors who do. Even in the limiting case, of course, many neo-Fordist firms would continue to supply standard, multi-purpose capital goods or components for more flexible firms. But subject to this reservation, the activities of the giant corporations would more closely resemble and actually blend into the activity of the industrial districts. An engine plant which participates in the design of the engine and depends on highly specialised local suppliers to produce it is both part of a multinational car firm *and* an independent industrial district. To pursue the implications of such developments for relations between industry and local government we have to shift perspective again and look at the changing self-perception of local economies.

Theory in Search of Practice: the Changing Perception of the Region as a Category of Analysis

Independent of the emergence of the new industrial districts and the shift in large firms' strategy, there has been a striking reorientation in the thinking of regional planners, local development officials, and the geographers, urbanists and regional economists who are their exponents and advisers. In the heyday of mass production poorer regions were conceived as blank spaces on the national map of industry, to be filled by the same development strategies as such voids were filled in the Third World. In more prosperous areas the region or municipality was seen as an administrative unit suited to dispensing welfare services.[79] Today, as increasing competition undermines the sense of security of even the most well-to-do areas and national welfare systems strain to meet their obligations, these two perspectives are giving way to a single view of the region as an economic entity full of under- or unused resources that range from traditional artisanal skills to petty commerce. Prosperity depends, according to the new doctrine of endogenous growth, on developing these resources rather than importing the equipment and skills of a mass-production economy from the rich exterior.

Much of this reorientation is just talk — sincere, often desperate talk, but detached from concrete projects. But in exceptional cases, the talk has inspired or been inspired by promising deeds. In any case, the new doctrines are so much of a piece with developments in the industrial districts and the corporations that, should these latter continue in the indicated directions, they will likely prompt elaboration of the idea of endogenous growth, which would in turn affect the new industrial organisations.

The new doctrine, like the old, is partly a reflection of current thinking about the Third World. The failure of many industrialisation projects, combined with the intractable problems of trade relations with the advanced countries, have encouraged 'neo-populist' calls for 'South–South' alliances based on semi-automatic strategies of growth 'from below'. Centres of declining industry at the mercy of uncontrollable markets can sympathise as easily with the spirit of such ideas as can perennially poor first-world regions who have lost the ear of fiscally strapped central authorities.[80]

But the new doctrines have deeper domestic sources. The failure of mass-production development strategies, combined with the welfare state's repudiation of its guarantee of prosperity — often expressed as decentralisation of authority for creating jobs and caring for the unemployed — have forced local communities to discard one promising growth model after another. The first to go was the notion of creating 'growth poles' and a regional 'export surplus' by attracting outside firms through subsidies.[81] Many of the new firms were low-wage, technically unsophisticated subsidiaries of larger corporations. They pulled up stakes at the first downturn, leaving few skilled workers or experienced managers behind. Fewer firms are currently willing to relocate (a result of slower growth and, presumably, the failures of the original corporate strategy of decentralisation to low-wage areas). Subsidies, as it turns out, seldom influenced location decisions: the unsophisticated firms were ignorant of them. The sophisticated ones found that every locality matched the others' offers.

These views are held clear across the political spectrum and in virtually all the advanced countries. In 1982 the British Labour Party's 'Alternative Regional Strategy' found 'with hindsight' that while the strategy of premiums 'succeeded in diverting new industry' to depressed areas until the mid-1970s, it 'failed to build up an economy capable of generating long-term growth'.[82] In 1984, the Council of State Planning Agencies, the research bureau of the US National Governors' Association, published a book on state development strategy which opened with an admonitory review of Mississippi's Balance Agriculture with Industry Program, established in 1936 to reduce the state's dependence on cotton. According to its authors:

> The most comprehensive financial incentive program of its time, BAWI proved to be a mixed blessing. It accelerated the pace of business diversification, but it also trapped Mississippi into a tradition of low-wage industries and denied tax coffers the resources for basic investments in education, infrastructures, and public health at levels enjoyed elsewhere. And, despite its leadership in establishing the prototype for state development economic strategy, Mississippi remains one of the poorest states in the nation.[83]

And this Prologue was introduced by an approving Foreword by the conservative Republican governor of New Hampshire, John H. Sununu.[84]

The second doctrine to go was what might be called municipal Keynesianism. During the late 1970s and early cities (or, in some West German cases, city-state) like Marseilles, London, Dortmund, Bremen, Hamburg, and Detroit tried to reduce or at least stabilise the local unemployment rate by funding public works — hospital construction, road improvement, and the like — or subsidising local employers on the verge of failure. The results were disappointing. Public works expenditures leaked from the region, so that most of the jobs they created were in other jurisdictions; the subsidies were insufficient for successful reconversion, or created too few jobs to justify the expense; the training programmes led to dead-end jobs or no jobs at all.[85]

The third false hope was the idea of a forward flight into the sunrise world of high-technology industrial parks. In the late 1970s and early 1980s almost the only industries with a future in the advanced industrial countries seemed to be related to micro-electronics, genetic engineering and such exotic materials as high-performance ceramics. Desperate to do something about rising unemployment rates, politicians tried to imitate the success of Silicon Valley and Route 128. But it soon became commonplace that the new firms created fewer jobs than anticipated; that industries like semiconductors and computers were as cyclical as other capital goods industries; that much of the money in high technology was to be made not by investing in breakthroughs, but by applying them to traditional products (as in the use of microprocessors to regulate motor-car engines). Moreover, even the successful regions did not have an institutionalisable understanding of their own success. To help revitalise depressed areas of the state, Massachusetts established university 'centres of excellence' modelled on Ohio's efforts to imitate the success of MIT and Route 128. Western Europeans — who were matching American industrial technology just as they discovered a new and thus more disconcerting technology gap

— still worried about keeping pace with the Americans and Japanese; but for most politicians, the blush was off the rose of high-tech industrial parks by the mid-1980s.

These pressures for reconsideration of development strategy were augmented, finally, by the new financial strains on local governments: The national state's willingness to cover shortfalls in local budgets declined as tax revenues from business activity decreased. In these cases the national state pursued a carrot-and-stick strategy. The stick was a reduction of subsidies to distressed firms and social welfare and vocational training benefits for displaced workers. The carrot was partial devolution of authority over vocational training, economic development, and social welfare programmes to local or regional authorities. The *Loi Defferre* of 1982–3 consolidated centrally controlled, piecemeal subsidies to local authorities into block grants which were to be principally under the latter's control.[86] The American Job Training Partnership Act (JTPA) of 1983 decreased the financial contribution of the federal government to vocational training, but increased the state's powers to dispose of the funds. It mandated that decisions about the allocation of grants be made in consultation with local Private Industry Councils (PICs) — boards created by the Act, and composed of representatives of local industry and government (but not, as the name already suggests, labour).[87] West Germany has pursued an analogous, though less unabashedly pro-industry, reduction of vocational training funds accompanied by increased subsidies to economically distressed regions.[88] Denmark and Sweden have been especially aggressive in what they explicitly call the 'regionalisation' of labour-market policy.[89] In other countries, however, there has only been the stick: in its efforts to reduce tax rates, the Thatcher government severely limited the power of local authorities to tax — in the case of Greater London, by abolishing the municipal council entirely.

Together, these changes created a new orthodoxy of endogenous local development that parallels the emergent orthodoxy in corporate strategy. Like the firms, the localities know that they must survive in a turbulent economic environment; like the firms, they must accommodate volatility through flexibility, though for localities this naturally means facilitating the recombination of resources among companies, so that the latter may better redeploy them internally. And as with the firms, many localities will renovate themselves only with the greatest difficulty.[90]

Certainly there are grounds for pessimism. Despite reduced resources, publicly discredited subsidies often continue new names. As usual, decentralisation by decree has had unspectacular results. The *Loi Defferre* has hardly allowed the regions to seize control from Paris;[91] in the Massachusetts state government no one, so far as I have been able to determine, has a comprehensive picture of what the PICs do, and the most informed persons say that many do nothing. Sustained efforts to diversify local (heavy) industrial 'monocultures' have frequently foundered, as in the now scandalous case of the state-owned Austrian steelmakers, because trade unionists, managers and local politicians from all parties have banded together to block change rather than trade old troubles for new.[92]

There are, however, also signs that the new ideas are combining in unanticipated ways with the firms' spontaneous efforts at restructuring to produce results akin to the reformers' intentions. Sometimes the successes are due largely to the capacity of local industrialists, bankers and development officials to co-ordinate many government programmes originally addressed to distinct economic problems. This is the case in Borken, where the head of the local development agency helped convince the local notables to restructure the old textile mills.[93] Elsewhere in West Germany, the district hospital, which depends on a strong local economy to keep firms' medical insurance payments within acceptable limits and hence its own finances in balance, could well become a nerve centre of economic planning. Because the hospitals' governing boards are composed of leading local industrialists and politicians whose own fate reflects the institutions', these committees provide a natural forum for discussion of the problems of co-ordination.[94]

Similar networks are forming in such traditional metalworking and garment districts of Massachusetts as Springfield (where labour participation is minimal) and Fall River (where it is substantial). In Springfield, the metalworking firms are creating a new apprenticeship system. The starting point is a demanding curriculum in machining technology planned in collaboration with the local community college. In combination with shop experience, this programme is designed to attract youngsters by validating metalworking as a 'computer' profession of the future, and provide them with high-level skills. In Massachusetts these developments are being encouraged by state programmes — the Cooperative Regional Industrial Laboratories — which provide for a discussion of local problems through the organisation of conferences and councils.[95] Governors in the American Mid-West encouraged a new generation of community activists to develop programmes for preserving the states' industrial base. Often the first step in such programmes — and an indication of how ill-prepared the states were for the task — was simply to take a detailed census of manufacturing establishments in key sectors. But many such programmes soon began to organise consulting services to individual firms, co-ordinate dispersed training facilities, and promote sustained, fundamental discussion of strategies for modernising the second- and third-tier supplier network: the firms most likely to be displaced by foreign manufacturers when the first-tier suppliers scramble to meet *their* customers' demands for a just-in-time delivery system.[96]

In France the major banks are becoming more willing to finance locally owned firms. Loans to the national champions proved riskier than anticipated, and the regional authorities, whatever their limitations, do have the power to secure the bank debt of firms in their jurisdiction. Of course, the guarantees could prop up hopelessly weakened firms; but given the banks' interest in profits and the state's general disappointment with policies of subsidisation, the result could be the promotion of regional economies.[97] Even in the UK, despite the central government's restrictions on local authorities, there are faint signs, discussed elsewhere in this volume, that a combination of strategic reorientation by the firms and local government is encouraging the formation of flexible, competitive industrial systems.

In extreme cases, local or regional authorities have comprehensive plans for economic revitalisation which overlap substantially with the more conscious practices of the new industrial districts. On the one hand, they encourage the formation of consortia of firms with complementary specialties. On the other, they provide an infrastructure of permanent innovation at the service of the new firm groups. At a minimum, the infrastructure plans call for vocational schools and research institutes. But they also provide for superbly maintained roads and other transportation facilities to ensure operation of just-in-time production systems; 'one-stop' negotiation of health and safety, unemployment insurance; and other social welfare regulations which take account of the ways firms are beginning to reduce insurance costs to the public through preventive medicine or job guarantees.

Here again the results are as provocative as they are inconclusive. There are signs of regional reconsolidation, but significant obstacles to it as well. Even in countries such as West Germany and Denmark with strong federalist traditions, prior efforts at administrative rationalisation of local governments, as instruments of the welfare state efforts to impose national fiscal discipline, obstruct efforts to increase regional autonomy. And these are the most favourable cases. But in these countries, and others as well, the new localists are pressing for an extension of their legal powers and no one is to say which forces will prevail.[98] But it is possible, I think, to indicate some ways political intervention can and has already encouraged the formation of successful regional entities. That is the task of the next section.

The Politics of Memory: Creating Regional Economies

To discuss the prospects of endogenous development and the multiplication of industrial districts it is necessary to return to the earlier questions about the constitution of the social solidarity on which both regional economies and the flexibly specialized corporations depend. The argument was that flexible economies rely on high-trust relations which they reinforce through their operation but cannot generate themselves: In a low-trust world no one wants to take the first step towards the high-trust alternative for fear of being caught out when others do not follow, so no one moves. If this initial, catalytic trust arises only under highly unusual conditions, flexibly specialised economies will be overshadowed by less exiguous neo-Fordist arrangements. Conversely, if there are many sources of trust, or rather if it is possible, as a common expression has it, to 'build' trust from diverse experiences, then there is more reason to think that efficiency considerations as currently defined will encourage their diffusion. The arguments for a restrictive view of the generation of trust have been developed most elaborately with regard to small-firm industrial districts; I shall therefore concentrate on these, although parallel claims and counter-claims can be made regarding trust relations in large corporations.

The explanation of the origins of trust in the regional economies focuses on the relation between pre-industrial land-tenure patterns and traditions of artisanal by-employments with their connections to world markets. In the Third Italy,[99] Jutland,[100] and Baden-Wüttemberg,[101] the argument in synthesis goes, agrarian conditions were similar to those which gave rise to flexible specialisation in the regional economies of nineteenth-century France. Land holdings were so small that proprietors had to supplement agricultural income with income from artisanal work (weaving, knitting, furniture making) or industrial employment (in, say, the urban construction industry during the agricultural off season). The property regime and connection to international trading networks which fostered these relations were different from case to case. *Mezzadria*, or sharecropping, combined with handicraft production exported via trade routes first opened by the Renaissance city states, were typical of parts of the Third Italy. In Jutland, eighteenth- and nineteenth-century state regulations kept peasants tied to land, allowed them to capture the return on their investments, but not to enlarge their holdings. This situation combined with proximity to the old Hanseatic sea routes to produce similar incentives and opportunities. The common results were the formation of entrepreneurial families which survived by shifting resources quickly from activity to activity, and the creation of local institutions such as banks and small merchant houses which helped the families move rapidly into national and international industrial markets when the opportunity arose. By contrast, areas in Denmark (Falster), Germany (East Elbia), and Italy (Sicily), where large estates were cultivated by farm labourers or peasants with scant possibilities for familial accumulation through astute management, have not produced modern industrial districts.

But such comparisons are misleadingly narrow. The finding that some areas are quick to adopt certain organisational forms does not warrant the conclusion that the history of the advantaged regions defines the only possible path to those forms. Nor does it warrant the conclusion that slower-moving regions lack the institutional or cultural reserves which could enable them to convert after some time to the promising alternative. In fact, even a slightly broader canvas of current cases is enough to show that there is no plausible list of the necessary and sufficient conditions — rare or otherwise — for the emergence of flexible economies. Moreover, many of the cases which suggest at first glance that such economies are the results of unreflective responses to the accidents of economic history are in fact full of just the kinds of political struggle over corporate, union, and state policy familiar from current debates. Some regions and firms have had an easier time than others adjusting to a volatile environment. But even the most favoured ones faced, and knew they faced, critical strategic choices. If they now appear to have arrived at their present organisation by following immemorial traditions, this is not least because they resolved those conflicts by redefining their past as traditionally harmonious or necessarily culminating in harmony. This is a kind of political intervention which is almost undetectable because it deliberately covers its tracks, but it is politics nevertheless.

The earlier discussion of new industrial districts immediately suggests the shortcomings of any current list of structural determinants of flexibility. Alongside Baden-Württemberg, Tuscany, the Marches, and Jutland are the cases of industrial automation in Turin, the electronic entertainment industry in Los Angeles, application-specific integrated circuits or engineering work-stations in Silicon Valley, and mini-computers in Route 128. None of these can be assimilated to the model of small-holder, family agriculture as the matrix of co-operative entre-preneurship which certainly helps explain the development of the former. Rather, trust is established through common educational and professional experiences, reinforced at times by ethnic allegiances or — cause or consequence of economic success? — local pride. These common experiences are often expressed in the language of family, as when certain persons or firms are said to be in the lineage of or descended from established laboratories, companies or researchers. But this metaphoric use of family is meant to mark off certain particu-larly intimate and formative professional experiences from others, not to identify and mystify them as 'truly' familial. Indeed it is conceivable that the understandings of 'family' will eventually converge in what I am here calling urban and rural industrial districts: biological family connections could come after several generations to play a greater role in structuring economic relations in the former (this has already hap-pened in the Los Angeles entertainment industry), while metaphoric family ties spread in the latter to resolve their recurrent succession crises.[102] But even if there is no convergence, professional solidarity is apparently an alternative to familial solidarity as a source of that mixture of individual responsibility and mutual dependence on which flexible economic relations depend. This conclusion is reinforced by Capecchi's observation that in Emilia-Romagna there is a distinct *urban* artisan tradition articulated and transmitted through publicly supported technical schools. Indeed, he found that the small-firm owners he surveyed were more likely to be children of workers or artisans and to have attended these schools than to have rural origins.[103]

The same point about solidarity as a social construct can be made the other way around by noting the cases of apparently traditional productive community which resulted in fact from repeated political compromises. In the nineteenth-century cases, conflicts arose out of efforts to construct an institutional regime which fostered flexible work relations and transmission of knowledge to succeeding generations through the old solidary craft organisations, while removing guild restrictions which blocked introduction of new technologies and products. The small manufacturers, who were as a rule the old guild masters or their heirs, pressed for substantial freedom; their employees, the guild journeymen or their descendants insisted on observation of traditional practices as their protection against the masters' caprice. The successful compromises in many of the German, Danish and French crafts typically depended on an exchange of rights: The journeymen granted the masters greater freedom of action in return for contractual guarantees to minimum wages and participation in dispute-resolution systems patterned on old-regime guild tribunals (for instance, the bipartite *conseils de prud'hommes*, established first in Lyons in 1806 as a court and 'quasi-legislature' for the regulation of the local silk-working industry).[104] Sometimes the state smoothed the way for these compromises by offering (as in Denmark)[105] aid to vocational schools under joint control of the parties or (as in the nineteenth-century Kingdom of Württemberg)[106] creating technical consultancies and information-gathering services which improved the competitive position of the small-firm sector and thus reduced pressure on the masters to insist on concessions.

The compromises were the result of conflicts. In Denmark it took a series of bitter strikes and lockouts from 1885 to 1899 as well as decades of struggle within the state ministries and between them and parliament to establish the rules of the new game.[107] Boch traces analogous conflicts at the municipal level in the Solingen cutlery industry.[108] And if conflict was an unavoidable prelude to compromise it was no guarantee of success. The Sheffield cutlery industry and the Birmingham hardware trades were competitively crippled by the kinds of dispute which led to renewal elsewhere.[109] The issue in all these disputes was precisely the meaning of traditions of co-operation; and however much the parties might in retrospect insist on the fidelity of their agreements to established principle, their conclusions could hardly be traditional in the conventional sense of a shared, indubitable, and self-explicating understanding of their rights and responsibilities.

Similar constitutive conflicts are common in the modern industrial districts, but if anything, harder to trace. First, there is the obvious problem that making peace often entails reinterpreting the events which led to conflict as an unfortunate misunderstanding best worth forgetting. Thus, despite his intimate knowledge of Prato and its post-war history, Triglia only recently discovered that between the time the integrated woolen mills began decentralising production in the 1940s and the consolidation of the decentralised system in the early 1960s, *no* collective bargaining agreements were signed between a union and employers' association currently regarded as traditionally co-operative.[110]

Second, the dominance of mass production has meant that unions and firms in the industrial districts have become extremely cautious about advertising their conflicts or co-operation to outsiders. The more the mass-production model spread as a standard of behaviour, the more deviant the craft practices of the industrial districts appeared to trade unions and employers' associations bent on negotiating standard agreements fixing working hours, wages and work conditions for entire economic sectors. For example, through the early 1970s the industrial unions accepted in principle that progress in the division of labour meant elimination of skill from manufacturing. Their strategy (frequently compromised by concessions to the craft workers who often remained their most loyal cadre) was to reduce pay differentials among different skill grades and raise the average wages of the increasingly central group of semi-skilled workers, whose augmented purchasing power helped ensure expansion. One consequence was that highly-paid semi-skilled workers were particularly likely to be laid off during downturns, with uncertain prospects for re-entering the firm or industry. In contrast, unionised workers in the industrial districts often pursued a strategy of *de facto* job sharing. The contractual wage was set low with respect to the employers' general capacity to pay, reducing the probability of layoffs during downturns and assuring the continuous participation in the industry and thus access to current information essential to flexible work practices. A complementary strategy was to invent administrative fictions allowing use of national unemployment insurance funds to support workers during slack seasons or periods. During upturns, the workers used the bargaining power conferred by their skills to raise wages without endangering employment.[111]

To avoid interference from the national organisations, local trade unions and employers' associations in the industrial districts made a policy of keeping to themselves. They typically have loosely formalised arrangements for settling differences over pay, working conditions and hours for the local labour market, and the establishment and maintenance of these arrangements is often accompanied by conflicts at that level rather than firm by firm; But such municipal unionism and the constant adjustment of rights and responsibilities on which it rests usually come to light as the accidental by-product of research directed to other questions. In the Baden-Württemberg machine-tool industry, Hildebrandt and his colleagues discovered that managers only realised how easily perturbed their relations with the work force were when their daily inspection tours that were informally used for elaborating the implicit social pact between the parties were replaced by information-gathering technologies — and conflict increased as a result.[112] In Denmark, Hull Kristensen found in the course of a study of individual reorganisation that the *tillidsmæn* or shop stewards in the metalworking industry were struggling to invent new payment, training and classification systems to increase the flexibility of production and increase the general skill level. Even though these efforts frequently entailed innovative use of public labour market institutions, the stewards were reticent to talk with national trade union officials about these matters for fear of inviting unwanted intervention.[113] Kochan, Katz, and I have observed the same combative inventiveness and detachment from the national union in frequent discussion with local officials of the United Automobile Workers from General Motors plants.

But this situation is changing rapidly. As the success of flexible economies attracts scholarly attention and as national unions and employers' association increasingly look to local experiments as a guide to rethinking their strategies, the informal or concealed practices of the regional economies are coming to light. Contarino's[114] study of local strategies of the Italian textile workers' union and Locke's[115] more recent work on the Italian textile, chemical and automobile workers are two examples of the studies to come.

But it may be objected that these arguments show at most that traditions of solidarity are in need of political repair under changing circumstances, not that it is possible to create such traditions once they have been totally destroyed. What, then, about the hard cases where the long-standing fragmentation of tasks in a mass-production regime has undercut the opportunities for acquiring the skills and exercising the initiative necessary in a system of flexible specialisation?

The evidence here is scant but dramatic. At Freemont, California, Toyota and General Motors have recently rebuilt an abandoned General Motors assembly plant, reorganised work according to Toyota's principles, and rehired selected employees from the old facility — which had a history of bitter labour disputes — to operate the new one.

The New United Motors Company is currently almost 50 per cent more efficient than the old General Motors plant on the same site, almost 50 per cent more efficient than comparable GM assembly plants which were modernised while Freemont was closed, and more than 90 per cent as efficient as an equivalent Toyota plant in Japan meeting the same standards of quality.[116] The difference in productivity, moreover, seems attributable to the Japanese plant's shorter supply lines for some components. This success is no proof that the workers could disperse to form a network of co-operating independent firms; but it does show that it is possible to reverse in an astonishingly short time a history of strife typical of mass production in its most exasperated form and move toward the kind of co-operation which makes the acqustion of skill and the exercise of initiative likely rather than exceptional. Studies of new, flexible firms growing up amidst the ruins of old Austrian centres of mass production such as Wiener-Neustadt[117] and Mürzuschlag[118] as well as the traditional centre of heavy industry in Sesto San Giovanni[117] near Milan point towards the same conclusion.

These empirical counter-examples, however, obscure the more fundamental point that the question about hard cases rests on an untenable assumption. It is misleading to ask about the prospects of regeneration of production systems when all forms of co-operation are destroyed because there can be no production — at least no industrial production — without some minimal degree of co-operation. Shop-floor managers and sociologists of work have long recognised that even the most exact plan of production must constantly be readjusted to meet changing circumstances; and that semi-skilled workers must draw on a large stock of 'tacit' — officially unrecognized — knowledge about particular machines, their workmates, or, say, the effect of humidity and heat on certain materials in order to maintain the flow of production. Workers demonstrate the indispensability of this knowledge everytime they shut down a plant simply by working precisely according to rule.[120]

The *source* of this co-operation is a matter for debate. A *marxisant* explanation is that work is collective in character and constitutive of individual identity; hence participation in production creates solidarity which cannot be fully destroyed even when the organisation of production belies its existence. Liberal explanations emphasise that parties which frequently contract with one another learn that the benefits of co-operation outweigh those of opportunism. Once it is generally understood that it pays to assume that the other party will not breach the agreement, contracts take on the cast of trust relations.[121] Efficiency-wage theories, for example, assume that by paying workers a premium above the rate necessary to elicit blind obedience to rules it is possible to induce them to use their initiative productively. Indeed, the exchange of a wage premium for an implicit promise to co-operate in raising efficiently is regarded in some of these theories as a 'quasi-gift' relation to underscore the break with purely contractual dealings.[122] On both views, however, co-operation in production is always necessary and possible, and the practical question is how to re-elaborate it according to the needs of the moment, not how to create it from nothing.

The numerous discredited theories of industrialisation are, moreover, so many admonitions against efforts to draw up a short list of necessary and sufficient conditions for competitive adjustment. To industrialise first meant to imitate Great Britain and the United States. When Germany, Russia, and Italy industrialised later in the nineteenth century, they defined new routes to mechanisation and cast doubts on explanations that overlooked the possibility of their success.[123] The growth of South Korea, Taiwan, Singapore and Brazil reveal still other paths and raise further explanatory questions.[124] No matter than an alleged precondition of industrialisation was a break with pre-industrial traditions of economically paralysing community and the issue here, on the contrary, is the (re)constitution of solidarity: the lesson is that structural explanations which simply make established cases into universal models overlook substantial reserves of organisational plasticity.

To argue that there are always diverse traditions which can serve as the source of high-trust social solidarity and that each of these is itself a political artefact is not to say that some situations are not more propitious than others for the emergence of flexible economies. Structural explanations such as the small-holder model of solidarity would have no bite were there no developmental regularities. But the arguments of this section do shift the burden of proof in debate over the expansive potential of flexible economies. To ask why flexible economies should not diffuse under competitive pressure is as reasonable as to ask why they should. The most disadvantaged regions or countries might adjust so slowly that they are ruined by swifter competitors. The winners, however, would be flexible economies, though they would not be identical: like the giant corporations of various nations in the heyday of mass production, each would bear the marks of its history and accordingly react (as did the mass producers) differently to future shocks. But all would be characterised by the greater integration of conception from execution which sets the new system off from the old.

Suppose that a short supply of solidarity does not impede the diffusion of industrial districts. Could these districts by themselves come to form a national economy? Or might their long-term survival some armature of higher-level, national institutions? These questions return attention to possible connections between changes in the organisation of production and the reconstruction of the welfare state.

The Localised Welfare State? Two Futures for Flexible Economies

Macro-economic regulation is at bottom a problem of reinsurance. Its aim is to reduce or spread the market risks which firms alone or in combination cannot escape or bear themselves. Mass-production corporations in the 1920s tried to stabilize their markets one by one through segmentation strategies or industry by industry through cartels. The lesson of the Great Depression was that control of aggregate purchasing power was a precondition for the success of any of these particular measures. The very nature of flexible specialisation suggests that it too will require complementary macro-economic institutions, different in kind but not in ultimate purpose from the Keynesian reinsurance system. And because of the conditions which favour its diffusion, furthermore, it is likely that even abstracting from the additional problems of creating an appropriate international trade regime, national economies will have no easier a time, and perhaps a harder one, discovering why and how to construct such institutions.

Flexible specialisation has been defined in two ways. It was introduced as the inverse of mass production: the manufacture of specialised goods by means of general-purpose resources rather than vice versa. Later it was defined as a system in which firms know that they do not know precisely what they will have to produce, and further that they must count on the collaboration of workers and subcontractors in meeting the market's eventual demand. This second definition clarifies some questions concerning the advantages of network production. It also better captures the actor's own fundamental strategic considerations, thus permitting a fuller understanding of their tactics in particular instances.

To draw out the macro-regulatory implications of flexible specialisation, however, it is necessary to examine more carefully the relation between flexibility and specialisation. The key point is that the former depends on the latter. In order to shift rapidly from product to product within one area of the economy, it is necessary to focus on that area to the neglect of others. The chief virtue of Bosch-model subcontracting systems is to free even the largest companies to concentrate on developing that portion of their expertise which they value most. Flexibly specialized firms are flexible by comparison to mass producers, and hence more competitive in volatile environments. But there are limits. They are hardly materializing machines capable of making any and all goods.

Specialisation of course entails market risk. Even the most flexible producer of woollens is in trouble when fashion shifts to other fabrics; and the sections of the Prato textile industry which currently face this situation know that their problems are not simply resolved because of their vast experience in running a network production system. If many governments subsidise domestic steel producers and block entry of imports, then, as West German steelmakers have discovered, even the most far-sighted strategy of specialisation will not guarantee security in the steel business.

These sorts of risk are mitigated for two reasons. First, specialisation can itself lead to diversification, which reduces reliance on any single type of market. For example, Trumpf, a West German manufacturer of sheet-metal bending and cutting equipment recently developed an industrial laser for its own purposes, discovered additional applications, and now plans to stabilise its earnings by entering new markets whose behaviour is not strictly tied to the demand for working sheet metal[125] Second, there are always analogies or overlaps between the manufacturing processes, materials, products or distribution channels serving one market and those serving others. Thus firms are constantly pulled by opportunity or pushed by crisis to shift their area of specialization by playing on the affinities between what they know and what they need to know. But even under favourable circumstances reconversion takes time, which firms under duress do not have.

Hence the need for a system of macro-regulatory stabilisation. In theory, the system as a whole should be flexible enough so that price changes — particularly the fall in interest rates accompanying a drop in economic activity — should lead to the redeployment of resources and the revival of investment which classical economics regarded as the re-equilibrating response to slowdowns. But no single district could rely on this mechanism to assure its long-term prosperity. Industrial districts which have already in effect insured themselves against substantial shifts in demand by increasing their internal flexibility should therefore want to reinsure themselves by pooling resources with other equally flexible regions. Such a confederation would be able to aid a distressed member by helping to provide the capital, technical assistance, vocational training, and unemployment payments required for reconversion to new markets. Whereas the Keynesian reinsurance system spread the residual risks of changes in the level of demand, this one spreads the uncovered risks of changes in its composition.

There is nothing novel about the idea of pooling resources to facilitate structural adjustment. Keynes and others in his camp hoped the International Monetary Fund created after the Second World War would collect funds from countries with a balance-of-payments surplus and lend it long-term to nations running a deficit. The debtors could then rebuild their industry and improve their trade balance by improving their export performance. This would have been a substitute for the austerity measures for reducing imports and increasing the share of public funds available to service foreign debt which the IMF in fact came to favour.[126] Within single countries, policies to aid poor regions, protect distressed industries from foreign competition, promote technological modernisation or ease labour market dislocations have long operated to facilitate structural adjustment.[127] But with a few marginal exceptions such as the confederations of Israeli *kibbutzim* (producer co-operatives which increasingly operate on flexible lines and pool resources in the indicated way),[128] these policies have been regarded at best as complements or correctives to the dominant Keynesian strategies. At worst they have been considered — sometimes correctly — as political payoffs to economic interests which have the ear of influential parties or ministries.

But the breakdown of Keynesianism and the concomitant spread of flexible production makes it less likely that such programme can operate in the shadows; and the state, industry, and labour will come to clarify their motives for pursuing them. In Scandinavia, for example, regional labour-market policy was viewed from the capitals for most of the post-war period as, among other things, a way of reducing the danger of wage inflation associated with demand stimulation by eliminating shortages of critical skills. At the same time, of course, these programmes contributed to the consolidation of regional economies; but these were not identified in public debate as such, and the effectiveness of the programmes was judged by their effect on national unemployment levels, not local reconversion. Today regional labour-market policy, understood broadly to include vocational and continuing education, is increasingly seen by the national political elite itself as part of regional programmes of job creation. Programmes to transfer technology from universities to industry or to encourage exports are being reinterpreted there and elsewhere in analogous ways. And these reinterpretations have their echoes in the internal discussions of national trade unions and employers' associations. Thus debate about the national implications of the emergent regional economies is slowly taking shape even as the regions begin to debate a future in which they can count less and less on the nation.[129]

Two contrary lines of development are imaginable. In the first, debate leads to the decision to reject systematic reform of the macro-regulatory institutions, or sputters out even before there is a considered judgement to do nothing. In that case, if the flexible economies spread, time will test how resilient to shocks each in isolation truly is. In the second, a new reinsurance system emerges with correspondingly new distribution of responsibility among national and local governments and the various levels of employers' associations and trade unions. Tracing these two lines of development points to the preconditions for two radically different kinds of industrial society based on flexible local economies.

The first possibility is a grim extrapolation of the most divisive tendencies in the diffusion of flexible specialisation. In this line of development in industrial districts combining small-firm networks and corporate operating units expand substantially as more and more regions discover the political secrets of reconversion. But this expansion stops short — depending on circumstances, far short — of encompassing the economically active population. Above all, there are no institutional incentives to extend the system past the limits reached by local initiatives. The new firm complexes depend as much on international as domestic markets; and in any case their flexibility protects them against shifts in the market. In contrast to the Keynesian epoch, they therefore have no interest in a steady, general increase of purchasing power, still less the expansion of employment which would make it possible. On the contrary, because they have to give something like an employment guarantee to the skilled workers on whom they depend, they are extremely chary about expanding the work-force even in boom times. As the power of national trade unions and industry associations declines with the atrophy of centralised macro-economic management, power in these organisations slides to the local level. Both begin to look out for the members in their industrial district or, at most, their branch narrowly defined (not metalworking, but medical instrument making, for example.) They too have no interest in pressing for the extensions of vocational training, technical consulting services, or credit facilities which could help create additional industrial districts and expand the circle of prosperity.

The welfare state would look like a more ramshackle version of its current self. The industrial districts would half surreptitiously reshape its services locally to meet their needs; wherever possible they would try to reduce their contributions to public revenues with the plausible argument that through their job guarantees and training programmes they already bear many of the risks and responsibilities once born by the state. At the same time, the national state would support the excluded — primarily unskilled workers, many of them women — through some combination of unemployment insurance and poor relief. In northern European countries with strong Social Democratic traditions some alliance of progressives urging the attractive possibilities of leisure in a post-material society and conservatives anxious to keep the poor off the streets might press for a legal right to a minimum income, thus removing poverty from the national political agenda and legitimating the silent coexistence of those inside and outside the new economies. In classically liberal societies such as the USA, much of the new underclass would scrape by serving the privileged. The rest would be grudgingly provided for, and constantly tested to determine its propensity to respond to various incentives to join the active labour force.

If this system is not shaken by the social divisions it tolerates, it is likely to fall victim to the very decentralisation of authority which makes possible competitive success through flexibility. The dilemma and the danger are the macro-social analogues to Perrow's account of the paradox of operating a potentially explosive continuous process plant.[130] To operate the unit efficiently, it is necessary to give operating teams authority to compensate for disturbances immediately so that problems are not amplified as they move from station to station. But if control is thus decentralised, it is unlikely that any central authority will have the knowledge, experience, or competence to stabilise situations which exceed the control of a sequence of stations. The price of higher efficiency under normal conditions is an increased chance of catastrophe. Similarly, the industrial districts could in this picture be lulled into a false sense of security by their superior resilience in the same way as the national institutions — state, trade unions, employers associations — which could respond to shocks beyond local control atrophy.

The second line of development supposes that circumstances favour the institutionalisation of motives to extend flexible specialization through the economy. In the rare cases such as Austria or Denmark where the trade unions have the *de facto* power to block major economic reform, the labour movement could almost achieve this unilaterally: If the unions insist — as they currently do — on expansion of vocational and technical training, with particular attention to requalification of the semi-skilled, as their price for acquiescence in industrial restructuring, the consequence will be an abundant supply of craft labour. The easy availability of skilled labour could then induce firms to use equipment in the most flexible way possible, thereby reinforcing the network production systems and creating demand for additional skills. This is the variant of Say's Law, frequently observed in West Germany, in which the supply of craft labour creates its own demand.

A more likely development concerns collaboration between national unions and national employers' associations faced with the common problem of unruly increases in local autonomy. Both have reason to identify and provide the industrial districts with services they can not provide themselves. In their search they come to see the benefits of co-operating with each other. Thus each can plausibly argue that the interests of its members and the other's are best served if the industrial districts do not cut too many ties to the national economy. To stay with the crucial example of education: the more broadly skilled a firm's workers, the less likely it is to lay them off and the more likely they are to find acceptable alternative employment if they are laid off. But any highly specialised group of firms and workers, however dedicated to training in principle, is likely to draw the circle of vocationally relevant skills too narrowly precisely because of its detailed knowledge of how much needs to be known to maintain current production. Managers and workers alike in such a setting will naturally discount the value of training in collateral or emergent skills with no clear connection to the indisputable core of necessary knowledge. In a period where technologies are constantly being recombined as each is advanced, however, these apparently marginal skills can suddenly decide the fate of reconversion projects. National institutions with sources of information in many sectors of the economy are of course in a better position to anticipate such possibilites than local ones. Hence the industrial districts have prudential motives for integrating into national training programmes monitored or advised by trade unions and employers' associations. The motives are all the stronger when, as typically happens, state subsidies are available to educational institutions which meet criteria set in consultation with the umbrella associations. And even when employers and trade unionists establish rival training programmes, the effects are similar: in this case, too, their respective members are forced to acknowledge bonds extending beyond regional boundaries, and these ties can become the first strands in a net of broader solidarity.

If the pooling of knowledge succeeds, it can easily become the political metaphor and matrix for the pooling of other resources as well. The more knowledge available to each industrial district, the less the probability of any being tripped up by costly ignorance; the greater the number of prosperous industrial districts, the more likely that each can draw on the resources of the others in its moments of distress. If firms, workers, trade associations and trade unions come to define their interests this way, then they will press for those policies — modelled perhaps on co-operation in education — which encourage the diffusion of regional economies. The result would be to draw currently marginal groups into the flexible economy while strengthening the armature of supra-local institutions which would eventually have to construct the macro-regulatory system of flexible specialisation. The division of labour between central and local authorities in such a system would differ from case to case, as would the organisation of flexibility in firms of different nations. But the emergent confederal states would all recognise in their constituent regions the same increased integration of conception and execution in economic strategy which is the distinguishing feature in flexibly specialised firms.

There is nothing utopian about this prospect. Many of the constitutive institutions of an eventual reinsurance system already exist, and national associations and agencies have not decayed beyond repair. Surely the situation is not very different from the decades that preceded the consolidation of the Keynesian model of macro-regulation, a model which was — typically — scarcely conceivable until it became almost self-evidently necessary.

Here my will to speculation is exhausted. If, as I have argued, flexible economies continue to spread through the fusion of large and small firms into industrial districts, the advanced capitalist societies are heading for a crisis. Either the circle of prosperity will remain closed to many, and the struggles between rich and poor, by themselves or in combination with the instability of uncoordinated economic decentralisation, will shake the foundations of divided societies. Or else the circle of prosperity will enlarge as both consequence and cause of new forms of institutionalised confederation. Then the capitalist democracies will face the problem of reconciling the new mechanisms of redistribution with their traditions of parliamentarism and equal treatment under law. Better the problems of prosperity.

Notes

1. See, on these regional economies, Charles Sabel and Jonathan Zeitlin, 'Historical Alternatives to Mass Production: Politics, Markets and Technology in Nineteenth-Century Industrialisation'', *Past and Present*, 108 (August 1985).

2. Alfred Marshall, *Industry and Trade* (London, 1919), pp. 283–8. For a detailed account of Marshall's ideas, see Giacomo Becattini, ed. *Mercato e forze locale: Il distretto industriale* (Bologna: Il Mulino, 1987).

3. For an account of the rise of mass production and Keynesianism which emphasises the link between the use of product-specific technologies, corporate organization and Keynesianism, but also the diversity of national experience, see Michael J. Piore and Charles F. Sabel, *The Second Industrial Divide* (New York: Basic Books, 1984).

4. See ibid., pp 165–93, for an analysis of the changes in the international conditions of competition.

5. The *locus classicus* of the neo-corporatism discussion is Philippe C. Schmitter, 'Still the Century of Corporatism?' *Review of Politics* 36.1 (1974), pp. 85–131. See also Gerhard Lehmbruch, 'Liberal Corporatism and Party Government'', *Comparative Political Studies*, 10.1 (April 1977), pp. 91–126.

6. For a clear formulation of the world-car strategy, see Marina von Neumann Whitman, 'Automobiles: Turning Around on a Dime?' *Challenge*, 24 (May–June 1981), pp. 37–39.

7. For a survey of the fate of neo-corporatist arrangements as of the early 1980s, see John Goldthorpe, ed., *Order and Conflict in Contemporary Capitalism* (Oxford: Clarendon Press, 1984); and Robert J. Flanagan, David Soskice and Lloyd Ulman, *Unionism, Economic Stabilization, and Incomes Policy: European Experience* (Washington,

DC: The Brookings Institutions, 1983).

8. For shifting views of the world-car strategy within the American automobile industry, see John Wormald, 'The World Car: Lessons of an Evolutionary Manufacturing Process", *Outlook*, 8 (1985), pp. 12–18. *Outlook* is the journal of the consulting firm Booz-Allen & Hamilton, New York.

9. See, for example, on banking and computer software, Sarah Kuhn, 'From Back Office to the Front Lines: The Computer Software Development Labor Process in a Changing Business Environment", unpublished PhD dissertation, Department of Urban Studies and Planning, MIT, Cambridge, MA, May 1987.

10. Arnaldo Bagnasco, *Tre Italie: La problematica territoriale dello sviluppo italiano* (Bologna: Il Mulino, 1977).

11. Angelo M. Michelsons, 'Turin between Fordism and Flexible Specialization", unpublished PhD dissertation, University of Cambridge, 1986; M.L. Bianco and A. Luciano, *La sindrome di Archimede* (Bologna: Il Mulino, 1982).

12. Giuseppe Berta and Angelo M. Michelsons, 'Olivetti' in Marino Regini and Charles F. Sabel, eds, *Strategie di flessibilità: Imprese, sindacati, governi locali* (forthcoming).

13. Gioacchino Garofoli, 'I sistemi produttivi in Lombardia: Meccanismi di funzionamento e politiche di intervento', in U. Leone, ed. *La rivalorizzazione territoriale in Italia* (Milano: Franco Angeli, 1986), pp. 83–110.

14. Serious scrutiny of the diffusion of these industrial systems to the South of Italy is just beginning. See Marcello Messori, 'Sistemi di imprese e svilluppo meridionale', unpublished paper, Program in Science, Technology and Society, MIT, Cambridge, MA, 1987.

15. Peer Hull Kristensen, 'Udkanternes industrielle miljo', unpublished manuscript, Copenhagen, 1987; P. Hartoft-Nielsen, *Den regionale erhverstruktur og Beskæftigelsudvikling* (Copenhagen: Landvistkommisionens Sekretariat, 1980).

16. See Bengt Ake Gustafsson, 'Kultur for entreprenorskap' in Bengt Johannison and Olav R. Spilling, ed, *Lokalnaeringsutvikling* (Oslo: Universitetsforlaget, 1982, pp. 79–96.

17. On the textile-machinery industry as a typical example of industrial organization in Baden-Württemberg, see Charles F. Sabel, *et al.*, 'How to Keep Mature Industries Innovative', *Technology Review* 90.3 (April 1987), pp. 26–35.

18. See AnnaLee Saxenian, 'Silicon Valley and Route 128: Regional Prototypes or Historical Exceptions?' in Manuel Castells, ed., *High Technology, Space and Society* (Beverly Hills, CA: Sage, 1985), pp. 81–105.

19. See, for example, the excellent study, Michael Storper and Susan Christopherson, 'Flexible Specialization and Regional Agglomera-

tions: The Case of the U.S. Motion Picture Industry', *Annals of the Association of American Geographers* (March 1987), pp. 104–17.

20. E.W. Soya and A.J. Scott, 'Los Angeles: Capital of the Late Twentieth Century', *Society and Space* (September 1986).

21. David Friedman, *The Misunderstood Miracle: Politics and Economic Decentralization in Japan* (Ithaca, NY: Cornell University Press, forthcoming).

22. Marie-Françoise Raveyre and Jean Saglio, 'Les systemes industriels localisés: éléments pour une analyse sociologique des ensembles de P.M.E. industriels', *Sociologie du travail*, 2 (1984), pp. 157–77.

23. Jean Saglio with the collaboration of Pierre Garrouste, Marie-Françoise Reveyre, and Geraldine Richoilley, 'Relations professionelles, strategies économiques et innovations technologiques dans les ensembles de P.M.E.,' Groupe Lyonnais de Sociologie Industrielle, Lyons, n.d.

24. Ma Theresa Costa Campi and Joan Trullen Thomas, 'Decentramiento productivo y difusión industrial', unpublished manuscript, Universidad de Barcelona and Universidad Autonoma de Barcelona, 1987.

25. For the most comprehensive and careful recent effort, see Werner Sengenberger and Gary Loveman, 'Smaller Units of Employment: A Synthesis Report on Industrial Reorganization in Industrialized Countries', Discussion Paper, International Institute for Labour Studies, Geneva, 1987.

26. Lothar Spaeth, *Wende in die Zukunft* (Hamburg: Rowohlt, 1986).

27. Chris Hull, 'Making Small Firms Grow: German Final Report', International Institute of Management, West Berlin, May, 1985.

28. Hans-Jürgen Ewers and Josef Klein, 'The Interregional Diffusion of New Processes in the German Mechanical Engineering Industry', Discussion Paper IIM/IP 83–2, International Institute of Management, West Berlin, January, 1983.

29. On the background of Italian developments see Charles F. Sabel, *Work and Politics* (New York: Cambridge University Press, 1982), pp. 145–67, and 220–1, which indicate further references.

30. A typical celebration of the new entrepreneuralism, which nevertheless casts interesting light on its unexpected communitarian aspects in Everett M. Rogers and Judith K. Larsen, *Silicon Valley Fever: Growth of High-Technology Culture* (New York: Basic Books, 1984).

31. Friedman, *The Misunderstood Miracle*.

32. Arnaldo Bagnasco and Rosella Pini, *Sviluppo economico e trasformazione sociopoltiche dei sistemi territoriali a economica diffusa*, Quaderni Fondazione Giangiacomo Feltrinelli 14 (Milan: Feltrinelli, 1981) esp. Table 4.1b, p. 105 (for wage data), and Table 3.9, p. 54 (for

investment data).

33. This view, held widely in Prato and Carpi, was confirmed by textile-machinery producers whom Gary Herrigel and I interviewed in Baden-Württemberg in July 1986.

34. Friedman, *The Misunderstood Miracle*.

35. Ewers and Klein, 'The Interregional Diffusion'.

36. Arnaldo Bagnasco, 'La costruzione sociale del mercato: strategie di impresa e esperimenti di scala in Italia' *Stato e mercato*, 13 (April 1985), pp. 9–45.

37. Michael Contarino, 'The Politics of Industrial Change: Textile Unions and Industrial Restructuring in Five Italian Localities', unpublished PhD dissertation, Department of Government, Harvard University, May 1984.

38. Rudiger Seltz and Eckart Hildebrandt, 'Production, Politik, und Kontrolle — Arbeitspolitische Varianten am Beispiel der Einführung von Productionsplanung and Steuerungssystemen im Machinenbau' in Frieder Naschhold, ed., *Arbeit und Politik* (Frankfurt am Main: Campus, 1986), pp. 91–125.

39. Arnaldo Bagnasco and Carlo Triglia, eds, *Società e politica nelle aree di piccola impresa. Il caso del Valdesa* (Milan: Franco Angeli, 1985), pp. 462–4.

40. 'Die Ärmel hochkrempelt. Baden-Württemberg ein Jahr nach dem Streik', *Frankfurter Allgemeine Zeitung*, 22 August 1985, p. 11.

41. See Carlo Triglia, 'Il caso di Prato' and Paolo Perulli 'Il distretto industriale di Modena' in Regini and Sabel, *Strategie di flessibilità*.

42. Saglio, 'Relations professionelles', p. 17.

43. Sabel *et al.*, 'Keeping Mature Industries Innovative', pp. 30–4.

44. See Perulli, 'Il distretto industriale di Modena'.

45. Sabel *et al.*, 'How to Keep Mature Industries Innovative', p. 32.

46. Interviews conducted by the author and Gary Herrigel with industrialists, bankers, and officials of the *Land* from several ministries, July 1986.

47. Fiorenza Belussi, 'Benetton: Information Technology in Production and Distribution: A Case Study of the Innovative Potential of Traditional Sectors', Occasional Paper Series, no. 25, Science Policy Research Unit, University of Sussex, 1987.

48. Triglia, 'Il caso di Prato', pp. 6–7.

49. For an excellent study of the vitality of small manufacturing firms in traditional sectors in Massachusetts, see Peter B. Doeringer, David G. Terrkla, and Gary Topakian, 'Crossing the Post-Maturity Frontier: Specialization, Product Cycles, and Other Invisible Factors in Local Economic Development', Institute for Employment Policy, Boston University, Boston, October 1986.

50. Triglia, 'Il caso di Prato'.

51. Michael Storper and Susan Christopherson, 'Flexible Specializa-

tion and New Forms of Labor Market Segmentation: The United States Motion Picture Industry', unpublished paper, Graduate School of Architecture and Urban Planning and Department of Geography, University of California, Los Angeles, January 1987.

52. On, for example, the fragmentation of the capital-goods producers in the American semi-conductor industry, and their uncertain relations with their customers, see Jay Stowsky, 'The Weakest Link: 'Semiconductor Production Equipment, Linkages, and the Limits to International Trade', Working Paper, Berkeley Round Table on the International Economy, Berkeley, August 1987.

53. Lauren A. Benton, 'The Role of the Informal Sector in Economic Development: Industrial Restructuring in Spain' unpublished PhD dissertation, Department of Anthropology, Johns Hopkins University, Baltimore, MD, 1986.

54. See the excellent study, William H. Sewell, Jr., *Work and Revolution in France* (New York: Cambridge University Press, 1980).

55. Friedman, *The Misunderstood Miracle*.

56. Bagnasco, 'La costruzione sociale del mercato'.

57. Piore and Sabel, *The Second Industrial Divide*

58. Seltz and Hildebrandt, 'Production, Politik und Kontrolle'.

59. These questions have been provoked by discussions with Luc Boltanski and Laurent Thevenot. See their *Les Économies de la grandeur* (Paris: Presses Universitaires de France, 1988).

60. Oliver B. Williamson, *Markets and Hierarchies, Analysis and Antitrust Implications: A Study in the Economics of Internal Organization* (New York: Free Press, 1975).

61. See Oliver E. Williamson and William G. Ouchi, 'The Markets and Hierarchies Program of Research: Origins, Implications, Prospects' in Andrew Van de Ven and William Joyce, eds., Perspectives on Organizational Design and Behaviour (New York: Wiley, 1981); William G. Ouchi, 'Markets, Bureaucracies, and Clans', *Administrative Science Quarterly*, vol. 25 (March 1980), pp. 120–42; and Oliver E. Williamson, *The Economic Institutions of Capitalism: Firms, Markets, Relational Contracting* (New York: The Free Press, 1985).

62. Michael Hannan and John Freeman, 'The Population Ecology of Organizations', *American Journal of Sociology*, 82 (1977), pp. 929–64.

63. Sanford Grossman, Oliver Hart, 'The Losses and Benefits of Ownership; A Theory of Vertical and Lateral Integration', *Journal of Political Economy*, 94.4 (1986), pp. 691–719.

64. Jan Johanson and Lars-Gunnar Mattson, 'Interorganizational Relations in Industrial Systems: A Network Approach Compared with the Transaction-Cost Approach', *International Studies of Management and Organization*, 17 (Spring 1987), pp. 34–48.

65. Except as otherwise noted, the following contrast between old-

and new-model corporations is based on interviews with managers in American, West German, and Italian multinationals between 1985 and 1987. The firms are regarded as innovative leaders of the motor car, automotive parts, chemical, machine-tool, telecommunications, computer, and food-processing industries. Many features of the new-model corporation have been described in management journals. See, for example, the following articles in the *Harvard Business Review*: Arnold O. Putnam, 'A Redesign of Engineering', 3 (May–June 1985), pp. 139–144; J.L. Bower and E.A. Rhenman, 'Benevolent Cartels', 4 (July–August 1985), pp. 124–132; D.N. Burnt and W.R. Soulcup, 'Purchasing's Role in New Product Development', 5 (September–October 1985), pp. 90–97; and, more synthetically, Hirotaka Takeuchi and Ikujiro Nonaka, 'The New Product Development Game', 1 (January–February 1986), pp. 137–46.

66. On the changing organization of corporate research and development, see John Frian and Mel Horwitch, 'The Emergence of Technology Strategy', *Technology in Society*, 7 (1985), pp. 143–78; and on the rise and fall of strategic planning, see Mel Horwitch, *Post-Modern Management: Its Emergence and Meaning for Strategy* (New York: Free Press, forthcoming).

67. This view of subcontracting has obvious affinities with Granovetter's view of 'weak' – frequent but not exclusive – social ties as a means of spreading information in labour markets. Familiarity facilitates co-operation; autonomy allows each partner to learn from the other's experiences. The expansion of network systems, and hence innovative capacity, is self-reinforcing in the same way as job mobility, 'The more different social and work settings one moves through, the larger the reservoir of contacts he has who may mediate further mobility'. Mark S. Granovetter, *Getting a Job: A Study of Contacts and Careers* (Cambridge, MA: Harvard University Press, 1974), p. 85.

68. Lorenzo Bordogna, 'Il caso del petrochimico Montedison di Ferrara' in Regini and Sabel, eds, *Strategie di flessibilità*.

69. Joel Cutcher-Gershenfeld, 'The Collective Governance of Industrial Relations', unpublished PhD Dissertation, Alfred P. Sloan School of Management, MIT, Cambridge, MA, November, 1987.

70. Stephen Herzenberg, John Chalykoff, and Joel Cutcher-Gershenfeld, 'But Does the Union Get the Management It Deserves?', unpublished paper, Department of Economics, MIT, Cambridge, MA, February, 1987, pp. 13–19.

71. Ann Lee Saxenian, personal communication, February 1988.

72. Interview with Horst Sandvoss, Purchasing Director, Robert Bosch GmbH, Gerlingen-Schillerhöhe, 10 July 1986. For that matter, the system might be the Olivetti model, since that firm publicly

follows identical principles. See the interview with Eliserino Poi, Head of the Office of General Strategy and Development, Olivetti, in *Industria Oggi*, 4 (March 1987), pp. 60–1. For a discussion of incipient tendencies in this direction in large Frence firms, see M.F. Raveyre, 'Une premieře approche du dispositif d'aide aux PME de Saint-Gobain Développement'. Groupe Lyonnais de Sociologie Industrielle, September, 1986, p. 43. For an overview of emerging subcontracting practices in the USA as an indicator of the changing relations between large and small firms, see *Electronics Purchasing*, special issue on *How Industry Buys Electronics*, 1987, and various numbers and special issues of its sister publication, *Purchasing Magazine*.

73. For an account of 'flexible mass manufacturing', see Michael J. Piore, 'Corporate Reform in American Manufacturing and the Challenge to Economic Theory', paper presented to the Conference on the Economics of Organization and Management, Yale School of Management, New Haven, CT, 24–25 October 1986.

74. Toshiro Nishiguchi, 'Competing Systems of Automotive Supply: An Examination of the Japanese "Clustered Control" Model and the "Alps" Model', paper prepared for the First Policy Forum, MIT International Motor Vehicle Program, Niagra-on-the-Lake, Canada, 5 May 1987, pp. 10–12.

75. Masayoshi Ikeda, 'An International Comparison of Subcontracting Systems in The Automotive Components Manufacturing Industry', paper prepared for the First Policy Forum, MIT International Motor Vehicle Program, Niagara-on-the-Lake, Canada, 5 May 1987; *idem*, 'The Japanese Auto Component Manufacturer's System for the Division of Production', Briefing Paper for the MIT Internal Motor Vehicles Program, 1987; *idem*, 'Small and Medium-sized Firms: Evolution of the Japanese subcontracting System', *Tradescope*, vol. 7, no. 7 (July 1987), pp. 2–6; *idem*, 'Production Network of Big Firms and Smaller Subcontractors in Japan', paper submitted to *Euro-Asian Business Review*, INSEAD, Paris, March, 1987.

76. Masahiko Aoki, 'Innovative Adaptation Through the Quasi-Tree Structure', cited — incorrectly — in Alexis Jacquemin, *The New Industrial Organization* (Cambridge, MA: MIT Press, 1987), pp. 150–1.

77. Nishiguchi, 'Competing Systems of Automobile Supply', p. 31.

78. Gary B. Herrigel, 'The Political Economy of Industry', paper prepared for 'The Case of the West German Machine-Tool Industry' in Peter Katzenstein, ed., *Industrial and Political Change in West Germany* (Ithaca, NY: Cornell University Press, forthcoming).

79. The rationalisation of the region as an administrative unit and the creation of regional economic development programmes from the

1950s until the 1970s intertwined in various complex ways in different countries depending on their constitutional history and the ways reform could alter the balance of local and national power. See, for example, on the UK, F.D. Lindley, 'The Framework of Regional Planning, 1964–1980' in Brian W. Hodgewood and Michael Keating, eds., *Regional Government in England* (Oxford: Clarendon Press, 1982), pp. 169–90; on France, J.C. Thoenig, 'Local Government Institutions and the Contemporary Evolution of French Society' in Jacques Lagraye and Vincent Wright, eds, *Local Government – Britain and France: Problems and Prospects* (London: George Allen & Unwin, 1979), pp. 74–104.

80. An excellent, historically sophisticated elaboration of the new development doctrines is Dieter Senghaas, *The European Experience* trans. by K.H. Kimmig (Leamington Spa and Dover, NH: Berg, 1985).

81. For a good review of this literature, see John B. Parr, 'Growth Poles, Regional Development, and Central Place Theory', *Papers of the Regional Science Association*, 31, 1973, pp. 173–212. A survey of findings on this topic and an excellent account of changing perceptions of regional development is Friederike Maier, 'Beschäftigungspolitik vor Ort: Die Politik der Kleinen Schritte', unpublished PhD dissertation, Department of Political Science. Freie Universtität Berlin, November 1987.

82. 'Alternative Regional Strategy: A Framework for Discussion', Parliamentary Spokesman's Working Group, September 1982, p. 10.

83. Roger Vaughan, Robert Pollard, and Barbara Dyer, *The Wealth of States: Policies for a Dynamic Economy* (Washington, DC: SPA, 1984), p. xi.

84. Ibid., pp. v–vii.

85. For a discussion of these problems in relation to job-creation programmes in, for example, Hamburg in the early 1980s, see Kurt Wand, 'Beschäftingungspolitische Initiativen in der norddeutschen Küstenregion', unpublished manuscript, GEWOS, Hamburg, January 1984.

86. For an account of the French reforms, see Yves Meny, 'Local Authorities and Economic Policy' in Howard Machin and Vincent Wright, eds., *Economic Policy and Policy-Making Under the Mitterand Presidency, 1981–1984* (London: Frances Pinter, 1985), pp. 187–99; for a discussion of the Socialists' goals at the time, Dominique Schmitt, ed., *La Region à l'heure de la decentralisation. Notes et études documentaires* (Paris: La Documentation Française, 1985).

87. For the history and structuring principles of the JTPA, see Robert Gutman, 'Job Training Partnership Act: New Help for the Unemployed', *Monthly Labor Review*, 106 (March 1983), pp. 3–7.

88. For a survey of West German labour-market policy in the 1970s and early 1980s, see Gunther Schmid, 'Arbeitsmarktpolitik in Schweden und in der Bundesrepublik' in Fritz W. Scharpf *et al.*, eds., *Aktive Arbeitsmarktpolitik. Erfahrungen und neue Wege* (Frankfurt am Main: Campus, 1982), pp. 29–62.

89. Per H. Jensen, 'Arbeidsloshedspolitiken i sverige' and Henning Jorgensen, 'Muligheder og grænsninger for regionaliseret arbeismarkeds- og geskaeftigelsespolitik' both in Henning Jorgensen and Jens. Chr. Tonboe, eds, *Fagbevægelse, stat, og kommuner* (Aalborg: Aalborg Universitetsforlag, 1985), pp. 77–102 and 138–83, respectively.

90. For a lapidary statement of the new orthodoxy and a good sample of the research, out of which it grows and to which it contributes, see David Keeble and Egbert Wever, eds, *New Firms and Regional Development in Europe* (London: Croom Helm, 1986). A critical view is Ernst A. Brugger, '"Endogene Entwicklung": Ein Konzept zwischen Utopie und Realität', *Information zur Raumentwicklung*, 1–2 (1984), pp. 1–19.

91. Michael Keating, 'Comment' on Meny, 'Local Authorities and Economic Policy', in Machin and Wright, *Economic Policy and Policy Making*, pp. 200–4.

92. Franz Summer, *Das VOEST Debakel* (Vienna: Orac, 1987).

93. Hull, 'Making Small Firms Grow'.

94. See Albrecht Goeschel, 'Krankenkassen Kommunalkörperschaften und Regionalwirtschaft', *Die Ortskrankenkasse*, no. 1 (1985), pp. 12–19.

95. Discussions with government officials, trade unionists, and industrialists participating in the Machine Action Project (Springfield) and the Needle Trades Action Project (Fall River), 1987. Both projects are part of the CRIL programme. One of the few studies of emerging inter-firm relations in the state metalworking industry is Sacha Page, 'Massachusetts' Policy Toward Changing Business Relationships in the Metalworking Industry', unpublished manuscript, Kennedy School of Government, February 1988.

96. Discussions from 1984 to the present with Jack Russell, founder of the Auto-In-Michigan (AIM) project, and other initiatives currently addressing these problems.

97. Didier Salvadori, 'Le Financement des systèmes productifs régionaux', *Revue d'économie industrielle*, vol. 35, no. 1 (1986), pp. 127–41.

98. For an example of new localists' attention to the complexities of tax reform in relation to their programmes, see A. Drack, 'Kommunale Steuerreform und dezentrale Autonomie' in U. Bullman and P. Gitschman, eds, *Kommune als Gegenmacht* (Hamburg: VSA, 1985), pp. 130–45.

99. For an excellent discussion of Italian debates on this subject, see Marzio Barbagli, Vittorio Capecchi and Antonio Cobalti, *La mobilità sociale in Emilia-Romagna* (Bologna: Il Mulino, 1988), esp. Chapter 3.

100. For a synthesis of the literature on Danish agrarian structure in relation to the formation of the artisan classes, see Peer Hull Kristensen and Charles F. Sabel, 'The Agrarian Background of the Small-Holders' Republic', unpublished paper, Program in Science, Technology, and Society, MIT, Cambridge, MA, September 1987.

101. Klaus Megerle, *Württemberg im Industrialisierungsprozess Deutschlands* (Stuttgart: Klett-Cotta, 1982), pp. 71–150, 197–242.

102. This view of the possible convergence of real and fictive kinship ties as the foundation of industrial structure arose in conversation with Michael Storper.

103. Barbagli et al, *La mobilità sociale in Emilia-Romagna*, Chapter 3.

104. Alain Cottereau, 'Justice et injustice ordinaire sur les lieux de travail d'après les audiences prud'homales (1806–1866)', *Le Mouvement social*, 141 (October–December 1987), pp. 25–59. The phrase 'quasi-legislature' is from p. 51.

105. Kristensen and Sabel, 'The Agrarian Background'.

106. J.J. Lee, 'Labor in German Industrialization' in M.M. Postan, D.C. Coleman, and Peter Mathias, eds., *The Cambridge Economic History of Europe* vol. vii, pt. I (New York: Cambridge University Press, 1978), pp. 442–90, esp. pp. 453–71. See, for a comparison with France, Jürgen Schriewer, 'Intermediäre Instanzen, Selbstverwaltung und berufliche Vergleich', *Zeitschrift für Pädegogik*, 32.1 (1986), pp. 69–113; For Baden-Württemberg, see Hermann Schindler, *Die Routlinger Wirtschaft von der Mitte des neunzehnten Jahrhunderts bis zum Beginn des Ersten Weltkrieges* (Tübingen: J.C.B. Mohr, 1969), esp. pp. 13–30.

107. Kristensen and Sabel, 'The Agrarian Background'.

108. Rudolph Boch, *Handwerker-Sozialisten gegen Fabrikgesellschaft. Lokale Fachvereine, Massengewerkschaft und industrielle Rationalisierung in Solingen 1870 bis 1914* (Göttingen: Vandenhoeck & Ruprecht, 1985).

109. On the decline of Sheffield see Sidney Pollard, *A History of Labour in Sheffield* (Liverpool: Liverpool University Press, 1959), pp. 65–77, 134–58; and G.I.H. Lloyd, *The Cutlery Trades* (London: Longmans, Green and Co, 1913), pp. 199–200, 348–9.

110. See Carlo Triglia, *Grandi partiti e piccole imprese. Communisti e democristiani nelle regioni a economia diffusa* (Bologna: Il Mulino, 1986), esp. pp. 133–205; and on the decade of conflict between the textile unions and the small firms, *idem*. 'Il caso di Prato' esp. p. 18. The Ilongot headhunters of northern Luzon in the Philippines provide a dramatic case of such negotiated forgetfulness. When

their blood feuds threaten the survival of their tribes, the aggrieved parties reinterpret their kin relations so that insults exchanged by their ancestors do not require murders of the descendants. See Renato Rosaldo, *Ilongot Headhunting, 1883–1974: A Study in Society and History* (Stanford CA: Stanford University Press, 1980).

111. See, for example, the discussion of American practices in Piore and Sabel, *The Second Industrial Divide*, pp. 111–20.

112. Seltz and Hildebrandt, 'Production, Politik, und Kontrolle', esp. pp. 102–3.

113. Peer Hull Kristensen, *Teknologiske projekter og organisatoriske processer* (Roskilde: Forlaget Samenfundsokonomi og Planlægning, 1986), pp. 414–16.

114. Contarino, 'The Politics of Industrial Change'.

115. Richard M. Locke, 'Redrawing the Boundaries of Italian Union Politics', paper presented to the American Political Science Association, Chicago, August, 1987.

116. John Krafcik, 'Learning from NUMI', Internal Working Paper, MIT International Motor Vehicle Program, Cambridge, MA, September, 1986.

117. See 'Die andere Obersteiermark', *Trend*, 1 (1987), pp. 96–101; Hans Glatz and Hans Moser, 'Innovationsorientierte Regionalpolitik Förderungsmoglichkeiten von kleinen und mittleren Unternehmen in der Obersteiermark', Institut für Höhere Studien, Vienna, February, 1987.

118. Gernot Grabher, 'Betriebliche Reorganisation in einer traditionellen Industrieregion Theoretische Grundlagen und empirische Ergebnisse für die Region Wr. Neustadt/Neukirchen', unpublished PhD dissertation, Department of Urban Studies, University of Vienna, 1987.

119. Ida Regalia, 'Processi di riaggiustamento nell'area di Sesto S. Giovanni' in Regini and Sabel, *Strategie di flessibilità*.

120. The classic reference is Stanley Bernard Mathewson, *Restriction of Output Among Unorganized Workers* (Carbondale: University of Southern Illinois Press, 1969; first published in 1931 by Viking Press, New York.)

121. For a recent game-theoretic exposition of this view see Robert M. Axlerod, *The Evolution of Cooperation* (New York: Basic Books, 1984). The clearest general formulation of this position is Arthur L. Stinchcombe, 'Norms of Exchange' in *idem.*, *Stratification and Organization* (Cambridge: Cambridge University Press, 1986), pp. 231–267. His key argument is that 'there are a lot of paths to complex normative developments in which an evolutionary sequence of Pareto-rational movements exists. In short, the pre-contractual element of contract can perfectly well be a previous contract.'

122. George A. Akerlof, 'Labor Contracts as Partial Gift Exchanges', *Quarterly Journal of Economics*, 97 (November 1982), pp. 543–69.

123. For a theory which generalised from these cases, see Alexander Gerschenkron, *Economic Backwardness in Historical Perspective* (Cambridge MA: Harvard University Press, 1966). A review of the criticism of the argument is Clive Trebilcock, *The Industrialization of the Continental Powers, 1780–1914* (London: Longman, 1981), esp. pp. 403–25.

124. See, for example, Alice M. Amsden, 'The State and Taiwan's Development' in Peter Evans and et al., eds, *Bringing the State Back In* (Cambridge: Cambridge University Press, 1985), pp. 78–106.

125. Interviews with managers of Trumpf GmbH and Co., Stuttgart, July 1986.

126. On Keynes's plan and its opponents, see Fred L. Block, *The Origins of International Economic Disorder* (Berkeley: University of California Press, 1977), pp. 1–108.

127. For a survey see Douglas Yuill, Kevin Allen, and Chris Hull, eds., *Regional Policy in the European Community* (New York: St. Martin's Press, 1980).

128. On the intricate interregional links among *kibbutzim* belonging to the same political groupings, see Bernd Biervert and Beate Finis, 'Zur Bestandssicherung des Kibbutz als relativ autonomes, offenes sozialsystem in einer kapitalistischen Umwelt', *Archiv für öffentliche und freigemeinnützige Unternehmen*, 14 (1985), pp. 1–19. For an overview of these extremely complex debates, see Jorgensen and Tonboe, *Fagbevægelse, stat, og kommuner*. On the rise of flexible technologies on the kibbutzim, see Menachem Rosner, 'New Technologies in the Kibbutzim', *Jerusalem Quarterly*, 39 (1986), pp. 82–9.

129. Jorgensen and Tonboe, *Fagbevægelse, stat, og kommuner*.

130. Charles Perrow, *Normal Accidents: Living with High-Risk Technologies* (New York: Basic Books, 1984).

2 Facing Up to Manufacturing Failure

Karel Williams, John Williams, Colin Haslam and Andrew Wardlow

After five years of economic recovery British manufacturing output is now (1987) no higher than it was in 1979 (and indeed is 10 per cent lower than it was in 1973). Despite wholesale scrapping of old capacity, labour productivity is growing no faster than 3 per cent, which was the rate achieved in the 1960s. More than 2 million, or 27 per cent, of all manufacturing jobs have been lost since 1979. Though the Conservative government and a few free-market economists must try and represent what has happened as a success, everybody else now accepts that there has been some kind of failure in British manufacturing and many believe that it will have dire consequences. But there is little agreement on the causes and nature of the problem or on remedies for decline; and we argue that much of the recent discussion does not adequately specify the problem or recognise its intractability. To be more specific, most of those who have contributed to the debate about causes and cures have underestimated the importance of the management problem in British industry and overestimated the benefits which can be obtained from orthodox policy instruments. If our analysis is pessimistic, our conclusions are not defeatist. The third and final section of this chapter shows how radical and unorthodox policy instruments such as value added content regulation and investment in import substitution can palliate our problems. The case for new policy initiatives rests on the basis of a definition of the problem proposed in the first two sections of the chapter. These sections analyse the nature and causes of failure and also provide us with an opportunity to indicate how much our position, and the debate on manufacturing failure, has moved on in the period since the publication of Williams *et al.* (1983).

The Problem

In the mid-1950s, more than 90 per cent of the manufactures consumed in the United Kingdom were British manufactures; thirty years later

71

only 65 per cent were British manufactures. The change has actually been more dramatic because, over the same period, the British content of the UK's national manufacturing output also declined sharply; by 1986, one-third of British manufactured imports were 'semi-manufactures' or components and kits of parts which were incorporated in British output. There were similar changes in other advanced countries. The old system under which each major industrial country supplied the bulk of its own consumer and producer goods was transformed in the 1960s and 1970s. In the new order there was a competitive interchange of manufactures among the advanced countries. As competition for home and export markets intensified, it revealed significant differences in the capacity of different advanced countries to organise production of high-quality manufactures whose non-price characteristics made them attractive to domestic and foreign buyers. The UK was the least capable of the advanced manufacturing countries and her relative inferiority was reflected in a decline in her share of world trade in manufactures. Over the past thirty years, her volume share of exports from the main manufacturing countries has fallen from over 20 per cent to well under 10 per cent. Most of the decline in percentage share occurred in the twenty years up to 1973 and this was followed by a period in the later 1970s when the British share stabilised around 10 per cent. During the long boom the UK's export volumes increased steadily as her share declined because world trade was growing rapidly; in the colder world economic climate after 1973, a stable share did not translate into substantial volume increases. Furthermore, since 1979 the British share of world trade has again begun to slip downwards. The best available official measure is provided by the Department of Trade and Industry (DTI), which measures the UK's share of manufactured exports from eleven 'major' industrial countries. As Table 2.1 shows, the DTI series discloses a fall of more than 2 per cent over the past decade. It is also worth noting that the DTI's list of major industrial countries excludes all the newly industrialising countries (NICs); if they were added to the list, Britain's trade share would fall by significantly more than 2 percentage points. When the six NICs, each with exports of over £30 billion, are added to the list, then Britain's trade share in 1986 is just 6.5 per cent.

The UK's relative failure in world export markets has had dramatic

Table 2.1. The UK's share in the volume of manufactured exports (per cent)

1975	1976	1977	1978	1979	1980	1981	1982	1983	1984	1985
11.2	10.9	11.2	10.7	10.0	9.7	8.9	9.3	9.0	8.9	9.1

Source: DTI

Table 2.2. Britain's balance of trade in manufactures
(SITC, divisions 5–8, £ millions)

1980	1981	1982	1983	1984	1985	1986
+ 3634	+ 2905	+ 199	– 4849	– 6308	– 5774	– 8239

Source: Central Statistical Office, *Monthly Digest of Statistics*, August 1987.

consequences because she has an average, or above average, propensity to import manufactures. The proportion of national manufacturing output exported has risen towards 30 per cent, but the fundamental point is that manufactured imports have not been compensated for by manufactured exports. The result has been a dramatic shift in the trade balance between manufactured exports and imports.

In the 1950s the value of the UK's manufactured exports was 2.5 times as large as the value of her manufactured imports. The surplus on manufactured trade was eroded as the values drifted towards parity in the 1960s and 1970s. There was then a disastrous deterioration in the position in the early 1980s; the UK's trade in manufactures went into deficit for the first time in 1983 and the deficit has since increased unsteadily but alarmingly. The recent record is summarised in Table 2.2, which shows how the deficit had increased to more than £8 billion by 1986. Since 1982, the depreciation of sterling has made British exports cheaper and imports dearer but it has not produced an export boom. It is true that manufactured export and import volumes have both grown by about 20 per cent since 1983. But that symmetry is deceptive because export volumes have been recovering from a depressed level which was actually lower than in 1977, while import volumes normally grow at around 20 per cent every three years. Any longer-run comparison shows a frightening disparity between the rate of growth of manufactured exports and imports. From 1975 to 1985, manufactured import volumes increased by 138 per cent while manufactured export volumes increased by 34 per cent.

The British economy had chronic payments difficulties in the 1950s and 1960s, and the deterioration in the balance of trade in manufactures after 1980 would, in the ordinary course of events, have produced a terminal payments crisis because the current account could not have been balanced. Crisis was averted by the windfall gain of North Sea oil which directly provided oil exports and indirectly saved oil imports. By 1985, when production peaked at 135 million tonnes, the UK was the world's fourth largest oil producer. She became self-sufficient in oil and a major oil exporter; in 1985, the North Sea produced 80 per cent more oil than was required for domestic consumption. It was always clear that the payments problems would return when the oil ran out, but that prospect was reassuringly remote when official estimates showed oil production would only decline by 5 per cent per annum. The fundamentals changed completely when the price of oil was halved in 1985 and the deficit on manufactured trade increased by £2.5 billion in 1986. The unfavourable trend on the oil account and the growing deficit on manufactured trade overwhelmed a favourable movement in invisibles. A £3 billion current account surplus in 1985 was more than wiped out in 1986 and most independent economic forecasters predict a substantial deficit in 1987. In these years the very large appreciation of the Deutschmark and the yen helped to contain the situation, but the crisis has been postponed, not abandoned.

Politicians on the right and left are still generally refusing to face up to the prospect of payments crisis. The Conservatives must deny the possibility because it does not fit their story-line about economic recovery. We have elsewhere (Cutler *et al.* 1986, pp. 110–16) examined and discounted the government alibis about currency depreciation, the rise of services and the sunrise industries which the Chancellor claims will avert a crisis in the medium term as the oil runs out. As for Labour, they are caught on a contradiction. The notion of a coming crisis provides them with a stick with which to beat Mrs Thatcher but the Party is also committed to a policy of reflation which must worsen the current account when consumer incomes are spent on imported manufactures. To their credit, the intellectuals of the centre and left are more realistically worried and anxious about the UK's short- and medium-term prospects. The 'problem of British manufacturing' has attracted increasing attention and concern over the past decade and the UK is now in the final phase of a dramatic change in academic perception of the problem. One is reminded of the old insurance company advertisement which featured little line drawings of the same individual at age 35, 45 and 55, with a caption beneath each drawing: 'they tell me my job is not pensionable'; 'unfortunately my job is not pensionable'; 'I do not know what I shall do when I retire'. The academic debate on manufacturing has developed in much the same way.

In phase one of this debate, in the 1960s, 'the problem of manufacturing' did not exist as such because it was buried in a broader discussion of economic growth. In this context, the slow growth of manufacturing output and productivity figured as a constraint on the increase of welfare because it limited increases in the resources available for private and social consumption. In phase two, in the late 1970s, a more threatening problem of 'deindustrialisation' was defined. Singh (1977) raised the possibility that, if national manufacturing performance was inferior, an economy might be prevented from utilising its resources fully by a 'payments constraint'. If such an economy moved towards full employment, then an influx of imported manufactures would produce a payments crisis. In phase three, after the early 1980s, the prospect of full employment had receded into the past. There was increasing concern that a weak manufacturing country might encounter a payments crisis when it was well away from full employment. The deflationary cure for the payments crisis might then have to be administered in an economy which was already running with more than 10 per cent unemployment. Smith (1984) introduced the notion of 'crisis' into the debate and raised the question of whether there would be a substantial general decline in living standards when the oil ran out. The House of Lords' Select Committee on Overseas Trade (1985) report trenchantly argued that such a crisis was inevitable.

The obvious question is how quickly the crisis will come. The answer must be more quickly than seemed possible in 1984 before the price of oil fell. It is difficult to be more precise about the timing and the scale of the crisis for two reasons. First, the connection between trade flows and currency dealing is much less direct than it was in the 1950s and 1960s. On the other hand, it does seem unlikely that foreigners will be prepared to hold sterling if the current account shows a large and increasing deficit in 1988 and 1989. Apart from this, the point that should be made is that the prospect of an external crisis has distracted attention from the internal crisis which the UK is already living through.

The decline of the uncompetitive British manufacturing sector has already produced dramatic changes in the level and composition of employment. Between 1970 and 1983, Britain lost 2.4 million manufacturing jobs. This large fall in the absolute numbers employed in manufacturing has no parallel elsewhere in the advanced countries. Of course, less than one-quarter of the workforce is now employed in manufacturing and the economy is creating jobs elsewhere in the service sector which have directly replaced lost manufacturing jobs on a one-for-one basis. But, in qualitative terms, these new jobs are no substitute. The jobs we have lost in manufacturing are full-time, well-paid jobs and those we have gained in services are part-time and ill-paid. There has been a dramatic deterioration in the composition of employment because the British economy is creating jobs, but not the kind of jobs which can support the traditional working-class household of man, wife and two children. On social justice grounds, the trend requires a redistributive response and a massive expansion of welfare payments; manufacturing decline changes income distribution so that a new Speenhamland system of wage subvention is required. But that is the last thing which any government will be able to afford by the end of this decade, when the International Monetary Fund (IMF) is likely to be insisting on a deflationary package to resolve the payments disequilibrium.

In our most recent work (Williams *et al*. 1987b) we have tried to take the argument further by analysing the connection between employ-

Table 2.3. Net output and employment in the advanced countries
(cyclical peaks to trough, after 1978)

Years	Country	Change in real net output (%)	Change from peak to trough, in numbers employed in manufacturing (%)
1980–81	Belgium	– 2.0	– 7.6
1980–82	France	– 1.1	– 3.7
1980–83	Italy	– 6.1	– 6.7
1980–82	Sweden	– 3.7	– 7.7
1978–82	UK	–18.6	–16.9
1979–82	USA	– 5.0	– 5.9

Source: United Nations, *National Accounts Statistics, Main Aggregates and Detailed Tables*. New York: 1983, Table 4.2.
Note: Net manufacturing output is defined as manufacturing value added.

ment loss and slow growth or decline of manufacturing output. It is necessary to distinguish between the trend of manufacturing employment on the upswing and on the downswing. In a cyclical upswing, manufacturing employment does not expand unless and until the rate of output growth outruns the rate of labour productivity increase. In a cyclical downswing, employment declines more or less proportionately with any decline of output because 70 per cent or more of net output is appropriated in the form of wages and social costs and any reduction in output quickly presses on the fund from which labour is paid. Because the British manufacturing sector is uncompetitive, export volumes have shown no steady upward trend since 1977 and import volumes have grown by an average 20 per cent every three years. In consequence, the British economy shows a unique pattern of weak upswing, severe downswing and no long-run growth in net output. Using manufacturing value added (MVA) as a measure of net output, there was a 10 per cent decline in manufacturing output between 1973 and 1976, in the wake of the oil crisis. In Mrs Thatcher's recession after 1978, manufacturing output declined by 19 per cent. In both downswings there was a more or less commensurate reduction in employment; two-thirds of the total job loss after 1970 occurred in these two recessions. Table 2.3 shows that the downswing relation between MVA and employment operates in much the same way in all the advanced countries and it also shows that the reduction in output and employment from peak to trough in Britain after 1978 was more than twice as large as in any other advanced country. On our rough calculation, around three-quarters of the output and employment loss after 1978 was caused by a displacement effect which arose as domestic output was replaced by manufactured imports.

It might be supposed that all this is past history. But we would argue that, just as the UK is leaving one policy-aggravated recession behind, another policy-induced recession is looming up. The only orthodox solution for a payments crisis is deflation, which will reduce output and employment.

The Causes

A variety of discourses, including economics, sociology and history, quarrel over whether and how British manufacturing failure might be explained. It would not be easy to classify the competing explanations and it is impossible to do justice to them all in the space of a few thousand words. Against this background, it is possible to describe our distinctive approach to the conditions of manufacturing failure. In a slightly solipsistic way, this does cover a fair amount of the ground because our approach was initially developed through criticism of other approaches and has progressed through self-criticism.

Explanations of manufacturing failure which emphasise the role of national character and attitudes continue to be popular. The point is proved by the favourable reception of Wiener's (1981) book on anti-industrial attitudes in Britain. We remain convinced that this approach has little to offer because it is impossible to establish any clear connection between a national ethos and specific failures at the industry and enterprise level. As the problem is immediately an economic one, many believe that it can be posed and answered within the framework of orthodox economic theory. But economics aims to provide a theory of the capitalist economy in general and necessarily abstracts from the specific institutional differences of particular national economies. That observation was our starting point when we began to work on the problem of manufacturing failure. In Williams *et al.* (1983) we were concerned to specify national differences and to emphasise the importance of the relevant institutions which directly handicapped British manufacturing. The book argued that British manufacturing's inferior performance was determined by unfavourable 'national conditions of enterprise calculation'.

If we were able to say something new and different in Williams *et al.* (1983) that was because the relevant institutional conditions had not been tightly specified and sceptically examined. There had, for example, been much general discussion about the British labour problem and the role of the City but very little analysis of how important and in what way.

We found that the importance of the labour problem had been generally exaggerated. Before the present recession changed the balance of power on the shop floor, bad work practices were widespread in British manufacturing. But these work practices did not have dire consequences. The aggregate evidence on the rate of growth of labour productivity was fairly reassuring because the British rate was rising towards the European norm during the 1960s. Of course, absolute levels of output per man were lower than in other northern European countries and British labour costs were increasing faster. But these points had to be seen in context. By the late 1970s, low levels of output per man were compensated by wages which were lower than in France and West Germany, while a depreciating currency ensured that British exporters were not seriously disadvantaged by increases in labour costs. Our scepticism about the labour problem was reinforced by case study material on motor cars. This showed that bad work practices imposed relatively modest cost penalties; the British car industry was more seriously handicapped by low model volume which ensured that development and tooling costs were spread over a small number of units. Furthermore, most of the non-price deficiencies of the British product were attributable to management.

In other areas we confirmed suspicions about, for example, the role of the banks and other financial institutions. We did not endorse the radical line that it was the overseas orientation of the City which caused the problems. The problems centred on what British financial institutions did and did not do for domestic enterprises. During the long boom of the 1950s and 1960s, the UK was the only advanced country whose banks refused to make loans to manufacturing enterprises for the purchase of capital equipment. And, although long-term loans for such purposes were available after 1973, the banks never changed their criteria for lending. They remain preoccupied with the taking of security over fixed assets. At the same time, the Stock Exchange did not provide generous finance to compensate for the deficiencies of the banks. In fact, the Stock Exchange made matters worse because the secondary market in issued shares made takeover on a share swap basis very easy. The consequence was a huge merger boom in the late 1960s in which nearly half the quoted companies vanished as a result of takeover.

Our conclusions of 1983 are not correct in every detail and some of them have been rendered obsolete by subsequent developments. We have restated our position on the labour problem in our more recent book on Austin Rover (Williams *et al.* 1987a) and would hope to revise our account of financial institutions in a way which takes note of the deregulation of financial markets. But we remain convinced that our 1983 approach to national institutional conditions does have explanatory power and does generate insights. The lending practices of the banks do help explain why the UK has an underdeveloped small business sector. The merger boom of the 1960s did produce giant firms which were difficult to manage and lacked strategic direction. For that matter, we predict that the renewed merger mania of the mid-1980s will have similar results. But, at the same time, after we had finished writing *Why Are the British Bad at Manufacturing?*, it was obvious that the institutional conditions approach had its limitations because it could not tackle the problem of the discretionary and variable nature of enterprise calculation. It is impossible to maintain a completely institutional determinist position. Institutions may condition and constrain but there clearly must be some kind of discretionary space for enterprise calculation. And institutional determinism does not explain what is this thing called enterprise calculation. Significantly in our 1983 book there is no general discussion of the nature of enterprise calculation which figures only as that which institutional conditions operate upon.

In taking up the issue of enterprise calculation, we started off from the observation that accounting profit was an ambiguous indicator of enterprise success. That much had emerged from our case study of GEC in Williams *et al.* (1983) which we originally undertook because we wanted to illustrate success. Instead we found that Lord Weinstock's use of financial ratios to guide the firm had produced perverse results. Profits had increased but the company's productive and market success was modest. GEC was a risk-averse company which had retreated from contested markets in civilian high-technology and consumer goods. The profits were being racked out of sheltered markets, especially in the cosy cost-plus world of defence. It does not surprise us that as these markets have become more difficult, GEC's technical competence has been called into question and its profitability has faltered. The conclusions of the GEC study were apparently confirmed and generalised by Hayes (1980) who argued that the investment techniques — net present value (NPV) and discounted cash flow (DCF) — favoured by large American and British firms had an inbuilt bias against large-scale strategic investment. This was a matter of simple arithmetic when such techniques applied a compound depreciation factor which reduced the value of distance returns. According to Hayes, the logic of financial control was a patching defensive approach to investment which ensured technological backwardness and market retreat.

But this view of the role of Western financial calculation was called into question by our further work on nationalised British coal, steel and cars (Cutler *et al.* 1985; Williams *et al.* 1986) where NPV techniques were used in the 1970s to justify massive strategic investment. What we found was that positive cash flows were projected after these enterprises had made highly optimistic assumptions about productive and market possibilities – BSC, for example, projected a steel market of 28–36 million tonnes by the early 1980s — and, in each case, the enterprises invested in giant new production facilities to meet the demand. BSC invested in basic oxygen steel converters and by the early 1980s had an installed capacity of 26 million tonnes. When demand ˙

failed to materialise, the fixed cost burden of the new facilities was sufficient to produce huge accounting losses, as in BSC where production has been running at around half of capacity since the early 1980s. The conclusion must be that the Western forms of financial calculation do not have one simple universal effect because everything depends on prior productive and market assumptions. If Western financial calculations do not guarantee sensible market and productive results, they are not uniquely responsible for manufacturing retreat and decline. After clarifying the limited role of financial calculation, in our latest book we have turned to examine productive miscalculation and the inability to relate production to the market. These are the themes of Williams *et al.* (1987a), which asks why the recovery strategy formulated by Sir Michael Edwardes for the volume cars division of Austin Rover after 1977 failed so dismally.

Management at Austin Rover failed to identify the hierarchy of interrelated production and market problems which faced the firm and inevitably then failed to tackle these problems in a sensible order of priority. Specifically, management privileged the reform of work practices which may have been a necessary condition but certainly was not a sufficient condition for the attainment of continuous high-volume production. Before or after work practices were reformed in 1981, the company has been unable to sell all the cars which the company can build; divisional labour productivity is now around nine cars per man year and that is no higher than it was in the early 1970s without the benefit of robots. The financial benefits of work practice reform were small because in motor cars (as in British manufacturing generally) labour costs normally account for no more than 15 per cent of total costs. The cost savings from this source were almost certainly outweighed by the cost penalties incurred through inept choice of production technology. In the new Longbridge body shop the company installed inflexible multi-welders. This body shop has been running at around 40 per cent of capacity since the Metro has failed to sell in the volume that was projected. Because the welding equipment is inflexible, it is not possible to use the excess capacity to build other models and it is carried as an extra fixed cost charge on each Metro built.

The cars division could never obtain any advantage from its investment in a docile work-force and automated body building inside the factories unless and until management solved the market problems outside the factories. Under Edwardes, the cars division aimed to take a substantial 20 per cent or more of the home market with a compact range of just three models — the Metro, Maestro and Montego — which were introduced between 1980 and 1984. The immediate problem was a new pattern of 'full line direct competition' on the home market. In each class Austin Rover's new models sold against competent offerings from Ford and Vauxhall. The inevitable result was market fragmentation as volume sales split three ways between the majors; the average best seller from a British major now claims just 5 per cent of the market. Even if Austin Rover's product and distribution were stronger, the division could not reach the Edwardes target. After all, three times 5 per cent will never equal 22 per cent. In this situation, the company's survival depended on export markets. But, under Edwardes after 1977, Austin Rover pulled out of the United States and export volumes to the EEC declined by 50 per cent to just 70,000 units; in effect, as sterling appreciated, the company pulled out of unprofitable export business. Management did not realise that, in so far as the cars division retreated onto the home market, it would never find a profit because that market would never absorb the output of Longbridge and Cowley. This point has now been taken on board in the Day plan of 1987 which seeks to stem financial losses by retreating from manufacture into low volume assembly.

Against the institutional background outlined in Williams *et al.* (1983), the later case-study work provides us with a distinctive concept of enterprise calculation which we can summarise in the form of two propositions.

The first of these is that enterprise calculation involves the exercise of managerial discretion within external limits and subject to specific institutional constraints. This point was first made in our brief treatment of the British motorbike industry in Williams *et al.* (1983). Given the disparity of productive scale and efficiency in comparison with those of the Japanese, the craft producers of British motorbikes had no option but to retreat up-market into superbikes. The British industry collapsed because, within these parameters, British management failed to develop a new range of high-quality superbikes which could justify a premium price. The variety of possible calculations is infinite, but most enterprises make financial, productive and market calculations and our second proposition concerns the relation between these calculations.

The second proposition is that enterprise calculation in each domain should be robust and realistic but, even more important, the aim should be to establish a harmonious relation between productive, market and financial calculations. The key to successful enterprise calculation is to make sure that one set of calculations does not preempt the achievement of objectives in other domains. The British case studies which we have considered in the discussion so far all provide textbook examples of how one calculation can pre-empt the others. The case of GEC showed how tight financial controls can be used to inhibit productive and market achievement while the case of Austin Rover showed how market miscalculation could nullify the effects of productive reorganisation and aggravate financial problems.

The virtue of this concept of enterprise calculation is that it allows us to escape from the rather dubious assumptions which have bedevilled most earlier discussions of enterprise calculation. First, our concept of enterprise calculation avoids reductionism. More specifically, the notion of three domains of enterprise calculation (financial, productive and market) allows us to resist the commonplace assumption that everything relevant to enterprise calculation can be represented in financial terms. This is the discursive error which is central to orthodox theory of the firm and it is the practical mistake which explains the failure of GEC's strategy. Second, our concept of enterprise calculation allows us to escape from the false choice between voluntarist and determinist accounts of what management can achieve. As the Austin Rover case study shows, some problems can be tackled and solved by management, while others, such as the limits established by market obstacles, must figure as external constraints. The lesson of Austin Rover is that management was free to privilege the labour problem in an unreasonable way but could not escape the pressures of demand fragmentation on the British car market.

If all this is, for us, an intellectually satisfying answer to what was an intriguing puzzle, it must be admitted that we did not begin work on manufacturing failure so that we could take up positions on enterprise calculation which were formally correct. Reconceptualisation is only a means to an end which remains the explanation of the causes of national manufacturing failure. From this point of view, the only question is what we have learnt about the causes of manufacturing failure which we did not know when we published *Why Are the British Bad at Manufacturing*? The answer is that our little group, which began by doubting the labour problem, has increasingly come to believe that the management problem is a crucial cause of manufacturing failure. The British management problem is that, within their area of discretion, British managers consistently take poor decisions about the priority of different problems and execute their strategies in a way that is generally inept. This point emerges not only from our case studies but also from recent survey evidence on the organisation of production in British manufacturing. Before the 1979–83 recession it was possible to blame poor organisation of production on the work-force and the unions. But that excuse is no longer plausible. The organisation of production inside the factory is now clearly within the prerogative of management.

Before we turn to examine the survey evidence, it is worth re-emphasising how and why the efficient organisation of production is a crucial prerequisite for manufacturing success. If production is not organised well then the results include reduced operating profits, poor quality, high cost, and poor delivery performance. Any enterprise which is handicapped in this way will find it difficult to achieve or maintain a healthy market share, and its lack of success in the marketplace is likely to create financial problems which can only be solved by retreat. To make the same point in a slightly different way: if the problem of production is not solved, then the result is likely to be a damaging disharmony between the different domains of calculation as productive inferiority compromises the enterprise's ability to achieve market and financial objectives. This is a point which the Japanese have always understood; their manufacturing success is built on the foundation of a superior capacity to organise production. If the Japanese have established a new standard of excellence in this area, the British are a natural polar opposite because British managers are specialists in the disorganisation of production.

The classic British mistake is to suppose that manufacturing efficiency can be obtained by buying in machines. All the surveys show that the stock of machinery in our engineering workshops is as up-to-date as in the shops of our European competitors. But, as the books on manufacturing techniques (for example, Schonberger 1983) emphasise, production is an activity where what counts is not what you have but how you use it. Daly *et al.*'s (1985) pilot survey shows how metalworking machinery in British factories is used less effectively than in West German factories which make the same simple engineering products such as coil springs, hydraulic valves and drill bits. In British factories machinery is poorly set up because numerical control devices and automatic feeders are not fitted; plant is poorly laid out so that work in progress cannot move quickly and easily from one work station to another; equipment in Britain is poorly maintained and frequently breaks down so that the quality and quantity of throughput is compromised; and, finally, line management in Britain often does not understand the capabilities of the more sophisticated equipment on the shop floor. Such problems about the organisation of production appear to be typical rather than exceptional right across British manufacturing.

The financial costs of the disorganisation of production cannot be calculated but the technical cost in terms of inefficiency has been devastatingly documented in the New and Myers (1987) survey, conducted in 1985, of 240 manufacturing plants selected to represent all the UK's major exporting industries. We know that the Japanese have a philosophy of no waste and this is applied to time as much as to manufacturing materials. The Japanese lay out their factories so that, via *kanban* and other methods, work in progress does not wait as inventory between production stations; capital equipment is modified so that downtime due to operations like die changes is minimised and bought-in components are delivered on a just-in-time basis. There is a huge gap between this ideal and current British achievement. According to the New and Myers survey, in component manufacturing, less than one-third of the total lead time is actually used for processing; for more than 70 per cent of the time, the components are idle awaiting the next operation. Despite leisurely schedules and large inventories British plants are often unable to deliver on time. In 1985 less than half the plants in the New and Myers survey managed to deliver more than 75 per cent of their product on time and one in four plants delivered more orders late than on time. This recent survey follows up an earlier survey undertaken in 1975 before the last recession when manufacturing output and capacity both fell by around 20 per cent. Despite the shakeout, according to New and Myers, there was no overall improvement in throughput efficiency and delivery performance in British manufacturing between 1975 and 1985.

This kind of general evidence demonstrates conclusively that Britain has a massive management problem which persists in a manufacturing sector which is leaner but not fitter. Like the general surveys, our case studies do not explain why British managers are unable to make sensible decisions on fundamentals which are within their prerogative. Some, such as Prais (1981), emphasise individual ignorance caused by the inadequacy of British education. And it is certain that management education is grossly deficient; the Handy (1987) report shows that 36 per cent of middle managers have had no management training since they started work and five of our top 100 companies made no provision for management training in 1986. Other writers would tend to emphasise corporate culture as an explanation of managerial performance. It is significant that many studies since the early 1950s show that American multinationals in the UK outperform native British firms; while Japanese success in consumer electronics assembly in the UK shows that, with the right organisational systems, the line managers and workers that we do have can achieve the highest standards of efficiency. The debate about the causes of the management problem is only just beginning. But already it is clear that the fact of pervasive managerial incompetence sets limits on the policy solutions that can work. That observation is the starting point of our analysis in the next section.

The Solutions

Williams *et al.* (1983) quite deliberately made no policy recommendations. But that book did briefly review the effects of government economic policies since the early 1950s. Keynesian and monetarist macro policies had been equally irrelevant to the problems of manufacturing and much micro policy had been damaging or ineffective. The record on detailed piecemeal intervention in the problems of specific enterprises and industries was dismal. Many policy initiatives, like the mergers promoted by the Labour Government's Industrial Reorganisation Corporation, had made matters worse, while others, like the little Neddies, had not helped because there was no machinery for implementing their recommendations. During the long boom, British manufacturing was generally harmed by an unfavourable environment setting policies such as the commitment to an overvalued pound before 1967. And, if *folie de grandeur* became less important after the mid-1970s, policy continued to engineer an unfavourable environment, mainly because a high-valued pound was the unintended consequence of Mrs Thatcher's monetarism in the early 1980s. In Williams *et al.* (1983) government policies rightly figured as one more unfavourable constraint on enterprise calculation.

It was equally obvious that in other advanced capitalist countries, such as France or Japan, economic policy was pushed to operational levels which were more closely specified and engaged constructively with enterprise calculation. This contrast naturally raised the question of what could be achieved through a more active industrial policy of the type which the centre-left was advocating in the early 1980s. This kind of industrial policy promised to improve competitive performance in two ways. Indirectly, it could change the conditions of enterprise calculation in a way which was beneficial. Thus, institutions, such as the National Investment Bank which the Labour Party proposed, could change the terms on which finance was supplied. Or, on a rather different front, new policy initiatives could rectify the gross deficiency of management education. Second, and more directly, industrial policy could make public funds available to assist research and development or finance process investment and more effective marketing in those industries or technologies which existing private institutions were not supporting adequately.

Cutler *et al.*, (1986) accepted that many of these initiatives were worth-while in the long term but argued they were unlikely to improve competitive performance dramatically in the medium term and would never avert the coming payments crisis. Even if the Labour Party had won the election of 1987 and had created a National Investment Bank, this one relatively small parallel institution working alongside the unreformed high street banks would never have produced an export boom in 1988. Improvements in management education could be more broadly based, but their effect on performance would necessarily be diffuse. As for policies of directly funding research and development or process technology, the problem here was the absence of clear criteria for supporting particular projects and enterprises and refusing others. It is not clear how a government agency could pick winners, particularly as there may be a conflict between desirable objects, such as the preservation or creation of employment and the development of high technology which is not labour-intensive. It must also be recognised that British civil servants have backed a disastrous series of losers. Their favoured civilian programmes from atomic power, through Concorde, to System X telephone exchanges have all had negligible market

potential. Civil research and development in the UK has never functioned as 'the process by which profitable opportunities for investment
are found' (Smith 1984).

A more active industrial policy is likely to have limited benefits in the
UK because it must operate in a national economy where the competence of our managers and civil servants is doubtful. Making funds
available on more favourable terms will only be beneficial if management strategy at the enterprise level identifies real problems and tackles
them in a sensible order. But, as the case of Austin Rover shows, that is
exactly what we cannot count on. This argument is rather hypothetical
because an active industrial policy has never been tried in Britain. But,
on the evidence we do have, the prognosis is fairly discouraging.
Under Mrs Thatcher, the government has sponsored a general change
in management culture; managers have been encouraged to reclaim the
right to manage from the unions and, through process and product
innovation, initiate a market-led recovery. There is no sign that such a
recovery is taking place. Are we to believe that, in partnership with the
DTI and local enterprise boards, the managers who have failed Mrs
Thatcher would have delivered the goods for a Labour or Alliance
government? And, if the enthusiasts for industrial policy will not take
on board the lessons of recent British experience, they are almost
certainly misreading the experience of countries such as Japan which
are presented as exemplars of successful industrial policy. As Cutler *et
al.* (1986) argue, industrial policy does not make Japanese productive
and marketing calculations work. The causal connections run the other
way because in Japan a superior production and marketing system
makes the task of picking winners less hazardous. The micro-economic
lesson of Japan is not that the UK could choose the right industrial
policy but that the UK is lumbered with a second-rate production and
marketing system. If it is grafted onto this kind of second-rate system,
industrial policy is likely to have very limited effects. The result, if
implemented in this form in the early 1990s, would be a reprise of our
disillusioning experience of French-style indicative planning in the
mid-1960s.

The fact of the matter is that the UK has a deep-seated management
problem which is not itself amenable to a political quick fix and which
limits the likely return on other policy initiatives such as industrial
policy. From this point of view, we have become interested in defensive policies which would curb payments crises and create a space
where we could live with, and work on, manufacturing failure. The
immediate problem which presents itself is an imbalance between
exports and imports. Since 1945, successive governments have encouraged exports and the question now must be whether it is not more
sensible to tackle the other side of the equation and restrict imports.
Cutler *et al.* (1986) argue the case for import substitution which could be

Table 2.4. British trade in manufactures with West Germany and Japan, 1986 (£ million)

Imports from W. Germany	13,082
Exports to W. Germany	6 368
Deficit	6 714
Imports from Japan	4 859
Exports to Japan	945
Deficit	3 914

Source: Central Statistical Office, *Overseas Trade Statistics*. London: HMSO, January 1987.

promoted through value added content regulation backed by state-sponsored investment in new capacity. The general aim of such policies would be to secure some kind of local balance between access to the British market and the location of productive capacity in the UK. This balance is not guaranteed by any market mechanism and has been undermined by our competitive inferiority.

Selective import controls would help to do the trick because, fundamentally, the British manufacturing trade deficit is a two-country, two-commodity problem. Eighty-six per cent of the total 1986 manufacturing trade deficit is accounted for by trade in just two types of commodity – motor vehicles, where the deficit was £4 billion, and electrical and electronic goods, where the deficit was £3.1 billion.[1] Most of the goods in the problem categories came from West Germany and Japan. Because we are in surplus with much of the rest of the world, the combined deficit with West Germany and Japan is actually larger than our overall manufacturing trade deficit (see Table 2.4).

The implication is that a narrowly focused policy of import regulation would be sufficient to curb the trade crisis. Such controls would hardly mean the end of the world as we know it because they would only extend the kind of protection which we all take for granted. All the advanced countries are protectionist against Japan; the trade figures show that, as the weakest of the industrial countries, the UK also needs relief from West Germany.

In proposing import controls limited to motor vehicles and electrical and electronic goods, we do not imply that the UK's manufacturing barrel is sound apart from these two bad apples. On the contrary in the decade after 1975 the value of imports rose faster than that of exports in all but two of the twenty-one sectors into which manufacturing divides at the SIC two-digit level. None the less a major feature is that, for the moment, a large proportion of the overall deficit is accounted for by vehicles and electricals. We would argue that this provides an opportunity, which may be fleeting, to adopt a highly selective policy of import controls. Such a policy is economically more desirable, politically more attainable and practically more effective than the imposition of a general tariff. These points are reinforced by the consideration that the two sectors are strategically placed in manufacturing industry: the linkages between motor vehicles and other sectors are especially strong; whilst electricals and electronics are crucial to the future development of the newer technologies.

It is also encouraging to find that the objective of curbing imports could be tackled through new kinds of policy instrument, without resort to quotas and tariffs of the old-fashioned kind. Motor vehicles and electronics present rather different problems and it is therefore worth considering them separately.

In the former, policy should initially aim to curb the £3 billion deficit which arises from the import of built-up motor vehicles. The most effective way of doing this is through value added content regulation on the company cars which account for half of new car sales in the UK. The existing tax depreciation allowances on company cars could be continued for those cars whose content was more than 80 per cent British and withdrawn for all others. Company purchasers of non-British cars would effectively pay a 'fine' of more than £1,000 over the two-and-a-half-year term of ownership. They could avoid this penalty by purchasing Ford Escorts and Sierras and Rover Group Maestros and Montegos which do meet the content requirement. The policy would be reinforced by similarly directing the public sector purchasing of cars towards those with a high British value-added content. The need is for an increase in British *manufacture* of cars with a high British value-added content. There are at least four recently modernised plants capable of such production in the UK (Longbridge, Cowley, Halewood and Dagenham) but to be viable these need a throughput sufficient to reduce the unit costs of manufacture. This throughput is equally essential for the domestic component-supplying industry. We estimate that our proposals would add at least 300,000 to British car production, leading to import substitution worth at least £1 billion. This benefit is much larger than the gain which will arise naturally as Ford and Vauxhall change their sourcing decisions in response to the appreciation of the Deutschmark. It is also more secure because value added content regulation would lock firms into British production, however currency relativities shift.

In electronics the approach would have to be different because the product lines are more diverse and British production capacity often does not exist. In our view, the appropriate response is investment in import substitution which could be sponsored by the state and enforced by suitable value added content regulation on major consumer electronic products like colour televisions and video-cassette recorders (VCRs). Wherever value added content regulation is imposed, investment in import substitution would in any case have to be regulated so that new entrants did not invest in excess capacity. Effective policy in electronics could start with positive measures aiming, first, to reduce the £400 million deficit on VCRs which accounts for around half the deficit in consumer electronics. In 1986, British consumers bought nearly 2 million VCRs, all of which were either imported or screwdriver assembled from kits. If the major suppliers were persuaded to incorporate one standard head in their different chassis, the British market (the largest in Europe) is big enough to sustain manufacture of the tape head which accounts for 40 per cent of total cost. Attention could also be given to curbing the import of television tubes. Some 2.5 million TV tubes are now imported each year because the multinational Philips only manufactures 20- and 21-inch sizes in Britain. More generally, consumer electronics is a suitable case for treatment because British interests have here been completely subordinated to multinational manufacturing strategies. The unprofitable and technically weak Ferguson division of Thorn EMI competes in an industry which is dominated by the Dutch firm Philips, which claims 25 per cent of the TV market, and by an assortment of Japanese assemblers which together hold a larger share of the TV market and completely dominate the VCR business. Here again, currency movements are influencing sourcing decisions but they will hardly sort out the problem when VCRs are at present virtually 100 per cent imported.

When import-substitution proposals of this kind are made, the conventional response is that they are economically unacceptable because value added content regulation would, like other forms of protection, featherbed inefficient producers and restrict consumer choice. In our view both of these objections cannot be sustained and rest on a misunderstanding of what has been proposed.

The counterargument about featherbedding rests on a complete misapprehension. The aim is not to emulate the East Europeans and move towards autarchy, where one (state) motor-car or television factory turns out a poor-quality and obsolete product which the consumer must buy. The aim is to emulate the Japanese, who protect their national market while they encourage stiff competition between domestic producers of differentiated goods; the home market may be reserved but the individual enterprise does not have a guaranteed share of that market. Value added content regulation in the UK would work in the same way, although it would often apply to multinationals rather than domestically owned majors. In cars value added content regulation would immediately benefit Ford and Rover by raising factory throughput. But one Japanese manufacturer, presumably Nissan, should be encouraged to manufacture light and medium cars which meet the 80 per cent standard and compete head on with domestic firms. In our view, Rover is too small and its management is too weak to cope with such competition, and the cars division should be handed over to

Honda, which could make a success of the business and benefit the UK if the Japanese firm were tied by value added content regulation. In consumer electronics, the approach would be slightly different because the aim here would be to encourage one or two private firms into volume production of commodity semi-manufactures. The policy would be to extend the existing pattern of competitive relationships. For example, with the exception of Sony, all the colour TV manufacturers in the UK already take their medium-sized tubes from Philips' British factories. Overall, in cars and consumer electronics, British manufacturing can plug into, and obtain the benefits of, industries which are increasingly organised on a global basis by American and Japanese multinationals. The policy of content regulation would ensure that, if these firms want to have a large share of the British market, they must undertake licensed manufacture here.

As for the issue of consumer choice, that has to be taken seriously. On any objective view, the difference between one small hatchback from Wolfsburg and another from Dagenham is trivial. But consumers have been educated into an appreciation of the differences over the import boom of the past twenty years. And when they have tasted of the fruit of the tree of product differentiation, they will not accept a sudden restriction of choice which leaves them with nothing but an 'inferior' British product. Any government of the left or centre which restricted choice in this way would almost certainly lose the election in which it sought a second term of office. But that is not a problem for us, because none of our proposals for cars and consumer electronics would dramatically reduce the present range of choice for the individual private consumer. A full range of imported European cars would be available for the private buyer, and the company user whose choice would effectively be restricted has always chosen from a list which excludes many imported makes and models. The availability of imported Japanese cars is already restricted by quota arrangement to 11 per cent of the British market. Further restriction on imports would be no hardship if at least one Japanese firm manufactured a range of two or three volume models in Britain. In consumer electronics equally there would be no problems about choice because a differentiated output of many brands and styles of TV or VCR could be produced from standardised 'national' commodity semi-manufactures. As Ford showed with its tied imports in the 1970s, and as Japanese firms are now demonstrating with British-assembled colour TVs, the British consumer does not care whether the product is manufactured or assembled in the UK, provided it embodies the qualities which he or she wants. That indifference is an opportunity which content regulation can exploit.

In conclusion, the economic costs of our new-style protectionism are negligible. The social benefits could be considerable because if output is maintained in British manufacturing, we can avoid further precipitous declines in manufacturing employment. In fact, it is the orthodox policy of deflation which turns out to have high economic and social costs, when it is used to curb payments crisis.

If there is an imbalance between manufactured exports and imports, the only orthodox way of reducing the consumption of imported goods is through deflation. This policy damps down the demand for imports by increasing the numbers of unemployed who have limited discretionary purchasing power and modest effective demand for imported manufactures. Two-thirds of the unemployed are on Supplementary Benefit and Bradshaw and Morgan's (1987) study shows that a family with two children on supplementary benefit spends just £6.68 on import-intensive clothing, footwear and durable household goods; according to the Family Expenditure Survey, the all-household average expenditure on these items is £36.20. The unemployed buy few new clothes, virtually no durable white and brown goods and cannot envisage owning a car. If the effects of unemployment on consumption of imported manufactures are dramatic, it is also the case that deflating to create unemployment is an extraordinarily indirect and wasteful way of regulating imports. If we look at those who are put into the dole queue, only a relatively small proportion of their reduction in income is taken out in the form of reduced consumption of imported manufactures. At £73.84, the income of Bradshaw and Morgan's model two-child family is £112 below the all-household average. So our 'average' unemployed family must be made more than £100 worse off so that their consumption of imports can be reduced by some £30. The creation of unemployment so as to reduce import consumption is also unjust in inter-class terms. In order that the middle classes can continue to satisfy their acquired taste for imported manufactures, the working classes must pay the price of unemployment and a dramatic reduction in their consumption choices.

With his usual perspicacity, Keynes saw these points in September 1931 when he was arguing for a revenue tariff and criticising the National Government's deflationary policies:

> Their policy is to reduce the standard of life of as many people as are within their reach in the hope that some small portion of the reduction of standard will be at the expense of imports. Deliberately to prefer this to a direct reduction of imports is to be *non compos mentis* (Keynes, 1972, p. 242).

Of course, more than fifty years ago circumstances were rather different. Keynes was arguing for a revenue tariff as a policy alternative to deflation which was being used to defend the fixed parity of sterling on the gold standard. But we would use much the same argument when arguing the case for selective import controls as a means of balancing the current account and preventing a precipitous decline in the value of sterling. After half a century it is still economically *non compos mentis* to prefer general deflation to a more limited surgical protectionist intervention. It would not be politically insane to acquiesce in deflation if there were now no alternative because EEC constraints prevent us from implementing necessary measures of protection. But the political difficulties of protection have been, and are being, exaggerated by dogmatic free-traders.

The policy that we are proposing is not a chauvinist one. It rests on the realisation that the system of competitive interchange of manufactures has reached its limits and that it is now unacceptable for the burden of deflationary output and employment-reducing adjustment to be placed more or less exclusively on peripheral and unsuccessful manufacturing countries. The Japanese can be told that we want their manufacturing techniques and value the stimulus which their competition provides, but the UK can do without manufactured imports from Japan which displace domestic output. In the long run no advanced country can live with unrestricted direct exports from Japan and, after much trade friction, the Japanese enterprises will have to undertake full manufacture overseas and accept slow output growth at home which requires the development of a welfare state so that the Japanese can cope with their share of unemployment. If the British government is free to set its own regulations on trade with Japan, West Germany is a more difficult case because British discrimination against imports from West Germany would break the free-trade rules of the EEC. But, the UK's current predicament is covered by article 109 of the Treaty of Rome, which states that 'when a sudden crisis in the balance of payments occurs . . . the member state may as a necessary precaution take the necessary protective measures' and envisages these measures would take the form of selective import controls. In an attempt to limit the concession, the protective measures are subject to approval by the Council of Ministers and the Commission. In a robust political argument, a radical British government would then have to defend policies of import substitution.

Those who claim that protection is politically impossible are, in effect, saying that they will only consider an economic policy fix which does not raise political problems and does not require institutional changes in the short and medium term. But there is no such policy fix for Britain which will do the trick and leave the institution of free trade (or, more specifically, the rules of the EEC) intact and unchallenged. The institutional conservatism which is commonplace on the centre left, as much as on the right, leads only to the quietist conclusion that nothing can be done except to manage industrial decline. At this juncture policies of benign neglect are not, or anyway should not be, an option for the left because manufacturing failure now has a distributional price which grows ever higher. In the 1950s and 1960s, poor manufacturing performance in a full employment economy simply meant that we all became better-off rather more slowly than the citizens of West Germany. Since unemployment started to rise in the 1970s, and especially since the recession which began in 1978, manufacturing failure means that a section of the British working class which is unemployed must accept large reductions in its living standards while the rest of us are growing better-off. If the left's socialism is about redistribution within the national economy, that result is intolerable. And if the curbing of unemployment is the first practical priority for the left, our argument is that, in the UK now, import controls must be a major instrument of policy.

Note

1. Motor vehicles includes cars, trucks and motor parts in SITC division 78. Electrical and electronic goods includes office machinery and data-processing equipment, telecommunications and sound-recording equipment and electrical and domestic appliances in divisions 75, 76 and 77

References

Bradshaw, J., and J. Morgan (1987), *Budgeting on Benefit*, London: Family Policy Studies Centre

Cutler, T., C. Haslam, J. Williams and K. Williams (1985), 'Aberystwyth Report on Coal', Aberystwyth, mimeo

Cutler, T., K. Williams, and J. Williams (1986), *Keynes, Beveridge and Beyond*, London: Routledge and Kegan Paul

Daly, A., D. Hitchens, and K. Wagner (1985) 'Productivity, Machinery and Skills in a Sample of British and German Manufacturing Plants', *National Institute Economic Review*, February, pp. 48–62

Handy, C. (1987) *The Making of Managers*, London: National Economic Development Office

Hayes, R.H. and W.J. Abernathy (1980). 'Managing our Way to Economic Decline', *Harvard Business Review*, 58.4, pp. 67–77

House of Lords Select Committee on Overseas Trade (1985), *The Causes and Implications of the Deficit in the UK Balance of Trade in Manufactures*, House of

Lords, session 1984–5, HL 238–I, London: HMSO

Keynes, J.M. (1972), *Collected Works*, Vol. ix, London: Macmillan

New, C.C. and A. Myers (1987), *Managing Manufacturing Operations in the UK 1975–85*, London: British Institute of Management

Prais, S.J. (1981), *Productivity and Industrial Structure*, Cambridge: Cambridge University Press

Schonberger, R. (1982), *Japanese Manufacturing Techniques*, New York: Free Press

Singh, A. (1977), 'UK Industry and the World Economy: A Case of Deindustrialisation?', *Cambridge Journal of Economics*, 1.2, pp. 113–36

Smith, K. (1984), *Britain's Economic Crisis*, Harmondsworth: Penguin

Wiener, M. (1981), *English Culture and the Decline of the Industrial Spirit*, Cambridge: Cambridge University Press

Williams, K., Williams, J. and Thomas, D. (1983). *Why Are the British Bad at Manufacturing?* London: Routledge and Kegan Paul

Williams, K., C. Haslam, J. Williams and A. Wardlaw (1986), 'Accounting for Failure in the Nationalised Industries', *Economy and Society*, 15.2, pp. 167–218

Williams, K., J. Williams and C. Haslam (1987a) *The Breakdown of Austin Rover*, Leamington Spa: Berg

Williams, K., J. Williams and C. Haslam (1987b), 'The Relation between Value Added and Employment in Manufacturing', *Aberystwyth Economic Papers*, no. 14, Aberystwyth: University College of Wales, Department of Economics

3   Flexible Automation and Factory Politics: The United Kingdom in Comparative Perspective

Bryn Jones

Introduction

Reindustrialisation and the resuscitation of manufacturing through new technologies are widely acknowledged to be a precondition for higher profitability and the revitalisation of product markets. It has been principally assumed that the new forms of computer-programmable automation provide an alternative to, and effective replacement for, production based on skilled workers. The aim of this chapter is to argue the contrary. Complex and uncertain relations between work roles and automated production systems persist and the organisation of the former can affect the operational success of the latter.

In the crucial sphere of *flexible automation*, operating methods, management systems and the role of labour may be developing in contrasting patterns. From a policy perspective industrial regeneration through technological advance could mean just fatter profits for established producers. However, different applications of similar technology can also mean differences in the quality of work life, workplace democracy, and the acquisition of skills and decision-making powers by rank-and-file workers, and can affect the broader political balance between labour and capital.

The use of programmable automation technology reduces times and changeovers in the marketing and design of products. It also speeds up the setting up and operation of manufacturing processes. The consequent transformation of plant organisation, jobs and managerial controls has stimulated two opposed interpretations of the implications for labour. For many radical and Marxist critics the attendant ethos of 'flexibility' is part of a more general recipe for more insecurity of employment, technological deskilling, segmentation of work-forces, effort intensification and the erosion of union checks upon managerial authority. From this perspective flexible manufacture is frequently labelled neo-Fordism: a more sophisticated system of exploiting labour and production technology than was possible under conventional, Fordist, mass production methods. An opposite conclusion is reached by those commentators who emphasise the new production goals and greater responsibility that the new systems require from production workers. On this view conventional mixtures of Fordist production organisation and Taylorised work roles are less relevant than skilled knowledge in the programming and maintenance of computer-controlled machinery.

These debates, therefore, largely turn on the extent to which narrowly specialised jobs controlled on hierarchical principles are replaced by genuinely expanded work roles and 'high trust' authority relations manifested in arrangements such as multi-skilled – polyvalent – and 'autonomous' work groups. A useful yardstick for clarifying these different interpretations is provided by the concept of flexible specialisation. Piore and Sabel's (1984) analysis suggests that a true break with Fordist production principles and Tayloristic work roles depends on whether the new technological systems are used to achieve shorter production runs, more frequent setting of machines and higher product quality rather than simply reductions in labour costs and other scale economies of standardised volume production.

The commercial application of flexible manufacturing systems (FMSs) provides such a clarification. It also gives an opportunity to reflect on the considerations that a future industrial policy ought to adopt in the promotion and utilisation of such advanced technologies. In the development of the 'computer-integrated' or automatic factory, FMSs constitute the operating core. Combinations of computer control systems and automatic machining and transfer equipment enable new and variable mixes of product to be initiated and repeated with only minimal operating staff and limited operational decision-making. In future and more sophisticated versions, integration with information flows from design, planning and inventory functions are envisaged as enabling almost instantaneous responsiveness of the production process to market requirements. In principle, therefore, FMSs could be the technological embodiment of post-Fordist flexible production.

It must be recognised that alternative models of labour organisation are not explicitly considered in managerial and technical debates on flexible manufacturing technology. However, in such disputes about its proper purpose there is concern with the rival merits of conventional Fordist production objectives and some of the elements of flexible specialisation. Contrasting types of jobs and labour-management systems are implicit in the different prescriptions. The engineers and manager's assessments, however, consist principally of disagreements about whether FMS technologies are best used to deliver Fordist-type cost economies into the previously refractory small and medium batch production processes, or whether their principal virtue consists of more qualitative gains. Amongst the latter are: enhanced product quality, simplication of managerial control arrangements, and a more flexible capacity to respond to design, product innovation and market changes.

Current patterns and future possibilities for either neo-Fordist or post-Fordist arrangements in factory automation can be gleaned from comparative studies of FMSs in the United Kingom, Japan, and the United States. On balance these suggest that a strict definition of flexible specialisation has yet to supersede Fordist-type orthodoxies in the planning and operation of automated factories. On the basis of comparable evidence from Italy, more authentic forms of flexible specialisation seem set to continue to be the preserve of smaller artisan-level enterprises rather than relocating in the automated plants of the larger firms. However, the significant national differences in the staffing and organisation of FMSs do suggest that these are influenced by politico-cultural choices and by the internal politics of the enterprise. Flexibility has different dimensions and different levels and outcomes are possible as between nations and firms.

Partly because of the intervention of political and practical difficulties, and also because of conflicting prescriptions for flexible automation, the present picture is one of a number of hybrid forms that are Fordist in some respects and more consistent with post-Fordist production roles in others. British applications of FMS are sufficiently tentative and *ad hoc* in their organisation to be influenced by coherent policies from outside the firm. However planners of industrial policy, or those aiming to influence the ways in which automation plans are implemented, should take account of this diversity and the crucial modifications of strategic-level designs by local institutions and practices.

The following account attempts to assess the potential for neo-Fordism and flexible specialisation and the extent to which they are accompanying and guiding the use of the flexible automation technology of FMSs. It is based principally upon plant visits and case studies in the USA, Japan, Italy and the UK.[1]

The material on Italy was gathered mainly from very small artisanal producers, rather than large-firm users of FMSs, in order to deal with a possibility often neglected in the current debates on flexible manufacturing. As Brusco and Sabel (1981) have shown, innovation and organisational flexibility have tended, at least in Italy, to be most effectively achieved by smaller firms, especially artisanal workshops, as part of the broader decentralisation of production away from large plants. Yet changing business strategy and the exploitation of programmable automation could be used successfully under either flexible specialisation or neo-Fordist regimes to reduce the numbers, and improve the quality and model-frequency of products.

Would this not represent a threat to small-firm specialisation; either by calling back subcontract jobs that were previously too small to put through the big firms' own plants, or by the larger businesses competing more directly on cost or product-quality grounds within the small-firms' own independent markets? To what extent can the empire strike back? This possibility is discussed below. To begin with, however, there is a need for a tighter definition of the terms used in the flexible manufacturing debate and for a description of the technologies involved.

Flexibility and Flexible Automation

Firms, industries and national economies have adjusted their production operations to the intensified competition associated with market contractions and instability in different ways. Commentaries and debates on manufacturing changes have not always distinguished clearly enough between the different adjustments that have been made by enterprises to avoid the instabilities of the mass manufacturing of standard products: the 'Fordist' approach. Not least amongst the problems is that, as Hyman (1988) and Tolliday and Zeitlin (1987) have pointed out, Fordism has not always, and particularly in the UK, been promoted or realised as a comprehensive system of manufacture by many mass manufacturers. Similar conceptual and practical variations apply to contemporary usage of manufacturing flexibility.

British commentators tend to merge together all business practices where there are systematic variations in the applications of finance, organisation, resources and labour to operations and products. The problem with these kinds of 'flexible' labellings is that they can apply almost as equally to the strict flexible specialisation model proposed in the work of Sabel (1982), and Piore and Sabel (1984), as to some mass production practices. Thus the flexible employment policies publicised by Atkinson (1984; Atkinson and Meager 1986) and the Institute of Manpower Studies (1985), whereby core and peripheral work-forces are created and managers seek flexibility in terms of numbers employed, can and have been pursued in the past to deal with seasonal fluctuations in the demand for *mass produced* goods, as Tolliday and Zeitlin (1987) have shown for the British motor-car industry.

Similarly, product flexibility can simply mean shortening the lifetimes of particular goods while continuing to manufacture them in high volumes over the shortened life cycle (see Child 1985). This strategy, associated often with the attempts of Japanese producers to increase global market shares, may make life more stimulating or harrowing for designers, engineers and marketing staff but will not necessarily change the content or quality of production workers' jobs. Conversely, flexibility may be sought and achieved in the work practices and roles of factory workers without any change towards more variation in products or processes of production. Some of the current vogue for 'multi-skilling', for example, is simply intended to minimise overhead costs of maintenance or to keep more complex and expensive electronic machinery working for longer periods (see Cross 1985). It is, therefore, important not to conflate these forms of flexibility, or others such as the Thatcher government's campaigns for 'flexibility' in wages and employment contracts, with flexible specialisation, as some commentaries are in danger of doing.

A strict definition of flexible specialisation would appear to require four interdependent elements: small or medium rather than large volumes of each part or product; frequent changes in the basics of product design and/or production methods; a product portfolio of several models for the same plant, rather than exclusive concentration on one, or a few, goods; reliance upon the greater task versatility, skills and decision-making abilities of production workers, because of the frequency of model changes and the irrelevance of detailed Tayloristic controls. As Sabel (1982) makes clear, the dividing line between this structure and compromises with more conventional Fordist arrangements (the ubiquitous neo-Fordism) may be blurred in practice. A comprehensive switch to flexible specialisation would push managements to 'high trust' relations with their work-forces, significantly affecting the latter's job satisfaction, decision-making powers and job security *vis-a-vis* management. In practice managers may attempt to minimise such trasformations. They may limit the scale and frequency of product changes, bank on pseudo-participatory schemes, or attempt to restrict the more responsible and skilled tasks within their own ranks or to a small elite of production workers (see Friedman 1977).

Yet another half-way house is to attempt *technological* substitutes for the risky policy of reskilling and decentralised controls. The purposes and applications of programmable automation are not an undifferentiated whole but can be used in different combinations of computer-aided design, computer-aided manufacturing (automatic planning and data communication for production process), computer-controlled machines, robots, and flexible manufacturing systems. Or, more ambitiously, these various systems can be integrated so as to provide automatic sequencing of different stages of production and preproduction. These complexities are thus another central element in the uncertainties about the direction in which the retreat from Fordist mass manufacture is leading. The problem is that these new technologies need not of themselves facilitate either post-Fordist flexible specialisation or neo-Fordist business and manufacturing practices. Yet there are commentators who have unequivocally identified flexible manufacturing with polyvalent, autonomous work organisation. Even among those who identify it with a more sophisticated but still highly exploitative industrial system, a misleading potency is often attributed to the technologies.

Robin Murray (1985, p. 31), for example, seems to conflate flexible specialisation with neo-Fordism because he singles out programmable technologies as the common thread in the new developments that lead to 'deskilling, fragmentation, and dualism'. He describes neo-Fordism/flexible specialisation as consisting of

> applying computer technology not only to each stage of the production process, from design to retailing, but also to the integration of all stages of the process into a single co-ordinated system. As a result, the economies of scale of mass production can now be achieved on much smaller runs, whether small batch engineering products, or clothes, shoes, furniture and even books. Instead of Fordism's specialised machinery producing standardised products, we now have flexible, all-purpose machinery producing a variety of products (Murray 1985, pp. 29–30).

As I shall explain below, managers of some of the world's most advanced automated factory systems would give their right arms for such comprehensive sophistication. Reality, for the vast majority, lags way behind such a shiny vision. Richard Hyman (1988) has provided a more clinical critique of the labour implications of flexible specialisation. Yet the more realistic threat, of oppressive surveillance and control, which he associates with flexible specialisation is also made against over-optimistic interpretations of computerised production as itself favouring decentralised decision-making and reskilling. Amongst this latter kind of post-Fordist interpretation we have as a prime example Hirschhorn's (1984) predictions. He identifies the advent of programmable automation in the manufacture of small and medium batch production with an industry-wide technical and organisational pressure to create autonomous work groups and polyvalent work roles.

As historical evidence demonstrates, the strict model of flexible specialisation does not depend upon new technologies (Sabel and Zeitlin 1985). Nevertheless the considerable potential of programmable automation and related computer aids for improving the relative profitability of variable product/small batch specialisation, and their direct impact upon labour, puts them at the centre of debates about the nature of post-Fordist manufacturing (see, for example, Williams *et al.* 1987). Preliminary to any more detailed resolution of possibilities with trends must be answers to three outstanding questions about existing applications of advanced manufacturing technology. How sophisticated are the actual technologies that have so far been applied to factory automation in terms of providing the opportunity to supersede traditional work practices and facilitate operational flexibility? Are managers seeking to apply these technologies in a systematic attempt to achieve variations in products and orders, or are they employed in order to continue Fordist objectives of cost minimisation and higher worker productivity? If the operation of the technologies is not itself sufficiently demanding to require more flexible and less hierarchical forms of work organisation and management what other social and economic factors intervene to promote or retard them?

The attempts to move small batch metalworking production towards more systematic computer-controlled flexibility, and the attendant claims of the relaxation of rigidly controlled job specialisms has a broader significance for the debate over flexible specialisation. The motor-car industry often figures as the primary test case for both proponents and critics of the thesis. But in terms of the impact of product and market versatility upon work it is an unsuitable case. Even with reduced batch sizes and more frequent model changes the volumes involved are still numbered in thousands and the numbers of resets of machines occur on weekly and daily bases. Under these circumstances only a minority of the more specialised workers is likely to be involved.[2]

In small-batch manufacture, on the other hand, resetting times may be hourly and the range of work requires broader skills and experiences. Taylorist influences long ago sought to limit the associated worker discretion by functional specialisation and a search for aggregations of more uniform types of batch. Programmed automation means that firms with these types of process no longer need simply to imitate the uniform specialisation of product types more successfully achieved by the mass manufacturers. To the extent that managements recognise that such a Fordist model is no longer the only route to technical efficiency and market success *then* polyvalence amongst production workers will appear relevant.

Technological Possibilities

Flexible manufacturing systems were first developed in the late 1960s and early 1970s as an attempt to achieve higher rates of machine utilisation in factories making small batches of components. In the late 1970s, in conjunction with the move to computer control of individual machine tools, came cheaper and more applicable computing power. This conjunction revitalised long-standing aspirations for automated factory units and, more ambitiously, the possibility of programming entire groups of automatic machines to operate simultaneously on diverse components until the finished parts or products left the system. However, despite enthusiastic ordering and publicity for FMSs in the early 1980s, debate has continued among technologists and industrial experts over the precise gains that have been and can be achieved.

Summarising a complex set of arguments, the principal differences can be said to hinge upon the definitions of flexibility that should be pursued.

For some it is sufficient that machine-tools systems should be capable of switching from one product or 'family' of parts by means of a change of computer program. This seems to be the technological trait which has led some commentators such as R. Murray to associate flexible manufacturing technology with a flexible specialisation business policy. Another, competing, technical definition of flexibility is that within a broadly defined range of products it should be possible to have any job randomly assigned to any part of the FMS by the appropriate software instructions without reprogramming or retooling. This arrangement would represent a much more sophisticated technological counterpart to flexible specialisation because different types of product for different orders and markets could be made at virtually the same time on the same equipment. Needless to say, this more ambitious approach has not yet been convincingly established to the satisfaction of theoretical engineering criteria, though some American firms claim practically to have achieved it.

Cross-cutting this debate is a managerial one about the kinds of commercial gain that can be achieved. Broadly the arguments here cluster around one set of 'quantitative' benefits that are fairly easy to calculate and record using conventional accounting techniques and another set of principally 'qualitative' gains (for an overview, see Jaikumar 1984). Plant engineers and production managers have tended to see the principal advantages of FMSs in terms of cutting labour costs, reducing stocks of semi-finished parts and increasing the throughput of work, thus improving the utilisation of machine tools and decreasing the payback period of their investment costs. 'Qualitative' benefits, on the other hand, are those that are more difficult to capture through existing accounting practices since they only contribute to long-term and generalised business gains. They are said to involve the improvement of product quality, less demands for managerial control and speedier responses to changes in market demand or product design.

Flexible specialisation requires that innovation is combined in the different spheres of design, marketing, production and work organisation in order to break with Fordist practice. Flexible manufacturing technology, on the other hand, may still be pursued with Fordist criteria in mind, and is, at present, mainly concerned with revitalising only the production side of business operations. However the engineering debates about the proper aims and applications of FMS also suggest that there is considerable uncertainty about the most appropriate role for these systems. There is the *potential* to use the technology to further a flexible specialisation strategy, but equally it can be used in a more restrictive fashion and still achieve certain operational and commercial gains. As to the implications for labour management and work roles, there are few clues in the technical literature. To identify these features there is no substitute for the study of appropriate working cases, to which we now turn.

The United States

General Trends

By 1981 there were already estimated to be between 20 and 30 FMSs operating in the USA. Objections could be raised about how many of these and subsequent installations satisfy engineering criteria of flexible manufacturing such as random assignment of parts to work stations. However, a few of these FMSs have been running successfully for a decade or more. In addition, in the opinion of some technologists, such as MIT's Nathaniel Cook, total flexibility of assignments to machines may be practically impossible to program.[3] So most of these systems are probably representative of current trends. In comparison with the experience of other countries there are five outstanding aspects to the adoption and operation of FMSs in the USA. First, emphasis tends to be placed upon technological sophistication, which is frequently bought in from systems suppliers rather than being generated within the user firms. Second, as a consequence of the resulting high costs, adoption has been almost exclusively by larger corporations. Third, hierarchical organisational principles are re-emphasised and shape the programming functions and process controls. Fourth, adherence to traditional forms of job classification and work roles limits the operational flexibility of the system. Fifth, the overwhelming, though not universal, emphasis in adoption motives and operating objectives tends to be conventional 'quantitative' rather than 'qualitative' gains.

Of the eight FMS firms that I visited during 1984, with one notable exception, none gave much emphasis to qualitative gains and the flexible specialisation principle of continuous product variation as operating objectives. By and large these were traditional small to medium batch manufacturers in the machine-tool, agricultural and construction equipment, and aerospace sectors. FMSs were being applied by them as singular technological solutions to bottlenecks that could not be dealt with by means of Fordist techniques. Unlike the current craze for flexible occupational roles and participative management arrangements, associated with the Quality of Working Life schemes in parts of the American motor-car industry (Katz 1985; Wood 1988), these employers operated with conventional forms of line management, work organisation and industrial relations. There was limited, and sometimes grudging, recognition of the importance of conventional skills in keeping the FMS running and adjusting machine operations yet there was little or no official rotation of jobs and a rigid barrier separated computer control and programming tasks from the mechanical operating duties. In some respects operators were treated as (and were capable of acting as) the new bottlenecks, hampering the required levels of FMS utilisation on jobs such as pallet and tool loading.

Hierarchy, occupational specialisation and the demarcation of computer-related tasks from the shop floor were largely attributable to the acceptance of industrial relations norms. Even if managements perceived the potential advantages of delegated authority and polyvalence (which seemed unlikely) they were generally too aware of the possible complications of conventional bargaining and work organisation arrangements in the rest of the plant to risk applying these principles to the FMS. Radical critics of automation in the USA, such as Shaiken (1985), have also observed the restriction of skilled programming tasks by and to management strata. While they associate such management practice with universal socio-economic imperatives for control, a comparative perspective suggests it is more an effect of national institutional conditions. By defining computer programming and controlling work as a managerial job, and therefore beyond the scope of collective bargaining, managements are conveniently able to avoid union influence over these jobs. For their part the tactics of unions are also generally circumscribed by industrial relations conventions. They possess a relative degree of security because of the existing system of occupational classifications and job transfers. Minor suggestions of job rotation or multi-skilling on production work are therefore resisted and the attraction of gaining a foothold in computing functions is obscured by management intransigence to relaxing their line of demarcation. Two case studies illustrate more clearly the institutional and micro-political obstacles and preconditions involved in combining flexible forms of work organisation with FMS technology in order to achieve flexible production methods. In the first case, Fordist orthodoxy won out over an experiment in work-group autonomy. In the second case a contingent combination of local circumstances favoured the development of such shop-floor independence and facilitated an operating philosophy that was much closer to flexible specialisation.

A Case for and a Case Against Post-Fordist Production

In a locomotive factory (which we will call 'Zeta') where the FMS had been introduced to improve the quality of the motor frames for diesel-electric locomotives the principal preoccupation was with speeding up the machining time. Despite being designed for only two small 'families' of parts, rather than extensive product variations, there were considerable debugging and mechanical adjustment problems during the early days of the system. Management and union evolved a provisional agreement on all-round work roles for loading, operating, tooling, and maintenance tasks together with a tentative plan to involve the operating crew in the computer-scheduling of the parts through the system.

The union local of the United Electrical Workers had a reputation for militancy and accountability to its members but was prepared to co-operate with the management provided the extra efforts and responsibilities involved in the new job classification were recognised by a higher pay grading system. The agreement collapsed with bitter complaints from the FMS crew and shop stewards when senior management revoked the payment system on the grounds of cost. Although there was only a difference of few thousand dollars per week between the original arrangement and the revised pay rates it was probably not coincidental that the revision took place when most of the running-in problems had been resolved. In revenge, however, the union and work crew dropped the co-operative work practices and reverted to a system of task specialisation by occupation title, also abandoning involvement in the scheduling of the system.

The second case, code-named Alpha, is more interesting as a case of 'what might have been' for other FMS users. At Zeta management appeared to calculate that once the implementation and running-in phase was complete there would be little dependence upon the operating crew and the formal attempts at flexible work organisation lapsed. At Alpha, by contrast, management found itself increasingly dependent upon an informal autonomous work group whose members rotated most of the key operating, maintenance and programming tasks amongst themselves on an *ad hoc* basis. This situation arose because of a failed management employment strategy, pragmatic trade unionism, and the adoption, by default, of a variable product policy; a *de facto* form of flexible specialisation.

The Alpha FMS was one of the earliest in the USA. It was set up in 1975 partly because the supplier company wanted to gain experience with FMS technology but had not the space at its own plants to undertake such practical experiments. Alpha was the small agricultural equipment division of a larger American corporation. The FMS was bought to machine the transmission parts for a new tractor and the production management adopted the FMS proposal largely because the supplier was willing to share costs, rather than because of any preference over other production systems. Managers, at that time, tried to avoid key provisions of the existing union contract being applied to the FMS. They feared that clauses on employee seniority and transfers within the plant could disrupt the efficiency of the FMS if and when rationalisation eliminated the jobs of more senior employees; because adherence to the contract would then allow older and possibly unsuitable workers with employment seniority to 'bump' out of the FMS members of the work crew with the most appropriate skills and aptitudes. Accordingly a new occupational classification of 'FMS Qualifier' was created that was not on the same 'job ladder' as other occupations in the plant. Almost an entire work crew was gradually recruited for the FMS from a small jobbing machine shop firm in the same district.

Over time, as the original engineering staff moved out of the plant or the company and the work crew developed their own methods and skills for resolving problems and meeting new requirements, *de facto* autonomy in operating methods and decision making was evolved. More task sharing developed and one of the operators was promoted to become the main programmer for the system after teaching himself the programming functions in his spare time. The skills and knowledge of the work group (of which the programmer regarded himself as an unofficial member and tacit leader) made it virtually independent of the normal authority and sanctions of line managers. The group's position was enhanced by the pragmatic decision of the union representatives to allow it to negotiate some of its interests for its members and by the company's drift into an operational form of flexible specialisation.

As the smallest of the American farm tractor manufacturers, Alpha was always at a disadvantage compared to the larger firms which could use resources such as their extensive dealer outlets to dominate the market. Technical improvements or model redesigns were the most appropriate competitive tactics for Alpha. In the late 1970s a new design was caught out by the slump in farmers' revenues. If the tractor parts had been machined on a dedicated transfer line there would not have been the volumes to justify its continued production. The FMS was used to produce the parts for the new model as demand required, mixing in other work as appropriate. On another occasion the FMS came to the rescue when new models with redesigned engine valves were to be launched through an important agricultural exhibition. The speedier resetting capability of the FMS was used to help out a dedicated transfer line on which machining of the necessary components had originally been planned so that the new models would be available for the show. More generally, the FMS staff could now claim that their ability to work the system flexibly had saved the division from possible closure by allowing it to maintain a small but healthy niche in a market dominated by volume producers.

Conclusion

American users of FMS have not sought, in the main, to use these as aids to a policy of flexible specialisation despite their undoubted potential for such an approach. FMSs have been purchased and used principally to achieve more conventional Fordist cost economies on fairly restricted product lines. Within these limits the systems exhibit considerable technical sophistication and several users seem committed to seeking additional technological solutions to some of the problems set by human inadequacies.

The role of the traditional adversarial and legal-contractual industrial relations system appears to lock both management and unions together in their indifference or anxiety to more responsible and flexible forms of work organisation. The trends towards 'participation' and broader work roles in the American motor-car industry have yet to make much impact upon firms in other metalworking sectors. However, contingent circumstances can allow a combination of flexible automation and polyvalent quasi-autonomous work groups with a variable product market strategy, as the Alpha case demonstrates.

Japan

As in other areas of industrial automation, Japanese use of computer-integrated manufacturing has acquired something approaching a legendary status in the Western business and industrial press. References to 'workerless factories' imply that technological virtuosity is responsible for Japanese manufacturing successes. Little thought is given to how such an American-style emphasis on high-technology substitution of labour is compatible with Japan's alleged reliance upon a willing and responsible work-force and reciprocal worker — management obligations. One particularly publicised feature of Japanese industrial organisation is the limited degree of direct management authority over the shop floor and the greater internal mobility of workers within the enterprise and plant (see, *inter alia*, Abbeglen and Stalk 1985, p. 206; Ouchi 1982; Dore 1973). Koike (1983) goes so far as to claim that job rotation takes place at half-day intervals in many plants. It might thus be conjectured that it is this organisational flexibility, rather than sheer technological commitment, that gives an optimal institutional framework, and hence successful operation of such schemes as FMS. In practice there are diverse implications.

Adoption and Diffusion: Enterprise Specificity

The dominance of the internal labour market in the Japanese corporate sector has been widely interpreted as a core element of its employment and industrial relations system. What is not, perhaps, so broadly acknowledged is the implication for working practices of the corresponding company-specific skills and qualifications. There is a more general particularistic character of production operations that accompanies and feeds off plant-specific jobs and work methods. All the FMS vendors that I spoke to commented on the buying firms' preference for customising the operating details of machines and systems to their own requirements. This preference was thought to be much more marked in Japanese than in European and American users who would be more willing to buy 'turn-key' systems. An interview with a Ministry of International Trade and Industry (MITI) representative revealed that further progress in the spread of FMSs in Japan could depend upon standardisation of machines.

Significantly it was also felt that software development was being impeded by *ad hoc* designs for, and by, particular users; and because of an insufficiency, in the relevant firms, of software engineering special- ists to develop and disseminate operating programs. A telling comment from FMS suppliers was that work-role flexibility was itself an *obstacle* to the development of systematic software controls and information processing as in computer-aided manufacturing systems. The tendency for decision-making by work groups and a reliance upon the on-the-job knowledge of all relevant individuals is facilitated by the famous long-service and 'life-time employment' arrangements. But these have the perverse effect of discouraging the formalisation and keeping of systematic paper records upon which the computerisation of produc- tion and methods planning would need to be based.

It is perhaps significant that the main reasons given for adopting FMS put little emphasis upon operating flexibility. Indeed one FMS user/vendor thought that FMS automation was about increasing vol- umes rather than product variety and flexibility of response. However, it was also conceded that smaller batch sizes and increasing product ranges, together with an overriding Japanese concern with product quality, were important considerations for customers. Financial consid- erations were given most emphasis. Round-the-clock working reduced the length of the payback period and the flexibility of the systems for resetting to different uses reduced or eliminated the need to purchase new or additional machinery.

FMS Operation and Division of Labour

The Japanese users interviewed reported few or no operating problems with their FMSs. There were two principal reasons for this happy situation. As in some of the British and American user firms, the FMSs were restricted to the production of a fixed family of parts with minimal reprogramming for 'true' flexibility. Such restrictions, of course, limit the scope for errors and unforeseen difficulties, as well as narrowing the extent to which engineers and operators have to exercise broader skills of adaptability and discretion. Such standardisation could be seen as simply an extension of the logic of Fordist manufacturing philo- sophy. However, the other factor that seemed to limit the importance of Japanese firms' operating problems was the delegated character of production management. Supervisors and operators are largely left to deal with the day-to-day running of the systems; a role that meant it was common for operators to undertake the reprogramming of individual machine-tools as well as, in some instances, the more risky adjustment of the computerised schedules that dispatch components between the work stations.

Unlike the American FMSs described above, there was much less specialisation into job categories. In addition to simple programming tasks, routine repairs and maintenance, tool and work-piece setting and quality inspection were the responsibility of a single class of 'operators'. However, these flexible arrangements were not specific to the FMS or other automated areas. They were simply an extension of normal practices in the rest of the plant. Operators who were interviewed said that they saw little difference between their work role in the FMS and in other machining processes. As far as *recruitment* was concerned there seemed to be no special qualities, training or out-of-the-ordinary experiences demanded of new FMS workers. The traditional British preference for workers with craft skills was, of course, irrelevant in a country without an industrial concept of craft specialisation and training.

FMS Case Studies

The relationship between FMS work roles and labour-management systems varied slightly but significantly in the FMS firms visited, suggesting two possible sub-types of the Japanese model. Two larger and more technologically sophisticated companies had made the major expansion of their operations, including the FMSs, on greenfield sites in rural areas so that the new recruitment tended to be mainly high school and university graduates (the average ages in these two plants were 28 and 29!). In Japan these tend to be recruited without regard to whether they have taken industrially specific course specialisms.

The consequence in one firm was that there was little movement out of the FMS areas because the extra time taken to develop machining skills limited the numbers of recruits with appropriate experience. Because a large proportion (perhaps half) of the shop floor are 'career workers' destined for eventual management positions, there is always a relative shortage of experience. In both these firms the operators seemed to have less discretion to make adjustments to the programs and the system was generally more 'rigid' in its range and usage. In the same firm, FMS and related developments had been accompanied by the formation of a specialised category of five programming staff (10 per cent of all staff employees at the plant) who worked as a central computer unit.

In the other two FMS firms the FMS workers seemed to have more discretion and also to produce a wider range of parts. In firm A the FMS was used to produce a wider range of parts, i.e. it was more authentically flexible, was used for a wider product range, and the operators appeared to have more discretion for part-programming and schedule modifications. Although the FMS was again situated on a greenfield site, a considerable proportion of the employees from the original factory had transferred, there was more recruitment of high school than university graduates into production jobs and the importance attached to previous experience meant that age was not so much of an obstacle to recruitment. In firm B there was also more dependence upon skilled production workers. There was a special skilled category called a 'cutting specialist' (unusual compared to most reports of Japanese factories) and, in general, production workers played a more important role and were more highly regarded. The company union was accorded high honorific status in corporate decisions and the managing director frequently resorted to paternalistic acts of generosity (salmon and sake outings) to keep favour with the highly skilled workers upon whom there is a recognised feeling of dependence.

Conclusion

As elsewhere Japanese FMSs are not particularly notable for being aimed at securing qualitative gains or more product variability. Sometimes they are fairly rigid in the range of parts that they can machine. The principal rationale for FMS seems to be cost savings on existing products with quality as a residual consideration. Since investment for the equipment (at least in the firms visited) mostly seems to come from retained profits rather than external sources this is probably quite a strong influence on design and usage.

Further spread and sophistication of FMSs are limited by the particularism of Japanese plants and enterprises. Production managers like to put together the constituent elements of the system themselves rather than buying complete turn-key systems. Co-operative working and work-role flexibility militate against detailed record-keeping and so make the transition to computerised information controls such as CAD/CAM more difficult. The rigidity of some FMS capabilities is offset by the work-role flexibility and delegated co-operative character of production workers and supervisors. The pressure is, on the whole, towards operator involvement in computer programming and controls of FMSs. Although the sample of firms was very small (though not necessarily unrepresentative of FMS usage) there were important variations: their internal labour-market practices did diverge and as a consequence so did the usage of production workers' skills. The approach in firm A is again suggestive confirmation of the hypothesis that greater flexibility of product range in an FMS corresponds to and presupposes more polyvalence and autonomy among production staff.

Italy

Background

The preceding argument is consistent with Sabel's (1982; 1985) arguments about the likely character of flexible manufacturing arising from larger firms' automation strategies. These will be timid or compromise attempts to break with Fordist manufacturing philosophy and practices. Authentic flexibility in product portfolios will be limited by rigidities in the management of operations and the full potential of the technology will be restricted by the perpetuation of specialised and low-trust work roles. If this picture is confirmed in large Western firms then the prospects for flexible specialisation may increasingly continue to depend upon the smaller-firm model developed in Italy.

The debate over flexible specialisation in Italy hinges on the changing character of the artisanal and neo-artisanal firms that often arose out of the larger firms' decentralisation and subcontracting of component and sub-assembly production. Critics of this small-firm expansion (R. Murray 1985, F. Murray 1983) have associated it with sweated labour, avoidance of trade union controls, and 'black economy' practices to avoid terms and conditions of employment regulations. Brusco and Sabel (1981) however, were amongst the first to point out that in certain industrial sectors and Italian regions artisanal subcontracting has taken off into a virtuous circle of product and process innovation, non-dependent product contracting, polyvalent work roles and enhanced personal incomes. In the Emilia-Romagna region the classic case of artisanal flexible specialisation would consist of a workshop where the artisan and his employees work collectively to design new products or devise new production methods by programming computer controlled machinery for a number of diverse customers.

Since the original specification of this 'Emilian model' of artisanal specialisation, technological and economic developments have challenged some of its conditions of existence. The recession has generally contracted market demand and may have eliminated customers for many artisanal products. Renewed competition on price grounds may have pushed some subcontractors towards exploitation of their workers, abandoning co-operative and polyvalent methods of working. The wider availability of a broader range of production technologies may also undermine artisanal flexibility both internally and externally.

Internally, task specialisation and a more conventionally hierarchical division of labour may develop as small firms acquire more sophisticated computer-controlled machines and computerised design and inspection systems, either because the owner-artisans themselves begin to monopolise this more strategic work, or because they hire specialist programmers and the like.

Externally, the artisanal enterprise could be negatively affected by the increasingly sophisticated technologies used among larger firms, either because the latter can use CAD/CAM data-generating systems or FMSs to produce, more flexibly, work which they might previously have had to subcontract to the artisans, or because CAD/CAM and the programs for computer numerically controlled (CNC) machine-tools can now specify much more tightly the specifications and standards for subcontracted parts. In the latter case the subcontracting artisans' scope for providing their own formulation of the customers' requirements and the experience and experimentation necessary to develop independently their own designs for other customers and markets would be eliminated. The organisational and technological reshaping of subcontracting relationships in the motor-car industry suggests that this scenario is possible. However, the regeneration of Fiat's motor-car production and its subcontracting structures in the late 1970s and early 1980s indicate the complexity of the changes and interdependencies that have been carried out amongst different sizes of firm.

Brusco (1986) hints at the possibility of a reversion to a division of labour between routine and complex tasks when and if artisans stabilise their product markets, and Sabel (1982, p. 228) suggests the existence of a category of unskilled workers excluded from the key tasks of flexible specialisation. It appears that the internal division of labour within the artisanal and small subcontracting firms may contain, or degenerate into, work roles that are as restrictive as those in larger Fordist or neo-Fordist enterprises.

Automated versus Artisanal Flexibility

Advanced factory automation of the FMS type has not (as of 1985) made any significant headway in Italian manufacturing. Experts interviewed were unable to name more than a half-dozen of firms with FMSs. Since several of these are also in the high-volume motor-car sector it seems unlikely that they are 'true' FMSs. The reasons for this limited spread do not seem to lie with any lack of relevant engineering expertise. Comau of Modena, for example, makes of the most advanced machining equipment and is also a system designer for FMSs. Yet it mostly utilises conventional, craft-intensive methods and machines. Rather it is the strategic business choices of these potential automaters, together with economic and political climate of their operations, which limits the extent of computerised production. By contrast, case-study and survey evidence suggest that the small and artisanal firms are continuing to achieve production superiority by flexible combinations of technology and labour skills.

The technology profiles of three large firms in Emilia-Romagna illustrate the contextual influences on technology adoption. A maker of packing machines and traffic controls, which has been described by one study as having developed a relatively concerted programme of production automation (Murray 1983) had made little advance towards CAD/CAM integration and none at all in the direction of FMSs. Instead business strategy emphasised market goals by enhancing product technology and computerising the design function. The reliability and quality of subcontractors (though the amount of subcontracted work had fallen significantly during the 1980s) together with the reduced mechanical content of products diminished the need for upgrading production technology. In this firm an unusual mixture of paternalistic management and militant unionism had led to a relatively high level of co-determination on production issues. These political matters provided a constraint on management's scope for dictating the terms of operation of new production technology. Union action had forced an agreement which meant 'polyvalence' for about fifty workers including some programming of CNC machine-tools on the shop floor by operators rather than technicians.

By contrast, a clear-cut example of a move to flexible automation in a Modena company producing luxury cars (in relatively small batches) shows how regional political culture cannot guarantee protection from managers intent upon Fordist labour-management and production methods. Here was a relative degradation of work roles. A two-line flexible machining system had been installed which was normally referred to as an FMS. Because different types of engine block could be switched between the two lines as demand changed, by reprogramming rather than retooling, it was, in motor industry terms, more flexible than standard transfer lines. However the batches were unchanging (twenty-four per day), changeovers were relatively infrequent and no new models had been introduced on the system since its inception. It was thought to be too inflexible to bring in any other kind of work. The main business objective was to minimise future capital expenditure because the system allowed modifications to be made to engine blocks in the event of model changes without further investment in new machines. All programming was in the hands of the shop manager and the operators were restricted to tool changing and mechanical fault rectification.

By the general standards of the motor-car industry skills and work roles were reasonably broad but, in the context of this particular firm, operators felt they had suffered a diminution of work autonomy. In other parts of the factory single workers build individual machines by hand and the concentration of programming tasks by the *capo* meant a loss of discretion by the operators. The plant had had a stormy industrial relations and financial history. The last reconstruction of the company involved its effective takeover by an individual tycoon who had centralised control over all aspects of the business in his own hands, including the decision to automate the engine line. Collective bargaining had broken down and had only been re-established the previous year.

A technically more advanced FMS, introduced in 1985, at an agricultural equipment producer in the same town provided more opportunity for product changes and hence for an injection of polyvalence. Its specific objectives were to facilitate responsiveness to market fluctuations and to provide a more rapid and cost-effective method of machining the wide range of associated components without repeated re-tooling and refixturing. In terms of work organisation this firm fell mid-way between the two previous cases. The FMS operators, selected for their previous high skills and craft experience, were responsible for optimising the part-programs and dealing with mechanical and some electronic breakdowns. However, countering this limited polyvalence, and similar to the American pattern, was the exclusive allocation of schedule programming and basic part-programming to a new specialised system programmer post. The strategy of the *delegati*, or shop stewards, had sought polyvalence, after the manner of the *professionalità* movement of the 1970s (see Barisi 1980) but had been checked by the lack of co-operation from technical staff and management insistence (shades of Alpha in the USA) on selecting workers for the FMS. A further obstacle to operator involvement had been the extent of advance programming before implementation of the FMS in the plant.

In both the motor-car manufacturer and the farm-equipment manufacturer automation was not planned as a means of changing the use of small-firm subcontractors. In the first firm this was because engine blocks had almost always been kept as an in-house operation, while in the case of the second firm it was because the management professed itself to be satisfied with exisiting quality and reliability arrangements with subcontractors and, perhaps more importantly, because even the FMS would still require an unmanagable increase in stock levels if it were used to take on previously subcontracted work.

In contrast to these minor and halting attempts at automated flexibility, artisanal firms in the metalworking sectors have essentially continued with their methods of organisational flexibility while adapting to the technological and macro-economic changes of the 1980s recession. Evidence from local surveys indicates that artisanal firms have responded by increasing the numbers of their products, orders and customers, — enhancing their market flexibility; in some cases investing in more computer-aided processes and computer-controlled equipment; and, in the Modena province, increasing the numbers of workers (Rieser and Franchi 1986; Jones 1986).

There are few clear indications that metalworking artisanal workshops have made their division of labour more specialised as a result of cost pressures or technological change. In typical artisanal enterprises, because legal recognition limits the number of employees to a maximum of fifteen, the owners do not have sufficient time themselves to combine all the skilled technical work with their own entrepreneurial tasks. The more orders they take on for market flexibility, of course, the more they have to develop or agree designs and liaise with customers, and so the less time they have for production-related tasks.

In Rieser and Franchi's Modena survey there had, however, been a large increase in numbers of office and, especially, technician employees. This could be associated with the adoption of a more specialised division of labour amongst the artisans' employees as a result of adopting new technology. However, as against such a trend there was a near two-thirds majority of artisans in the Modena survey who agreed that computerisation needed 'diffuse, polyvalent and flexible skills'. Observational visits to workshops in both Bologna and Modena confirmed a willingness born of necessity on the part of the artisanal owners to involve machine operators in tasks such as programming.

Summary

Flexible specialisation, as defined by Brusco, Sabel, Piore, and Zeitlin, is not, of course, a strategy only for the large and artisanal enterprises. Many intermediate types of firm could be affected by the economic and technological shifts referred to above. However there do, at the moment, seem to be more clear-cut options of flexible manufacturing for firms at the extremes of the size range rather than those in the middle. In the larger firms automated flexibility through FMSs is financially more plausible (because of the high investment costs) and methodologically more congenial because of management by professional engineers, Tayloristic mistrust of production workers, and susceptibility to technological fashions. In the artisanal enterprise, largely because of quite opposite limitations on formalised work organisation, technologically assisted flexibility through polyvalent work on unintegrated computerised equipment seems the most developed alternative possibility. Because of their quite complex specific circumstances, the medium-sized firms will be pulled in different directions between these two poles of flexible automation.

However, in the specifically Italian context the artisanal model has more scope, success, and indeed virtue, as a vehicle for flexible specialisation. Large-firm automated flexibility is constrained by many of the same types of institutional forces as in other countries. For this reason, and because of inappropriate levels of technical sophistication and corporate resources and strategy, the automation path represented by FMSs will continue to compare unfavourably with artisanal organisational flexibility for some time to come, while a multitude of local industrial relations contexts will influence what seems likely to be a shifting balance between polyvalence and work-group autonomy, on the one hand, and more marginalised workers under more centralised control, on the other.

The United Kingdom: Ignoring the Advantages of Late Development?

Despite having established the world's first operational prototype of today's FMSs, at the Molins company's cigarette-machine factory in the 1960s, the UK has only developed an FMS presence in the last five years. Unlike most of the other major nations with FMS plants, both the manufacturing philosophy and the crucial financial support for most of the installations have come from state initiatives. This factor needs to be emphasised because it has helped give a pronounced Fordist bias to the management objectives, though not always the operational running, of most of the systems currently in use. Under the then Labour government a Department-of-Industry-sponsored working party known as the Automated Small-Batch Production (ASP) Committee reported on the commercial and technical benefits of adopting FMS-type automation in British firms. The report heavily emphasised quantitative gains such as reduced inventory and work-in-progress; reductions of direct labour costs; and higher machine utilisation. The quantitatively more ambiguous gain of reduced lead times between design and production was also cited. Consequent funding made available by the Labour government, and a similar successor scheme by the subsequent Conservative government, may have transmitted this emphasis to the firms that have used state support to adopt FMS. For in Peter Scott's (1987) survey of nine of the thirty British FMSs running in 1985 the above features were all cited as FMS goals and achievements.

The official philosophy is summed up in the words of the ASP committee chairman that small batch automation would allow British firms to use 'very high technology to manufacture low technology products cheaper than the rest of the world' (*Production Engineer* 1981).

Flexibility versus Fordist Criteria

Some plant managements have been seeking to achieve some of the advantages of flexible specialisation through their FMSs. However, they have been handicapped by initial systems designs, rigid managerial structures and practices and the imposition of volume manufacturing criteria of efficiency by their senior managers. In several of the cases studied engineers had difficulty in achieving speedy changeovers of hardware and software in order to make components that were outside the immediate part-family for which their FMS was first set up. In three cases engineers had found it difficult to reach the lower batch sizes that

FMS is supposed to put within the capabilities of automated production. Commercially economic times and uses of resources clashed with these attempts. The engineers seemed to be settling for larger batches than they had planned for both technical and commercial reasons.

However, economic returns were sought on grounds that both satisfied and conflicted with the ASP committee chairman's claim. Contrary to FMS purists' philosophy, some systems were used to make high-volume orders. But in other firms, jobs with a long cycle, but high value, were put through the FMS. Lack of flexibility tended to become self-reinforcing because expansion of the product range for FMS can only be achieved if there are sufficient time and resources for experimentation. Often, however, insufficient development time was allocated and, in at least one case, there was clear evidence that it was the senior management who pressured production managers and engineers to maximise running time. This left insufficient opportunity for the development work required to introduce new types of component into the FMS. Contrary to the advice of the noted international FMS consultants, Ingersoll Engineers, there was little evidence of a coherent flexible manufacturing philosophy being applied to the companies' various support functions. Furthermore, in most cases there was no computerised integration of production processes with pre-production functions, through CAD, CAM or materials requirements planning systems.

Coming to Terms with Labour

The introduction of most of the British FMSs has coincided with a catastrophic period for the traditional strengths and countervailing powers of British plant unions (for a summary of some of the evidence on this change of fortunes, see Jones and Rose 1986). There has been erosion of some of the traditional tactics of skilled production workers and, if some of the more dramatic accounts were to be believed, it might be thought that managers would be able to redesign from scratch what they expected from their new FMS workforces. But in the UK skilled manufacturing labour is relatively cheap and in the plants studied it was plentiful. Perhaps partly because the FMSs did create major savings in direct labour costs, in line with the ASP philosophy, managements tended to take little interest in job redesigns for the remaining workers. In most cases they played safe by transferring not necessarily the youngest and most adaptable workers but those with considerable mechanical, especially machine-tool setting, skills. Managements still tend to regard them as 'craft' jobs and do not explicitly recognise the complex overlap of empirical craft knowledge and abstract systems thinking that the new work roles require. Training was almost invariably provided internally, often in an on-the-job fashion.

There was, with a couple of exceptions, little attempt at systematic design of occupations for the FMS personnel. By and large managements seemed to have adopted a relaxed, almost diffident attitude to specification of their duties. This has no doubt been encouraged by the near-absence of union opposition to management plans for factory automation. However, it seems to have been often recognised, after the event, that the small numbers now employed on these systems require, *de facto*, greater occupational flexibility simply to get things done. Perhaps as a reflection on the general flux and uncertainty in industrial activity and labour relations in the UK it was possible to find the whole gamut of job combinations amongst the FMS crews. In some they were specialised into well-defined mechanical and maintenance jobs, in others there was a management injunction to swap tasks flexibly. In most there was an embargo on involvement in programming but in a couple of cases of smaller cells the polyvalent operator did most of the subsidiary programming!

Between Flexible Specialisation and Neo-Fordism?

If informal or 'pragmatic polyvalence' is burgeoning then this development may owe something to the fact that, in most cases, these are mainly early days for of the management of British FMSs. Moreover, a clear signal of the role of factory politics that recalls the American experiences is exemplified in the one firm where a systematic FMS philosophy was applied to job design. Here semi-autonomy for a polyvalent work group, schooled to participate in computer programming, was encouraged from the start by the initial management team. However, when the FMS was switched to a new and more routine set of production requirements in the main plant, a battle ensued with the personnel department. These managers were anxious to maintain existing occupational status and pay gradings in order to hold the line against potential union demands. In the eventual compromise arrangement there was a virtual regression to specialised work roles (for a broader description and discussion of these developments, see Jones and Scott 1987).

But remember the American Alpha case in the USA. Where there is a relaxation, but not a destruction, of normal industrial relations as may well be happening in many British plants that can adopt FMS; and where Fordist intentions are disrupted by the pressures of the market then a pragmatic form of flexible specialisation may emerge as a result of adoption of the technology.

In more general terms the comparison of British developments in flexible automation with the longer-established Japanese and North American cases suggests both continuities with previous episodes of manufacturing change and the potential for radical breaks with previous practices. Flexible automation technology seems, at the moment, to be viewed from a managerial perspective based upon Fordist manufacturing principles. But there is considerable heterogeneity in this respect and the new fluidity and pragmatism in shop-floor labour management could lead to work practices closer to the Japanese than the American model. The increase in Japanese manufacturing plants in this country may provide a more direct influence on British managers in this respect.

It can be confirmed with more certainty that flexible automation strategies are, in the main, distinct from the flexible specialisation approach. Whether the former are successful in their own terms is a matter for further analysis. Yet they, or a second-hand Japanisation, may well falter. In that event the contrary examples of flexible speciali- sation based upon flexible automation suggest that, at least in specific cases, it could be realised outside of the Italian context. The current plasticity of the British situation is favourable. What is needed are industrial policies that recognise the interdependence between changes in production systems and work roles for optimal exploitation of technological potential.

Notes

1. The overseas fieldwork and the study leave involved was financed by a grant from the Economic and Social Research Council.
2. For the British motor-car industry Marsden *et al.* (1985 pp. 88–9) argue that technological and organisational changes have meant greater proportionate reliance upon technical white collar and craft workers, in isolation from the semi-skilled work-force, whose num- bers continue to fall. They also comment on flexible automation that 'it is still by no means certain that market demand will encourage full use of the technical potential of such equipment' (p. 47).
3. Interview with Nathaniel Cook, MIT, May 1984.

References

Abbeglen, J.C. and Stalk, G. (1985), *Kaisha: The Japanese Corporation*, New York: Basic Books

Atkinson, J. (1984), *Flexibility, Uncertainty and Manpower Management*, Brighton: Institute of Manpower Studies, Report no. 89

Atkinson, J. and N. Meager (1986), *New Forms of Work Organization*, Brighton: Institute of Manpower Studies, Report no. 121

Barisi, G. (1980), 'La notion de professionalità pour les syndicats en Italie', paper presented at the 'Colloque Politique d'Emploi et Rapports Sociaux du Travail' 10–12 December.

Brusco, S. (1982), 'The Emilian Model: Productive Decentralisation and Social Integration', *Cambridge Journal of Economics*, 6.

Brusco, S. (1986) 'Small Firms and Industrial Districts: The Experience of Italy', in D. Keeble and E. Warner, eds, *New Firms and Regional Development in Europe*, London: Groom Helm

Brusco, S. and Sabel, C. (1981), 'Artisan Production and Economic Growth' in Wilkinson (1981)

Child, J. (1985), 'Managerial Strategies, New Technology and The Labour Process' in Knights *et al.* (1985)

Cross, M. (1985), *Towards The Flexible Craftsman*, London: Technical Change Centre

Dore, R. (1973), *British Factory — Japanese Factory*, London: Allen & Unwin

Friedman, A. (1977), *Industry and Labour*, London: Macmillan

Hirschhorn, L. (1985), *Beyond Mechanisation*, Cambridge, MA: MIT Press

Hyman, R. (1988), 'Flexible Specialisation: Miracle or Myth?' in Hyman and Streeck (1988)

Hyman, R. and W. Streeck eds. (1988), *New Technology and Industrial Relations: International Experiences*, Oxford: Basil Blackwell

IMS (1985). Flexibility, Working Practices and the Labour Market, Brighton: IMS, Commentary no. 32

Ingersoll Engineers (1982), *The FMS Report*, Bedford: IFS Publications

Jaikumar, J. (1984), 'Flexible Manufacturing Systems: A Managerial Perspective', Harvard Business School Working Paper 1–74–078

Jones, B. (1986), 'Industrial Decentralisation and New Technology in Emilia Romagna', University of Bath, mimeo

Jones, B. and M.J. Rose (1986), 'Redividing Labour: Factory Politics and Work Reorganisation in the Current Industrial Transition' in Purcell *et al.* (1986)

Jones, B. and P.J. Scott (1987), 'Working The System: FMS in Britain and the USA', *New Technology, Work and Employment*, 2.1

Kamata, S. (1983), *Japan in The Passing Lane*, London: Unwin Paperbacks

Katz, H. (1985), *Shifting Gears: Changing Labor Relations in the US Automobile Industry*, Cambridge, MA: MIT Press

Knights, D., H. Willmott and D. Collinson (1985), *Job Redesign: Organisation and Control of the Labour Process*, Aldershot: Gower

Koike, K. (1983), 'Internal Labour Markets: Workers in Large Firms' in Shirai (1983)

Marsden, D., T. Morris, P. Willman and S. Wood (1985), *The Car Industry: Labour Relations and Industrial Adjustment*, London: Tavistock

Michelsons, A., ed. (1985), *Tre incognite per lo sviluppo: strutture di mercato, scelte technologiche, e ruolo delle istituzioni nell'ultimo decennio*. Milan: F. Angeli

Murray, F. (1983), 'The Decentralization of Production and the Decline of the Mass-Collective Worker', *Capital and Class*, 19

Murray, R. (1985), 'Benetton Britain: The New Economic Order', *Marxism Today*, 29.11.

Ouchi- W. (1982), *Theory Z*, Reading, MA: Addison-Wesley

Piore M, and C. Sabel (1984), *The Second Industrial Divide*, New York: Basic Books

Production Engineer (1981), 'ASP Is Alive and Well but Going in a Different Direction', 60.4, pp. 17–19

Purcell, K.,S. Wood, A. Waton and S. Allen eds. (1986), *The Changing Experience of Employment*, London: Macmillan

Reiser, V. and M. Franchi (1986), *Innovazione technologica e mutamento organizzativo nell'impresa artigiana: una ricerca sull'artigianato metalmeccanico di produzione nella provincia di Modena*, Modena: Confederazione Nazionale dell' Artigianato

Sabel, C. (1982), *Work and Politics*, Cambridge: Cambridge University Press

Sabel, C. (1985), 'A Strategy for Flexible Specialization in the Italian Capital Goods Sector' in Michelsons (1985)

Sabel, C. and J. Zeitlin (1985), 'Historical Alternatives to Mass Production', *Past and Present*, 108

Scott, P.J. (1987), 'Craft Skills in Flexible Manufacturing Systems', University of Bath Ph.D. thesis

Shaiken, H. (1985), *Work Transformed: Automation and Labour in the Computer Age*, New York: Holt, Reinhart and Winston

Shaiken, H., S. Hertzenberg, and S. Kuhn (1986), 'The Work Process under More Flexible Production', *Industrial Relations*, 25.2, pp. 167–83

Shirai, T., ed. (1983), *Contemporary Industrial Relations in Japan*, Madison: University of Wisconsin Press

Tolliday, S. and J. Zeitlin eds (1987), *The Automobile Industry and Its Workers: Between Fordism and Flexibility*, Cambridge: Policy Press

Wilkinson, F., ed. (1981), *The Dynamics of Labour Market Segmentation*, Cambridge: Cambridge University Press

Williams, K., T. Cutler, J. Williams and C. Haslam (1987), 'The End of Mass Production? ' *Economy and Society*, 16.3.

Wood, S. (1988), 'Between Fordism and Flexibility?: The Case of the US Car Industry', in Hyman and Streeck (1988)

4 The Search for Flexibility: Subcontracting Networks in British and French Engineering[1]

Edward H. Lorenz

This chapter examines the issues of subcontracting and flexibility from a comparative perspective. Conditions in the Lyons region in France, where subcontracting is used extensively and in novel ways, are contrasted with conditions in the West Midlands region of the UK, where the possibilities remain comparatively unexplored.

More speculatively, the chapter considers whether the West Midlands might benefit from some version of the policies adopted by employers in Lyons. These reflections are not intended as a crude exercise in identifying features of a comparatively successful region and simply arguing that their wholesale transfer to another region would be beneficial. Each region's distinctive economic and institutional context is kept in mind.

With respect to questions of industrial policy, this research is directly relevant to the debate on mass production versus flexible specialisation associated notably with the work of Piore and Sabel (1984). We all have a good idea of what is meant by an economy based on mass production. This refers to an industrial structure in which large vertically integrated firms are dominant. These giants have sufficient market power to stabilise the demand they face for a standardised product. Stable product market demand is the precondition for their willingness to risk investing in a capital-intensive and product-specific technology with few alternative uses.

Piore and Sabel identify the current crisis in the United States and Western Europe as a crisis of mass production. Critical to their argument is the idea that uncertainty in international product markets has made it increasingly difficult for large firms to consolidate mass markets as in the 1950s and 1960s. They argue that adopting some version of flexible specialisation will provide a solution.

What is flexible specialisation? Much of the early literature focused on the possibly beneficial role in the economy of small dynamic firms.

Subsequent work has made it clear that size is not the critical factor. The key to flexible specialisation is the development of organisational forms that achieve a balance between co-operation and competition and encourage competition on the basis of product and process innovation rather than price as in the standard neo-classical model. Innovation in the context of market uncertainty is highly risky and some sort of co-operative arrangements are required if individuals are to bear these risks. An example would be a locally financed unemployment scheme such as some nineteenth-century French municipalities operated. But co-operation between the actors cannot stifle all competition or the incentives to innovate will be eliminated. Think of the Japanese lifetime employment system. In principle you have a guaranteed position but you can be up or down the ladder depending on your performance.

Flexible specialisation does not draw a sharp line between economy and society, the firm and the wider community. This partly reflects the fact that the community may finance and organise the co-operative arrangements (for example, a municipal insurance scheme or an industrial training scheme). This can also be understood by seeing that flexible specialisation incorporates a set of rules of the game which regulate competition. Violating these rules, for example by competing on the basis of low wages, not only invites retaliation but also exclusion from the community. Reputation effects become very important.

With these general comments in mind, I will turn to the case-study material. I will argue that subcontracting arrangements in France are successful in comparison with the British case precisely because of the way they balance co-operation and competition.

A Tale of Two Regions

In order to motivate the discussion I will say something about the context in which I decided to focus on the theme of subcontracting and flexibility. In 1984 I began a comparative study of the introduction of new technology, primarily numerically controlled (NC) and computer numerically controlled (CNC) machine-tools, in small and medium-sized British and French engineering firms (of less than 500 employees). This was motivated by a number of intriguing pieces of information: first, the improved performance of firms in this size category relative to that of large firms from the mid-1970s in terms of growth of output and employment (Dellatre 1982); second, that small and medium-sized firms have been some of the most dynamic investors in new technology.[2]

This picture of a comparatively rapid growth and technological sophistication contradicted established views of the role of small firms in the British and French economies. In particular, it was inconsistent with the dualist model predicting technological backwardness in accordance with the confinement of small firms to unstable portions of the product market (Berger and Piore 1980). To arrive at some understanding of these unanticipated shifts in relative performance, I decided to investigate the process of mechanisation in a selected number of small and medium-sized engineering firms in the Birmingham and Lyons conurbations.

A preliminary visit to French firms in 1985 in the 200–500 employee range producing a variety of types of machinery revealed that most had reduced their employment levels since 1980. The value of their sales, however, had in most cases increased, after a dip in 1982–3. This could be explained in part by improvements in their productivity but also by a substantial increase in their use of subcontracting for intermediate component production.

All the firms, of course, had used subcontracting to some extent. Few had been of sufficient scale in their operations to warrant investing in plant for such specialised operations as gear grinding or producing heavy castings. All had made use of subcontracting to meet temporary capacity constraints. What I was observing, however, was different. It was a shift to subcontracting on a permanent basis for such standard operations as turning, milling and drilling. It allowed the firms to avoid making investments in up-to-date machine-tools and frequently was the occasion for a reduction in capacity, with some existing plant being scrapped.

I should stress that while the general type of machining operations being subcontracted was not specialised or specific to the particular firm in question, the design and specifications of the components were. It was not a case of substituting in-house production for standardised components available in the market. Rather, it was a case of specific components being machined by subcontractors according to firm-specific plans produced in the design offices of the client firms.

French firms used a suggestive word to describe these evolving relations with their subcontractors: partnership. In the course of my interviews with management, other equally suggestive language was used to characterise inter-firm relations: the existence of a moral contract, the importance of loyalty and the need for mutual trust. This language, I will argue, reflects a growing perception of the mutual dependency that exists between client and subcontractor.

My previous fieldwork in the West Midlands had uncovered little evidence of similar tendencies among comparable firms. Certain firms had decided to buy in specialised capital intensive operations (for example, heavy casting and forging work) formerly done in-house. The explanation was the dramatic contraction of their markets and scale of production which precluded undertaking these operations profitably, unless the firms were to go into the business of being subcontractors themselves. I had only come across one example, a Birmingham machine-tool producer, of a firm moving in the direction of scrapping existing machine-shop capacity and using subcontracting on a regular basis. The majority, though recognising that increased subcontracting might offer potential benefits, saw the quality problem as insurmountable. Subcontracting was used solely to meet temporary capacity constraints.

This finding had initially discouraged me from investigating subcontracting relations in Britain in depth. The developments in Lyons, however, encouraged me to reconsider subcontracting in the West Midlands context. If the quality problem had been satisfactorily solved in Lyons, why was it apparently insurmountable in the Birmingham area? French firms claimed to be benefiting from increased use of subcontracting and saw it as contributing to their improved financial performance after the losses of the early 1980s. Were West Midlands firms in a position similarly to benefit?

With such questions in mind I decided–to retrace some of my steps and investigate the character of supplier–buyer relations in more detail. What follows are some preliminary observations based on this research in progress.

Before proceeding with this I will present some background information on the firms. The Lyons case study is based on ten firms I visited in 1985. Five of these were revisited approximately a year later. In the case of the West Midlands, I visited six firms in 1984. More recently I returned to three of these for more in-depth discussions on their subcontracting policies. In the Lyons region I also visited five subcontractors working for client firms. These interviews were less systematic than those conducted with the clients. The aim was to check for discrepancies between the two sides' characterisations of the subcontracting relation. This part of the research remains to be done for the West Midlands.

All the client firms produce high-precision machinery. The West Midlands sample is weighted towards machine-tool producers: four of the six firms. I also included a Coventry producer of engines and fork-lift trucks and a Coventry producer of small turbo engines which engages in some sub-assembly production for Rolls Royce. The Lyons sample is more diversified. It included machine-tools, textile machinery, packaging machinery, mining equipment and industrial filters. With the exception of the fork-lift trucks producer, these firms do not aim for mass production.Their products tend to be large, complex, customised and expensive. As production is to order, they find it difficult to predict their requirements with any accuracy beyond a horizon of six months to a year. On average there is a high dependency on export orders, over 50 per cent in some cases.

The size of the firms varies from 150 to 700 employees. As I noted, employment levels have declined in the French firms since the mid- to late 1970s, primarily due to improvements in productivity and increased use of subcontracting. The employment decline has been more severe in the case of the British firms and contracting markets and declining sales have been important and in some cases the dominant factors in this process. Employment at the fork-lift trucks producer and the largest machine-tool producer declined from about 2,000 in the mid-1970s to about 700 in 1984. Employment in the second largest machine-tool producer declined from 1,000 to about 400 over the same period.

This difference in economic adversity is also apparent in the performance of the regional economies as a whole. Firms in both regions benefit from large and diverse engineering sectors and are potentially well placed for subcontracting. In 1980, excluding vehicles, the engineering sector accounted for about 15 per cent of manufacturing employment in the Rhône-Alpes and about 13 per cent in the West Midlands. If vehicles are included, the figures are 40 and 53 per cent respectively. In the West Midlands, employment in engineering fell by some 20 per cent between 1976 and 1981, in contrast to a 3 per cent decline for the Rhône-Alpes. Between 1982 and 1984 employment in the sector in the West Midlands fell by a full 19 per cent while in the Rhône-Alpes the decline was only 7 per cent.[3]

Subcontracting and Trust

With this background in mind, let us consider the potential benefits and costs of shifting machining operations from in-house to external sourcing. What incentives have been operating in the case of Lyons machinery producers? When questioned, manufacturers generally dated the decision to increase subcontracting to the 1982–3 recession in engineering in conjunction with the tremendous productivity improvements then being made possible through the introduction of CNC machine-tools. Most of the Lyons producers argued that given the slow growing and uncertain markets they operated in, it would be impossible to amortise investments in CNC equipment. They were not in a position to operate continuously the equipment for the 12–16 hours a day required to achieve a satisfactory return on the investment. Smaller specialists, they argued, were in a position to do this, in part because such specialists aggregated demands from multiple clients and in part because of their greater internal flexibility both in terms of job allocation and use of overtime. In short, subcontractors could do it more cheaply. Significantly, wage differentials were not a factor. The evidence I collected for both France and the UK showed that on average small high-technology subcontractors pay rates comparable or superior to large firms.

While subcontracting offers potential savings, it also poses risks of a contractual nature. Let us consider these first from the subcontractor's point of view and then from the client's. For the subcontractor, the risks can be illustrated by the example of a Coventry-based firm I investigated. In 1983, on the basis of an order for large batch production of connectors from Plessey Engineering, the firm invested in additional premises and equipment. Plessey, possibly because of a turnaround in its market, subsequently only agreed to take delivery of small batches. The subcontractor's demand for a renegotiation of the contract price to take account of higher unit costs was refused, leading to a deterioration in relations and an eventual breakoff. The subcontractor sustained an annual loss of £20,000 during 1984 and 1985.

It is possible that Plessey made an honest mistake, though one has to wonder whether they would have made this mistake quite as easily if it had been a question of expanding their own capacity. In any case, the subcontractor viewed the change of order, combined with the refusal to consider a renegotiation of price allowing a return on the investment, as a violation of trust.

My discussions with subcontractors in the West Midlands make it clear that there is nothing exceptional about this account. The only exceptional point is this subcontractor's stubborn refusal to accept Plessey's terms, so that it sustained an even larger loss than otherwise. A recent report on the car-components industry commissioned by the West Midlands County Council provides ample documentation of this sort of problem for the case of Austin Rover and its suppliers (Bessant *et al.* 1984):

Inevitably the uncertain vehicle build, multisourcing and destocking exercises of the 1970s gave rise to a general mistrust on the part of the component supplier who was asked to deliver items to the builder under the cover of a blanket purchase order and specific material control requirements schedules issued at irregular intervals. Examples of legitimate suppliers being turned round at the customer's gates were a common feature of our interviews.

The report concluded that much of the deterioration in relations could have been avoided if buyers had fully shared information with suppliers on their expected future requirements.

In the case of subcontractors, then, risks develop when the firm is locked into relations because of a generalised capacity expansion only made because of the prospect of selling a large amount of the product to a particular client. Clearly, if the capacity were specific to the requirements of the client, the risks would increase (Williamson 1985). In the case of the Coventry-based subcontractor I mentioned, this was avoided and the firm still hopes to make a return on the investment in the long run.

What are the risks from the client's perspective? Interestingly, the main concern is not a fair price. Recall that these are general (milling, turning, drilling, etc.) as opposed to specific types of machining operations and client firms expressed confidence in their ability to make reasonably accurate estimates of production costs. As a check, the rule is to request two to three tenders on each contract to preclude any opportunistic pricing.

More important than price is the problem of quality. Concern in this area has increased as slow-growing markets have increased competitive pressures. As a rule, client firms inspect individual components upon delivery and payment is only made after ascertaining that components have been produced to the required standard. Quality can still pose a problem, though, if the component is delivered at the last moment, holding up the completion of the machine. This is costly, since firms generally face stiff penalties for late delivery on contracts which in some cases are for over £1,000,000. Late delivery, accompanied by poor quality or not, seems to be the main concern. Recall, too, that these are not standardised components. It is not possible to turn to the market for an instantaneous replacement, nor increasingly can the firm produce the components in-house.

All client firms allow for the inevitable mistake, the unexpected machine breakdown. They also are aware that subcontractors often find it difficult to turn down work even with full knowledge that they lack the necessary capacity to complete the order on time or the expertise to produce to the required standard. Repeated problems of delivery or quality lead inevitably to the latter interpretation and a breakoff of relations.

With this discussion of why buyer–supplier relations can break down in mind, I will turn to a characterisation of the partnership strategy being used by Lyons machinery producers. I want to argue that the strategy is designed to build up mutual trust and to balance competition with co-operation. There are four basic elements.[4]

First, partial guarantees are given to the subcontractor as to the amount of work on a long-term basis. The uncertainty clients face in their own markets precludes long-term guarantees on the absolute level of work. The policy of a number of firms I visited is to guarantee their partners a percentage of the work available. Client firms do not pull all the work back in-house, assuming this were possible, whenever final demand falls.

Second, partners are not instantaneously dropped if a differential in terms of price or quality emerges with respect to competitors. Rather, a system of advance warnings is used. A reasonable amount of time is allowed the subcontractor to match the competition.

Third, there is what client firms call the 10–15 per cent rule of subcontracting. This sets a client's orders at between 10 and 15 per cent of a subcontractor's sales. On the face of it, this is surprising. Why would a firm want to lessen its bargaining power by limiting a subcontractor's dependency? The minimum is set at 10 per cent because anything less would imply too insignificant a position in the subcontractor's order book to warrant the desired consideration. The maximum is set at 15 per cent to avoid the possibility of uncertainty in the client's market having a damaging effect on the subcontractor's financial position, possibly resulting in a deterioration of relations. In short, the 10–15 per cent figure both allows the client a degree of flexibility without undermining the viability of the subcontractor and at the same time assures the client is considered a sufficiently important customer to make continuing relations of interest.

Fourth, there is the importance of geographical proximity. Firms prefer to deal with subcontractors within a 50 km radius. The issue is not transportation costs. Rather, it is the importance of personal contacts. Client firms only establish partnerships with firms of which they have considerable experience and managers argued that personal contacts with their opposite number were essential to building up viable relations. Economic relations are thus embedded in a network of personal relations. A number of factors are no doubt involved. Personal contacts facilitate the exchange of information as each side learns about the other's idiosyncrasies. It is possible that personal integrity is involved. Naturally one feels more confident in undertaking a risky proposition when personal integrity is mutually at stake (Granovetter 1985).

To summarise, the partnership strategy involves a set of policies designed to foster mutual trust in recognition of the importance of co-operation between client and subcontractor.

I will now turn more speculatively to consider the possibility of instituting in the West Midlands a version of the subcontracting practices used by firms in Lyons. In so far as the trust and co-operation underlying the success of subcontracting in Lyons can be explained pragmatically or as resulting from the intentional actions of producers, a positive assessment can be made. However, if trust between firms in Lyons can be explained better as a by-product of values or norms held for other reasons, we would have to lower our estimate of the possibility of instituting the Lyons system elsewhere.[5]

The West Midlands firms, as I noted, use subcontracting of machining operations to solve capacity problems. They generally request tenders from two or three firms they have prior experience with and then contract with the one offering the lowest tender, other things equal. Management, when questioned about the benefits of offering long-term guarantees in terms of improved relations and performance, generally appreciated the point. Invariably it was claimed that their own market uncertainties precluded such policies. Even the one firm using subcontracting on a regular basis ruled out the giving of guarantees to suppliers.

The Lyons example suggests, however, that there is value in offering partial guarantees in the form of a percentage of the work available and that this, combined with the 10–15 per cent rule and a system of advance warnings, could result in substantially improved relations and performance. Of course, it is important to keep in mind the regional context. Economic adversity pushed the Lyons firms into rethinking their subcontracting practices. But, clearly, too much adversity would work against their solution. The greater severity of the economic crisis in the West Midlands should be kept in mind in formulating realistic policies. Implicit in my discussion is the idea that offering guarantees you know you cannot keep is worse than no guarantees at all.

The social embeddedness of economic relations is clearly important here. I have touched on one aspect of this, personal contacts and the exchange of information between buyer and supplier. Another aspect is the network of personal relations between the managers of the different client firms. It should be clear from the description I have given of subcontracting in Lyons, that it only works as well as it does because client firms as a group tend to pursue the same sorts of policies. The situation is not comparable, say, to Japanese subcontracting networks associated with such giants as Toyota, whose large size and successful performance allow it to provide a steady level of work to subcontractors who frequently rely on Toyota for over 80 per cent of their business. In the case of Lyons, as the 10–15 per cent rule implies, the environment the subcontractors operate in is only stabilised to the degree that it is because the clients collectively operate the same sort of policies. Take this away, and subcontractors would find it much more difficult to make the right sorts of investment in new technology.

I am not suggesting that Lyons machinery producers meet and collectively commit themselves to a common strategy. But it is clear they communicate. My interviews showed that producers were well aware of the subcontracting policies of others and to a much greater extent than their West Midlands counterparts. One factor of probable importance in explaining this is differences in the ownership structure of the firms in the two regions. With one exception, the West Midlands firms are part of larger national or multinational groups, whereas the majority of the Lyons producers are independent. Two were family-owned and -managed. The interview evidence gave the impression that management of the West Midlands firms saw themselves more as members of national groups and less as members of a local community of employers as compared with their Lyons counterparts.

History is also no doubt important in shaping attitudes. Lyons has the recent historical example of a famous system of decentralised production, the local silk industry or *fabrique Lyonnaise*. An employee of the *préfecture* suggested to me that employers found recourse to sub-contracting an obvious solution because of this historical example.

All these differences between the West Midlands and the Rhône-Alpes are important. They mean that the regionally specific context has to be taken into account in formulating policies for the improvement of subcontracting. Yet, by and large, they speak favourably for a transfer of the Lyons system to the West Midlands. There is nothing to preclude West Midlands machinery producers from adopting the partnership strategy with due regard for the constraints imposed by the greater severity of the economic crisis in that region. Differences in the owner-ship structure of the firms between the regions could be compensated for by the creation of regional institutions designed to bring the major employers together to discuss and possibly co-ordinate their subcon-tracting policies. In so far as co-operative behaviour was in part a by-product of attitudes explained by the unique history of Lyons, the assessment is less positive. But nothing in my discussions with French employers suggested that this was a determinant factor. Rather, they pointed to economic and technical changes in explaining their decisions to promote more co-operative relations with their suppliers.

Let there be no misunderstanding. My argument is not that subcon-tracting is a *panacea*, the solution to the ills of the West Midlands engineering sector. Clearly, competitive performance depends on a variety of factors including product development, marketing, training and skill acquisition, not to mention the impact of macro policy. But I do want to argue that subcontracting can contribute via lower-cost and higher-quality component production, and that the Lyons partnership strategy provides a model for achieving that end.

Notes

1. I would like to thank Gerry Berk, Diego Gambetta, Teresa Ghilar-ducci, Jean Saglio and Jonathan Zeitlin for their useful comments on earlier drafts of this article. I am also indebted to Jean Saglio for providing me with access to the facilities of the Groupe Lyonnais de Sociologie Industrielle while I was undertaking fieldwork in the Lyons region. The article is based on research funded by the Eco-nomic and Social Research Council (UK) under its Postdoctoral Research Fellowship Scheme. Its contents are the responsibility of the author and do not necessarily reflect the views of the Economic and Social Research Council.
2. For the British case, see *Metal Working Production*'s 1982 survey

which showed that firms with less than 500 employees increased their share of the British stock of NC and CNC machine tools between 1976 and 1982. Most of the increase was attributed to firms in the 10–49 employee range. For the case of France, see Cavestro (1984).

3. The statistics on the Rhône-Alpes region are taken from *Les Entreprises en Rhône-Alpes: Enquête Annuelle*, Banque de France. The figures on the West Midlands are from various numbers of the *Department of Employment Gazette*.

4. For a more complete discussion of the importance of trust for co-operative subcontracting relations, see Lorenz (1988).

5. For a general discussion of how trust can be brought about, see Gambetta (1988).

References

Berger, S. and M. Piore (1980), *Dualism and Discontinuity in Industrial Societies*, Cambridge: Cambridge University Press

Bessant, J., D. Jones, R. Lamming and A. Pollard (1984), *The West Midlands Automobile Components Industry*, Birmingham: West Midlands County Council Economic Development Committee

Cavestro, W. (1984), 'Automisation, organisation du travail et qualification dans les PME: le cas des machines-outils à commande numérique', *Sociologie du travail*, 4

Dellatre, M. (1982), 'Les PME face aux grandes entreprises', *Economie et statistique*, 148

Gambetta, D. (1988), 'Can we trust?', in D. Gambetta, (ed.), *Trust: Making and Breaking Cooperative Relations*, Oxford: Basil Blackwell

Granovetter, M. (1985), 'Economic Action and Social Structure: The Problem of Embeddedness', *American Journal of Sociology*, 91

Lorenz, E. (1988), 'Neither Friends nor Strangers: Informal Networks of Subcontracting in French Industry', in Gambetta ed. (1988)

Piore, M. and C. Sabel (1984), *The Second Industrial Divide: Possibilities of Prosperity*, New York: Basic Books

Williamson, O.E. (1985), *The Economic Institutions of Capitalism*. New York: Free Press

5   Innovation, Skills and Training: Micro-electronics and Manpower in the United Kingdom and West Germany

Adrian Campbell, Wendy Currie, and Malcolm Warner

National Settings

This chapter argues that the responses of industrial societies to technical and economic challenges differ significantly along national lines.[1]
In particular we are concerned with the variation between the strategies
adopted in the engineering industries of the United Kingdom and West
Germany. To this end we shall be presenting the main lessons derived
from four research projects with which the authors have been associated. Two of these projects are still in progress and three have
involved Anglo-German comparisons.

Our main contention is that the education and training systems of a
given country will inform work organisation patterns and hierarchical
structures within industry. Depending on how these patterns and
structures 'fit' with technical and economic exigencies, there will be a
significant effect on the performance of that country's industry. To
anticipate our conclusion, we argue that among the main reasons for
the continuing poor performance of British manufacturing is not only
the country's well-documented parsimony regarding training in general (Coopers and Lybrand 1985), but also the form that its training
takes and the 'elitist' vicious circle that is set in motion by these factors,
a vicious circle that helps explain the otherwise puzzling coincidence of
high unemployment and skill shortages.

New Technology and the Crisis of Mass Production

In recent years, managements, notably in the Anglo-Saxon world,
brought up on Taylorism have found it difficult to comprehend the
forms of competition engendered by the 'crisis of mass production'
(Piore and Sabel 1984). Where they have, their control systems, such as
the emphasis on machine uptime required for capital budgeting, as

133

well as an orientation towards short-term profits, have proved obstacles to progress. They have also experienced skill shortages as labour markets and training systems geared to standardised production have failed to provide for the demands arising from the need to customise and modify products, or the hybrid skills required to integrate increasingly complex technologies (Campbell and Warner 1987).

This crisis of mass production has been accompanied by a second crisis, that of 'bureaucratic control' (Ray 1986). This crisis has emerged in two complementary ways. On the one hand, the traditional bureaucratic organisation embodying a division of labour into segmented specialisms has been strained in its attempts to keep pace with technical developments, and has lost credibility as a result. The changes wrought within it in an attempt to use technology more effectively have in turn destabilised company cultures and their supporting values (loyalty, demarcation, career stability). The forms of work organisation associated with the new technology (where these changes occur) may make the control previously exercised problematic or less appropriate than before.

The Skills Problem

One of the major symptoms of the current confusion is the much-publicised skill shortage. This problem is one that first began to surface on a large scale with the limited economic recovery from 1983–4 onwards. Previously the question was seen to be one of oversupply, not shortages. From the recession of 1979 onwards companies began accelerating their restructuring programme and eliminating labour in successive 'shakeouts' (which are still continuing). Technological advance and 'restructuring' did in fact provide an effective smokescreen for the disappearance of large sections of British industry. Reductions in the number of technical workers were generally seen to result from technological advance, whereas in fact they were, overall, due to the collapse of manufacturing (Manpower Services Commission 1985). A further smokescreen for these developments was provided by the received opinion that 'old' manufacturing was giving way to 'new' services. The element of truth contained in this view prevented many commentators from noticing that, of the advanced industrial nations, only the UK saw an absolute (as opposed to relative) decline in manufacturing in favour of services.

By way of counterattack, the period saw a series of attempts to underline the importance of engineering for the country's prosperity, notably the Finniston Report (Committee of Inquiry 1980). This debate began to centre itself on the priorities of the education and training system. One problem was that the worse the situation grew the fewer resources were available to remedy it. Meager (1986) has claimed that no proven link exists between skill shortages and economic performance, at least no direct link, since each may be a symptom of the other. However, not only does this sanguine view underplay the seriousness of the shortages, particularly in the 'information technology' sector (see Pearson and Connor 1986), it also ignores the ways in which the British patterns of education, training and work organisation render the country more vulnerable to the effects of skill shortages than are the UK's European competitors, who also suffer such shortages but with less obvious repercussions. To clarify the sources of this greater vulnerability, we now set out the main characteristics of the British and West German systems, emphasising that the latter is better equipped to deal not only with skill shortages, but with integrated skill-intensive technologies and the 'crisis of mass production' in general.

Education and Training in the United Kingdom and West Germany

The regulation of skilled trades in both countries may be traced back to the dominance of the incorporated guilds in the Middle Ages. Differences between the two cases were, however, early to emerge. In Germany, policies towards the power of the guilds were subject to frequent change, the cutting back of guild privileges being followed by a later renaissance, notably in nineteenth-century Prussia. Guild controls applied specifically to handicrafts at first, but most journeyman trained in handicrafts went to work in manufacturing. Unlike in Britain, the differences between manufacturing and traditional handicrafts were not reduced through liberalisation of the latter, but through regulation of the former by government. The process made headway notably between the wars, in both the Weimar Republic and the Third Reich. As a general framework of qualification developed in all sectors, disputes arose between trade unions and employers, and between industry and handicrafts. Government policy gave training jurisdiction to chambers of industry and commerce, on the model of craft guilds. This tendency continued in the Federal Republic, culminating in the *Berufsbildungsgesetz* (Vocational Education and Training Act) of 1969. The training system became increasingly generalised, based on both apprenticeships and technical colleges, and acquired a corporatist dimension both at the local level, where trade unions participated in chambers of industry, and at national level, where the parameters of training were agreed between government, unions and employers.

In Britain, government policies for most of the period since the Middle Ages have tended towards 'liberalisation' and a reduction of guild power. The regulatory model provided by the medieval guilds survived intact only in the case of the professions and semi-professions, at a higher social level than the occupations covered in Germany. Furthermore, the doctrine of liberal non-interference in Britain minimised the role of the state in training and education (Sorge and Warner 1987). Indeed, British governments held back from compulsory schooling or any kind of obligatory education until the latter part of the nineteenth century. This contrasted with continental Europe, where the state generally took the leading role in the provision of education from Napoleonic times onwards.

Skill Composition and Work Organisation in the United Kingdom and West Germany

In the post-war era, notably during the 1960s, a number of attempts were made to bring British training provision in line with continental norms. The Industrial Training Act 1964 and the establishment of the Engineering Industry Training Board, combined with a greater co-operation between companies and educational institutions, represented major advances. However, the British apprenticeship system, compared with that of West Germany, remained restricted in its application to certain trades, and became perhaps too closely connected to a rigid system of demarcation. Although the British apprenticeship was a four-year rather than a three-year course, it included practical (as opposed to written) examination to a much smaller extent. Thus even in apprentice training the British concern with the dichotomy of theory and practice remained central. As Fores and Rey (1977) describe, no notion took hold in the UK which could correspond with the German concept of 'technik', incorporating applied skill or science. In addition, the gap between the numbers of apprentices in each country began to widen, so that in the 1970s there were three times as many apprentices in West Germany as in the UK, growing to eight times as many by the early 1980s.

Despite the new initiatives of the 1960s, training practices in the UK and West Germany have moved further apart since 1945. Whereas in both countries, before that date, technical apprenticeships were only undertaken on completion of craft apprenticeships, latterly British training for technicians has become wholly differentiated from the craft apprenticeship. This was facilitated by the absence in the UK of a two-tier technical college structure. In West Germany the *Berufsschule* and the *Technikerschule* provided for craft and technical levels, ensuring that they were approached successively. In the UK, students in the same colleges would be 'streamed' into craft and technical courses at an early stage.

This change emphasises the other differences already described. The implications of the national differences can now be summarised in this fashion: with the separation of craft and technical training, the declining number of craft apprenticeships in the UK affects ultimately the supply of technicians. Whereas in West Germany a large reserve army of craft workers is available for technical training, the early extraction of elites in the UK means that the system there is less responsive to demand changes. Where the West Germans have no shortage of candidates who have carried out the basic training to which technical training can be added, in the UK the pressure to recruit and train technicians as quickly as possible regardless of experience means an even earlier selection (so that the process becomes a self-reinforcing cycle) and throws a greater burden on school and college education, which is not equipped to redress the balance. The shortage of qualified technical labour leads to an even more elitist recruitment and training policy by companies, given the expensive nature of the training thus necessitated (Sorge and Warner 1987).

A further twist is provided by the scarce resources traditionally devoted to formal training in British companies. In an attempt to increase the number of skills available to them, companies develop a bias towards university graduates. To an extent it is, of course, clear that advances in technology have required a far greater emphasis on skills at graduate and post-graduate levels, a trend which has been taking place both in the UK and West Germany. At the same time, we would suggest that in the UK the inadequacy of training provisions below graduate level rendered industry unnecessarily dependent on the recruitment of graduates. Strains are put on a university system that has traditionally developed at more than one remove from industry and which has not been designed or funded to meet the increasing demand for specialists in new technical disciplines (let alone generalists or those trained in hybrid disciplines). When shortages of graduates occur, it follows that West German industry will have more skills in reserve to fall back on.

The greater emphasis on non-apprenticeship-linked training for technicians in schools and colleges and the need to cover as much ground as possible at these stages leads to a differentiation between technical and craft skills in the UK that does not occur under the West German system. In the UK, newly-recruited technicians will have a more academic background and no work experience. Craft workers, on the other hand, will have work experience but less college experience. The number who have both is thus dwindling. The position is made the more serious in that the policy of 'early extraction of elites' means that the most gifted will be denied work experience and those working at the craft level will be of a lower standard than in West Germany.

It is easy to see how the process outlined above leads to greater specialisation in British industry. The scarcer the skills, the more they will be differentiated and specialised. This also leads to a self-reinforcing cycle — greater specialisation leads to a greater demand for specialists, requiring more specialised training, the difficulties associated with which lead to renewed shortages.

During the period in question, there has of course been an increased specialisation of activities, largely in response to technological developments. Child and Kieser (1979) found this trend to have taken place in both the UK and West Germany according to the same pattern. In the UK, as one would expect, the process has gone substantially further, entailing a greater organisational burden regarding the co-ordination of specialised activities. The current position in manufacturing, where product integration and complication has occurred following the introduction of micro-electronics into products (Campbell and Warner 1986) and the introduction of CAD/CAM favours the organisational integration of different steps of the engineering and production processes the British organisation is arguably in a worse starting position that the West German, having dispensed with the integrative principle at an earlier stage and to a greater extent, as a result of the training and labour market trends outlined above. The British enterprise is more clearly demarcated not only in terms of labour generally but also in terms of distinct professions, a notion that seems relatively weak in West Germany (Sorge and Warner 1987). The limitations arising from this specialisation are accentuated by the fact that higher education in the UK is concluded at a much earlier age than in West Germany (21 rather than 25). Thus the British engineer has a weaker occupational identity, to which the traditional weakness of the professional engineering institutions has also contributed (Smith 1984). The continuing education of the British engineer 'on the job' will, in its turn, lead to more, not less specialisation.

Thus, a system of education geared to academic-technological as opposed to technical training, largely separated from vocational practice, leads to higher specialisation, and greater division of labour. It also leads to a more bureaucratic work organisation, as the integration of specialised inputs is co-ordinated. Decisions need to be taken further up the hierarchy and away from the point of design or production. Technology applied in this context threatens to increase this division between concept and execution, particularly if combined with the finance-driven priorities characteristic of Anglo-Saxon engineering, as described earlier. This can occur even when technological developments could be interpreted as favouring a shift in the opposite direction.

Four Research Studies

In this section we review the findings of the four research studies mentioned earlier, dealing with management, technology and skills in manufacturing industry.

Societal Differences in Organization

The first of the four studies (Maurice *et al.*, 1980) took issue with the assumption of organisational universality which the authors saw as prevalent in much organisational literature. Cross-national comparisons of closely matched factories in France, the UK and West Germany were undertaken. The major overall finding was that 'organizational processes of differentiation and integration can be seen to interact with processes of educating, training, recruiting and promoting manpower, so that both develop within an institutional logic that is particular to a society, and bring about nationally different shapes of organization'. With respect to particular national differences, the following stand out as relevant to this chapter.

Regarding the deployment of labour, West Germany firms were seen to use production labour more flexibly in the sense that workers were trained in a variety of jobs, rather than learning only when moved to a new job, as was the case in the UK. Flexible deployment was as pronounced in British maintenance work as in West German. However the distinction between production and maintenance was less rigid in West Germany. French practices were closer to the British than to the West German.

Regarding autonomy, supervisory authority was strongest in France, whilst in the UK and France work schedules were usually worked out in advance by production planning and control functions. West German workers tended to use the supervisor more as a go-between to exert their influence on the scheduling and manning of work. In this way disputes over particulars were less likely to manifest themselves in labour–management conflict. In West Germany the equivalent of the chargehand was responsible for more aspects of supervision than in the other countries. This meant fewer layers of supervision in the production area. An associated characteristic of West German enterprises was the way in which production planning and control, or technical services in general, were seen as providing production workers with a service, rather than the other way round, as was the case in France and the UK. Accompanying this in turn was a greater 'technicity' of line management and supervision in West Germany. Unlike in France and the UK, technical expertise was not concentrated away from the central line of operations, so that staff hierarchies were lighter.

Regarding qualifications, the authors used the notion of 'professionality' to distinguish between the findings of the three national cases. Differences in the level and mode of training and education of employees were reflected in the relation between their functions in the enterprise. Differences between line and staff regarding education were proportional to the distance between the functions. Thus, in the UK technical tasks are split off from the line of authority, the demarcation being reflected in different qualifications — for staff specialists, engineering qualifications; for line managers, natural science qualifications. Similar conditions have established the separation of production and maintenance in the UK to a greater degree than in West Germany. The authors found also that the differentiation and professionalisation of non-line management was inversely related to the degree of professionalisation of workers, technicians and line managers. Also, the more profession-alised the latter jobs were, the less differentiation, or division of labour, was required. The UK, although to a lesser extent than France, exem-plified the first type of professionalization, West Germany the second. These findings have been confirmed by other studies, notably Child *et al.* (1983).

The upshot is that in West Germany highly trained workers at the centre of operations, through technical, supervisory and line manage-ment levels, means a lesser requirement in terms of staff specialists. In the UK, what Sorge *et al.* (1983) were later to call 'the flight of skills from the factory floor' means that far more staff specialists are required, leading both to problems of co-ordination and to skill shortages.

To anticipate our conclusion, we may say that in the UK graduate skill shortages coincide with the introduction of new technology which favours (but does not necessarily deliver) the integration of functions and specialist disciplines both organisationally and through hybrid skills. One way to minimise the ill-effects of the shortage would, on the basis of this analysis, be to strengthen intermediate levels of training, notably apprenticeships, doing so with a longer-term perspective (avoiding the vicious circle engendered by the 'extraction of elites') and in doing so, achieve the broader objectives regarding integration and co-ordination.

The CNC Study

Sorge *et al.* (1983) took the cross-national investigation further with regard to the forms of work organisation associated with the applica-tion of computer numerically-controlled (CNC) machine tools. Varia-tions were classified against the parameters of the firms studied — the size of the firms and the size of the batches they were manufacturing. Through matching case studies, controlling for these variables in British and West German firms, an attempt was made to delineate national differences, in particular the effects of national traditions regarding skills and training.

A number of interesting national differences emerged, over and above differences between large and small plants and large and small batch sizes. First, operator programming of equipment was far more widespread in West Germany than in the UK. As such it was not an isolated development, but served as the focus of a more general reintegration of functions and personnel. Whereas earlier technical advances, in a mass production/homogenous market context, had been accompanied by the 'flight' of skills and personnel away from the sphere of direct labour, in West Germany, particularly in the larger plants producing smaller batches, programming, troubleshooting and job-changing brought together a whole range of categories – operators, planners, production engineers, managers, chargehands, and foremen. This shift of focus back to the shop floor is seen by the authors as representing a new paradigm for manufacturing in the conditions of the 1980s. Failure to perceive its relevance, and continuing to extrapolate the centralising tendencies of the 1940s to 1970s automation is seen as potentially disastrous. This tendency was more evident in the UK both on the macro level, with its neglect of craft and intermediate skills and training in favour of a 'technology fetishism' over information technology and a 'post-industrial society' obsession with 'information work' as opposed to traditional skills. This in turn brings us back to the fallacy of the workerless factory archetype, again more popular in the UK than in Japan, from where it is assumed to have been copied. As Takamiya (1979) has argued, efficiency and productivity in Japanese plants is more rooted in the skills and delegated responsibilities of workers than in their small numbers, often larger than in British plants of comparable size. In the UK an often legitimate concern with over-manning has led to a simplistic and over-quantitative approach to productivity, and has turned attention away from the inappropriateness of structures as a factor in inefficiency.

The emphasis on the separateness of 'information work' from practical skill is repeated in the organisation of work in British plants, particularly larger ones. Whereas integration in West Germany is assisted by its system of qualification that appears to avoid clear class distinctions, in the UK the traditional hiatus between craft and technical work forms a barrier, just as does the emphasis on programming and planning as a white-collar activity, which was found to be greater in the UK than in West Germany.

A national difference which is worth commenting on, but which does not so easily permit judgement, was the way in which the West German formal system of qualifications held sway in large and small plants equally, whilst in the UK there was a distinct difference between the two. Whereas larger plants tended to be organisationally segmented with an emphasis on formal engineering qualifications, smaller plants were pragmatically flexible with regard to skills, qualifications and in some cases those in charge were openly hostile to formal apprenticeships, seeing them as favouring dilletantism. Such criticism was not encountered regarding the formal training system in West Germany. Regarding the latter, we should stress that, in contrast with the UK, technical apprenticeship was only embarked on subsequent to finishing a craft apprenticeship.

Overall, the arguments in favour of the West German approach could be mitigated by stressing the flexibility of the informal training in the UK, particularly in small plants, and contrasting this with the time-consuming, laborious and bureaucratic nature of the West German system of training and qualification. We should, however, mention that manufacturing in the UK is far more concentrated in larger plants than it is in West Germany and Japan, and it is in these larger plants that the greater inflexibility of white–blue-collar, craft–technician divisions holds sway. It would appear that the West German system, while ponderous in its dimensions, provides a rigid overall framework within which the opportunities for strategic choice, flexibility and integration are less trammelled. It is not, of course, to be recommended that a system such as the West German one be copied slavishly; such initiatives frequently involve simplification and shallowness and may even make the inflexibilities of the British mode of organisation work to greater detriment. It is not the bones of the West German system that are crucial but the strategic values that inform them and which they facilitate. It is the twin fallacies of the 'workerless factory' (cf. Senker and Beesley 1986) and the 'post-industrial society' conception of information work, grafted onto an older and increasingly irrational distinction between white- and blue-collar work, that obstructs the reorientation that appears to be required in the present decade.

The authors reject the workless factory paradigm, not only on account of its inappropriateness at the present time, but also on account of the facile linear approach to technical advance and its relation to society that it embodies. The workerless factory idea cannot conceive of itself as ever being inappropriate since it ignores the extent that choices are available with any given technology regarding manning, skills, role in production process, and the fact that these choices (including choices regarding the design of the equipment concerned) are guided by the economic context in which the organisations using the technology are obliged to operate. It is understandable that those who have a vested interest in explaining away unemployment find refuge in the concept of a post-industrial society determined by technological change. It is more surprising that many of those who do not, nevertheless blame unemployment on technology as if it were an ahistorical force. The context which the authors of this study observed and its implications for technology and work organisation are as follows: slow economic growth led to a concentration on small market niches and a consequent increase in customisation and the provision of more differentiated products. Market expansion and increased market share are only thought feasible with increased production variety.

This process leads to increased product complexity. To keep this development within reasonable bounds there is then an increase in the complexity of parts. In the case of machining, this will result in the need for more demanding cuts and a greater number of such cuts to be carried out on a single work-piece. As a result, numerically controlled (NC) machining has, in this context, a *qualitative* justification which is of such importance that it makes any parallel justification based on quantitative increases in productivity almost irrelevant. In this context the 'new technology' cannot be seen as a destroyer of jobs, since the trend is dependent on, and causal to, a wider diffusion of NC machining.

It cannot either be seen as a destroyer or polariser of skill (of itself), since in the context described choices in the direction of a work organisation more dependent on shop-floor skills have seemed the more logical, and have been applied in West Germany, aided by the greater availability of skilled labour in the intermediate range in that country. Technology and markets have positioned the focus of variability at the point of production itself, close bureaucratic control being innappropriate to the handling of large numbers of highly variable batches with increasingly complex parameters. This is not to say that technology and organisation may not be developed so as to enable a continuation of bureaucratic control which does not have too severe an effect on efficiency. In the UK, where engineers and engineering managers are as aware as their West German counterparts of the qualitative rationale for NC technology, there are signs that this is being done, for which our most recent study has found new evidence. While we may say that the 'locus of variability' is now firmly placed at the point of production, it does not follow that the 'locus of control' of that variability need reside there. In the West German case, traditions of work organisation that favour a renewed emphasis on craft-centred production appear to integrate the two to a larger extent than in the UK. British engineers appear to be applying themselves to moving the locus of variability control higher up the hierarchy (hence the general preoccupation with software and design engineering skills to some extent).

If current market conditions favour the diffusion of technologies suited to coping with complexity and variability, such as NC, CAD and, by extension, CAD/CAM, these conditions do not necessarily determine the best way of utilising these technologies. This is not to say that they can be seen as a *tabula rasa* as far as work organisation is concerned, but that they are like the two sides of a coin. One national tradition may develop their propensity for 'democratic' delegated integration, another may develop their potential for integration at a higher point. We should remember that the technology concerned can, for some, represent an attempt to conquer the very variability to which it owes its rationale.

The CAD Study

A number of the themes from the CNC study reoccur in the findings of a study, recently completed at Henley, the Management College, on the decision-making process regarding computer-aided design (CAD) in twenty British engineering companies. Whilst the study found further evidence of a bias towards narrowly quantitative investment criteria, which may be attributed to the dominance of the accounting perspective (see Armstrong 1987) the study was significant in finding evidence of a reaction amongst engineers and sections of engineering management against this type of approach.

Those implementing the CAD had in many cases a different view of the benefits of computer-aided design to those held by senior management. The former tended to emphasise qualitative benefits such as the improved quality of drawings, the drawing of designs hitherto impossible, the potential for greater system integration and related 'global' benefits (Senker 1984; and Primrose *et al*. 1985) including improved lead times, the latter seen from the qualitative angle, as part of a trend towards non-price-related competition. Senior management, particularly in the largest firms, were more likely to emphasise quantitative criteria such as drawing office productivity and lead times in the narrow sense related to direct productivity.

These differences complicated the process of investment justification and evaluation. Senior management demanded that qualitative benefits be quantified, the assumption being that if this could not be done they could not be admitted as relevant. In one case this went as far as requiring that a precise estimate should be given as to the amount of incremental business that could be derived from the appearance of a working CAD system in the company's brochure (a more common reason for introducing innovations such as CAD than might have been expected).

For their part, the advocates of CAD and its qualitative benefits responded by presenting their arguments under a quantitative smokescreen. This could mean simply restating the figures given by CAD suppliers regarding the likely productivity gains in drawing office, so as to be seen to be 'speaking the same language' as senior management. The advertising literature, for the very reason that it was geared to the perceptions and priorities of senior management, tended, in the early 1980s particularly, to emphasise direct productivity advantages and underplay training requirements.

This process of 'false dialogue' between technical champions and senior decision-makers could lead to difficulties. In more than one case, managers in charge of the design function were subsequently preoccupied with staving off senior management demands for their delivery of drawing office productivity targets. These had usually not been met, since those doing the implementation were more concerned with objectives such as greater inter-functional communication and more accurate information transfer. Moreover, predictions regarding the potential of CAD to erode jobs have tended to be exaggerated, since, as with CNC, the work-load is likely to increase along with the capability.

Thus design and drawing office managers were left hoping that senior management would be impressed soon enough by the indirect benefits of CAD to ignore the fact that their productivity targets were not being met. Some managers viewed senior management's insistence on the fulfilment of such productivity targets to be partly bluff, based on the need to maintain a quantitative control system, as well as being rooted in senior management anxiety about their legitimacy given their lack, in most cases, of up-to-date technical understanding. This was, of course, a sanguine view, but not without some basis in fact in a number of companies. Productivity targets were, in any case, met indirectly through systems integration and fewer repeats.

Conflict was, of course, not only intra-managerial. The draughtsmen's union, TASS (the former Technical and Supervisory Section of the engineers' union), were strong supporters of CAD, through which they hoped to achieve their demands for training and upgrading. The Amalgamated Engineering Union (AEU) which organised the machineshop floor tended to resent the wider repercussions of CAD via CAD/CAM (see below).

TASS[2] have often resented the way managements have ignored the importance of the 'middle' stage of design work, whereby the general framework provided by design engineers is interpreted by draughtsmen and then committed to paper (or screen). As a result, the introduction of CAD has sometimes proceeded without full understanding of the nature of the function which is actually being automated (Currie and Campbell 1987). In one case, for example, implementation foundered at first on account of a misconceived strategy of having manual and CAD draughting as successive stages of the same work process, in the hope of maximising system utilisation. The scheme failed since in splitting the task in half, it ignored the skills required in interpreting rough sketches.

In several sites visited, TASS were demanding the acquisition of more terminals and universal CAD training for their members, in response to attempts by management to divide the drawing office into two groups, one more broadly trained than the other, and the associated attempt to improve utilisation of the system through the introduction of shift work (not usual for technical staff) for those with CAD training. Where TASS negotiators felt obliged to accept shift work there was conflict with management over TASS's demand that those involved should receive both shift payments and CAD skill premiums. Where TASS was successfully resisting shift work, drawing office and engineering management were caught between TASS's demands and those of senior management. Whether or not the companies concerned had enough business, there would probably be no way that in such cases senior management would allow one terminal per person (plus the relevant training) since their understanding of the technology was geared to cutting back manpower and skill requirements. Which scenario emerges thus depends on the values and organisational skills underpinning the balancing act of the implementation managers.

The politics of the implementation process is thus linked to routine conflicts from the departmental level upwards, which traditionally operate around the budgeting structure. Senior management will generally attempt to extract the same or greater level of performance from them whilst giving them fewer resources, whether in the form of capital investment or 'head count'. It is thus in middle management's interest to maintain 'slack' against such demands, and they are thus less likely to seize every potential for reducing numbers and skills under their control. This should be even more the case where such simple rationalisation is seen to be irrelevant to the potential of the technology to be used as part of a strategy for organisational change.

Resistance to the qualitative approach comes not only from higher levels, but also from junior and middle management whose careers have been governed through the short-term, control-intensive approach that has characterised many British company cultures. In some cases senior managers in charge of implementing CAD were pressurised from below to include (otherwise unnecessary) control mechanisms in CAD packages so as to enable the ease of supervision that could be obtained under the manual system. In one large company a large-scale training initiative had been set in motion to wean supervisors and junior managers away from styles of supervision that were seen as no longer appropriate given the more integrated organisation with more fluid boundaries that was being implemented along with CAD/CAM.

There does, however, seem to be some substance in the view that a more pervasive tendency exists in British organisations for the system to have discretion 'spillover' at a higher (i.e. more cerebral) level of skill than in a more production-centred industrial culture such as that existing in West Germany. CAD/CAM, for example, had often meant a shift of skill and discretion from machine shop to automated drawing office in which machine-programming tapes were produced, a development strongly resented by the machine operators. Although managers were in favour of this shift (perceiving the dispute that occurred as being purely inter-union in nature), they were concerned that the shift in this case made them more dependent on the good will of the more militant union (TASS), particularly given that the planned merger between TASS and the more moderate Association of Scientific, Technical and Managerial Staff (ASTMS) was likely to rob them of one possible strategy, namely the splitting of the drawing office into two groups, with the more skilled draughtsmen being transferred to ASTMS. They were also concerned that shop-floor skills, and the craft workers' good will might gradually wither in the process, so they would no longer be on hand when crises occurred.

At the same time, the company in question provided a rare example (in the UK) of the survival of a comprehensive apprentice training system. Although there was a significant shift from craft to technical apprenticeships, involving many direct transfers (unlike the West German practice described in an earlier section), a shift which reflected the direction of the company's technical strategy, it was guaranteed that those graduating had a grounding in basic skills that were no longer needed on a day-to-day basis, as well as those which were always required.

What emerged from the CAD study overall was the extent to which advances in technology and skill provision depended in large part on skilful manoeuvering on the part of managers below the most senior levels, often highly individualised, and diverse strategies which contrasted with the greater level of consensus and codified practice that characterised the West German system. Such strategies (in training as well as in technology implementation), were often conducted in ways that were half-hidden from those above and below who might oppose them, making use of the complex possibilities of the budgeting structure (Campbell and Currie, 1987).

Thus, just as there are engineering managers who have (correctly, from a strategic point of view) maintained drawing office manpower and increased training despite assurances that they would reduce both as a condition of the technology's introduction, there are also more than a few training managers who have managed, through a variety of means, to spend more than twice their allocated budget on training, within an overall culture that demands such expenditure to be kept at a minimum.

The above is not meant to detract from the criticisms of British practice overall made in the following section, but to emphasise the extent to which a potential for change exists within the 'repertoire' of the British system, albeit informally for the most part. This potential perhaps deserves more attention, given the difficulties involved in translating directly the other lessons of another tradition.

The Micro-electronics in Product Applications Study

With this study the focus shifted to product rather than process applications of micro-electronics. The data gained from British firms with such applications will shortly be compared with data from similar West German firms currently being investigated by the International Institute of Management, Berlin, team. A total of twenty-seven British firms have been investigated.

As we review the data, the most striking aspect of the findings is the overriding concern with graduate engineering skills. Although a number of (usually smaller) firms reported serious shortages of technicians and skilled prototype workers, almost all shortages in the larger firms were shortages of graduates, shortages of electronics hardware or software, and perhaps most importantly, shortages of 'firmware' and systems engineers.

While such shortages (particularly those in the last-named category) are undoubtedly important, and are likely to be predominant on West Germany as well, we might perhaps question their centrality to the skills and training debate as evident in the Butcher Report produced by the Department of Trade and Industry (DTI 1985). The Butcher Report takes a rather simple 'pump-priming' approach to training in the economy. Interviews with DTI officials seemed to suggest that their general view was that training was the responsibility of industry, and that government could merely provide the overall strategic skills (high-technology graduates) that industry could not be expected to provide. For the rest, the traditional British approach of 'on-the-job' training (not to be dismissed, since it could be claimed, as it was by several managers, that formal training is less efficient and only serves to create the framework whereby learning can occur through on-the-job experience) would make most of the running for the rest. To an extent, the DTI was merely reflecting the emphases of company recruitment and training policies. The second part of the Butcher Report, intended to deal with skills at technician level (the shop-floor or intermediate levels were not covered at all) could only work with generalities, since companies appeared to have very little precise information on the numbers and qualities of skills either posessed or required at this level. At the graduate level, on the contrary, the most precise figures can be obtained almost instantly. Immediately it comes too mind that the graduate shortage is given attention because it is bureaucratically the most comprehensible and the most accessible. Furthermore, the emphasis on the need for high-technology graduates plays a part in the pressure on universities to concentrate on vocational courses — the much publicised 'switch' of funds from arts and social science to new-technology subjects meant a drop in the total number of students, since more money is required per student in the latter subjects. This emphasis on the universities ignores the fact that countries such as Japan have, if anything, a less vocational university syllabus, the emphasis being on vocational training in the firm itself.

Overall, large British companies appear to prefer recruitment to training. Skills are bought off the shelf wherever possible, the simplest (though in the long run of the most difficult) means of doing this being to recruit 'ready-made' graduates. Smaller companies, and in particular companies with fewer than fifty employees, placed a greater emphasis on training and development of staff, with a high premium on versatility made necessary because of the need to overlap with such small numbers. In these companies one often found people with Ordinary National Certificate (ONC) or Higher National Certificate (HNC) qualifications doing work which in larger companies would be seen as wholly the preserve of graduates. Interestingly, it was the smaller companies which made proportionately greater use of local educational establishments. Often they could only recruit school-leavers by offering them day-release at a local college to study for an HNC. On gaining the HNC after four or five years, these trainees would invariably leave to join a larger company which was able to offer them a career structure in line with their increased expectations. The only advantage of small firms was that they offered the possibility of more varied and interesting work at each level of skill than the large companies.

In these firms the diminishing returns from graduate skill were a problem. Although an effective 'half-life' of five years was seen as an inevitable result of a high-technology industry where skills were quickly superseded, the problem may in part be due to such large organisations themselves where initiative tends to become submerged in the large concentrations of graduate specialists. Even if it is more a question of the speed of technological change, the problem is exacerbated by the emphasis on recruitment of new graduates rather than the training or the retraining of the old. The group training manager of a large electronics company strongly repudiated the 'Butcher approach' in this respect, and was organising a substantial retraining drive to redevelop the existing personnel in the company. Interestingly, he was also instrumental in keeping the apprenticeship and technician training programmes at full strength, with some mixing of mechanical and electronic disciplines, despite the relative decline of craft and technical labour in the production process.

Apart from the waste of human resources implied, the national emphasis on recruitment rather than training has other drawbacks. One engineering manager was attempting to recruit more women engineers through speaking to local schools. Those in charge of girls' education refused such initiatives, with the view that such a career was not appropriate. The engineering manager's motive was practical — the increase in engineering graduates (mostly male) had only brought in more second-rate engineers who were only in the area for career purposes, and had no engineering talent. Women's engineering ability has not been tapped to anything like its full potential. This was another area where traditional recruiting practices had failed.

Companies frequently complained about the nature of the skills they were so assiduously buying in from the universities. Companies wanted company specialists whereas universities provided subject specialists. In addition, the direction taken by product technology meant that greater integration between disciplines would be required. Technical complexity has, in the higher-technology areas, become such that it is knowledge of the product as a system that counts, not specialist knowledge of one of its parts or one of the required disciplines. As one mechanical systems engineer remarked, 'I want someone who is interested in how the engine as a whole is going to turn out, not just one of its component units'.

In the CNC study, it was suggested that parts become more complex so that the product as a whole can be kept within manageable limits of complexity. This process appears to have reversed. Under the continual pressure to customise, micro-electronics has been applied to simplify component units so that more functions of a system can be confined in a smaller space. The customer then demands that the remaining space be 'filled' up with new functions. The result is an increasingly elaborate system with increasingly simple parts. The kind of expertise required is of a different order than before, when the needs of complex part could be met by subject specialists. Complex wholes require a different approach, with generalist and integrating abilities, hybrid skills and an experience of the system as a product not as a scientific creation. How this is solved depends on the level of technology involved. In one company making alarm systems, this need was said to call for good ONC-grade 'jack-of-all-trades' technicians. In another, where integration of the whole had become 'a matter of luck', it was highly-qualified systems engineers that were called for.

With the arrival of CAD/CAM it is possible that the designs of many components will become 'repeats' from a central data base. In this way graduate skill shortages may force their own solution, since smaller numbers of graduates will be required to produce 'routine' designs from scratch. Other innovations, such as application-specific integrated circuits (ASICs) may reduce the requirement for electronic engineers. What will remain will be an emphasis on system design, packaging and assembly. This will require a smaller number of generalist engineers, people with intermediate mechanical skills, and assemblers and craft workers able to deal with a variety of different arrangements for the customised systems that will be the company products. Here we are talking about the larger, more strategic engineering companies who, in addition to contracting for each other, do also rely (increasingly as value added is based in many cases on systems design and assembly and not on component manufacture) on large numbers of small subcontractors. It is not to be assumed, however, that these smaller component manufacturers all work on strict mass production lines. Their small size, and the likelihood that they provide components of some variety, suggest that they will be organised on flexible lines, although this flexibility may sometimes be at the employees' expense, particularly if they are unskilled in conventional terms. Skill shortages in the intermediate range mean that, as with graduates, those who posess such skills are often in a sellers' market, and are able to demand conditions for their employment, notably training (as in the example of school-leavers given earlier). That this is occurring at the graduate level is explicit in the increased status being granted to the training function for graduates in a number of engineering companies in the last couple of years. To some extent this is to remedy the problem of technology having outpaced existing expertise in the company (in the area of product/system complexity as described earlier); it is also a reflection that training is now taken into account when graduates 'shop around' for employment.

We conclude this brief review by summarising the major points that have arisen, in addition to the ones set out above. First, if management strategies have a tendency to focus on key constraints on their decision-making power, then shortages of 'off-the-shelf' graduates have become such a key constraint that we must expect steps to be taken to eliminate them. This can be done either through technical or organisational initiatives or through training of existing graduates or other staff.

Second, the history and traditions of an organisation have a major influence on how decisions concerning product or skills development will be tackled, as will regional and cultural factors — Scottish firms, for example, placed a greater emphasis on training, despite their access to as many university graduates as they wanted via their proximity to a wide range of universities and technical colleges.

Third, the decay of skills within companies through lack of training is as much a cause of the skills shortage as is inadequacy of initiatives outside.

Fourth, design expertise is becoming more product-orientated and groomed to deal with specific constraints put forward by customers.

Fifth, technology and skills appear to follow a pendulum effect. Paradoxically, the pendulum begins to swing back on itself before it has reached the extremity of one movement. In other words, the rise of one group contains the seeds of its fall. In many cases specialists in electronics, for example, were still the key constraint but, whilst still recruiting them, more than one company was thinking of what to do with them when, as was expected, the pendulum began to swing further towards mechanical packaging as a selling point.

Sixth, in advanced small batch engineering, the experience of the past both protected and eroded skills. The need to update past products in the posession of or on order by the customer kept older skills alive. At the same time, the need to generate the appropriate information for these repeats and updates encouraged greater automaticity in design.

Seventh, there appears, in some larger companies, to be an indissoluble antagonism between the skills of certain groups – as with the drawing office and the machine-shop — since skills could not be gained in one area without being eroded or underutilised in the other. How and where this surfaces depends on where and how integration is focused, which in turn rests with company product and work organisation strategies.

Finally, small-batch production favours hybrid skills, most particularly in small companies and plants.

Training Implications

According to a Manpower Services Commission-sponsored survey of 500 firms in the UK (*Times Higher Education Supplement*, 29 November 1985, p. 8) British firms spend only 0.15 per cent of their sales turnover on adult training, whereas a high proportion of American counterparts disburse 2 or even 3 per cent.

The absolute quantity of training is less a problem than the need for increasingly frequent updating of ideas, as existing knowledge becomes more rapidly obselete. According to the MSC Chairman, Mr Bryan Nicholson, 'Between half and three-quarters of Britain's workforce will need to up-date their skills and knowledge during the next five years just to keep pace with new technology' (*THES*, 29 November 1985, p. 8).

As training thus requires greater investment by employing organisations, it is likely that the latter will be more selective in recruitment to find employees with the most appropriate prior qualifications and aptitudes, and to minimise the risks of selecting those who may not appear be good long-term 'training investments'.

Many firms are unwilling to face the costs of training skilled people, leading to shortages of technical and maintenance manpower. Other reasons for such shortages include lack of suitable candidates for apprenticeships, dismissal of skilled staff early in the recession, inadequate training schemes, the legacy of demarcation practices, and vast interregional differentials in house prices.

Recruiting is one thing, holding onto graduate or technician trainees is another. For example, in one plant studied, graduate intake for the plant (all engineers) was 14 in 1985, compared with 25 for 1984, out of the total of 330 employees. The turnover for the year was over 20 per cent. Labour turnover is a problem under the skills shortage.

Concluding Remarks

The gap between the demand for highly skilled labour and the supply of indiscriminately qualified labour partly results from the rapid pace of technological change in key sectors, unanticipated by employers, trade unions and government agencies, as well as the effects of recession. There is little evidence in the UK that the gap is being bridged in spite of well-publicised government initiatives.

While there are both skills shortages specifically and job shortages generally, these trends need not persist if there were the political will to do something about it. At the macro-economic level human resources investment is still a fraction of physical capital investment. As one training manager put it: 'Training is cheaper than ignorance'.

Notes

1. This chapter is based on the results of a series of research projects, three of which were funded by the Anglo-German Foundation for the Study of Industrial Society, and carried out in collaboration with Arndt Sorge and colleagues from the International Institute of Management, West Berlin. The fourth, on CAD, was funded by the SERC.
2. TASS was subsequently to merge with ASTMS to form Manufacturing, Science and Finance (MSF).

References

Armstrong, P. (1987), 'The Abandonment of Productive Intervention in Management Teaching Syllabi', Warwick Papers in Industrial Relations No. 15, Industrial Relations Research Unit, School of Industrial and Business Studies, University of Warwick

Campbell, A. and W. Currie (1987), 'Rationality, Politics and Culture: Management Strategies Regarding New Technology and Engineering Skills', Paper presented at Conference of the British Universities Industrial Relations Association, Strathclyde, July

Campbell, A. and M. Warner (1986), 'Product Innovation, Skill Needs and Manpower Training: A Study of Microelectronics Applications in Selected British Firms', in T. Lupton, ed 'Human 3 — Proceedings of the 3rd International Conference on Human Factors in Manufacturing. Amsterdam: North-Holland

Campbell, A. and M. Warner (1987), 'New Technology, Innovation and Training; a Survey of British Firms', New Technology, Work and Employment, 2.2, pp. 86–99

Child, J., M. Fores, I. Glover and P. Lawrence (1983), 'A Price to Pay — Professionalism and Work Organization in Britain and West Germany', Sociology, 17, pp 63–78.

Child, J. and A. Kieser (1979), 'Organization and Managerial Roles in British and West German Companies: an Examination of the Culture-Free Thesis' in C.J. Lammers and D.J. Hickson, eds, Organizations: Like and Unlike, London: Routledge and Kegan Paul

Committee of Inquiry into the Engineering Profession, Engineering Our Future (The Finniston Report), Cmnd. 7794, London: HMSO, 1980

Coopers and Lybrand (1985), 'A Challenge to Complacency', Report to the Manpower Services Commission, MSC: Sheffield

Currie, W. and A. Campbell (1987), 'Skills and Strategies in Design Engineering'. Paper presented to 5th Aston/UMIST Conference of the Organization and Control of the Labour Process, April

Department of Trade and Industry, IT Skills Shortages Committee (1985) First Report: The Human Factor. The Supply Side and Second Report: Changing Technology, Changing Skills, London: DTI.

Fores, M. and L. Rey (1977). 'Technik: The Relevance of a Missing Concept', Higher Education Review, Spring, pp. 43–57

Manpower Services Commission (1985), *The Impacu of New Technology on Skills in Manufacturing and Services*, MSC: Sheffield

Maurice, M., A. Sorge and M. Warner (1980), 'Societal Differences in Organising Manufacturing Units: A Comparison of France, West Germany and Great Britain', *Organization Studies*, 1, pp. 59–86

Meager, N, (1986), 'Skill Shortages again in the British Economy', *Industrial Relations Journal*, 17.3, pp. 236–48

Pearson, R. and H. Connor (1986), 'Tapping the Manpower Pool', *Times Higher Education Supplement*, 27 June

Piore, M.J. and C.F. Sabel (1984). *The Second Industrial Divide*, New York: Basic Books

Primrose, P.L., G.D. Creamer and R. Leonard (1985), 'Identifying and Quantifying the "Company-Wide" Benefits of CAD within the Structure of a Comprehensive Investment Programme' in E. Rhodes and D. Wield, eds, *Implementing New Technologies*, Oxford: Blackwell, pp. 291–302

Ray, C.A. (1986), 'Corporate Culture: The Last Frontier of Control?', *Journal of Management Studies*, 23.3, pp. 287–97

Senker, P. (1984), 'The Implications of CAD/CAM for Management', *Omega*, 12.3 pp. 225–301

Senker, P. and M. Beesley, (1986) 'The Need for Skills in the Factory of the Future', *New Technology, Work and Employment*, 1.1 pp. 9–17

Smith, C. (1984), 'Design Engineers and the Capitalist Firm'. Working Paper, Work Organization Research Centre, University of Aston

Sorge, A., G. Hartmann, I. Nicholas and M. Warner (1983), *Microelectronics and Manpower in Manufacturing*, Gower: Aldershot

Takamiya, M. (1979), 'Japanese Multi-Nationals in Europe: International Operations and their Policy Implications', Discussion Paper 79–86, International Institute of Management, Wissenschaftszentrum, Berlin (West)

6 Markets, Technology and Local Intervention: The Case of Clothing

Jonathan Zeitlin and Peter Totterdill

Clothing manufacture is widely considered a 'sunset' industry with little future in countries like the United Kingdom. Simple products, static technology and low capital requirements, it is often argued, make labour costs the central focus of competition in the industry and give low-wage developing countries an insurmountable comparative advantage. Public policies, on this view, should not aim to maintain clothing production in the advanced economies through protection and subsidy, but rather to smooth the course of the unavoidable process of adjustment (for more or less sophisticated expressions of these views, see Keesing and Wolf 1980; Silberston 1984; de la Torre 1986).

At first glance, the recent history of the British clothing industry appears to support this line of argument. Between 1971 and 1984, the industry shed 126,000 jobs, or 43 per cent of total employment. Over the same period, imports increased rapidly, while exports lagged behind, giving rise to a trade deficit of £1.2 billion in 1986. Average levels of profitability in clothing manufacture are below the levels obtained in other sectors, while capital investment in 1984 stood at just over half the 1979 level and has fallen as a proportion of manufacturing as a whole. Average gross weekly wages in 1984 for manual workers in full-time employment were 72 per cent of the average for manufacturing for men and 83 per cent for women (who make up more than 80 per cent of the total labour force) (Lancashire County Council 1986; Greater London Council 1986; *Hollings Apparel Industry Review*, Spring 1987).

Despite its contraction, however, the clothing industry remains a major sector of British manufacturing, accounting for 4.3 per cent of total employment in 1986. Clothing and textiles together employ some 480,000 people — 200,000 more than motor vehicles and components, and their contribution to value added is also greater. Activity is heavily concentrated in particular regions such as London, the East and West Midlands, Yorkshire and Lancashire, and clothing is a major source of employment for women and ethnic minorities, particularly in the inner cities (Department of Trade and Industry 1987; British Textile Confederation 1987).

Nor is its continued decline by any means inevitable. This chapter argues that recent developments in the market for clothing and retailer strategies have expanded the demand for better-quality, more fashionable garments, while related changes in technology and manufacturing methods have reduced the cost penalty associated with the production of a variety of styles in shorter runs. These shifts, which reflect a broader movement from mass production towards flexible specialisation also visible in other sectors (Piore and Sabel 1984; Sabel and Zeitlin 1985), have tilted the balance of competitive advantage for many types of garment away from low-wage suppliers in developing countries, and have opened up new and remunerative opportunities for clothing production in the advanced economies. In the UK itself, the growth of import penetration has slowed down since the early 1980s, output has risen by 20 per cent above the trough of 1980, and employment has also begun to pick up (Department of Trade and Industry 1987). But given the underlying weaknesses of the British clothing industry, there is little reason to believe that market forces alone will ensure the necessary adjustments, and the role of the public authorities is therefore crucial. While few positive initiatives have been forthcoming from national government, clothing has been a major site for new forms of local industrial intervention such as direct investment in firms and the provision of collective services, whose strengths and weaknesses are examined in the concluding section of this chapter.

Markets

Retail Distribution and Industrial Structure

The clothing industry has never been a classic site for mass production. The volatility of fashion and the instability of limp cloth as a working material have always set greater limits to production economies of scale than in other industries. A relatively open and fragmented industrial structure has therefore persisted even in the United States, where the adaptation of mass production methods to garment manufacture has progressed furthest, though firms are generally larger and production runs longer in menswear and workwear than in womenswear (Chandler 1977; Fraser 1983; Arpan *et al.* 1982). But even for the most standardised types of garment such as men's suits and shirts, a recent study shows that the cost penalty resulting from production at one-third of the minimum efficient scale of operation is only 2–3 per cent at the level of the plant and 4–10 per cent at the level of the individual product.[1]

In the UK, however, the major impetus towards more standardised, longer-run garment manufacture came from the growing concentration of retail distribution during the inter-war and post-war periods (Jefferys 1954). By 1977, as Table 6.1 shows, multiple retailers, department and variety stores controlled 70 per cent of all clothing sales in the UK, a larger proportion than any other Western economy, including the United States; in Italy and France, by contrast, these outlets accounted for only some 15 per cent of the market.[2] With the market divided into relatively stable segments by age, sex and price, the major retailers such as Marks and Spencer were largely able to set the pace and direction of fashion change, and pressed the manufacturers dependent on them to capture available production economies of scale by adopting garment engineering techniques developed in the United States. Within the core segments of the mass market, therefore, competition among the retail chains and their manufacturers revolved mainly around price and the physical quality of garment manufacture, with design relegated to a subsidiary role outside the high-fashion sector (Wray 1957; Rees 1969; Rainnie 1984).

These patterns of distribution and marketing in turn gave rise to a profoundly segmented industrial structure. By the early 1970s, as Table 6.2 shows, the British clothing industry had become the most concentrated in Europe, with 53 per cent of employment in enterprises with 200 or more workers;[3] while behind this aggregate pattern stood even greater disparities among different types of firm, as can be seen from Table 6.3. At one extreme stood a small cluster of multi-plant enterprises with 1,000 or more workers, often affiliated to diversified textile groups such as Courtaulds, Tootal and Coats-Viyella, whose large provincial factories were predominantly engaged in contract manufacturing for the major retailers: in 1982, twenty-seven such firms operating 150 plants accounted for 29 per cent of employment, 30.5 per cent of net output and 33.1 per cent of net capital expenditure in the industry as a whole. At the other extreme stood a vast penumbra of small firms employing less than 100 workers, concentrated in London and other urban centres, which catered for the less stable segments of demand at the top and bottom of the market: in 1982, 5,561 such enterprises accounted for 36.2 per cent of employment, 35.1 per cent of net output and 30.0 per cent of net capital expenditure in the industry. The remaining third of the industry consisted of some 286 medium-sized firms, often family-owned, the bulk of which shared the mass-market orientation of the larger multi-plant companies without the benefit of their financial resources.

The Crisis of the 1970s

The salience of price competition and the industry's concentration on the high-volume manufacture of a slowly changing range of garments with a low design content left domestic producers extremely vulnerable

Table 6.1. The market share (as a percentage of sales) of major clothing and textile outlets, 1977

	Multiple retailers	Department and variety stores	Co-operatives	Mail order	Independents	Others
UK*†	53.2	16.9	6.3	8.0	8.7	6.9
USA*	31.4	38.0	–	3.9	–	27.7
Netherlands	22.3	10.7	–	2.0	48.5	16.5
Switzerland	19.7	9.9	11.4	2.5	32.5	24.0
Belgium	13.5	11.0	0.5	3.0	72.0	–
West Germany	12.9	20.0	5.2	7.3	25.8	28.8
Italy	7.5	8.0	0.4	1.3	80.8	2.0
France	5.2	9.8	0.7	4.2	70.3	9.8

* Clothing only
† 1976
Source: Retail Trade International (1977), cited in Clairmonte and Cavanagh (1981), p. 213.

Table 6.2. The structure of the European clothing industry, 1971

(No. of employees)	West Germany		Belgium		France		Italy		The Netherlands		UK		Denmark	
	Firms	Employees	Firms	Employees	Firms	Employees	Firms	Employees	Firms	Employees	Firms	Employees	Firms	Employees
10 – 19	21.4	4.2	⎱74.8	⎱35.3	30.7	5.2	47.0	12.3	⎱44.7	⎱12.0	⎱60.9	⎱16.5	32.7	⎱36.8
20 – 49	36.7	16.1	⎰	⎰	33.3	12.9	30.8	17.8					40.2	⎰
50 – 99	21.6	20.7	14.0	19.9	17.2	14.7	11.7	15.4	⎰	⎰	18.7	14.5	16.9	⎱63.2
100 – 199	13.2	24.9	7.4	20.0	10.1	17.2	⎱10.5	⎱54.5	55.3	88.0	10.9	15.9	7.5	
200+	7.1	34.2	3.8	24.8	8.7	50.0	⎰	⎰			9.5	53.1	2.7	⎰
Average no. of employees per firm (firms with 10 or more employees)	90		49		82		52		65		100		42	

Source: Fornengo (1978).

Table 6.3. British clothing industry enterprises by size of total employment, 1982

Size of Enterprise	Enterprises	Establishments	Employment (000s)	Employment (%)	Net output (£m)	Net output (%)	Gross value added (£m)	Gross value added (%)	net capital expenditure (£m)	net capital expenditure (%)
1–99	5,561	5,689	80.3	36.2	524.0	35.1	556.8	43.8	17.3	30.0
100–199	146	182	20.7	9.3	134.7	9.0			5.6	9.7
200–499	108	160	34.1	15.4	235.2	15.8	200.8	15.8	10.7	18.5
500–999	32	92	22.4	10.1	142.2	9.5	118.4	9.3	4.8	8.3
1000+	27	150	64.2	29.0	455.0	30.5	396.0	31.1	19.1	33.1
Total	5 874	6 273	221.6	100.0	1 491.1	100.0	1 272.0	100.0	57.7	100.0

Source: UK Business Statistics Office, *Report on the Census of Production 1982*, Business Monitor PA 1002, cited in Lancashire County Council (1985), p. 67.

Table 6.4. UK imports and exports of made-up clothing (£ millions)

	1981	1982	1983	1984	1985	1986
Sales	2911.0	2987.2	3253.3	3700.7	4134.7	4338.1
Exports	558.7	540.2	560.8	643.9	762.5	789.8
Imports	997.1	1051.0	1121.2	1415.5	1532.0	1686.3
Home market	3349.4	3498.0	3813.7	4472.3	4904.2	5234.6
Import						
penetration (%)	29.8	30.0	29.4	31.7	31.2	32.2
Exports/sales (%)	19.2	18.1	17.2	17.4	18.4	18.2

Source: Department of Trade and Industry (1987).

to the upheavals in the international economy during the 1970s. As Third World countries such as Hong Kong, South Korea, Taiwan and the Philippines acquired the relatively simple skills and transferable technology associated with the manufacture of standard garments in long runs, the low wages and non-union conditions of their work-forces enabled them to undercut domestic production costs by a wide margin. Given the financial separation of production and distribution in the UK, moreover, there was a ready incentive for many domestic retailers themselves to begin importing Third World garments on a large scale, particularly for new entrants aiming at the bottom of the market such as the food chains Tesco and ASDA. Despite restrictive quotas imposed under international agreements, therefore, import penetration in the British market shot up dramatically to reach a level of just under 30 per cent in 1981 (Table 6.4: cf. also Rush and Soete, 1984).

The British clothing industry's commitment to mass production and price competition likewise left it unprepared for the onset of the world recession at the end of the 1970s. The depression of consumer demand at home and abroad left retailers competing for shares of a slowly growing market and touched off a major price war among the high street retail chains. Unpredictable fluctuations in demand, low-cost import penetration and static retail prices all combined to squeeze domestic clothing manufacturers no longer able to achieve the sales volumes needed to cover the high overheads of long-run garment production (Rainnie 1984). The result has been a rapid decline in employment from 320,000 in 1974 to 290,000 in 1978, 216,000 in 1981 and 194,000 in 1984, with closures concentrated among large and medium-sized firms. Thus Courtaulds, for example, shed 43,000 jobs in the UK between 1980 and 1984, while its Nottingham subsidiaries reduced their work-force by one-third between 1978 and 1983. In London and other inner-city areas such as the West Midlands, employers' efforts to shed overheads and cut labour costs have also produced a widespread revival of outwork, much of it unregistered in official employment statistics (West Midlands County Council 1983; Greater London Council 1984; 1986; Lancashire County Council 1985; Mitter 1986; London Strategic Policy Unit 1987).[4]

The Fragmentation of the Mass Market

Since the beginning of the 1980s, however, the conditions of competition in the British clothing industry have shifted decisively away from those prevailing in previous decades. Changes in consumer tastes and the demographic structure of the population, the volatility of demand and the high capital costs of stocks and work in progress, and the industry's own efforts at product differentiation have together fragmented the mass market in the advanced countries and eroded the advantages of long-run garment manufacture. While price remains important, particularly at the lower end of the market, the struggle for competitive advantage has come to centre increasingly on retailers' and manufacturers' efforts to target specific groups of consumers defined in new ways; to seduce customers with attractive, fashionable garments; and to respond rapidly to short-term trends in the sales of individual product lines.

There is widespread agreement among industry observers that consumer demand for clothing has become at once more fragmented and more discerning in recent years, with no single fashion or style dominant as in the past. Demographic and economic changes in the advanced countries have made 25–40-year-old women rather than more easily influenced teenagers the most important group of clothing buyers, at the same time as the recession has fuelled the trend towards purchasing fewer but more expensive and durable garments. The rise of casualwear and 'lifestyle' dressing has undermined established divisions within the market, as has the growing sensitivity to fashion of menswear, childrenswear and even workwear. Increased international competition has likewise added to the cacophony of styles within each national market. The result has been a reconfiguration of demand in which, as one study puts it, 'fashion is becoming more a question of individual taste than of trends set by designers' (Rosen 1984, p. 36); and as recent studies confirm, a large section of consumers are prepared to pay a price premium for clothing 'catering to my taste' (Ody 1984a, p. 43; *Apparel International*, June 1984, p. 22).

The New Retail Competition

The growing fragmentation and sophistication of the mass market has made it increasingly difficult to sell a single, rigidly planned 'look' to broad categories of consumers, and high street retailers have therefore begun to target narrowly defined segments of the market with loosely structured garment ranges which allow the individual shopper to construct a more 'customised' wardrobe. The outstanding success for this strategy in the UK has been the rapid growth of the Hepworth chain, Next, whose 'co-ordinated' separates aimed at fashion-conscious women between 25 and 40 boosted sales from £20 million in 1983 to £70 million in 1984. Group sales rose from £108 million in 1984 to £190 million in 1986. This strategy has been extended to new market segments with the creation of Next for Men in 1984 and Next Interiors in 1985, followed by new ventures in childrenswear and mail order; significantly, the company has split its core womenswear chain into two components in order to target customer preferences more precisely (Ody 1984b; 'What's Next', *The Economist*, 15 September 1984, p. 79; Polan 1985; *Investors Chronicle* 31 October 1986; 12 December 1986; *Financial Weekly* 21 May 1987).

Next's success has set off shock waves in rival boardrooms, sparking off a series of takeovers and imitative responses from retailers whose markets have been invaded. Richard Shops, which caters for the same age bracket of women as Next, has been taken over by Terence Conran's Habitat-Mothercare group and is making a determined effort to regain its customers through improved design and garment quality. In addition to taking over Debenhams, the Burton group has launched a new chain, Principles, explicitly aimed at translating high fashion into high-street terms: 'Vogue designs at Next prices' according to one description, with looser co-ordination than the Hepworth chain. Under pressure of poor results in 1984 and 1985, even Marks and Spencer was forced to follow suit with the establishment of a specialist co-ordination department and a belated effort to upgrade its design profile; though overall profits have recovered, Marks and Spencer's share of the clothing market appears to have been permanently reduced, particularly in womenswear (Polan 1984; Taylor 1984; 'Market Fit', *Apparel International*, July 1984; Rosen 1984; Beach 1985; Peston 1985; *Investors Chronicle* 1 November 1985).

While these developments are most pronounced in the upper and middle segments of the women's market, they are clearly visible throughout the British clothing industry. C&A, for example, has been successfully pursuing a strategy of increased variety and fashionability across a number of market segments, moving away from commodity marketing towards garment ranges targeted by lifestyle such as sportswear, outdoorwear and young fashions. Woolworth, now under new management, has likewise sought to upgrade its image with more fashionable, better-made clothes, especially in childrenswear; as have other mass market dinosaurs such as Littlewoods, Great Universal Stores and British Home Stores, another recent Conran acquisition.

On an international scale, however, it is the Italian chain Benetton which has pioneered and perfected the new marketing strategies. Beginning in the domestic market and progressively extending its operations to Western Europe, the United States and Japan, Benetton has targeted its products at the most sophisticated and remunerative segment of the youth market. By offering a wide variety of styles and colours in its numerous franchised shops (each catering for a narrowly defined sub-market and geographical location) and rapidly adjusting its output to the pattern of sales, Benetton enables individual consumers to participate in the construction of a product range tailored to the requirements of the local market. The result of this formula has been a spectacular growth of sales from 55 billion lire in 1978 to 623 billion lire in 1984 and 850 billion lire in 1985, 55 per cent of which were obtained from exports (Correale and Gaeta 1983; Rullani and Zanfei 1984; Belussi 1987; *Apparel International*, October 1986).

Design as a Two-way Process

The shift of retailer strategies from price competition to fashion and variety has transformed relationships with suppliers as well as consumers. Whereas in the past garments were designed by retailers or manufacturers in relative isolation from one another, now the trend is for fabric selection and range development to become a two-way process based on consultation between buyers for retail chains and suppliers' in-house design teams. At the same time, the votatility of fashion and the riskiness of a design-led strategy requires production to be tailored more closely to demand and places a premium on suppliers' ability to shift output rapidly from slow to fast-selling garment lines.[5]

Through much of the post-war period, the design process in the British clothing industry followed two main patterns. Many large retail chains such as Marks and Spencer designed the bulk of their garments themselves, bought the fabrics and put them out with detailed specifications to manufacturers on something close to a cut, make and trim (CMT) basis. In other cases, manufacturers or wholesalers designed the garments and retailers selected from their ranges almost as if from a catalogue. These patterns still persist at the top and bottom ends of the market, respectively, as designer firms sell their collections to retailers with little modification, while CMT firms produce rush orders using cloth and specifications provided by the manufacturer.

But an increasing proportion of British clothing manufacturers now reduce the risks of fashion production by developing their ranges in collaboration with the buyers for retail chains, many of whom themselves have a design training. Like the new emphasis on design itself, this trend is most visible in the upper and middle segments of the women's market but extends to other areas as well. Thus, according to an interview with its managing director, 'Next does *not* believe in simply contracting out its own in-house designs to a garment-maker. It prefers a two-way process with design input coming from manufacturers as well as its own staff.' At Marks and Spencer, too, the main design impetus is now expected to come from the manufacturer rather than the chain's in-house staff, since, as one company spokesman observes, 'We can't change our styles fast enough if we have to plan everything in advance ourselves'; and Marks and Spencer selectors now suggest modifications to ranges developed by suppliers and pick out fabrics jointly at international exhibitions. Even retailers whose relationship with suppliers has historically been looser, such as Woolworth, C&A and Richard Shops, are moving in this direction, attending fabric fairs with manufacturers, extending informal commitments to cover cloth purchases, and participating in the development of garment ranges (Ody 1984a; 1984b; 1984c; *Apparel International* July 1984, p. 10).

Tailoring Supply to Demand

Just as retailers' new emphasis on fashion and variety demands increased design input from suppliers, so too does it demand enhanced flexibility to manufacture a wider range of styles and switch production between them in response to short-run in sales. While the selection of colours and fabrics takes place well in advance, especially among retailers concerned with exclusivity and co-ordination, lead times for garment manufacture have become much shorter than in the past. Next, for example, finalises only 70 per cent of its range by the beginning of the preceding season, while Marks and Spencer is switching to three fashion seasons instead of two. Woolworth used to receive its merchandise in a single massive shipment at the beginning of the season, but buyers now stagger orders over three deliveries and keep back a portion of their budget for last-minute impulse purchases; at the opposite end of the market, the fashionable Reiss menswear chain buys only 30 per cent of its merchandise in advance and the rest during the course of the season. A number of chains will now book production time with manufacturers while reserving the right to allocate it among specific styles as the season progresses, and lead times of six to eight weeks from order to delivery have become commonplace (Ody 1984b; O'Dwyer 1984; *The Economist*, 15 September 1984, p. 79; Taylor 1984).

Crucial to this process has been the development of Electronic Point of Sale (EPOS) systems which enable retailers to gather precise data on each style's sales performance and adjust orders with suppliers accordingly. The growth of Benetton, in particular, is closely tied to its pioneering use of EPOS systems. Each of its 3,200 shops is linked into a data collection centre in its regional or national market which transmits detailed sales information to company headquarters (by satellite in the case of Japan and the USA), facilitating rapid analysis of market trends. Production scheduling from its own factories and 200 associated subcontractors is thus tied as closely as possible to actual orders from the shops, and Benetton has developed a fully-automated warehousing system for the Italian market to cope with the resulting fragmentation of deliveries into small lots (Belussi 1987; Rullani and Zanfei 1984).

The proliferation of styles and their rapid permutation have reduced the average length of production runs as well as compressed lead times for garment manufacture. As the chairman of a leading Marks and Spencer supplier ruefully comments:

> In the old days . . . Marks and Spencer was buying *bulk* just to fill the shelves. We would supply 1,000 dozen in one style and that was it. Today they're buying *merchandise* — styles have to be tried and tested and the runs could be as little as 50 or 100 dozen, although much larger orders are still commonplace. It means certainly that we lose a lot of the economies of scale which we used to find with the long production runs of the old days' (*Apparel International*, July 1984: 11).

Many clothing manufacturers, of course, are now obliged to cope with still shorter runs, since order quantities from the smaller, more fashion-conscious retail chains average between 1,000 and 3,000 garments per style.

But the decline of scale economies in direct production is more than counterbalanced by savings in the costs of inventories and work in progress, as well improved profit margins resulting from a closer correlation between orders and sales. Thus a study by Kurt Salmon Associates (Frazier 1986; cf. also Kurt Salmon Associates 1986) demonstrates that 83 per cent of the time from raw material production to final sale for a typical garment is spent in inventory rather than in process, and concludes that quicker response of production to sales can save up to 25 per cent of the retail price of a garment through reductions in inventory costs (6.4 per cent), forced markdowns (14.6 per cent) and sales losses from 'stock-outs' (4 per cent).

These new demands on clothing manufacturers for design capacity and productive flexibility carry with them profound implications for relationships between retailers and suppliers. Most retail chains are now looking for long-term relationships with a smaller number of suppliers, whom they also expect to become more independent than in the past. The more successful manufacturers have diversified their customer base, and many retailers now prefer to be responsible for no more than a fixed proportion of their suppliers' business, normally below 50 per cent. This process of diversification puts manufacturers in touch with a wider range of design currents and enhances their ability to develop new styles at the same time as it reduces the retailers' responsibility for unsuccessful garment lines. While many established suppliers have been dropped and some retailers have taken advantage of high levels of competition to squeeze manufacturers' margins, the new pattern of production and distribution promises to create a more balanced relationship between the two parties in the longer term. As manufacturers broaden their order books they become less vulnerable to monopsonistic pressure on their profit margins, while retailers themselves become more dependent on those suppliers able to come up with saleable designs and adjust rapidly to changing market trends.[6]

Domestic Sourcing and International Trade

The growth of non-price competition and the new relationship emerging between retailers and suppliers has reduced the importance of clothing imports from low-wage developing countries. Lead times are too long, minimum production runs too large, quality control too difficult, and the capital costs of stocks too high to make sourcing in the Far East worthwhile for many of the more fashion-sensitive types of garment. Wages and prices have gone up significantly in the more established countries such as Hong Kong, which have themselves begun to move upmarket to escape low-wage competition elsewhere in the Third World and to overcome fixed-volume import quotas in the West (OECD 1983, pp. 85–9; Mower 1986; Milburn 1986). Physical proximity is also important for collaboration between retailers and suppliers in range development and rapid adjustment of production to sales. Thus Marks and Spencer have always bought 90 per cent of its garments in the UK, and new fashion chains such as Next and Principles source more than 80 per cent of their merchandise domestically. Even such downmarket retailers as Littlewoods and British Home Stores now aim to obtain some 70 per cent of their clothing needs from British manufacturers (Ody, 1984a; 1984b; 1984c; Silberston 1984, p. 46).

Within the British market, as Tables 6.4 and 6.5 show, the growth of import penetration has slowed down since the early 1980s, though exchange rate fluctuations have influenced the precise balance between imports and exports.[7] Thus import penetration fell back from 31.7 per cent of the domestic market in 1984 to 31.2 per cent in 1985, only to rise again to 32.2 per cent in 1986. There has also been a pronounced shift in the composition of imports away from developing countries and towards Western Europe: as Table 6.6 illustrates, the share of developing countries in British imports fell from 50.3 per cent in 1980 to 45.2 per cent in 1986, while that of the EEC and Western Europe rose from 40.7 per cent to 50 per cent. Some of this movement, to be sure, reflects the restrictive effects of the Multi-Fibre Arrangement (MFA) on imports from developing countries, as well as the diversion of trade to lower-cost countries with privileged access to the EEC such as Portugal and Spain (Silberston 1984; Fornengo 1984). But Italy is now the second largest source of British clothing imports (after Hong Kong), and a number of reports by manufacturer-retailer panels of the National Economic Development Council confirm that imports from other European countries are concentrated at the upper end of the market, competing on the basis of design and quality rather than price alone (National Economic

Table 6.5. UK trade balance in clothing (SITC division 84 £ thousands)

Year	Imports	Exports	Balance
1978	920746	670004	−250742
1979	1194446	751088	−443358
1980	1231122	807558	−423564
1981*	N/A	N/A	N/A
1982	1500755	840351	−660404
1983	1601480	865394	−736086
1984	2013149	996392	−1016757
1985	2094680	1171923	−922757
1986	2386678	1228286	−1158392

* 1981 figures affected by Civil Service strike.
Source: Overseas Trade Statistics of the UK (December 1986), cited in *Hollings Apparel Industry Review* (Spring 1987).

Development Office 1985; 1986; cf. also Euromonitor 1985a).

Perhaps the most striking example of these trends has been the emergence of Italy as the world's largest net exporter of textile and clothing products, ahead of Hong Kong, South Korea and Taiwan, with a positive trade balance in 1982 of $3.7 billion in clothing alone (Economist Intelligence Unit 1983; Euromonitor 1985b, p. 12; de la Torre 1986, p. 39; Correale and Gaeta 1983). Alone among developed countries, Italy also increased its employment in clothing manufacturing between 1971 and 1981 from 416,000 to 443,000 (Fornengo 1983). The international success of the Italian clothing industry is particularly remarkable since wage costs per direct employee (including social costs) are nearly twice those in the UK, four times those in Hong Kong and nearly twenty times those in countries such as Sri Lanka.[8]

The Italian industry, which specialises in high- and medium-priced fashion garments, is extremely fragmented, with an average of 5.5 employees per firm, including those with less than ten employees (Fornengo 1978; 1983; Mariotti, 1982). Offsetting the formal fragmentation of productive units, however, is the concentration of firms in a series of 'industrial districts' which permits substantial economies of specialisation and provision of common services (including fashion forecasting, market research and technological information), as well as access to pools of skilled labour (Brusco 1982; Solinas 1982; Piore and Sabel 1983; 1984). According to a recent report by the OECD, these small Italian clothing firms, which have been active in adopting the best available technology and computerised management methods, have also proved more profitable than most of their larger counterparts. The result has been a far-reaching process of vertical disintegration whereby 'the large groups have not necessarily disappeared, but, when surviving, they now have a more flexible organization, and a number of

Table 6.6. Clothing (SITC division 84) imports by main trading area (£ thousands and percentage of total)

Imports from	1980	1983	1984	1985	1986
EEC*	322989 (26.2)	516998 (32.3)	655547 (32.6)	759230 (36.2)	1032496 (43.3)
Rest of W. Europe*	178495 (14.5)	233694 (14.6)	289784 (14.4)	305304 (14.6)	159235 (6.7)
Other developed countries	16512 (1.3)	20645 (1.3)	26085 (1.3)	20118 (1.0)	19421 (0.8)
Latin America	5527 (0.4)	5389 (0.3)	8686 (0.4)	7483 (0.4)	5839 (0.2)
Middle East and N. Africa	51636 (4.2)	78219 (4.9)	85343 (4.2)	89660 (4.3)	100366 (4.2)
Other developing countries	562773 (45.7)	663282 (41.3)	861556 (42.8)	814793 (38.9)	974735 (40.8)
Centrally planned economies	34202 (2.8)	46548 (2.9)	53999 (2.7)	67768 (3.2)	71537 (3.0)
North America	59028 (4.8)	36707 (2.4)	32149 (1.6)	30324 (1.4)	23049 (1.0)

* Greece has been included in the EEC since 1981. Spain and Portugal are also included in the figures for the EEC since 1986. The Rest of W. Europe includes Gibraltar, Malta and Turkey. In 1980, if we transfer the Greek figure from the Rest of W. Europe into the EEC, this raises the latter to £337,514,000 (27.4%) and reduces the Rest of W. Europe figure to £163,970,000 (13.3%). The increase in EEC share since 1986 must be treated with care because of the inclusion of Spain and Portugal. In 1985, for instance, the two contributed £149,558,000 which would have raised the EEC figure for 1985 to £908,788,000 (43.0%). In 1984 the percentage would have been 38.9 while in 1983 it would have been 38.3.

Source: Overseas Trade Statistics, elaborated in *Hollings Apparel Industry Review* (Spring 1987).

small independent firms are connected with the parent company only through financial (and sometimes marketing) linkages' (OECD 1983, pp. 25–8, 137–9).

Technology

Changing market trends and retailer strategies have transformed the conditions for efficient garment manufacture over the past decade. The challenge facing clothing suppliers is no longer that of turning out long runs of individual garments at the lowest possible unit cost, but rather of designing and manufacturing the widest possible range of styles at the lowest cumulative cost. The central problem here has been to overcome the traditional trade-off in the industry between flexibility and productive efficiency, and there has been considerable progress in this direction through the use of computer-based technologies and revised methods of manufacture (Hoffman and Rush 1984; Rush and Soete 1984; Trent Polytechnic 1986).[9]

Computer-aided Design

On the technological side, the most important recent innovation in clothing manufacture has been the emergence of sophisticated computer-aided design (CAD) systems for the pre-assembly stages of pattern development, grading and lay planning, linked in many firms to computer-controlled cutting (discussed below). There are a number of competing CAD systems now available, but most involve some combination of the following components: a digitiser, a mini-computer linked to one or more graphic display screens, and a high-speed marker or plotter. Using the digitiser or a photographic scanning table, the shapes of existing pattern pieces are entered into the system, and house rules applied to them at a series of points to generate automatically a nest of graded patterns in a variety of sizes. The operator can then manipulate the graded pattern pieces on the screen to work out the best possible lay, while the system calculates the fabric utilisation ratios for different combinations. The finished lay is then plotted out at high speed to yield a full-size marker for manual cloth cutting, while a magnetic tape can also be generated to guide a numerically-controlled cutter.

The most recent addition to the CAD facilities now available are pattern development systems, whereby the two-dimensional pattern blocks can be created on the screen and existing pattern pieces rapidly modified. Computers are not yet able to simulate the drape of three-dimensional fabrics, so that the scope for producing original designs directly on the screen remains severely limited. A number of companies have also brought out automatic marker-making programmes, which can be used for rapid costing exercises while remaining less effective than the operator-assisted version.

Manual pattern grading and lay planning are highly skilled and time-consuming activities performed by well-paid, experienced crafts-people in most clothing firms. The main effect of CAD systems is to enhance existing skills and increase their productivity rather than to eliminate the need for skilled operators. This is clearest in the case of lay planning, where the operator makes the final decision on the arrangement of the pattern pieces, and experienced marker-makers can beat an unassisted computer both for speed and fabric utilisation. But even in the case of grading, where a larger proportion of the task has been automated, many industry experts believe that considerable operator judgement is still required in the formulation of new grade rules and their application to new styles.

Labour costs in grading and marker-making form a tiny fraction of total manufacturing costs, and their reduction has not played a major part in decisions to purchase CAD equipment, though shortages of qualified personnel have sometimes been a factor. Far more important in firms' calculations have been improvements in fabric utilisation and reductions in the time needed to grade and mark out new styles. Since fabric comprises 40–60 per cent of garment costs, cloth savings from tighter lays were the main initial justification for the installation of CAD systems in larger firms. More recently, however, clothing manufac-turers have become aware of the possibilities offered by CAD systems for more rapid generation and modification of new styles. Grading and marker-making times have been reduced by a factor of between two and six, and tasks which previously took days can be performed in a few hours. The full range of a firm's existing pattern blocks can be stored on the system for easy modification, decisions on which styles to cut can be delayed until sales information becomes available, and samples which may never go into production at all can be offered to buyers already graded, lay-planned and costed. The more rapid turn-around and increased flexibility available from CAD systems have thus proved crucial to suppliers in meeting the retailers' demands for an ever greater variety of styles produced to shorter lead times.

CAD systems are expensive, with prices ranging from £40,000 to £200,000 and more, depending on their size and sophistication, and normally need to be utilised on a shift-work basis. But despite their cost, such systems are not characterised by significant economies of scale: indeed the shorter the production run, the larger are grading and marker-making as a proportion of total costs, and the more frequent the style change the more crucial reductions in turnaround time become. Hence both equipment suppliers and users have become increasingly concerned to bring CAD facilities within the reach of smaller clothing manufacturers. As the suppliers start to saturate the demand for their products among larger firms, they have naturally begun to experiment with simpler, less expensive systems suitable for a wider market. The industry leader, Gerber Garment Technology, has dropped its prices significantly and now offers highly sophisticated systems on a modular basis, as have a number of smaller European and American manufacturers (Disher 1983; 1985; 1987a). So far, however, the quantity of information processing required for CAD in clothing remains beyond the capacities of existing micro-computers, limiting the scope of potential cost reductions.[10]

An alternative method of giving smaller firms access to the full range of CAD facilities is through the establishment of a service bureau. Commercial CAD bureaux have been operating successfully in the USA, France, Italy, Japan and Scandinavia since the early 1970s, while a Leeds-based bureau has been servicing a range of different-sized clothing firms in the North of England since 1981. A number of large multi-plant clothing firms now maintain centralised facilities which operate like bureaux for the factories in their group, while the Baird Group has been leasing time to other firms on its Manchester-based CAD system. Beyond these strictly commercial operations, local authority-funded CAD bureaux are being established in a number of areas (see pp. 181–2).

Computer-controlled Cutting

The other major micro-electronics-based innovation in clothing manufacture has been the spread of computer-controlled cutting systems to replace manually guided methods. By far the most successful of these systems is the Gerber cutter, in which a numerically-controlled servo-motor following a computerised pattern guides a reciprocating, self-sharpening knife across a cutting table on which many ply of cloth have been compressed by a vacuum mechanism. Linked to CAD systems, the Gerber cutter offers substantial gains in the speed and accuracy of the cutting process, resulting in improved fabric utilisation and fewer defective parts in the assembly process. While 'knife intelligence' enables the machine to compensate partially for faults in the cloth, the wide range of fabrics used and their different cutting characteristics have led most firms to retrain existing skilled staff on the new equipment, though the number of cutters required has fallen substantially by comparison with manual methods (estimates of staffing reductions range from 25 per cent to 60 per cent depending on whether a shift system is introduced at the same time).

Like CAD systems, Gerber cutters are expensive, though prices have come down dramatically since the early 1980s. Three systems are currently available, at prices ranging from $295,000 to $145,000, though second-hand equipment can be bought for as little as $60,000 in some cases. The principal advantage of the more expensive systems is their ability to cut larger quantities of fabric in a single batch, but the lighter construction and lower capacity of the smaller systems also enables them to operate more rapidly. There are also advantages associated with lower-ply cutting such as reduced time and space involved in material handling and storage. The high-ply systems require minimum batch sizes of 880–1,000 garments, and most buyers have been large, multi-plant companies (23 of 39 Gerber cutters in the UK in 1984 belonged to Marks and Spencer suppliers), who have centralised their cutting facilities to feed a network of satellite sewing factories. But the lower-ply systems can cope with batches of 150–200 garments and are aimed at medium- and small-sized firms; sales have been reported to companies with as few as forty employees, though typical customers are still much larger (Clark 1986). The major obstacle for smaller firms in using this equipment arises from the need to keep it fully occupied in order to amortise the costs of the investment, and a number of commercial cutting bureaux are reported to be operating successfully in Italy and Scandinavia. For very low-ply cutting (between one- and five-ply), laser systems are available from a number of suppliers, but these are mainly used for marker-making and their broader commercial application will depend on progress in continuous fabric spreading.

Management Information and Production Control

Clothing managers themselves believe that the most immediate and far-reaching effects of new technology will be the application of computers to management information and production control, traditional problems of the industry which have been multiplied by the pressures of shorter lead times and wider product ranges. Software packages have long been available for such traditional computing applications as accounting, invoicing and payrolls, and the spread of cheap microcomputers has now brought these within the means of even the smallest clothing firms. CAD systems can be used for decisions on product costing, cut order planning and production scheduling, while new software packages are being developed to assist firms with the preparation of work dockets, stock control and fabric sourcing. In the sphere of production control, periodic reviews of factory performance are giving way to 'real-time' systems which monitor work-in-progress and assist managers in production planning, line balancing and work measurement. These systems range in size and sophistication from individually engineered work stations linked by automatic garment-moving rails to simple bar-code readers linked to a central computer suitable for smaller firms. As these systems of management information and production control become cheaper and more flexible, they should prove of special assistance to smaller clothing firms constrained by limited managerial resources (Chuter 1986; *Financial Times*, 18 July 1984).

The Sewing Machine and the Micro-chip

Labour costs in garment assembly account for a large proportion of total manufacturing costs, yet there has been less technological innovation in the sewing room than in any other area of the production process. The main reason for this lies in the unstable properties of limp fabric which necessitates extensive manual positioning by the sewing machine operator. Between the late nineteenth century and the 1970s, there were three main lines of innovation in sewing technology: increased stitching speeds and machine durability; the development of work aids such as needle positioners and underbed trimmers; and the emergence of dedicated machines for special tasks such as buttonholing and button attachment. While each of these innovations brought significant productivity gains, most came at the expense of flexibility, limiting the possibilities for their diffusion in a volatile, fashion-sensitive industry like clothing to a small parts assembly and more standardised products such as men's shirts and industrial workwear.

Much of the initial application of micro-electronics to sewing machinery has followed the course of previous technological innovation in the industry towards the development of special-purpose equipment for high-volume, repetitive operations. Thus dedicated micro-processors and numerical control units have been introduced for tasks such as beltloop attachment and collar stitching, and preprogrammed convertible units for more variable tasks such as contour seaming, pocket setting and decorative stitching. While substantial productivity gains can be achieved, this equipment is expensive, costing anywhere from $15,000 to $35,000 (as opposed to between $500 and $1,500 for an ordinary lockstitch machine) and its flexibility remains limited, though adjustment to style changes is easier than with the previous generation of dedicated machines, particularly for those with convertible programming units.

The major departure from this pattern of productivity gains achieved at the expense of flexibility has been the development of operator-programmable sewing machines. While these machines use a variety of methods to speed up and simplify the manipulation of the fabric including stitch counters, edge sensors and record/playback mechanisms (whereby the operator teaches the machine a sequence of operations it can then repeat), manual intervention in guiding the material remains crucial for the effective use of the equipment. Operator-programmable machines are general-purpose equipment which can cope easily with style changes, cost much less than special-purpose ones (between $2,500 and $7,500), and offer significant improvements in sewing accuracy and reductions in the length of the learning curve for new operations. So far, however, this equipment is in the early stages of development, and has mainly been used for small parts assembly operations such as top-stitching collars and cuffs and pocket setting, though programmable controls for basic operations such as back-tacking are becoming common on the latest generation of ordinary sewing machines.

Much more ambitious forms of flexible automation in garment assembly are currently being pursued by large firms and public authorities in a variety of countries. The highest-profile initiative is Japan's Automated Sewing System project, established in 1982 by the Ministry of International Trade and Industry with $60 million of public support and the collaboration of leading clothing and machinery manufacturers. But the US government has also provided financial support for experiments in apparel automation at the Massachusetts Institute of Technology's Draper Laboratories by the Textile/Clothing Technology Corporation $(TC)^2$, a tripartite body established jointly with organised labour and private industry. And the European Community is likewise sponsoring the efforts of large manufacturers such as Courtaulds to develop flexible manufacturing systems for garment assembly under the Basic Research in Industrial Technologies for Europe (BRITE) programme. Whatever their differences in approach, each of these initiatives has concentrated on the development of a programmable transfer line which can identify and pick up a single ply of fabric from a larger stack, position the piece and join it to another without further human intervention (Hoffman and Rush 1984; Commission of the European Communities, Directorate-General for Science, Research and Development 1985; US Congress, Office of Technology Assessment 1987, pp. 69–73).

If successful, the diffusion of automated sewing systems along these lines would have a dramatic impact on cost structures and employment patterns, pushing the clothing industry in a decisively more capital-intensive direction. But despite initial progress in automating sub-assembly operations on more standardised types of menswear, the wider applicability of this approach to the requirements of the contemporary clothing industry appears quite limited. In West Germany, for example, the consensus among machinery manufacturers is that automated transfer lines such as those exhibited at the 1987 Japan International Apparel Machinery fair will be unable to meet the high-quality standards, smaller batch sizes and increased variety demanded by the market, while also displaying great vulnerability to costly breakdowns (Gebbert 1988). Similarly, a recent review of Japanese experiments with flexible automation in sewing found that the most promising departure, the Toyota Sewing System (pioneered by the car firm's garment subsidiary, Aikin Seiki) was based on a 'combination of group working practices, manual skills, electronic sewing machines and careful line planning'. Most crucially, the Toyota system depends on the operators' ability to work several different general-purpose machines to produce garments in small lots, rather than attempting to remove the need for operator discretion through hard automation, as in other Japanese experiments such as the Mitsubishi Automatic Sewing System, which is only capable of handling two-dimensional shapes in a narrow range of predetermined patterns (Tyler 1985).[11]

Multi-skilling and Productive Flexibility

As the preceding discussion indicates, perhaps the most important key to increased flexibility of production lies not in new technology but in the skills and training of the workers themselves. Given the persistence of manual methods in garment assembly, a major source of scale economies on longer production runs has been the increased productivity of machinists as they move up the learning curve for each style. The tendency in larger firms has therefore been to subdivide the sewing process as finely as possible to allow each machinist to concentrate on a single operation and augment her/his productivity through the use of work aids and special machinery for complex tasks. But as production runs become shorter and style changes more frequent in the industry as a whole, even the larger firms have been forced to encourage their machinists to become proficient at a wider range of sewing operations to avoid costly bottlenecks and line imbalances. Broader initial training and continuous retraining, higher basic wages for more versatile operatives, and video-taped work aids for unfamiliar tasks are all being used by larger clothing companies in their efforts to shorten the learning curve and reduce the cost penalty associated with frequent style changes.

Local Intervention

Opportunities and Dangers

Current trends in markets and technology create new opportunities and new dangers for each section of the British clothing industry. Small firms in inner-city areas such as London stand to benefit from increased demand for the flexible, short-run garment production in which they specialise, while computer-based technologies and management methods have reduced the cost penalties associated with frequent style changes. By taking advantage of these developments to move into higher-quality, better-remunerated work and improve the organisation of production, such firms can achieve the increased profit margins needed to sustain high inner-city rents and rates and to upgrade wages and employment practices. But inner-city firms could also lose out as large provincial manufacturers themselves become more flexible, particularly if sweatshop conditions and heavy reliance on outwork prevent them from meeting the higher-quality standards increasingly demanded at every level of the market. In London, for example, there are clear signs that local firms are losing orders because of quality problems and a growing shortage of labour arising from the rundown of training programmes and the reluctance of outworkers to re-enter the factory in the face of high off-the-book payments obtainable from unscrupulous employers evading tax and national insurance contributions (Zeitlin 1985; Davenport *et al*. 1986; London Strategic Policy Unit 1987).

These trends also open up potential benefits for the provincial contract manufacturers which make up the core of the British clothing industry. The growing importance of fashion and variety in the market for clothing reduces the importance of sourcing from low-wage countries, and offers opportunities for domestic manufacturers to expand their order books and upgrade their product lines. For suppliers who can come up with saleable designs and adjust rapidly to changing market patterns, these developments hold out the prospect of more collaborative relationships with a wider range of retailers and improved profit margins on higher-value garments. But where managerial conservatism and lack of investment lock suppliers into overstocked markets for low-value garments, they face increasing pressure on their prices and the loss of crucial contracts with long-established customers. Nor can it be taken for granted that the current trends towards domestic sourcing will persist indefinitely. If British manufacturers fail to meet the new standards of design and productive flexibility required, domestic retailers will turn to suppliers elsewhere in Western Europe, as even Marks and Spencer now seems to be doing, while low-cost producers such as Hong Kong are themselves moving upmarket and learning to compete on the basis of design and flexibility as well as price (*Daily Telegraph* 1 December 1986; Milburn 1986). In this context, the surge of import penetration in 1986 may signal a renewed phase of intensified competition for British clothing manufacturers in the domestic market.

National Policy and Local Intervention

Recent developments in markets and technology create new, potentially favourable opportunities for clothing production in Britain. But neither the seizure of these opportunities nor their translation into benefits for the work-force will necessarily happen by themselves, and there are also dangers of a further rundown of employment if the underlying weaknesses of the industry are not tackled. Much therefore depends on strategic intervention by the public authorities to create a policy framework which can encourage firms to offer an innovative response to the challenges which confront the British clothing industry.

But little by way of a co-ordinated strategy for the clothing industry has been forthcoming from national government. The major form of state intervention in the industry over the past two decades has been the restriction of imports from low-wage countries through participation in the MFA. The MFA may have provided a valuable breathing space for British clothing producers, particularly during the 1970s, slowing down the decline of employment at the cost of modest price increases for consumers (for assessments of the costs and benefits of the MFA in the UK and Europe, see Silberston 1984 and Fornengo 1984; for a discussion of its effects on the USA, see Nehmer and Love 1985). But by itself the MFA provides no mechanism for encouraging positive adjustment within the industry; while as we have seen, alternative sources of low-cost garments remain available within the EEC from Portugal and other Mediterranean affiliates, and other advanced countries such as Italy account for an increasing share of British clothing imports.

Beyond the partial protection of the domestic market, moreover, central government schemes aimed at promoting the restructuring of the clothing industry have largely been conspicuous by their absence. In the 1970s the National Economic Development Office (NEDO) and its sectoral Economic Development Councils saw the future of the industry in rationalisation and capital investment by the large textile groups such as Courtaulds; in the 1980s, it has advocated increased attention to product design and closer co-ordination between retailers, garment manufacturers and fabric producers. But as in other sectors, NEDO's lack of executive powers and independent resources left it little means for securing the implementation of these recommendations beyond persuasion and exhortation (Pearce and Totterdill 1986; National Economic Development Office 1982; 1985; 1986; Cotton and Allied Textiles Economic Development Council 1983; 1984). Only the 1975 Clothing Industry Scheme linked selective financial assistance to clothing firms with NEDO's objectives for sectoral restructuring, and it was wound up in 1977 despite modest success in encouraging the use of management consultancy and promoting capital investment (Lambert 1983; Totterdill 1986a, Appendix I). Most recently, in 1984 the government proposed to spend £20 million over five years to support investment in advanced technology by small and medium-sized clothing, footwear and textile firms; but despite its limited scope, which was widely criticised by the industries concerned, the 'CLOFT' scheme was rejected by the European Commission as incompatible with EEC competition policy (Pearce and Totterdill 1986a).

Nor has the industry fared better in obtaining assistance from central government under Regional Aid and National Selective Assistance schemes administered by the Department of Trade and Industry (DTI). Clothing and footwear together received less than 1 per cent of the £1,055 million spent on Regional Development Grants between 1981 and 1984, and a similar proportion of the £4,437 million paid out in

Regional Selective Assistance over the whole period from 1972 to 1984. Many of the more specific schemes aimed at supporting innovation and providing technical advice to firms are restricted to companies with at least sixty employees or require large minimum investments, and takeup by the clothing industry has been well below that of other sectors. A number of the programmes most useful to clothing firms such as the Design Advisory Service Funded Consultancy Scheme and the CAD/CAM Scheme have also been cut back severely or allowed to expire. Despite its importance in the national economy, DTI officials have often tended to consider clothing a 'sunset' industry, and this judgement is reflected in the allocation of priorities for expenditure (Totterdill 1986a, Appendix II).

In this context, local authorities have increasingly become the major source of policy initiatives for the sector. In areas such as London, Nottingham, Leeds and the West Midlands, clothing remains a major source of manufacturing employment, and local authorities have felt obliged to fill the gap left by the absence of central government policies. Since the late 1970s, moreover, there has been a growing interest in local economic initiatives more broadly, particularly among authorities controlled by the Labour Party. Rising unemployment in the cities and in many regions has encouraged local authorities to bring employment and economic development to the forefront of their activities, despite the lack of specific statutory powers in these areas. No longer concerned exclusively with issues such as land and premises, authorities have undertaken detailed analyses of local industrial structure and moved into new areas of intervention such as industrial finance and the provision of collective services to firms, often on a sectoral basis. Clothing, together with textiles, has been a major site for these new forms of local intervention.

As in the case of industrial policy more generally (Thompson 1987), local intervention in clothing has been informed by a set of competing and sometimes contradictory objectives. The most general aim has undoubtedly been to create a net increase (or at least to prevent a further decline) in local employment by supporting firms in their efforts to adapt to changing market conditions. In this respect, the new wave of local intervention marks an open break with traditional approaches to regional development based on the attraction of inward investment by footloose companies. But many authorities have also sought to improve the position of low-paid workers by assisting firms to move towards higher value-added areas of production. In some cases, as in London, local authorities have argued that an absolute priority should be given to intervention aimed at strengthening worker organization, promoting better wages and working conditions, and discriminating positively in favour of disadvantaged groups (Greater London Council 1984; 1985; Gough 1986a; 1986b; London Strategic Policy Unit 1987).

Direct Assistance to Firms

Perhaps the most widespread form of local intervention in the clothing industry has been direct financial support to individual firms. In many of the smaller authorities, such as the London boroughs or provincial city councils, a large proportion of economic development expenditure has been devoted to grants or loans to individual firms for assistance with rates, rents, refurbishment or interest payments (Totterdill 1986a; London Strategic Policy Unit 1987, Part B.[12] But this form of intervention has been widely criticized for its *ad hoc* and reactive character, as well as for the lack of accountability in the utilisation of public money. Labour-controlled local authorities have therefore moved increasingly towards direct investment in manufacturing firms, often through the establishment of Enterprise Boards, as in London, the West Midlands, West Yorkshire and Lancashire. Equity investment is seen as offering the company a sound financial basis for carrying out an agreed programme of restructuring, while at the same time offering the authority some control over company policy, working conditions, equal opportunities and work-force involvement. In London, in particular, local authorities have argued that direct investment in larger firms is a crucial means of overcoming the fragmentation of the work-force and encouraging the growth of unionisation (Pearce and Totterdill 1986; Greater London Council 1984; 1985; London Strategic Policy Unit 1987).

The undercapitalisation of many clothing manufacturers and the unresponsive attitudes of British banks and financial institutions clearly give enterprise boards and direct investment an important part to play in local authority policies for the sector. While a number of clothing companies have been acquired in whole or part by enterprise boards across the country, however, considerable difficulties with direct investment have also been experienced. The fragmented structure of the industry in many areas and the small size of most companies makes them unattractive candidates for investment, while few local authorities have either the financial or managerial resources to become involved with a sufficiently broad group of firms to achieve substantial influence over the sector as a whole. In the extreme case of London, there are fewer than thirty firms with fifty or more employees, and individual approaches by the Greater London Enterprise Board (GLEB) failed to generate any willing candidates for equity investment in the industry.[13] Nor is it clear from GLEB's experience with Bassetts, a large workwear manufacturer bought from the receiver in 1983, that wages, employment conditions and work-force involvement in larger firms are necessarily superior to those elsewhere even when wholly owned by a local authority (Pearce and Totterdill 1986; Zeitlin 1985).

The Provision of Collective Services

The other major form of local intervention in the clothing industry has been the provision of collective services which are beyond the capacity of individual firms to supply for themselves. Through the provision of such services, proponents argue, firms can be guided towards appropriate business strategies, given access to advanced technologies, and assisted to improve their management practices. In exchange, local authorities can promote unionisation and insist that the users of their services follow legitimate business practices and upgrade the wages and employment conditions of their work-forces. Where collective bargaining is weak, as in many inner-city areas, local authorities can thus potentially play an important part in encouraging employers to compete through innovation in products and processes rather than through reliance on sweated labour (Zeitlin 1985).

The principal vehicle for the provision of collective services to the clothing industry has been the creation of Fashion or Resource Centres with financial support from local authorities (often assisted initially by Urban Programme grants from central government). Clothing Centres have been established in Hackney (now defunct), Tower Hamlets, Nottingham and Birmingham, and plans are well under way for similar initiatives in Lambeth, Leeds, Coventry, Newcastle, Glasgow and Lancashire (see Pearce and Totterdill 1986; Newcastle City Council 1986; Lancashire County Council 1986; London Strategic Policy Unit 1987, Part A; and Chapter 8 of this volume). The older Fashion Centres were focused around the provision of joint showroom and exhibition facilities, export promotion, and the compilation of a CMT register to put potential customers in touch with local subcontractors. But permanent showrooms have tended to give way to one-off events aimed at attracting buyers from the major retail chains, while the newer centres have placed increasing emphasis on the provision of fashion forecasting facilities to guide firms in designing their garment ranges. In a number of localities, for example, the textile departments of local polytechnics are expected to become involved in elaborating information bought in from commercial design intelligence agencies, while Nottingham has also established contact with the Centro Informazione Tessile Emilia Romagna (CITER), a public–private agency which has pioneered the provision of these services in the garment and knitwear centre of Carpi (see Brusco and Righi 1985).

On the production side, a CAD bureau has been established in Birmingham, and there are plans to set up similar facilities in Nottingham, Newcastle, Lancashire and Glasgow in the near future.[14] A major function of all the Centres is the provision of technical information and business advice through regular seminars and consultations with individual firms, together with training courses for managers and supervisors in some cases. Operative training, by contrast, normally remains outside their sphere of activity, though several authorities have set up off-the-job training centres for the industry in response to widespread labour shortages and the need to upgrade the skills of existing workers for increased flexibility (Totterdill 1986b). Most of the Centres, finally, have established Codes of Conduct which specify minimum employment conditions and trade union access for firms using their services; and even the Tower Hamlets Clothing Centre, which maintains an open-door policy, has been active in promoting organisation among local employers as a means of improving employment practices.[15]

While individual authorities may begin with a restricted range of services reflecting their perception of local needs, the functions described above should be understood as elements of a systematic strategy which might give rise to the emergence of flexible industrial districts composed of interdependent firms on the Italian model. Thus marketing assistance helps firms diversify their products and move into better-paid work; technical assistance helps them to achieve the necessary combination of flexibility and efficiency in production; training helps firms develop the wider skills and versatility required of their work-force; while monitoring employment conditions pushes them to compete through innovation rather than sweating, a role facilitated by the growing involvement of the Clothing Centres in mediating relationships between firms. The 'social' aims of local intervention in regulating conditions of competition thus form an integral part of this wider 'economic' strategy, particularly in areas where weak unions and employers' associations have been unable to overcome the disorganisation of product and labour markets through their own resources.

This strategy has proved an attractive approach to local intervention in the clothing industry, as the proliferation of projected Centres testifies. But, as in the case of direct investment, a number of important difficulties have also been encountered. One difficulty concerns the relationship between the Clothing Centres and the local authorities themselves. A number of the Centres have been set up as publicly funded companies with independent management boards, and this arrangement has often given rise to bitter disputes over financial accountability and political control. The Hackney Fashion Centre, for example, was closed down in 1986 amid allegations of financial mismanagement and pervasive discontent within the Council about the policies of its director, particularly towards the monitoring of employment conditions in firms using its services (London Strategic Policy Unit 1987, pp. 64–74). Another difficulty concerns the relationship between the Centres and the firms they are intended to service. On the one hand, the Centres set out to attract the active participation of local manufacturers, while on the other, they seek to influence firms' business policies and employment practices. The unavoidable tension between these objectives, finally, is exacerbated by the need to maintain trade union support for the Centres by establishing minimum standards for user firms and monitoring their subsequent performance. Each of these difficulties illustrates in turn the impossibility of imposing from above an industrial strategy which depends on co-operation and mutual trust among the parties involved; and local authorities will need to take the lead in a delicate process of consensus-building and the construction of common interests if the provision of collective services is to achieve its objectives.

The Limits of Local Intervention

The devolution of industrial policy to local authorities opens up new possibilities for the development of initiatives based on intimate knowledge of local circumstances and tailored to local needs. But despite its evident benefits, this shift in the locus of industrial intervention also creates new problems of co-ordination between local initiatives and national policies. Thus local authorities attempting to develop a strategic approach to sectoral intervention are often frustrated by the fragmented and uncoordinated policies of national government agencies. DTI schemes for aid to manufacturing industry typically lack any clear sectoral dimension, and available assistance is dispersed on an individual casework basis without any attempt to evaluate the broader consequences of assisting any one firm. Similarly, the Urban Partnership/Programme schemes, a major source of funding for local economic intervention, are aimed at alleviating deprivation in the inner cities without an overview of industrial priorities or any attempt to co-ordinate initiatives in different areas. Although the Manpower Services Commission, now the major agency responsible for training initiatives, does formulate policies for individual sectors, its current emphasis on 'employer-led' training largely confines it to narrowly reactive forms of provision.

One response to this misfit between national policies and local intervention has been the emergence of new forms of co-ordination among the local authorities themselves. Local Action for Textiles and Clothing (LATC) was formally constituted in 1986 as a result of growing collaboration between a number of authorities actively engaged in the development of policy initiatives in these sectors (Pearce and Totterdill 1986). With financial support from some fifteen member authorities and one full-time staff officer, this organisation is intended to perform three principal functions. First, it aims to co-ordinate local initiatives in these sectors by acting as a forum for the exchange of information through the organisation of seminars, the production of discussion papers, and the commissioning of policy research. In this way, local authorities can be made aware of promising initiatives elsewhere and discouraged from seeking to maintain employment by competing for inward investment with other areas. Second, LATC aims to develop collaborative initiatives among participating authorities on issues which extend beyond the boundaries and resources of individual localities. Thus, for example, it is currently exploring the possibility of setting up a merchant converting enterprise controlled by a consortium of local authorities in order to bridge the gap between British fabric manufactures and their potential customers among smaller garment manufacturers (Gillingwater 1986; Local Action for Textiles and Clothing 1987). Finally, the organisation aims to provide a vehicle for obtaining modifications in the policies of central government agencies such as the DTI and the MSC, as well as a voice for influencing the direction of national policies towards clothing and textiles more broadly.

But whatever the co-ordination of local initiatives, their potential effectiveness will be limited if the national policy framework remains unsupportive. While, in many Western economies, central governments have welcomed, or at least acquiesced in, the growing involvement of local authorities in industrial restructuring and employment creation, the thrust of recent policy in the UK has moved sharply in the opposite direction. In the name of increased accountability and control of public spending, the Conservative governments in power since 1979 have progressively reduced the autonomy of local authorities in both financial and policy terms, and there must be considerable doubt as to the scope for local industrial initiatives if these trends continue. The response of the British clothing industry to the opportunities created by recent shifts in markets and technology may depend as much on the emergent balance of responsibilities between central and local government as on the strategic choices of the firms themselves.

Notes

1. The minimum efficient size of plant required 175 workers in men's shirts and 375–500 workers in men's suits, depending on the quality and complexity of the product, though additional scale economies for the latter could be obtained at the level of the enterprise through the specialisation of operations in three associated plants (see Mariotti 1982, pp. 85–136, 189–94).
2. These figures conceal significant differences among multiple chains of different sizes. In 1984, multiple chains with 100 or more outlets were responsible for 38.8 per cent of clothing sales in the UK, compared to 19.8 per cent for chains with 10–99 outlets and 15 per

cent for chains with between two and nine outlets (data from *Business Monitor SDO25 Retailing 1984* elaborated in London Strategic Policy Unit 1987, Table 3, p. 123a).

3. The contrast with countries such as Italy would have been even sharper if firms with less than ten employees had been included in the calculations: see p. 168.

4. The 1981 *Census of Employment* assessed Greater London employment in 'clothing, hats and gloves' at 29,000. The economic activity component of the *Census of Population* based on a 10 per cent sample of households indicated a total of 56,000 in 'clothing and footwear' for the same year, while borough-level data also show approximately twice as many people engaged in clothing as the number reported by the *Census of Employment*. For a fuller discussion of estimates of the number of outworkers in clothing, see Mitter (1986); and London Strategic Policy Unit (1987, pp. 131–2, 139–40).

5. In addition to the sources cited, this section draws on interviews with buyers for retail chains conducted mainly in 1984; for a fuller account of the research, see Zeitlin (1985).

6. According to a recent report on the knitwear industry, however, the investment needed to obtain more rapid response to market trends would not be justified for British manufacturers unless the retailers were prepared to pay a price premium for improved service (Kurt Salmon Associates 1986).

7. Measures of import penetration are strongly affected by the precise choice of industry classification. Import penetration for clothing and footwear together stood at 35 per cent in the first quarter of 1986: see *Hollings Apparel Industry Review* (Spring 1987, Table 35).

8. Research by Kurt Salmon Associates reported in *Apparel International* (February 1984).

9. In addition to the sources cited, this section also draws on information obtained through interviews with machinery suppliers in 1984–5 and 1987.

10. For a detailed guide to CAD systems currently available in the UK, see Trent Polytechnic (1986, Appendix XIX).

11. A similar production system has been displayed by an Italian company, F.K. Arna: see *Manufacturing Clothier* August 1986; and *Apparel International*, September 1986. As Disher (1987b) points out, both the Japanese and the Italian systems recall earlier experiments with autonomous work groups in the British clothing industry: cf. Clothing and Allied Products Training Board (1978); and 'How Sugden's Succeed with Work Group Systems', *Apparel International*, October 1986.

12. Since 1979, for example, the London Borough of Hackney has provided grants or loans to about seventy-five clothing firms, and despite significant differences in approach, financial assistance to

companies also remains an important form of intervention in Haringey, Islington, Lambeth and Tower Hamlets.

13. Detailed proposals for investment in smaller clothing firms were rejected by the GLEB Board on several occasions despite support from its own sector strategy division: see Greater London Enterprise Board (1983; 1984a; 1984b).

14. A CAD bureau was briefly established in London with financial support from the Greater London Council, but was shut down as a result of the closure of the Hackney Fashion Centre with which it was associated.

15. Tower Hamlets has helped to set up two employers' associations, the London Clothing Association and the East London Leather Clothing Association. According to a recent review of its policies, 'the council now often makes it a condition of receiving grants that employers should join one of the associations', and the resultant contacts with local employers are used 'to encourage better employment practices, "on the books" payments, etc., and to help spread the examples of companies doing well in improved premises with the council's help' (London Strategic Policy Unit 1987, p. 104).

References

Arpan, J., J. de la Torre, and B. Toyne (1982), *The US Apparel Industry: International Challenge, Domestic Response*. Atlanta, GA: Business Publishing Division. College of Business Administration, Georgia State University

Beach, S. (1985), 'Branching Out', *Manufacturing Clothier*, September

Belussi, F. (1987), 'Benetton: Information Technology in Production and Distribution: A Case Study of the Innovative Potential of Traditional Sectors', Occasional Paper Series no. 25, Science Policy Research Unit, University of Sussex

British Textile Confederation (1987), *Review of 1986/7 and Annual Report for 1986*. London

Brusco, S. (1982), 'The "Emilian Model": Productive Decentralization and Social Integration', *Cambridge Journal of Economics*, 6.2

Brusco, S. and E. Righi (1985), 'Local Government, Industrial Policy and Social Consensus: The Experience of Modena', unpublished paper presented to the OECD/Italy seminar, 'Opportunities for Urban Economic Development', Venice, 25–27 June

Chandler, A. (1977), *The Visible Hand: The Managerial Revolution in American Business*, Cambridge, MA: Harvard University Press

Chuter, A.J. (1986), 'Making Sense of the New Production Control Technology', *Apparel International*, July

Clairmonte, F. and Cavanagh, J. (1981), *The World in Their Web: The Dynamics of Textile Multinationals*. London: Zed Press

Clark, K. (1986), 'Gerber's Factory of the Future', *Apparel International*, November

Clothing and Allied Products training Board (1978), *Self-Organised Work Groups*. Leeds: CAPITB

Commission of the European Communities, Directorate-General for Science, Research and Development (1985), *Basic Research in Industrial Technology for Europe (BRITE): Projects Supported under the First Call for Proposals*. Brussels

Correale, G. and Gaeta, R. (1983), 'Mutamenti strutturali nell'industria tessile-abbigliamento mondiale: posizione competitiva e strategie internazionali delle aziende italiane', *Economia e politica industriale*, 38

Cotton and Allied Textiles Economic Development Council (1983), *Structure and Prospects of the Finishing Sector*. London: NEDO

Cotton and Allied Textiles Economic Development Council (1984), *Designing for Success: Approaches to Managing Textile Design*, London: NEDO

Davenport, E., P. Totterdill, and J. Zeitlin, (1986) 'Training for the Clothing Industry: A Strategy for Local Government Intervention', unpublished report prepared for the Greater London Council

de la Torre, J. (1986), *Clothing-Industry Adjustment in Developed Countries*, London: Macmillan

Department of Trade and Industry (1987), *Bulletin of Textile and Clothing Statistics, 1986*, London: DTI

Disher, M. (1983), 'A Spanish Giant Using Computers to Service High Fashion', *Manufacturing Clothier*, September

Disher, M. (1985), 'Modular CAD', *Manufacturing Clothier*, May

Disher, M. (1987a), 'CAD: Cost-Effective Adaptive Developments', *Manufacturing Clothier*, March

Disher, M. (1987b), 'Turning the Tables', *Manufacturing Clothier*, October

Economist Intelligence Unit (1983), *World Textile Trade and Production Trends*. London: EIU

Euromonitor (1985a), *UK Clothing Report 1985*. London: Euromonitor

Euromonitor (1985b), *European Clothing and Footwear Report 1985*. London: Euromonitor

Fornengo, G.P. (1978), *L'industria italiana dell'abbigliamento*. Bologna: Il Mulino

Fornengo, G.P. (1983), 'Tessile-Abbigliamento', unpublished paper, Faculty of Political Science, University of Turin

Fornengo, G.P. (1984), 'Gli effetti del protezionismo nel settore tessile abbigliamento', *L'industria*, new series, 5.3

Fraser, S. (1983), 'Combined and Uneven Development in the Men's Clothing Industry', *Business History Review*, 57

Frazier, R. (1986), 'How Industry Can Deliver the Quick Response'. *Apparel International*, February

Gebbert, C. (1988), 'Application of Technology and Working Conditions in the German Clothing Industry'. Paper presented to the EEC conference on 'Information Technology and the Clothing Industry', Brighton Polytechnic, 26–28 February

Gillingwater, D. (1986), 'The Significance of Fabric Manufacturers and Finishers in the Garment Manufacturing Industry in Britain: The Potential for Intervention', unpublished report commissioned by the Greater London Council

Gough, J. (1986a), *Socialist Strategy and Local Economic Initiatives*, Labour Economic Strategies Group Working Paper no. 4

Gough, J. (1986b), 'Industrial Policy and Socialist Strategy: Restructuring and the Unity of the Working Class', *Capital and Class*, 29

Greater London Council (1984), *The London Clothing Industry*, Economic Policy Group Strategy Document no. 37

Greater London Council (1985), *The London Clothing Strategy: A Debate*, Economic Policy Group Strategy Document no. 39

Greater London Council (1986), *Textiles and Clothing: Sunset Industries?* London: GLC

Greater London Enterprise Board (1983), *Proposals for GLEB's Investment in London's Clothing Industry*, Sector Strategy Division, November

Greater London Enterprise Board (1984a), *The Fashion Centre Outline Investment Proposal*, Sector Strategy Division, March

Greater London Enterprise Board (1984b), *A Strategy for Intervention in Smaller Clothing Firms*, May

Hoffman, K. and H. Rush (1984), *Microelectronics and Clothing: The Impact of Technological Change on a Global Industry*, Geneva: International Labour Organisation

Jefferys, J.B. (1954), *Retail Trading in Britain, 1850–1950*, Cambridge: Cambridge University Press

Keesing, D.B. and M. Wolf (1980), *Textile Quotas Against Developing Countries*, Thames Essay no. 23, London: Trade Policy Research Centre

Kurt Salmon Associates (1986), *'Dynamic Response': An Opportunity for Retailers and the UK Knitwear Supply System to Improve Profits and Become More Competitive by Working Together*, report prepared for the Knitting Economic Development Council

Lambert, J. (1983), *The Clothing Industry Scheme: An Assessment of the Effects of Selective Assistance under the Industry Act 1972*, Government Economic Service Working Paper no. 61, Department of Trade and Industry

Lancashire County Council (1985), *The Lancashire Clothing Industry*, Economic Intelligence Unit, County Planning Department

Lancashire County Council (1986), *A Lancashire Clothing and Textile Centre*, Economic Intelligence Unit, County Planning Department

Local Action for Textiles and Clothing (1987), *A Strategy for Textiles and Clothing*, Manchester: LATC

London Strategic Policy Unit (1987), *Sewing Up the Pieces: Local Authority Strategies for the Clothing Industry*, Economic Policy Group

Mariotti, P. (1982), *Efficienza e struttura economica: il caso tessile-abbigliamento*, Milano: F. Angeli

Milburn, R. (1986), 'Made in Hong Kong', *Manufacturing Clothier*, October

Mitter, S. (1986), 'Industrial Restructuring and Manufacturing Homework: Immigrant Women in the UK Clothing Industry', *Capital and Class*, 27

Mower, S. (1986), 'Designed in Hong Kong', *Guardian*, 6 February

National Economic Development Office (1982), *Changing Needs and Relationships in the UK Apparel Fabric Market*, Textiles Section, London: Nedo

National Economic Development Office (1985), *Ways Forward in the Better Womenswear Market*, Communique from the Garment Manufacturer-Retailer

Panels of the Joint Textile Committee no. 26, London: NEDO

National Economic Development Office (1986), *Challenges in the Upper Menswear Market*, Communique from the Garment Manufacturer-Retailer Panels of the Joint Textile Committee no. 29, London: NEDO

Nehmer, S. and M.W. Love (1985), 'Textiles and Apparel: A Negotiated Approach to International Competition' in B.R. Scott and G.C. Lodge, eds, *U.S. Competitiveness in the World Economy*. Boston, MA: Harvard Business School Press

Newcastle Economic Development Committee (1986), 'Newcastle Fashion Centre', unpublished report by the Employment Group

O'Dwyer, T. (1984), 'Searching for the Newest Sources', *Men's Wear*, 5 April

Ody, P. (1984a), 'What Today's Retailer Seeks from Suppliers', *Apparel International*, March

Ody, P. (1984b), 'The "Next" Success Factors', *Apparel International*, May

Ody, P. (1984c), 'The New High Street Manufacturers', *Apparel International*, September

OECD (1983), *Textile and Clothing Industries: Structural Problems and Policies in OECD Countries*, Paris: OECD

Pearce, S. and P. Totterdill (1986), *Prospects for Local Authority Intervention in the Textile and Clothing Industries*, Manchester: Centre for Local Economic Strategies

Peston, R. (1985), 'St. Michael Charges Back', *Investors Chronicle*, 29 May

Piore, M. and C. Sabel (1983), 'Italian Small Business Development: Lessons for U.S. Industrial Policy' in J. Zysman and L. Tyson, eds, *American Industry in International Competition*, Ithaca, NY: Cornell University Press

Piore, M. and C. Sabel (1984), *The Second Industrial Divide: Possibilities for Prosperity*, New York: Basic Books

Polan, B. (1984), 'Sophisticated Principles', *Guardian*, 15 September

Polan, B. (1985), 'At the Sharp End', *Guardian*, 24 January

Rainnie, A. (1984), 'Combined and Uneven Development in the Clothing Industry', *Capital and Class*

Rees, G. (1969), *St. Michael: A History of Marks and Spencer*. London: Weidenfeld and Nicolson

Rosen, M. (1984), 'A Study of Market Segmentation and Target Marketing', *Hollings Apparel Industry Review*, May

Rullani, E. and Zanfei (1984), 'Benetton: invenzione e consolidamento di un sistema internazionale', *Bolletino OSPRI*, 1

Rush, H. and L. Soete (1984), 'Clothing' in K. Guy, ed., *Technological Trends and Employment, vol. I: Basic Consumer Goods*. Aldershot: Gower

Sabel, C. and J. Zeitlin (1985), 'Historical Alternatives to Mass Production: Politics, Markets and Technology in Nineteenth-Century Industrialization', *Past and Present*, 108

Silberston, Z.A. (1984), *The Multi-Fibre Arrangement and the UK Economy*. London: HMSO

Solinas, G. (1982), 'Labour Market Segmentation and Workers' Careers: The Case of the Italian Knitwear Industry', *Cambridge Journal of Economics*, 6.2.

Taylor, S. (1984), 'High Technology Fashion', *Manufacturing Clothier*, April

Thompson, G. (1987), 'The American Industrial Policy Debate: Any Lessons for Britain?', *Economy and Society*, 16.1.

190 Zeitlin and Totterdill

Totterdill, P. (1986a), 'Local Action for the Textiles and Clothing Industry in the UK: The Experience of Nottingham', in *European Assistance for Textiles and Clothing: Action at the Local Level*, proceedings of a consultative conference sponsored by Nottingham City Council, with assistance from the European Economic Community through the Centre for Employment Initiatives, 20–1 June

Totterdill, P. (1986b), *Towards a Strategy for Clothing Operative Training*. Manchester: Local Action for Textiles and Clothing

Trent Polytechnic (1986). *How Knowledge of New Technology Can Be Made Available to the Clothing Industry*, report of Local Collaborative Project No. 703, MSC/DES Pickup Programme

Tyler, D. (1985). 'Flexible Apparel Automation and Japanese Initiatives'. *Hollings Apparel Industry Review*, Spring

US Congress, Office of Technology Assessment (1987), *The U.S. Textile and Apparel Industry: A Revolution in Progress — Special Report*, OTA-TET-332. Washington, DC: U.S. Government Printing Office

Wray, M. (1957). *The Women's Outerwear Industry*. London: Duckworth

Zeitlin, J. (1985). 'Markets, Technology and Collective Services: A Strategy for Local Government Intervention in the London Clothing Industry' in Greater London Council (1985)

7 Sector Strategies and Industrial Policy: The Furniture Industry and The Greater London Enterprise Board

Michael H. Best

Introduction

The United Kingdom of the twentieth century has revealed how rapidly industrial centres can become depressed areas and how deeply seated the barriers to reversing industrial decline can be. The last two decades have revealed that the processes are not peculiar to Britain. Numerous American and European communities have witnessed an erosion of their economic base as once viable local business enterprises have become exposed to foreign competition. Increasingly regional governments have come under pressure to do something about firm closures and job losses.

The challenge is formidable. Local or state/regional governments cannot appeal to prevailing economic theory for guidelines to counter or harness the powerful economic forces that can relegate their communities to economic stagnation. Keynesianism offers mainly national, demand-side policies but neglects attention to the organisation of production, national or local.

Monetarism, the only supply-side theory, locates the causes of poor industrial performance in 'regulated' markets and the solution in terms of 'perfecting' markets and improving the efficiency of production. Persistent unemployment is attributed to wages not declining to market clearing levels. Once prices and wages are freed regions with high unemployment will have a comparative advantage in labour-intensive goods.

My purpose is to elaborate an alternative supply-side analysis to that of monetarism, one which locates the sources of declining industrial performance in organisational failure as against market failure. Gaining competitive advantage means upgrading the organisations of work, firm and sector to match or surpass the competition. Matching the competition today means developing firms with the capacity perpetually to upgrade their performance. This capacity is enhanced by firm and sector organisations which promote institutional learning and co-operative inter-firm relations.

If the monetarist position best captures the dynamics of competition then the opportunities for local government industrial policy-making are limited to market deregulation activities, and communities faced with declining tradable goods sectors must resign themselves to deteriorating wages and employment opportunities. If the alternative supply-side theory is a better explanation of the sources of decline and growth of sectors then local government industrial policy-making initiatives can positively affect the economic destiny of communities. But they can also harden the barriers to organisational development. Only strategically orientated industrial policy can relax, as opposed to harden, the barriers to reorganising production for competitive advantage.

A strategically orientated industrial policy is based upon two notions: first, the replacement of comparative with competitive advantage; and second, the indirect link between tradables and job promotion. The next section explores these two notions. Then a sector analysis is applied to the European furniture industry. Three strategies for establishing competitive advantage are compared along with the implications for production organisation. This is followed by a look at the implications for a reconstituted theory of the firm. The chapter concludes with a critical examination of the sector strategy instruments applied by the Greater London Enterprise Board to revitalise London industry.

Competitive Advantage and Industrial Policy

Competitive Versus Comparative Advantage

A crack in the edifice of comparative advantage theory has emerged in recent years as a result of the successful industrial policy experience of Japan. The leaders of the Japanese Ministry of International Trade and Industry (MITI) deliberately repudiated comparative advantage theory (Johnson 1982). Comparative advantage theory dictates that regions specialise according to cost criteria and that free-market prices provide all the information that is necessary to make sector choices. A region's comparative advantage will be 'revealed' by the relative costs of resources. Entrepreneurs will use that information to make sector choices which are optimal in the sense of the most efficient possible use of the region's resources. For post-war Japan, which lacked both natural resources and capital, labour was the cheap resource which meant that Japan would maximise national income by targeting labour-intensive products.

Japanese economic policy-makers did not choose to specialise according to resource endowments. They instead sought to maximise growth by specialising in those sectors where a competitive advantage could be established by organisational superiority. This required information that was not embedded in prices. It meant developing competitive strategies based upon a comparison of the organisational strengths and weaknesses of foreign firms, sector by sector. They gambled that organisation, a non-marketable input and the intermediate variable between the cost of resources and the value of output, can be the basis of competitive advantage, at least in certain sectors. Unlike natural resources, organisation could not be sold and purchased in the market. Therefore competitive advantage based upon organisational superiority, once established, would be difficult and take time for competitors to match even by those from countries with superior resource endowments.

The idea of competitive advantage gives explanatory power to strategy and organisation. The success of firms in the market depends less upon resource endowment of the nation than upon the organisations of work, firm and sector and their interrelationships. Post-war Japan represents a nation starting with minimal resources, both physical and human, but which has set new standards for production performance. As noted, organisation is not a marketable resource and does not have a price. For this reason the information required by the theory of comparative advantage is no longer embedded in market prices. Comparative advantage theory depends upon supply being responsive to price, but in the case of factors without a price, supply responses will not be automatically forthcoming in the 'market'.

Japanese industrial policy has been about sequential targeting of strategic sectors to maximise industrial growth. Strategic sectors are those where an international competitive advantage can be secured at any one point in time. But the target is a moving one. For Japan it may have started with low-skill, labour-intensive goods but with the intention of moving to medium capital and raw-material-intensive followed by medium capital and resource-intensive and eventually to knowledge-intensive sectors (Magaziner and Hout 1980). Moving through such a hierarchy of sectors meant increasing the value added of existing resources by shifting to products with greater labour skill and refined organisational capabilities.

In the past, Japan strategically marched through sectors picking off the competition where it had become lethargic and incapable of responding to the new competitive threat. Today, they are increasingly moving into new sectors a step ahead of the competition. The policy has worked. But it has depended, in part, upon the lack of sector strategic planning capability elsewhere. What happens when many governments imitate the industrial policy instruments of the Japanese development state and simultaneously pursue the same strategic march through sectors? Today, the Four Tigers (Hong Kong, Singapore, South Korea and Taiwan) are following suit and the very success of the Asian challenge is generating pressures for Western European welfare-regulation states to adopt more strategic industrial policy roles.

Does the Japanese model of industrial policy have lessons to offer regions tied to declining sectors? Can anything be done about improving economic conditions in communities faced with declining sectors particularly under conditions of slower economic growth? Japan has enjoyed sufficient growth in the expanding sectors to soften the impact on communities with declining sectors. Communities linked to 'mature' sectors in the United States and the UK, where growth is slower, are unlikely to receive large interregional resource transfers. What is the role for industrial policy here? Can certain sectors be defined as strategic to regional governments and can regional governments act to promote international competitiveness?

The sector-strategy approach to industrial policy is about developing intra- and inter-firm organisational responses to industrial decline which presumes that competitive advantage is not pre-given but can be created. It intends to carve out a space for government involvement outside both the 'lemon' socialism of bailing out firms with no hope of remaining or becoming internationally competitive and the 'picking winners' approach which concentrates on individual firms to the neglect of sector organisation.

Industrial Policy, Tradables and Jobs

Industrial policy implies a priority to industry over services. It would perhaps more appropriately be described as tradables policy because, whereas the industry versus services is not a distinction relevant to economic policy, the distinction between tradables and non-tradables is fundamental.

The focus on tradables follows from an asymmetry between tradables and non-tradables: firms that produce tradables face the discipline of world-wide competition whereas non-tradables face only regional competition. This asymmetry has a profound implication for local production and jobs. If a firm producing tradables shuts down it means that local jobs are destroyed, whereas the closing of a non-tradables firm will result in a shift of production to other local firms. Thus the direct effect of a factory closing that produces tradables on the number of jobs is immediate. Indirect employment-reduction effects follow in supplier firms and in the diversion of expenditures outside the region.

The asymmetry is based on the fact that non-tradable production and employment levels are not affected by the costs of production. Whatever the level of local efficiency relative to foreign producers of non-tradables, the local producers are insulated from the disciplining effects of more efficient production elsewhere. Local haircutters, plumbers, brick-makers and restaurants may be inefficient by international standards but, whatever the cost of production, they will not collectively be shut down.

The tradable – non-tradable asymmetry has important implications for local-level industrial policy. Promoting non-tradables can shift production within the region but will not increase the level of production. Promoting tradable goods production, on the other hand, can increase the level of production in a region. To the extent that tradables production within a region is expanded, local employment can grow.

A tradables policy (industrial policy) is the foundation of an employment policy, but the two should not be confused. Jobs will come mainly from an expansion in non-tradable sectors such as construction, health and education, not from the expansion of firms that produce tradables, but the critical constraint on the expansion of non-tradable employment is the level of tradable production.

The question becomes, how a local government can promote internationally competitive firms. Traditionally the answer has been to improve the environment for business enterprises in the form of tax relief and material infrastructure. Increasingly, these passive policies have been replaced by direct intervention in firms. Particularly metropolitan authorities faced with declining private sector initiatives have sought to promote indigenous enterprise development as opposed to engaging in competitive bidding campaigns with other local authorities for potentially movable firms.

In some cases, such as regional government enterprise boards in the UK this has meant the creation of public sector venture-capital funds that invest long-term in private enterprises. These publically funded enterprise boards are different from private venture capital, in part because of their commitment to restructuring sectors and promoting sector strategies. The concept of sector strategy has thus emerged to provide a criterion for investing in firms. The idea of sector strategy has great appeal. It implies, first, that industrial policy should intervene to promote strategic sectors, and second, that industrial policy can be more effective if it has spill-over effects on a whole sector as opposed to only a single firm within the sector.

The development of firm and sector intervention marks an entirely new dimension to local and metropolitan government activities. Local governments have long experience in managing public services for non-tradables such as public transportation, housing and education. It is not immediately obvious that enterprise boards could achieve the goal of promoting tradables with direct investments. It might be so if the major constraint to enterprise promotion is lack of finance. I will argue that it is not.

But effective local government industrial policy initiatives depend upon an understanding of the constraints on the development on business enterprises. The notion of sector strategy alone does not answer this question. It might if it were grounded in a political economic analysis, but to date it has not been. The fault does not lie in the concept alone but in the inadequacy of economic theory, in particular the lack of strategic orientation and the plan–market dichotomy that informs it.

Competing Inter-firm Strategies in the European Furniture Industry

Increasing Internationalisation

Between 1973 and 1981, world-wide exports of wooden furniture increased nearly 2.5 times (see Table 7.1). The overwhelming single fact is the emergence of Italy as the leading force in the world furniture industry. Italian exports increased fivefold between 1973 and 1981. Over the same period, Italian furniture exports went from less than half to more than double those of the Federal Republic of Germany, the other major furniture exporter in the world.

Within the European community import penetration varies from 2.1 per cent of furniture sales in Italy to 36.1 per cent in the Netherlands (see Table 7.2). Italy and the Federal Republic of Germany stand out as the major exporters with nearly two-thirds of total furniture exports over the 1978 to 1984 period. But whereas the Federal Republic is also the major furniture importer, Italy imports less than all but Spain and Belgium. Italy's nearly $2 billion furniture trade surplus in 1980 is further evidence of her leading role in the European and world furniture industry (see Table 7.3).

The Decline of the Old Competition

Internationalisation of the furniture market meant that furniture firms where less insulated from competition by geographical boundaries. National or local customer loyalty could no longer be taken for granted as the retail shops were offering products from firms located throughout Europe. Local firms that failed to adapt with strategic and organisational adjustments suffered from declining sales. The collapse of the North London furniture industry demonstrates how rapidly fortunes can change. Today only B. & I. Nathan and Stonehill remain out of the twenty-five furniture firms listed in Table 7.4. Together Nathan and Stonehill employ roughly 550 people in a furniture district that employed over 16,000 in the 1960s. The demise of the North London furniture firms provides a lesson on how not to respond to the new competition.

Faced with shrinking sales, the North London firms sought to main-

Table 7.1. World export of furniture by major furniture exporters ($ thousands)

	1973	1974	1975	1976	1977	1978	1979	1980	1981
World	2 547 068	3 152 951	NA	NA	2 095 259	3 149 033	3 869 644	4 511 271	6 275 655
Federal Republic of Germany	615 880	772 896	853 166	NA	685 543	886 178	987 745	1 061 014	881 067
Italy	275 247	370 716	481 630	NA	447 151	673 737	1 009 668	1 187 384	1 672 383
Belgium	347 196	384 284	396 771	NA	232 488	284 337	302 010	366 789	480 535
Sweden	NA	NA	NA	NA	196 448	230 900	295 449	342 648	302 336

Source: United Nations, *Yearbook of International Trade Statistics*.

Table 7.2. Furniture consumption and imports* in various European countries ($ millions) 1983

	Furniture consumption	Imports of wooden furniture	Imports/Consumption (%)
Belgium	1 490	315	21.1
France	8 700	1 048	12.0
Italy	4 130	86	2.1
The Netherlands	1 400	506	36.1
Sweden	1 380	170	12.3
United Kingdom	4 180	653	15.6
West Germany	8 320	1 132	13.6
Total	29 600	3 910	

* The table is only indicative. The data for imports include only wooden furniture but also include office furniture; the data for internal consumption include furniture made from all materials but exclude office furniture.

Source: Centro Studi Industria Leggera (1986)

Table 7.3. Furniture trade balance, 1980 and 1984 ($ millions, current)

| | 1980 | | | 1984 | | |
	Exports	Imports	Balance	Exports	Imports	Balance
Austria	142	302	−160	118	246	−128
Belgium	636	608	28	467	249	218
France	506	1 178	−672	449	968	−519
Germany	1 672	1 506	166	1 362	1 109	253
Italy	1 929	112	1 817	1 783	99	1 684
The Netherlands	264	882	−618	221	467	−246
Spain*	151	54	97	167	34	133
Sweden	436	279	157	396	192	204
Switzerland	89	458	−369	83	407	−324
United Kingdom	432	561	−129	302	696	−394

* 1978 and 1984.

Source: As Table 7.2.

tain market share by cutting prices and costs. The result was a worsening in labor relations, slimmer margins and, eventually, insufficient financial capacity to survive. Unfortunately, the North London furniture manufacturers failed to identify the roots of the problem until it was too late. They perceived the problem in terms of excessive wages and competition from their neighbours in the same or nearby industrial estates. So they reacted to the perceived excessive wage rates by hiring less-skilled workers, increasing the intensity of work and substituting machines for labour. And they reacted against their perceived competitors by cutting prices in order to drive them out of business after which they could pick up their order books. In fact, both responses left the North London firms less able to respond to the real problem.

The real problem was neither their labour force nor their local competitors but the emergence of foreign competitors organised around different principles. Consequently, each round of cost reductions and bankruptcies did not result in the expected expansion in orders. Instead it merely sealed the fate of the survivors as it had the losers in the previous round. The eventual winners were, first, firms promoting product development, mainly foreign, who were expanding the supply of specialised, design-orientated furniture for selling in the quality market, and second, discount retailers in the commodity market. While the English furniture firms were cutting costs and seeking volume sales by selling to discount retailers, import penetration rose from 3.5 per cent in 1968 through 7 per cent in 1973 to 15 per cent in 1978. Most of increased imports were from high-wage Western European countries, particularly Italy.

Table 7.4. Losers and survivors in the North London furniture industry

Firms closing down before 1983	Workforce	Firms closing down, 1983-6	Workforce 1970	1984	Survivors	Workforce 1970	1986
Angel Colony							
Great Eastern Cabinet Co.	300	Carasell	130	30	B. & I. Nathan	400	150
Sparrow & Simmons	130						
Coller	200						
Supasuite	200						
Beautility	1 000						
Ely's Estate							
Homeworthy	500	Howard	130	100	Stonehill	900	400
Cabinet Industry	1 000	Welsell	300	130			
Wrighton	500	Uniflex	400	100			
John Citizen	100						
Lea Bridge							
Berrys	100	Bluestone	300	150			
Henry Wilkes	100	Austin	500	200			
Grant	100						
Liden (Whitewood)	300						
Others in North London							
Lebus	3 010						
Eyelock	400						
Summers	300						
Schreiber (Harlow)	1 000						
Totals	13 430	Lost jobs (1970–84):	1 050 (remaining jobs)	710	Lost jobs (1970–86):	750	550 (remaining jobs)

Source: Michael H. Best, interviews with North London furniture manufacturers and workers.

The New Competition

The manufacturing winners in the new competition compete less on price than on product development. One common organisational feature they share is that the successful firms rely upon a business system that co-ordinates product development across six functions, namely: technology; design; production; distribution; marketing; and sales. Effective product development depends upon consultative co-ordination across each of these functions. This does not mean that a furniture firm has to internalise each business function within its business entity, although some do, but that a successful furniture firm must have consultative, not simply market, access to each business function. Simple market co-ordination is insufficient. Consultative co-ordination enhances the capability of co-ordinating the six functions under the guidance of an enterprise *strategy* for gaining competitive advantage.

Two principal strategies are discernible. The first is the pursuit of global products that can be marketed in homogeneous market segments in all high-income nations. The second is the market-niche, flexible specialisation strategy that pursues market segments too heterogenous or small for the mass producers.

Both strategic orientations emphasise product development, international marketing, market segmentation, flexible production and the importance of design. Enterprises that cling to the old standardised product, price-led competition have been retarded in such consultative co-ordination and have been unable to engage in product development. Some of them have survived by introducing flow-line principles of production and seeking just-in-time supplier relations but they remain dependent upon retailing giants both for sales and design. The purely market mode of co-ordination means that the mass retailer is constantly sourcing the world seeking the lowest-cost producer of homogeneous products. It is usually only a matter of time before a low-wage country sets up a turnkey factory and threatens to drive sales levels below the break-even point for the pre-existing firms, whose highly dedicated machinery is suddenly threatened by obsolescence in the fast-moving commodity-producing segment of the industry.

The new competitors share a second organizational feature: networked inter-firm co-ordination. The new competitors are members of furniture industrial districts in which individual firms specialise in particular products, parts, processes or services. Together the district supplies the whole range of furniture. The advantage to an individual firm is that it has access to all of the requisite business services as demanded and in a quantity that is appropriate at the time. To gain the same business services by engaging a specialist in an employee relation inhibits flexibility both of quantity and adaptability to changing conditions. The disadvantage is that the autonomy of the firm is reduced; each firm is mutually interdependent with a network of suppliers and buyers.

The accomplishment of a successful industrial district is to establish the links of association among firms so that the inevitable tension between the opposite poles of internalisation and externalisation of enterprise functions is negotiated in the direction of externalisation. Only with such links of association do firms have the confidence to specialise, a prerequisite to increased productive efficiency in a small firm.

The North London furniture firms were never able to make the transition to an interdependent and networked furniture district. Instead, they remained locked within a mutually destructive system producing the same products, unable to benefit from a supplier network of specialised products, parts, and activities.

The price-competition strategy and the lack of links of inter-firm association are intertwined. An individual North London firm could not pursue a strategy of specialisation because it alone could not create the networks that constitute a vibrant industrial district. Thus a firm strategy is contingent upon the form of inter-firm co-ordination, and the greater the networking, the more opportunities for pursuing a strategy of specialisation.

Mass-Production, Retailer-Led Strategies

Mass production came late to the furniture industry. It is an industry in which bigness did not lead to success. In the USA, for example, no furniture firm has entered and remained on the *Fortune* 500 list. In both the USA and the UK ambitious furniture-manufacturing enterprises unsuccessfully sought to gain commanding market shares by vertical integration. Internationally the furniture industry has remained highly disaggregated as well. However, two retailing giants emerged in Europe in the 1970s that have altered the dynamics of the industry.

The Swedish transnational retailer, IKEA, is the biggest furniture retailer in Europe and the most dynamic in the world. IKEA pioneered the combination showroom/warehouse concept which relies upon substituting consumer participation for dealer expertise in the sales process. In effect, they eliminated the salesperson much as interchangeable parts had eliminated the fitter in the metal-working industry a century before.

The previously mentioned technological developments in flatpack and containerisation plus the application of flow-line principles to wood materials were preconditions for the successful penetration of foreign markets. IKEA, which opened its first showroom in 1953, opened its first foreign store in 1963 when it accounted for only 6 per cent of Swedish furniture sales. By 1979, IKEA had 10 megastores (over

200,000 square feet, not counting car parks) in the Federal Republic of Germany, two in Switzerland, one each in Austria and the Netherlands, and franchising outlets in Australia, Canada, Hong Kong, Singapore and Japan. By 1984, IKEA was printing 44 million catalogues per year and demanding that all suppliers produce homogeneous products for its world-wide system of outlets. IKEA's great strength is value for money as retailing overheads and manufacturing costs have been driven down by unprecedented rates of stock turnover and throughput. But costs are also driven down by the leverage that IKEA has over its suppliers.

IKEA is a discount retailer that sells 'designed' commodities. IKEA has a large and active designer staff which will send the same specifications to a range of manufacturers throughout the world who will bid for the contract. Thus IKEA relies upon the market not for product ideas but as a monitoring device. A firm that cannot meet both the cost and volume requirements is dropped for one that can. The market tie gives IKEA responsiveness to shifts in demand but at the expense of the manufacturer. Since IKEA has forsaken vertical integration, shifts in sales can be translated into orders without consideration for paying for plant and equipment geared to last year's products. Thus IKEA enjoys flexibility and efficiency but at the expense of mass producers whose products are no longer in demand in the volume required to finance the large fixed costs.

MFI is a British follower of IKEA's showroom/warehouse strategy. Both have recently opened outlets in Philadelphia in the USA where for the first time they are competing in the same city.

In the early 1970s, MFI was a small mail-order firm. But a change in strategy to an edge of town, self-delivery showroom/warehouse concept led to rapid growth fuelled by trade credit. MFI successfully used the finance-generating formula of opening new outlets, selling for cash and paying on 60 to 90 days' credit. By 1983, MFI had 13 per cent of the British market, followed by Harris Queensway with 4 per cent. The strategy worked as MFI reached the volume required to become a self-sustaining discount retailer. MFI's success was not only at the expense of traditional retailers; MFI also captured profits at the expense of manufacturers. This is indicated by a comparison of the profit margins of MFI and a group of 'successful' UK furniture manufacturers surveyed by a British market research agency (Keynote 1984): MFI's profit margin rose from 8.1 per cent in the year ending May 1982, to 12.3 per cent (1983) and 13 per cent (1984); while the group of 'successful' UK manufacturers recorded figures of 2.2 per cent (1982), 2.5 per cent (1983) and 4 per cent (1984).

MFI's strengths are low price and immediate delivery; its weakness is the requirements of huge volume sales for every item. The pursuit of a mass market in the United Kingdom dictates that MFI must produce a low-cost commodity that can be purchased by low-income families. In fact, MFI has brought furniture to many families that could not afford traditional retailers. At the same time, satisfying this market has led to a corporate image and supplier relations that would make it difficult for MFI to supply, for example, specialist, assembled, solid or otherwise upmarket furniture.

The subordination of design by the domination of powerful mass-market retailers has turned British manufacturers into subcontractors with little product-development capability. Partly for this reason and partly because of squeezed margins and lack of investable funds, suppliers to the retailing giants have not made the necessary invest-ment in a changeover from mass production to flexible specialisation. As long as manufacturers compete as subcontractors, such firms will be threatened by both Eastern European and Third World, low-wage commodity producers and high-wage producers of specialised pro-ducts.

The market-dominating retailing chains in the United Kingdom are very appealing to manufacturers. A furniture manufacturer can gain access to a sizeable portion of the British furniture market by establish-ing a relationship with the purchasing agents of half a dozen retailing giants. But once a manufacturer has installed high-volume, dedicated equipment for producing products defined by a Harris Queensway or MFI, its future is at risk from the retailer's incessant world-wide search for lower-cost producers.

Terence Conran's Habitat, has a product range similar to IKEA but its retailing strategy is to counter the trend to edge-of-town megastores with 'gallerias' or small, speciality shops along the lines of Mothercare, part of the same group of companies. This 'localism' counter-trend seeks to offer greater product specialisation. Habitat's share of the British market is only 1–2 per cent of sales, which offers greater opportunity for medium-sized manufacturers. But even Habitat seeks the market-orientated supplier relationship. Manufacturers are offered contracts but only on the understanding that they produce designs specified by Habitat. Thus Habitat insists that an independent design capability not be developed by its suppliers.

Mass-Production, Manufacturer-Led Strategies

Poggenpohl, the large West German Kitchen manufacturer, has an annual turnover exceeding $120 million. It specialises in kitchens and utilises a large franchise dealer network staffed by people trained in a facility shared with several other West German kitchen manufacturers. The franchisee offers a customised fitted kitchen according to the specifications of the customer. Poggenpohl subcontracts the doors for the panels to enhance the range of door designs and minimise the commitment to any one design. Companies such as Poggenpohl are a formidable opponent as they have pursued the principles of modularisation and flow-line production. Within six years of entering the British market, mainly West German mass producers controlled nearly 50 per cent of the kitchen market. But again the very strength of Poggenpohl is also a weakness. The firm can produce at low cost only at a volume which threatens market saturation and thereby the need continuously to seek new markets.

West German firms are unparalleled in the production of panel-based units. Firms can draw upon world-class production engineering in the form of hired personnel or consultants. The consultants Gerhard Schüler, for example, have layouts for 2,200 plants around the world. The Rosenheim Woodworking School is also the world leader in the teaching of furniture production engineering. The German craft tradition and leadership in the machine-tool industry also contribute to a highly competitive furniture industry. West German firms subject themselves to performance tests such as work-in-process turns, capital-utilisation rates and quality testing that are highly advanced by conventional furniture industry standards (Haas nd(a); nd(b)).

But the powerful West German furniture industry has not stopped imports of over $1 billion in furniture annually. To understand why we must turn to flexible specialisation as an alternative to mass production. The best example is Italy.

Flexible Specialisation and the Italian Furniture Industry

Italy's economy has performed comparatively well in recent years. In real terms Italian industrial output increased by 16 per cent between 1978 and 1984; over the same period, the Italian furniture industry expanded by over 50 per cent. Between 1967 and 1981 money output per employee increased by 15.75 times, value added per employee increased by 10.78 times, fixed investment per employee increased by 8.14 times, and pay per employee increased by 9.89 times (Silvestrelli 1985) for furniture firms with over 20 employees (the consumer price index rose nearly five times from an index of 100 in 1967 to 472 in 1981). Annual changes in turnover, value added, fixed investment, pay and employees are shown in Table 7.5.

The second feature of the Italian furniture industry is the prevalence of small-scale producers. In 1981, over 86 per cent of the furniture firms employed less than ten workers and only two employed more than 500 workers (see Table 7.6). The average number of employees per firm increased from 4.7 in 1961 to 5.8 in 1981 (see Table 7.7). The employment share of artisanal (between one and nine employees) did drop sharply from 53.4 per cent in 1961 to 37.2 per cent in 1971, but was still 35.8 per cent in 1981 (see Table 7.7). But the shift of employment has never been to firms with more than 100 employees. In fact, firms with between 10 and 49 employees increased their share from 27.8 per cent

Table 7.5. Macro-economic data for Italian furniture firms with over 20 employees, 1967–81

Year	Turnover billions of current lire	Turnover annual change (%)	Value added billions of current lire	Value added annual change (%)	Fixed investment billions of current lire	Fixed investment annual change (%)	Personnel expenses billions of current lire	Personnel expenses annual change (%)	Number employed (000s)	Number employed annual change (%)
1967	196.0	–	97.4	–	12.5	–	72.6	–	58.8	–
1968	242.3	+23.6	117.5	+20.6	20.1	+61.1	86.9	+19.6	64.2	+ 9.2
1969	290.9	+20.1	137.4	+17.0	21.0	+ 4.0	102.4	+17.8	68.6	+ 6.8
1970	336.8	+15.8	155.7	+13.4	20.1	– 4.3	119.9	+17.1	69.4	+ 1.2
1971	387.4	+15.0	187.6	+20.5	24.1	+20.4	148.8	+24.1	71.1	+ 2.4
1972	499.6	+29.0	223/7	+19.2	41.6	+72.3	171.3	+15.2	80.9	+13.8
1973	707.9	+41.7	304.3	+36.1	61.5	+47.9	225.1	+31.4	83.8	+ 3.5
1974	1,001.1	+41.4	406.4	+33.5	89.3	–45.2	296.1	+31.5	85.5	– 2.1
1975	929.8	– 7.1	421.1	+ 3.6	47.3	–47.1	327.5	+10.6	79.0	– 7.6
1976	1,408.1	+51.4	570.2	+35.5	79.9	+69.0	416.9	+27.3	78.7	– 0.3
1977	1,651.5	+17.2	674.0	+18.2	101.3	+26.7	501.1	–20.2	77.5	– 1.5
1978	1,922.4	+16.4	764.4	+13.4	86.5	–14.6	575.4	+14.8	76.3	– 1.6
1979	2,661.9	+38.4	940.2	+22.9	108.7	+25.6	686.2	+19.2	74.5	– 2.3
1980	3,674.5	+38.0	1,226.9	+30.5	147.1	+35.3	820.8	+19.6	73.8	– 0.9
1981	3,881.9	+ 5.6	1,365.2	+11.2	135.1	– 8.1	925.8	+12.7	70.2	– 4.8

Source: Silvestrelli (1985).

Table 7.6. Composition of Italian furniture and wood furnishing business units by number of employees, 1961–81

Class size (number of employees)	Typology of business unit	1961 Bus. units	(%)	1971 Bus. units	(%)	1981 Bus. units	(%)	Change 1961–71 (%)	Change 1971–81 (%)
1–9	artisanal	26,689	92.8	25,517	88.6	29,207	86.3	+ 3	+ 6
10–49	small	1,815	6.3	3,013	9.7	3,954	11.68	+66	+31
50–99	medium	195	0.7	393	1.25	364	1.1	+101	– 7
100–499	medium-large	69	0.2	132	0.4	149	0.4	+91	+13
500 and over	large	1	0.003	4	0.01	2	0.006	+300	–50
Total industrial units	10 and over	2,080	7.2	3,542	11.4	4,469	13.2	+70	+26
Units without employees				13	0.04	182	0.54	+ 8	–
Total business units		28,769	100.0	31,072	100.0	33,858	100.0	+ 8	+ 9

Source: Silvestrelli (1985).

Table 7.7. Composition of the work-force in Italian furniture firms, 1961–81

Class size (number of employees)	Typology of business unit	1961 Number employed	1961 (%)	1961 Average number employed	1971 Number employed	1971 (%)	1971 Average number employed	1981 Number employed	1981 (%)	1981 Average number employed	Change 1961–71 (%)	Change 1971–81 (%)
1–9	artisanal	72,179	53.4	2.7	65,393	37.2	2.4	70,122	35.8	2.4	– 9	+ 7
10–49	small	37,480	27.8	20.6	59,342	33.8	19.7	75,046	38.3	19	+ 58	+26
50–99	medium	13,325	9.9	68.3	26,885	15.3	68.4	24,468	12.5	67.2	+102	– 9
100–499	medium-large	11,455	8.5	166.0	20,966	11.9	158.8	24,635	12.6	165.3	+ 83	+17
500 and over	large	592	0.4	592.0	2,946	1.7	736.5	1,470	0.7	735	+398	–50
Total industrial units (10 and over)		62,852	46.5	30.2	110,139	62.7	31.1	125,619	64.2	28.1	+ 75	+14
Total industrial units		135,031	100.0	4.7	175,532	100.0	5.6	195,741	100.0	5.8	+ 30	+11

Source: Silvestrelli (1985).

in 1961 to 33.8 per cent in 1971 to 38.3 per cent in 1981. And the category of firms with 99 and less employees included 86.3 per cent of all furniture workers in 1971 and 86.6 per cent in 1981.

The important implication to draw from these empirical details is that the enormous growth and improvement in competitiveness of the Italian furniture was not associated with an emergence of big firms. The increase in productive efficiency came primarily from increased specialisation which, in turn, was a consequense of improved organisation. As noted earlier, success in the European furniture industry in the 1970s depended upon the development of industrial districts. Such industrial districts allowed small, flexible firms to specialise and have ready access to the full range of requisite business services. Activities of firms within such industrial districts are co-ordinated through consultative networks that facilitate tailorised consortia.

The Italian *consorzio* is one institution that facilitates inter-firm networking. The structure of the *consorzio* is fixed by law. It is an association of enterprises designed to provide a common service which cannot be profit-seeking and must be accountable to its members. Joint marketing and financial *consorzi* are the most prevalent form. The number of co-operative marketing ventures in Italy increased from 48,000 in 1970 to 79,000 in 1979 (Economists Advisory Group 1983).

An example of such a co-operative marketing venture in the furniture sector is the *Consorzio Poggibonsi*, established in 1965. In 1983 it had a staff of six and 85 member firms which together employed about 2,000 people. Total turnover of the consortium was about $150 million with 30 per cent coming from exports. Sixty-three of the member firms were in furniture with the other twenty-two distributed across a broad range of ancillary products and services including interior decoration, lamps and lighting fixtures, doors and windows, glassware, marble, shipping, paints and varnishes, metallurgical products, printing and graphic arts, building construction, wood-working machines and ceiling tiles.

Membership in the consortium cost about $6,000 per year. The services provided included the following:

export promotion

fair and exhibition organisation

sales missions to foreign markets

maintainance of contact with governmental bodies that promote trade market research

maintainance of an export office with translation facilities in Florence

promotion of domestic and export catalogues. Twice a year the consortium publishes a glossy review.

keeping files on financial soundness of existing and potental clients

organising bulk buying of raw material and other inputs. These materials are often stored in the consortium's warehouse.

provision of a range of business services including computer and
telex facilities, advice on compiling budgets and tax returns, a
weekly newsletter, job advertisements and exchange-rate
movements

provision of training facilities

The members' fees cover about half of the consortium's expenses.
The rest is covered by grants and loans from the Italian Foreign Affairs
Ministry, the Tuscany Regional Administration and municipal government (Economists Advisory Group 1983). Thus the government provides a crucial input into the marketing co-operative. The effect is to
reward private collective action as opposed to subsidising individual
firms.

Marketing consortia are an alternative to co-ordination by either
managerial hierarchy within a big business or by prices in the market.
They allow small firms to gain access to collective services that are
provided to divisions within multi-divisional firms but without sacrif-
icing entrepreneurial activity and organisational flexibility, both of
which are crucial to the furniture industry. They also allow firms to
co-ordinate product lines and thereby specialise but without common
ownership. Thus without forming a multi-divisional organisation production units can avoid the tendency to producing the same products
and competing over price as was done by the North London furniture
firms.

Finance can also be the subject of a consortium's activities. Loan-
guarantee consortia are co-operative associations created to provide
credit guarantees for members to borrow from banks. Borrowings are
guaranteed by the consortium which collects contributions from members and federal, regional and local governments. For example, the
regional government contributes 3 per cent of the negotiated interest
rate to the Consorzi Fidi of Emilia-Romagna.

Any member enterprise that desires a loan must go first to the local
branch of the National Confederation of Artisans, which is an association
of firms with twenty or less employees. The NCA secretary 'asks for
detailed information on the overall situation of the firm, its long and short
term credit exposure, its main customers and suppliers, receipt and
payment periods. He then sends a report to the Board of Directors adding
his own opinion on the personal characteristics of the applicant, his
trustworthiness and his professional standing' (Brusco and Righi 1985).

What the loan-guarantee consortium supplies to the bank is an
assessment of the enterprise's prospects based on intimate knowledge
of fellow artisans and a loan guarantee. These additional inputs open
up the credit market for small firms, a market that depends upon trust,
a non-commercial input. In the case of the Credit Co-operative of
Modena, founded in 1976, a total of about $6 million in loan guarantees
by 1985 had resulted in only about $45,000 of unrecovered loans. The

reason according to Brusco is 'the person who receives a loan from the cooperative will stay up at night thinking up ways of repaying his loan. Whereas the person who receives a bank loan will stay awake at night thinking up ways of *not* repaying his loan' (emphasis in original).

Municipal governments also actively promote industrial districts among small networked firms with land-planning programmes. The passage of the Plan for Industrial Parks in 1972 gave municipalities the power to expropriate and plan large areas for industrial parks for artisanal and medium or small firms. In 1974 the municipality of Modena passed the Plan for Small Firm Areas which focused on the following objectives (Brusco and Righi 1985):

> Assist the interrelationships of manufacturing districts by means of carefully planned location within the territory of those companies which are seeking alternative premises.
> Increase the range of the availability of areas less than 800–1000 square meters.
> Support and create incentives for the development of artisan consortia as an alternative to big companies.

Thus the industrial parks foster joint private–public organisations to promote co-operation and competition. A group of small firms, in conjunction with the government, can effect land use arrangements in ways that only large firms could in most countries.

Marketing and financial consortia and industrial parks do not exhaust the forms of sector infrastructure institutions that have been developed in Italy, but they illustrate the principle that such institutions allow the co-ordination of the six business functions required by the new competition. What is most significant about these developments is that they provide an alternative path to productive efficiency. In fact, in the case of furniture, they may well be the only path. The provision of collective services within a single firm generates large overhead expenses which require volume production. This big enterprise organisational form inhibits the production flexibility and design responsiveness that have become trademarks of the most successful furniture-producing regions.

Co-operation and the Theory of the Firm

The existence of co-operative inter-firm relations is not limited to groups of Italian furniture firms. The existence of 'shared network norms' amongst Japanese suppliers (Ken-ichi *et al.* 1985) and the 'external suppliers as collaborators' of the Boeing Company (Piore and Sabel 1984) are examples of co-operative inter-firm relations co-ordinated by a large firm. Richardson (1972) has suggested a criterion for categorising co-ordination within a market–plan–co-operation framework that is built on Penrose's (1959) theory of the firm. Richardson's framework gives theoretical underpinning to co-operation as an alternative to either market or bureaucratic co-ordination.

Penrose (1959, p. 52) posed a theory of the firm based upon human organisation and tacit or practical knowledge derived from specific experience and teamwork. In her words:

> When men (*sic*) have become used to working in a particular firm or with a particular group of other men, they become individually and as a group more valuable to the firm in that the services they can render are enhanced by their knowledge of their fellow-workers, of the methods of the firm, and of the best way of doing things in the particular circumstances in which they are working.

Richardson takes from Penrose the notion that industries comprise a large range of activities each of which has to be carried out by an organisation with the appropriate knowledge, skills and experience. The capability of an enterprise depends upon developing a distinctive competence in one or more activities. Richardson distinguishes similar activities that utilise the same capability from complementary activities as those that utilise distinct capabilities.

Firms will internalise similar activities and go outside for complementary activities. A metalworking job shop, for example, will require general tools and skilled craftspeople capable of creating prototypes for a range of metal-fabricating and assembling firms. To maintain a distinctive competence such firms will continuously update skills and machines that enhance prototyping and small-batch capabilities. Organisational flexibility can be enhanced by developing workers' capacities to operate, maintain, set up and modify a variety of metalworking machines, to be aware of the whole production system and able to respond rapidly to new opportunities.

By making the simple distinction between similar and complementary activities, Richardson is able to redefine the boundaries of the firm and the notion of a sector. The plan–market dichotomy of the conventional theory of the firm draws the boundary of the firm by comparing the transactions costs of market versus administrative co-ordination (Coase 1937). Competition in the market would select those firms with the optimum internalisation. Any firm with a different extent of internalisation would not survive in the market.

The Penrose–Richardson vision, on the other hand, suggests that firms will internalise similar activities and externalise complementary activities. This implies that firms will specialise for reasons of production performance and not transaction costs. The distinctive competences that are built up in human organisations that specialise in single activities cannot be replicated in the market or in organisations that combine dissimilar activities. This means that to obtain the benefits of complementary specialist activities a firm must develop a co-operative relationship: it is the only way to get the highest-quality product. An analysis of comparative transaction costs misses the point, because the comparison is between different products and production organisations with different distinctive competencies.

The Penrose–Richardson theory of the firm is consistent with two images that are crucial to the flexible specialization perspective. The first is an image of the firm in which the capacity to learn is a productive asset. Nurturing this capacity is what makes an organisation flexible. Conversely, denying this capacity is built into Taylorist scientific management' principles of specialisation by simplification and predetermined rules to guide workers actions.

The second is an image of a sector as an association of producers of complementary products. Sectors in which firms specialise by activity will have a different dynamic than sectors composed of identical firms producing the same product. The first requires co-operation amongst firms; the second fits the formal plan–market dichotomy of economic theory in which firms are linked spontaneously by markets.

This has implications for the regional rise and fall of sectors. For competition within a sector does not ensure that the optimal form of sector specialisation will emerge and, in fact, market competition can thwart the emergence of specialisation based on similar activities. The reason is that a single firm that specialises by activity is dependent upon firms specialising in complementary activities. If complementary products are not available or are only available from firms that seek to exploit short-run market advantages, then the firm is likely to fail in the market.

A sector in which firms are co-ordinated by the market alone can persist even though firms have not specialised by activity as long as the sector is insulated from competition. But the whole sector will come under competitive pressure from other sectors that have so specialised once the barriers to trade are relaxed. Thus a specific sector can be outcompeted in the international marketplace, even though individual firms within it have organised themselves according to minimum transactions costs.

Thus business and sector organisation is not determined by technology or transactions costs but negotiated within a context of competing and co-operating firms. Co-ordination and coherence across activities can be by market, co-operative inter-firm relations within a sector or by inter-departmental hierarchy within an enterprise. In this version, sectors and the firms that constitute them are shaped, in part, by the specific forms of inter-firm co-operation that are collectively developed.

Sector Strategy and the Greater London Enterprise Board

The Greater London Enterprise Board (GLEB) was established by the Greater London Council in January 1983 as an industrial development agency with an annual budget of about £30 million. Approximately one-third of the budget was designated for property purchases, one-tenth for overheads, and the rest for a variety of projects (GLEB 1985–6). When the Greater London Council was abolished in March 1986, control of GLEB was transferred to twelve London boroughs. The budget for 1987–8 is estimated to be about £7 million of which about £2 million is provided by the boroughs, £2 million from selling assets and £3–5 million is being sought externally, primarily from pension funds and various European Economic Community programmes.

GLEB's corporate plan for 1985–6 listed three primary objectives: these were to

1. create and improve the quality of jobs in London;
2. regenerate London's economic base by investing in London's industry; and
3. widen the control that Londoners have over their economic future, particularly at work.

It also listed nine secondary objectives: the promotion of novel forms of social ownership and control, co-operatives, equal opportunities, new forms of property development, technological change, company restructuring, sector restructuring, information on problems facing London, and open communication and staff development within GLEB.

As an industrial policy instrument, GLEB's charter was shaped by two propositions. The first was a 'capital-gap' explanation of industrial decline in London. In the words of the Chief Executive: 'By providing loan and investment finance to enterprises, both private and co-operative, the GLEB can help to plug the "capital gap" which is so often a threat to survival or growth for new or established enterprises' (GLEB 1985).

The second proposition was that past industrial policy initiatives in Britain had failed from a lack of governmental influence over private business management and the failure to involve workers in the management of government-supported or -owned enterprises. The tripartite National Economic Development Office, for example, has long conducted sector studies but lacks power over business management. The National Plan of the Wilson government was judged to have failed because it abandoned compulsory for voluntary planning agreements. Both of these institutions, plus the National Enterprise Board, the Industrial Reconstruction Corporation and the nationalised industries were criticised for failure to promote industrial democracy in the work-place.

These propositions implied a theory of industrial decline and a strategy for economic development. Industry had declined because of a lack of capital, the incapacity of private enterprises to co-ordinate investment decisions and because workers were systematically excluded from business decision-making. The implied development strategy was for GLEB to make equity investments in private companies. Such investments could simultaneously fill the capital gap, create a basis for inter-firm planning and implement industrial democracy in the work-place.

Private companies became the target of GLEB's investment strategy both because the capital gap was deemed greater in companies with non-tradable shares and because their small asset base meant that a GLEB investment would ensure greater influence. A private company is defined by the Companies Act 1980 as a 'company which is not a public company'. Like a public company, a private company is a non-human legal person which enjoys the benefits of limited liability. But, unlike a public company, a private company cannot market its shares or debentures to the public. The number of public companies in England and Wales is small (7,000) compared to the number of private companies (740,000) (Oliver 1982, p. 9).

Investment in a private company involves redrafting its articles of association in compliance with the Companies Acts. The articles of association form a registered document which includes compulsory clauses, such as the object of the company, the limitation of liability of the members and the amount and forms of share capital. But the articles of association also include discretionary clauses that are agreed amongst the shareholders. The novelty of GLEB, and similar metropolitan enterprise boards in the UK, was to become shareholders in private companies in order to draft the discretionary clauses of the articles of association so as to give enterprise boards power over the strategies and operations of business enterprises.

It was taken for granted that GLEB finance would be attractive to the manager-owners of private companies because of the 'capital gap'. The manager-owners of private companies were assumed to have a list of investment projects that were finance-constrained because private financial institutions lacked the capacity to assess long-term industrial investment projects. It was assumed that the unmet demand for finance capital was sufficiently large that GLEB could extract partnership in management in exchange for the provision of finance. The existing shareholders of a private company would have to write GLEB social goals into the articles of association and give GLEB appointees influence within the enterprise. In most cases GLEB demanded a seat or seats on the board of directors and in all cases GLEB demanded access to all financial and operational information used by management.

The foremost social goal was worker participation in enterprise governance. GLEB required that an agreement to enterprise planning in principle was written into the articles of association. The actual planning agreements were to be negotiated later and signed by representatives of the work-force and/or unions, management and GLEB. The enterprise plans would cover product and market strategy, future investment and technical change, location, pricing policy, employment levels and conditions, skill levels and training, and equal opportunities.

Thus, to achieve its objectives, GLEB was constituted as a public sector venture-capital fund but with a different motivation. Both invest equity capital in private companies. The motivation for a private sector venture-capital fund is the windfall profit that can be made by either converting a private company into a public company, by which its shares become tradeable, or selling a private company to a public company. Either eventuality involves a multiple increase in the value of each share as the value of a private company can jump from a multiple of around 5 times earnings to a multiple of around 15 times common for a public company. GLEB had a different motivation: invest in private companies as a means of pursuing economic and social goals of the Greater London Council. The presumption was that investment gave control over economic decision-making. The purpose of this control was not to maximise return on shareholders' investment but to promote jobs and revitalise industry.

The focus was on 'key' firms with over forty employees (Economic Policy Group 1983). This was for two reasons. First, the costs of identifying and analysing a company for investment and articles of association are roughly the same for large and small investments, which meant the administrative costs per pound invested were much higher for small investments. Second, bigger companies employed more people and had more influence on their sector and the London economy.

GLEB also promoted co-operatives as an alternative form of ownership but investments in co-operatives were largely in the form of loans rather than equity stakes. Since the essence of co-operatives is shared ownership among the working members of the enterprise, an equity investment by an outsider is against the principles of the co-operative movement. Interest charges on loans limit the capacity of firms to borrow.

Given its goals, GLEB was both less and more constrained than private venture-capital funds. It was less constrained in that its charter enabled it to invest according to a social and not private rate of return. This meant that GLEB could account for non-market returns. But GLEB investments were more constrained in that they must account for potential negative effects on London competitors.

The concept of sector strategy was developed as a method to address the problem of negative effects of GLEB investments on other firms. It was quickly realised that rescuing firms to save jobs could have just such counter-productive effects. In one early case, GLEB funding saved a firm that was pursuing a price-cutting strategy to drive other London firms into bankruptcy.

To avoid counter-productive investments the GLEB board approved the following set of sector and enterprise guidelines for interventions (Best 1984):

1. Intervene in key firms that can influence strategic planning and business organisation of the entire sector.
2. Intervene where sector wide competitive advantage could be created.
3. Intervene to promote industrial districts.

These criteria distinguished *proactive* from *reactive* investments. Reactive investments meant acting as a lender of last resort by rescuing firms that were failing in the market, and proactive investments meant seeking out firms that could become catalysts for sector revitalisation.

To identify proactive investments, a sector strategy methodology was developed. It involved one-to-one discussions with manager-owners of all the firms with more than forty employees in a sector. The purpose was to determine the challenges and opportunties facing a sector from the perspective of sector insiders both in the UK and abroad. This entailed an assessment of the strengths and weaknesses of the London firms with the strengths and weaknesses of firms located elsewhere in the same sector. Based upon this information a sector strategy was shaped which included a vision of the restructuring required for London firms to gain a competitive advantage. GLC (1985) describes strategies for over twenty sectors in the London economy. The sectors judged to be most promising for GLEB interventions were clothing, cultural industries, food, furniture and printing.

GLEB was and is a bold experiment in local government industrial policy-making. But its potential as a model for revitalising structurally depressed industries and regions is not clear. If enterprise boards are to become an instrument of industrial revitalisation they must transcend the lender-of-last-resort role and become a catalyst for sector restructuring. One way to do this is to pursue equity investments in private companies with a sector strategy orientation. The infrastructure-led approach of the 'Third Italy' is another.

To access the GLEB firm-investment approach, I will examine its consistency with the analysis of sector strategy based upon the market–plan–co-operation framework outlined in the preceding sections. That framework suggests a three-part criterion for testing sector strategy approaches. Unless enterprise boards systematically pursue a sector strategy orientation consistent with this criterion they are likely to remain trapped in rearguard actions, victimised by the 'market'.

The Theory of the Firm as an Organic Social Institution

The basic proposition of GLEB was that equity investment gave GLEB power over enterprise decision-making and governance. In practice, equity investment gave GLEB less power over firms than anticipated. GLEB investments were dependent upon their private partners who had the intimate knowledge of the firm and the sector. This power gave the private owners maximum leverage once the investment was made. GLEB could demand financial information, but it could not threaten a manager-owner with the sack if he did not perform unless GLEB was prepared to buy out the private owner or sell off its shares to the existing owner at a price agreed with the private owner.

GLEB's power was less than had been anticipated because of the implicit theory of the firm. GLEB took for granted the neo-classical concept of the firm as a bundle of exchange relations, as opposed to the Penrosian notion of the firm as a collection of human resources. Both neo-classical theory and GLEB perceived that senior mangement and productive resources are, first, controlled by capital (the owners in neo-classical and Marxian theory) and second, purchasable in the market. But as Penrose argued, human resources in a firm are developed over time by shared experiences and their productivity is firm-specific.

The fact that knowledge of a firm is embedded in the human resources that make up the firm limited the power of GLEB in two ways. First, it would take time for GLEB-appointed management to become effective within a firm. Second, GLEB became dependent upon existing management because the loss of such resources could destroy such knowledge. GLEB found itself dependent upon existing managers, just as managers were dependent upon existing workers. These resources were not replaceable in the marketplace without a considerable drop in productive capability.

The image of the firm as a bundle of exchange relations also underlay GLEB's approach to enterprise planning. The presumption was that this could be enforced by contract. The possibility that the very enforcement of the contract could undermine the trust required for co-operation and enterprise success was ignored. Although the acceptance of the principle of enterprise planning was written into the articles of association of every GLEB contract, the planning agreements were rarely drawn up with the participation of the workforce and when they were they were not often followed.

Enterprise planning agreements were opposed even by managers who saw their work-force as their company's most valuable asset and worker involvement in decision-making as conducive to competitiveness. Some within GLEB interpreted this as evidence that capitalism could not be reformed; others saw the formal agreements as ineffective against managers, who signed them but ignored them in practice, insulting to managers who practised progressive industrial relations as a matter of principle, and redundant to managers who understood the principles of flexible specialisation. Too often the potential for GLEB to act as an intellectual midwife for the reorganisation of work required for the transition from Taylorist to flexible specialisation production methods was lost in an environment dominated by debate over legal agreements and suspicions of hidden motives.

Sector Strategy and Consensus

The idea of a sector strategy rested on the notion of a consensus, but the firm-led approach was predicated on confidentiality. The delicate financial relations between firms and their banks and suppliers are easily upset, with potentially devastating consequences for a firm. Every firm is hesitant to subject these issues to public debate, but no investment in a company can be made without a thorough considera- tion of such matters. Thus the confidentiality that management de- manded if it were to participate in discussions about financial restructuring was antithetical to the dialogue that was required for developing a sector strategy. The compromise resulted in a closed dialogue in which confidentiality won out and financial matters domi- nated production matters.

Secrecy was also built into GLEB's top-down conception of sector restructuring. The assumption was that sector restructuring required strong-man leadership. J.P. Morgan and Henry Ford cast long sha- dows. The alternative notion of sector restructuring as an ongoing process promulgated by inter-firm co-operation was not seriously con- sidered. It was simply assumed that a strong man in a key firm was required with the willingness and capacity to make tough decisions about which firms would win and which would lose in the restructur- ing process. The J.P. Morgan approach, above all, demanded secrecy, and lent itself to covert politicisation. The market, when competition does prevail, does not offer the same opportunity for bureaucratic manipulation.

Administrative Guidance and Institutional Focus

GLEB did not specialise and build an organisation with conceptual focus. Instead it attempted to be a bank, management consultancy, rescue and turnaround agency, property manager, and technology- transfer institution. There are no models of institutions, public or private, that internalise such a broad range of activities. GLEB did not pursue what is essential to any organisation and what it advised its clients: focus. Consequently, GLEB lacked clarity as to mission, and members worked at cross-purposes.

Cross-purposes turned into crossfire for GLEB-appointed board

members of client firms. From within GLEB came pressure to achieve
by imposition the wide-ranging social goals that single-issue factions
deemed paramount. The implicit notion was that firms are planned,
therefore control of the firm could give senior management, which now
included a GLEB official, the power to direct organisational practices at
will. At the same time GLEB board appointees were working alongside
management of the firms who saw themselves as caught between
survival in a marketplace increasingly dominated by better-organised
foreign firms and a band of social reformers seeking to establish a
work-place utopia from the security of government offices.

In practice, the firm-led sector strategy approach simply gave way to
a firm-led approach and the sector strategy dimension withered away.
This was for many reasons. Some GLEB divisions rejected the sector
strategy as being too ambitious and others as diverting attention from
the social goals of GLEB. But perhaps the biggest reason was the
diversion of GLEB personnel into the operational activities of firms. A
failing firm, in particular, consumed inordinate amounts of GLEB's
staff resources and left little time for strategic concerns. The concept of
sector strategy itself was abandoned when the Greater London Council
was abolished and GLEB was taken over by the boroughs.

Many lessons can be drawn from the GLEB experience. First, as
noted, a firm-led sector strategy approach will likely turn away from a
sector strategy orientation. This is for the reasons given above, particularly the inconsistency between the confidentiality demanded in investment decisions and the openness required to achieve the consensus
upon which a sector strategy depends. For inter-firm co-operation and
a sector infrastructure depend upon a capacity for shaping consensus.
Thus successful industrial policy efforts elsewhere have separated the
sector strategy and sector infrastructure institutions from the financial
institutions. The two functions demand different organisational styles
and, if mixed, the financial demands for confidentiality will undermine
the openness required to develop co-operation amongst firms.

Second, the firm-led sector strategy approach was based on the
presumption that state control could force enterprises to adjust to
GLEB-imposed goals. The lesson of GLEB, like MITI before it, is that
industrial policy based upon administrative guidance is superior to
industrial policy based on either state control or private control. Administrative guidance or planning through the market means forging a
sector strategy by ongoing deliberation, formally or informally, amongst
actors in the sector. It cannot be imposed by right of ownership or
contract alone.

Third, the purpose of an enterprise board should not be to fill a
finance gap. It is rather to promote the competitiveness of firms producing tradables. Unintentionally, GLEB slipped into the role of a
lender of last resort and, in the process, played only a limited restruc-

turing role. Unintentionally, it became overwhelmed by efforts to save client firms to the neglect of promoting the adoption of new principles of production organisation which involves changing relations between worker and manager, worker and machine, and between firm and firm. These notions cannot be imposed by ownership, either within or outside the firm. They must be negotiated and, ultimately, seen as in the interests of the managers and workers themselves or they will not be pursued. One can argue that they are in the long run interests of both groups, but if managers do not want to adapt to the new principles of production then GLEB cannot have impact on the industry with or without financial investments.

The implication is that an effective industrial policy, like modern production itself, depends upon flexible specialisation. Enterprise boards should specialise in developing sector strategies and promoting sector infrastructures; financial institutions should specialise in the provision of finance. But rather than locating both activities, and others as well, in one organisation, they should be in separate networked organisations. This is not to say that public sector venture-capital funds will inevitably fail, but that success will be greatly enhanced if such agencies can draw upon sector infrastructural institutions that provide an independent basis for forging a sector strategy and evaluating individual business plans.

Finally, these criticisms are easy in hindsight. GLEB faced severe challenges. It did not have the luxury of development-finance institutions with which it could co-ordinate efforts. And, given the practical realities of rapidly disappearing sectors, it had little choice but to invest in firms in order to maintain the presence of a critical mass of enterprises to build a sector strategy. GLC (1985) documents the decimation of large portions of London's manufacturing base. In many cases, one could argue that GLEB did not have the luxury of developing a sector infrastructure. There would have been no enterprises left to use it.

References

Best, M. (1984), 'Strategic planning and industrial renewal: principles to guide the Greater London Enterprise Board's selection of sectors and firms', Greater London Enterprise Board, mimeo

Brusco, S. and E. Righi (1985), Local government, industrial policy and social consensus in the experience of Modena (Italy), mimeo

Centro Studi Industria Leggera (1986), *L'industria del legno e del mobile*, Milan: CSIL, September–October

Coase, R. (1937), 'The Nature of the Firm', *Economica*, n.s. no. 4

Economists Advisory Group (1983), Cooperative Marketing and Joint Trading for Small Firms, London: EAG

Elbaum, B. and W. Lazonick eds (1986), *The Decline of the British Economy*, Oxford University Press

Greater London Council, Economic Policy Group (1983), *Small Firms and the London Industrial Strategy*, London

Greater London Council (1985), *The London Industrial Strategy*

Greater London Enterprise Board (1985), *Annual Report and Accounts*, London

Greater London Enterprise Board (1985–6), *Corporate Plan*, London

Haas, D. (n d (a)), 'Basic Principles of Corporate Performance', Pfalzgrafen-weiler, West Germany, Gerhard Schüler Consultancy

Haas, D. (n d (b)), 'Replanning Furniture Production', reprint from *Cabinet Maker and Retailer Furnisher*, Oxted, Surrey

Johnson, C. (1982), *MITI and the Japanese Miracle*, Stanford, CA: Stanford University Press

Ken-ichi, I., N. Ikujiro and T. Hirotaka (1985), 'Managing the New Product Development Process', in K. Clark, R. Háyes and C. Lorenz *The Uneasy Alliance*, Boston: Harvard Business School Press

Keynote (1984), *Furniture Sector Overview*, London: Keynote

Magaziner, I. and T. Hout (1980), *Japanese Industrial Policy*, London: Policy Studies Institute

Oliver, M. (1982), *Company Law*, 9th ed. London: MacDonald and Evans

Penrose, E. (1959), *The Theory of the Growth of the Firm*, Oxford: Basil Blackwell

Piore, M. and C. Sabel (1984), *The Second Industrial Divide*, New York: Basic Books

Richardson, G. (1972), 'The Organization of Industry', *The Economic Journal*, September

Silvestrelli, S. (1985), 'Progresso technico e rapporti tra imprese nel settore del mobile in Italia e nelle Marche', *Economia Marche*, June

8 Sector Strategy in the West Midlands

David Elliott and Michael Marshall

Introduction

During the five years to March 1986 the West Midlands County Council developed and implemented a wide-ranging economic strategy aimed at regenerating industry, employment and living standards in the West Midlands conurbation. The centrepiece of this strategy was the West Midlands Enterprise Board (WMEB), established by the County Council in 1982 as a source of development capital for investment in the local manufacturing sector. With the support of the West Midlands metropolitan district councils, the WMEB continued after the abolition of the County Council in 1986 and took on a wider range of economic development functions enabling it to fulfil the role of a strategic, conurbation-wide agency for economic regeneration.

One of the distinctive characteristics of the County Council and WMEB's economic intervention was, and remains, its reliance on a sector-based industrial strategy (Elliott 1986). This sector strategy was developed as an alternative not only to the Conservative government's anti-interventionist stance towards industrial policy but also to the attempts at sectoral intervention pursued by past Labour governments. In this sense, the West Midlands experience discussed in this chapter represents a radical departure from previous approaches at national level.

There is nothing new *per se* in sector strategies as part of a national industrial policy. However, the idea that industrial and economic intervention in the economy should be based on sectoral, as distinct from but complementary to enterprise- or company-based, strategies has had a far from distinguished history. The West Midlands' experience indicates that a large part of the explanation for past failures lies in the simplistic and generalised approaches adopted rather than deficiencies in the underlying concepts. This over-simplification in turn partly reflects a reluctance or inability to acknowledge the differences in structure and culture between industrial sectors as well as the complexities of relationships within and between sectors. The National

Plan of 1965 is judged to have failed because the sectoral targets were unrealistic and those companies and workers who were set the task of achieving them had not been involved in determining, and consequently had no commitment to, the Plan's objectives. Sectoral intervention by the 1974–9 Labour government through the National Enterprise Board and Sector Working Parties failed because of the absence of any overall strategy across sectors and the predictable failure of tripartite committees to agree on development strategies for sectors as a whole (Elliott 1984). Both attempts at sectoral planning were, in any case, abandoned in the face of adverse macro-economic circumstances.

While it is not the purpose of this chapter to explore the lessons of previous sectoral strategies at national level, it is important to introduce the context in which sectoral strategies have been more recently tried at regional and, increasingly, local levels. The WMEB has gained widespread recognition for the implementation of its approach to sector strategy and for the lessons the West Midlands' experience might yield for other regions and localities as well as national government. This chapter discusses the origins, principles and practice of the WMEB's sector strategy and its underlying rationale.

Industrial Change in the West Midlands Economy

The County Council's sector strategy originated and evolved against the backcloth of an unprecedented downturn in the fortunes of West Midlands industry (Spencer *et al.* 1986). The West Midlands conurbation of Birmingham, Coventry and the Black Country is the largest concentration of manufacturing industry and employment in the United Kingdom. As such, the West Midlands has suffered heavily from the contraction of these industries over the past decade. At the height of the recession and its aftermath between 1979 and 1984 an estimated one-third of the county's manufacturing employment disappeared, involving 225,000 job losses and a trebling of the local unemployment rate, as illustrated by Figure 8.1.

Although the slow stagnation of West Midlands manufacturing had been apparent since at least the mid-1960s and had intensified sharply during the 1974–5 recession, the dramatic downturn in the region's industrial performance after 1979 came as a major shock to a region which was still widely regarded as the prosperous heartland of British industry. The present-day industrial structure of the West Midlands is the product of successive historical waves of economic change and adaptation (Marshall 1987, p. 115). From the late eighteenth century the regional economy was founded on its basic industries of coal, iron, steel and metal working trades. Following the Great Depression of the late nineteenth century, these industries developed into the familiar

Figure 8.1. Unemployment rates in the West Midlands and UK

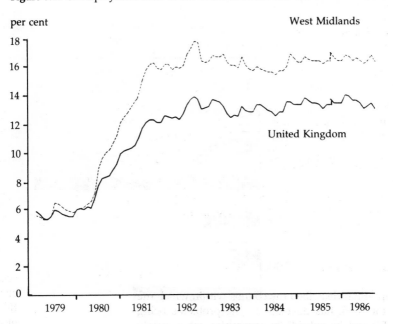

Source: West Midlands Districts Joint Planning and Transportation Data Team.

modern engineering industries, notably motor vehicles, cycles, aircraft and machine-tools which were founded upon the old-established metalworking skills.

The rapid growth and dynamism of the West Midlands economy during this period rested upon the wide diversity of craft skills and the predominance of small-scale, workshop production. This dynamism shielded the region from the worst effects of the inter-war depression and continued into the post-war period when the region reinforced its position as the UK's foremost manufacturing centre. During the economic cycles of the 1950s and early 1960s West Midlands industries suffered less acutely during the downturns and were the first to emerge from each trough, leading the rest of the country.

From the mid-1960s, however, the former dynamism of the West Midlands began to give way to stagnation as the region's key sectors, in common with most of British manufacturing, failed to match the levels of investment and productivity achieved by their major international competitors. West Midlands manufacturing entered the 1970s in a poor position to withstand the economic shocks of the decade. By its conclusion, successive recessions and intensified competition had combined

Figure 8.2. Employment structure of the West Midlands and the UK, 1981

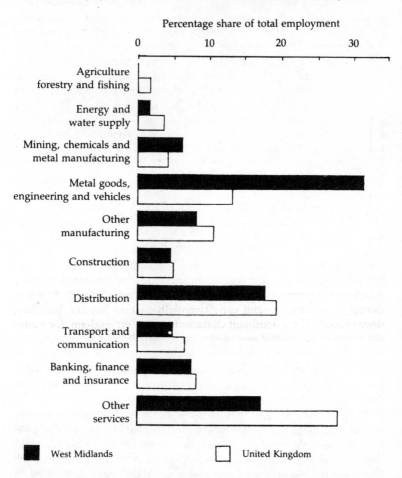

Source: Census of Employment.

to bring about the imminent collapse of the region's industrial base.

At the time the Labour Party took control of the West Midlands County Council in 1981, manufacturing accounted for 43 per cent of employment in the conurbation compared to 28 per cent for the UK as a whole. Within the County's manufacturing sector, some 67 per cent of the work-force were employed in four key industries: motor vehicles, mechanical engineering, metal manufacture and metal goods (see Figure 8.2). These industries fall into large-scale, mass production activities, notably motor vehicles, and smaller-scale, often craft-based activities, such as lock and key manufacture. The industries which characterise the present-day West Midlands industrial structure have not developed in isolation from each other. They are dynamically interlinked within the production process as the output of one producer becomes the component for a further process or assembly by another. Their fortunes are also closely related through the extent to which they draw upon a skilled and experienced pool of labour. Vehicle manufacture and assembly, for example, is supported by an industrial sub-structure of foundries, pressing and machining shops, electrical and electronic sub-assembly, tyres, windscreens, trim, upholstery, and so on, which employs far more people than the vehicle industry itself. It was estimated in 1984 that 60,000 jobs in the West Midlands motor vehicles sector were directly dependent upon the Rover Group which itself employed a further 17,600 in the area (Bessant *et al*. 1984).

This interdependent industrial structure is represented in a hierarchy of customer–supplier linkages focusing on a limited number of large firms. Irrespective of plant size and economies of scale in production, there has been an accelerating trend throughout the century towards concentration of ownership in multinational enterprises. By the late-1970s, the jungle of small traders and independent manufacturers, which was a prominent feature of much of West Midlands industry during its nineteenth- and early twentieth-century heyday, had long since ceased to be a dominant characteristic. In Birmingham, for example, some 43 per cent of manufacturing employment was accounted for by ten companies in thirty plants. In 1977, ten major multinationals (GEC, Lucas, GKN, Tube Investments, Glynwed, Dunlop, BSR, Cadbury, Delta and IMI) employed an estimated 27 per cent of their combined British work-force of 507,000 in the West Midlands. From the mid-1970s, many of these companies were faced with market decline, overcapacity and falling profitability, and began to rationalise and restructure their activities (Gaffikin and Nickson 1984). In many cases this involved disruption of their links with the region's traditional industries in their search for new markets outside the West Midlands. Between 1978 and 1982 the British work-force of these ten companies fell by 30 per cent, many of these job losses taking place in the West Midlands.

The corporate strategies pursued by these and other major manufacturers, particularly British Leyland, have had serious effects on the West Midlands' base of component, materials and equipment producers, many of whom saw their traditional markets collapse practically overnight during the 1979–81 recession. The knock-on effects of the recession in demand for industrial equipment are well illustrated by the experience of the West Midlands machine-tool industry. In 1980 this industry employed over 10,000 workers in the West Midlands. By 1983 the work-force had slumped by 67 per cent with what remained of the sector increasingly foreign-owned, especially by American multinationals (West Midlands County Council Economic Development Unit 1983).

Since 1979 the West Midlands has been trapped in a downward economic spiral as its former strengths in interlinked, diverse metal-based manufacturing have become structural weaknesses. During the early 1980s a sequence of redundancies and plant closures followed one another with the predictability of a line of dominoes while unemployment in the county climbed from 6 per cent in 1979 to 16 per cent by 1986. Over half the region's 340,000 jobless have been out of work for over a year. Average wages for male manual workers in the West Midlands fell from top of the ten-region pay hierarchy in 1972 to eighth a decade later, while it has been estimated that one in three households in this once prosperous area now live on poverty incomes no more than 40 per cent above supplementary benefit level (West Midlands Enterprise Board, 1986a).

Underlying these trends is a history of underinvestment, technological backwardness and a collapse in skill training. Latest figures for 1983 show that capital expenditure per employee in West Midlands manufacturing was a mere £946, the lowest for all regions of the UK and 21 per cent below the national average. Significantly, a survey of the country's top thirty-one pension funds in 1983 found that most considered the West Midlands a poor investment prospect and many were considering withdrawing from the area altogether (Debenham, Tewson and Chinnocks 1983). Underinvestment in new capital equipment has been accompanied by the collapse of investment in the skilled work-force which has traditionally been one of the West Midlands' strongest economic assets. The number of engineering apprenticeships in the region fell by 69 per cent between 1978 and 1985, during which time thirty major regional skill training centres closed. Underinvestment in research and development, new equipment and skills has been reflected in the West Midlands' poor rate of adoption of new product and process technologies. The number of new product innovations per employee in West Midlands manufacturing during the 1960s and 1970s was only one-third of that in the South-East (Oakey *et al.* 1980). On the process side, a survey in 1983 found that over 30 per cent of machine-tools in West Midlands industry were over 35 years old and only 1 per cent were modern numerically controlled models (Metal Working Production 1983). Another recent survey of West Midlands engineering plants revealed that the introduction of computer-aided design was often rejected by manufacturers because of the absence of suitably skilled personnel (Armstrong and Lewis 1986).

It is against this background of long-term industrial restructuring and decline that the impact of past government policies on the region should be considered. It is clear that public policies have failed adequately to respond to the West Midlands' needs and may even have exaccerbated the region's economic problems (Marshall and Mawson 1987). Although the Conservative governments since 1979 have taken a number of limited measures to support West Midlands industry, most notably the award of Intermediate Assisted Area status in 1984, these steps were taken against a backcloth of macro-economic polices which have had damaging consequences for manufacturing in the UK in general and in the West Midlands in particular. The abolition of exchange controls in 1979 facilitated the ability of West Midlands-based multinationals to transfer investment overseas. Rationalisation and closures in the nationalised industries, such as steel, have directly contributed to job losses. At the same time, tight monetary restraint, together with relatively high exchange and interest rates, have constrained West Midlands exporters, encouraged import penetration and inhibited the long-term investment required to rebuild the region's manufacturing base.

It would be mistaken, however, to lay all blame for the West Midlands' economic malaise on the Conservative government. It is clear that past attempts by the 1964–70 and 1974–9 Labour governments to intervene in the restructuring of major West Midlands companies and sectors, initially via the Industrial Reorganisation Corporation (IRC) and later through the National Enterprise Board (NEB) and Sector Working Parties, had mixed consequences for the region. Thus whatever its effects on the subsequent performance of the company, the restructuring of British Leyland was pursued with scant regard for the interlinked component, materials and equipment sectors which were left to 'sink or swim'.

In broad outline, these are the structure and problems of the West Midlands economy which the sector strategy discussed in the remainder of this chapter is intended to confront. It would be misleading, however, to leave the impression that all is doom and gloom. While the overall picture is one of crisis and decay, this pattern is far from evenly represented within and between industrial sectors. For example, while the machine-tool industry as a whole has suffered a disastrous decline, the past five years have seen the emergence of a new robotic equipment sub-sector. The decline of the region's traditional metal-based industries has been accompanied by the rapid growth of the clothing sector. Although manufacturing in the West Midlands has clearly been through and is still experiencing traumatic times, it remains the dominant feature of the regional economic, industrial and social landscape. The development of new industries and growth of services may play a role in the future of the regional economy, but they will in many cases be closely related to the fortunes of manufacturing industry and their impact will be relatively marginal (West Midlands Enterprise Board 1987). Analysis of prospects for the West Midlands' future economic development points to no realistic alternative other than to retain and build upon the region's existing manufacturing base.

Principles for Intervention

The preceeding overview of changes in the West Midlands economy provides the context in which the West Midlands County Council's Economic Development Committee (EDC) and the WMEB developed their approach to industrial intervention. Before proceeding to examine their record of intervention in detail, it is necessary briefly to describe the political and organisational features of policy development in the West Midlands in order to provide an appreciation of the principles on which intervention has been based and sector strategy developed.

For some of the reasons alluded to in the introduction to this chapter, 1979 was a watershed in socialist thinking on industrial policy and intervention in general and sector strategy in particular. The election of a Conservative government committed to an anti-interventionist economic programme, coupled with dissatisfaction over the past record of Labour governments in office, prompted a reassessment of socialist models for industrial strategy and intervention. In these circumstances, it is not surprising that the more original and innovative thinking on the policy and practice of industrial intervention over the next seven years should take place at local and regional levels of the Labour Party and government.

Labour took control of the West Midlands County Council in May 1981 with a manifesto commitment to embark on a radical economic development strategy. The essential elements of this strategy had been mapped out by various individuals and working parties grouped loosely around the West Midlands Labour Party and the Conference of Socialist Planners. Several of those involved had broader national policy interests and were later to play a prominent role in the implementation of the strategy, not least Geoff Edge who became chair of the County Council's newly-created EDC and, subsequently, the WMEB. It would be easy to overstate the continuity through all stages from ideas to policies to practice, but it would be equally misleading to underestimate the importance of this long-term process in building a collective commitment to the tasks ahead.

Following the county elections, the new economic strategy was given its first fully articulated public presentation in the chairman's statement to the EDC in November 1981 on *Policies and Priorities for Economic Development in the West Midlands* (Edge 1981). This set out the basis for a new approach to the development of local economic policies and initiatives. The central element of this programme was an explicit industrial strategy whose first priority was to revive investment and employment in West Midlands manufacturing while making all public investment accountable to those who lived and worked in the area. The principal agency for accomplishing this was to be the West Midlands Enterprise Board. The industrial strategy was to be paralleled by a community strategy designed to improve the economic circumstances of the unemployed and disadvantaged groups through training projects, support for worker co-operatives, welfare rights campaigns and work with the voluntary sector, drawing in particular on resources from the Urban Programme for inner city projects.

The WMEB was established in February 1982 as a source of investment capital for indigenous manufacturing firms with over 100 employees, although this size requirement was later reduced to fifty. Investment was provided in the form of equity stakes and long-term loans, replacing the practice of providing grant aid to industry. By March 1986 the WMEB had approved investments totalling £14.2 million in thirty-nine companies with a combined work-force of around 5,000.

The WMEB was always conceived as one element within a much broader economic strategy and the abolition of the County Council in March 1986 and subsequent transfer of control to the seven metropolitan district councils enabled it to adopt a wider role in regenerating the West Midlands economy. This enlarged role involved the establishment of four subsidiary companies: West Midlands Technology Transfer Ltd; West Midlands (Tyseley) Training Ltd; West Midlands Cooperative Finance Ltd; and West Midlands Clothing Resource Centre Ltd which was a specific sectoral initiative set up as part of a broader strategy for the clothing sector. Together with the WMEB's existing investment activities and the formation of an enhanced research, analysis and policy function, it was now possible for the WMEB to provide a comprehensive economic development service for the West Midlands under local democratic control.

The WMEB's future development was to be guided by seven principles for economic regeneration which reaffirmed and extended the approach pioneered by the County Council since 1981. These principles were set out by the chairman of the WMEB in January 1986, announcing the enhanced future role for the WMEB in the face of the County Council's imminent abolition (Edge 1986). These were:

1. The future prosperity of the West Midlands lies in the survival and strengthening of its indigenous industries.
2. There is an urgent need to increase the flow of long-term investment funds into the West Midlands.
3. There is a need to ensure public accountability and a commensurate return on investment where public funds are used to support private industrial and commercial activity.
4. There is a need to invest in human skills as well as industrial and economic infrastructure.

5. There are within the community a whole series of energies and talents which may be mobilised to create employment opportunities.

6. Poverty is an integral part of the West Midlands' economic problems and direct measures are needed to reduce it.

7. Positive steps should be taken to redress inequalities by promoting equal opportunities for women, ethnic minorities, disabled people and other disadvantaged groups throughout the full range of policies and initiatives.

These seven principles were designed to guide the WMEB and its subsidiary companies in implementing an overall economic strategy. Implementation was to be through a combination of: *intervention* using existing, if limited, resources; *research and analysis* in order further to investigate economic problems and polices as a guide to intervention; and *advocacy* on the basis of past successes in intervention and the extent to which research and analysis showed this intervention to be generalisable or complementary to the activities of other economic agents and agencies.

The Objectives and Practice of Industrial Sector Work

The first half of this chapter has described the context within which the WMEB's industrial sector work has developed. The problems being addressed by the WMEB and its subsidiary companies are precisely those which emerge from an analysis of industrial restructuring and decline in West Midlands manufacturing industry. Underinvestment is being tackled; outdated technologies in products and processes are being upgraded; the work-force is being trained and retrained with new skills; and the industrial infrastructure of one industry — clothing — is being enhanced.

The direct impact of these initiatives is, of course, quite limited. However, the WMEB's sector work has played an important role in maximising their impact in three ways. Sector work has guided the choice of priorities for deployment of limited resources. It has highlighted the extent to which specific interventions are generalisable, indicating the scope for further action by other agencies. Last, but not least, it has provided a mechanism for co-ordinating the range of interventions to focus on key problems of the core industries.

The original objectives for the County Council and WMEB's sector work were set out in a report approved by the EDC in September 1982. These were: to contribute to a broad analysis of the West Midlands economy which will provide a rationale for EDC policy and initiatives; to identify areas where EDC intervention is required and likely to be effective; to form the basis for advocacy of policy change towards the region by central government and related agencies; and to provide a context for WMEB investment decisions. These objectives have remained unaltered and the WMEB has continued to apply them subsequent to the abolition of the County Council. As the work has developed, however, increasing emphasis has been placed on dissemination of research findings, on translation of analysis into implementation of initiatives, and on extending the coverage of research in terms of both depth and range.

The pursuit of each of the above four objectives is best illustrated by examples. It should be stressed, however, that all four objectives have been pursued simultaneously wherever possible, depending upon the nature of the objective, the character of the particular sector, the availability of resources, and the extent to which it is possible to influence external agencies.

Policy Research and Analysis

In contributing to a broad analysis of the West Midlands economy and providing a rationale for policies and interventions, it is important to recognise that industrial sector work provides only one dimension, albeit the most important, of the WMEB's research and analysis programmes (West Midlands County Council Economic Development Unit 1986). The WMEB also undertakes extensive analysis of macroeconomic trends in the economy and their impact on the West Midlands, most notably using forecasts based on the Cambridge Econometrics national model (Marshall 1986) and a regional occupation-by-industry matrix developed by the Institute for Employment Research at Warwick University. In both cases, sector work has informed trend prediction of employment and occupational categories and has fed into separate but related research on industrial land-use planning and future skill requirements. At the micro-economic level, analysis has been regularly undertaken of particular West Midlands firms, providing a strategic and sectoral context for WMEB investments.

The WMEB's main programme of sectoral and sub-sectoral research lies between and links these macro and micro levels of economic analysis. To date the WMEB and the former County Council have published twenty-four major sector reports. Most of this work has been commissioned externally, drawing on outside expertise on the industry concerned. Externally commissioned studies are, however, treated as consultation documents and not as WMEB policy statements. While outside researchers are encouraged to make recommendations on policy and initiatives, the final recommendations and follow-up work take account not just of the research itself but also of internal accumulated evidence and the consultation process.

Identification of Target Sectors for Intervention

The role of the WMEB's sector strategy in identifying sectors where intervention is required and likely to be most effective is best illustrated by initiatives towards the clothing industry. A report on the clothing industry in the West Midlands was commissioned in Autumn 1983 when qualitative observation and research by other bodies suggested that the sector was of growing importance in both relative and absolute terms (Leigh and North 1983). The most rapidly growing sub-sector consisted of predominantly Asian-owned firms in the West Midlands' inner-urban areas. This sub-sector had experienced rapid growth largely due to low entry costs and the existence of a large pool of cheap female labour within the Asian community. The research study indicated that there were about 500 firms in the County area employing around 20,000 workers, substantially more than indicated by official statistics, with many of the newer entrants to the sector characterised by poor managerial experience, archaic production techniques, poor working conditions and a low-paid, non-unionised Asian female workforce. On the basis of this study, together with consultations with relevant bodies such as the Clothing Industries Training Board, Asian Traders' Association and the National Union of Tailoring and Garment Workers, it was resolved to pursue a number of policies and initiatives addressing a range of interrelated problems.

It was clear from the outset that any programme of intervention in the sector had to assist not only firms through investment, management advice and training provision but also labour by tackling low wages and poor conditions, especially among homeworkers, which are endemic to the industry. Initiatives were developed to address each of these problems. Direct investments were made by the WMEB in some of the larger, high-volume, established clothing firms. A business advice scheme aimed at ethnic minority businesses and a clothing design project were also initiated. Training courses for operatives, managers and senior technical staff were set up in collaboration with Handsworth Technical College, the Manpower Services Commission the Asian Traders' Association and the Federation of Clothing Designers and Executives. Measures to improve pay and conditions in the industry involved working with and through the West Midlands Low Pay Unit, a specific clothing action research project and a campaign on the issue of homeworking.

The tension implicit in a strategy which sought to strengthen the interests of both capital and labour was always accepted but it was also recognised that intervention which simply sought to strengthen one side of the industrial divide would ultimately destabilise the industry to the benefit of neither group. The overall aim was to upgrade the industry as a whole from a low-wage, low-investment and low-productivity sector to one where higher levels of investment and productivity could support improved wages and working conditions.⚹ The disparate range of initiatives listed above clearly could not achieve this in isolation. There was a need to ensure co-ordination and consolidation of the different initiatives as well as to build links with other local clothing initiatives being developed elsewhere in the country.

The West Midlands Clothing Resource Centre (WMCRC) was established in 1986 as a self-supporting subsidiary of the WMEB, providing a physical and organisational focus for initiatives towards the sector. In contrast to the Fashion Centres set up by several local authorities in other areas to address marketing deficiencies, the WMCRC was aimed directly at intervention in production. It houses computer-aided pattern laying and marking facilities to which local firms subscribe on a bureau basis as a means of improving production efficiency. Other types of business assistance, such as management and operative training, are built around this core activity. Links between the WMCRC and other local initiatives in the UK have been developed through the formation of a joint working and campaign group, Local Authority Action for Clothing and Textiles, which co-ordinates, supports and informs local authority initiatives while advocating national policies to provide targeted support for the clothing and textile industries, building on experience at local level.

Although the clothing industry provides the most fully developed example of sectoral intervention by the WMEB, there are others such as the audio-visual industries where research was used to clarify funding policies, to encourage organisations to form development plans in the overall sectoral context and to identify major new initiatives. Both the clothing and audio-visual industries are sectors where meaningful intervention is possible within the resource constraints of regional and local authorities. In other industries, including the key West Midlands vehicles and engineering sectors, local initiatives can only have a limited impact. More meaningful intervention would require policy change at national level and significantly enhanced regional resources. The WMEB has sought to address the problems of these industries through its advocacy work.

Advocacy

The WMEB's work on the motor vehicle and component industries exemplifies the importance of advocacy in regional and local sectoral intervention. Advocacy is most effective when based on detailed analysis of the structure and problems of an industry together with small-scale initiatives which demonstrate the forms of intervention required and maximise the use of available resources. The WMEB's analysis of issues facing the motor industry has been based upon a series of major research reports commissioned from outside industry experts combined with in-house monitoring of trends and development. The main form of direct intervention by the WMEB has been investment in seven component firms. Direct investment has been supplemented by training courses in electronics, robotics, pneumatics and hydraulics to equip engineers with the skills to deal with new technologies. The industry has been identified as a priority for both a strategic business consultancy scheme and the work of the WMEB subsidiary company, West Midlands Technology Transfer Ltd, based at Aston Science Park.

Drawing on research and analysis as well as this experience of intervention in the sector, the WMEB's advocacy work on the motor and components industries has been undertaken within a broader policy framework. This consists of a strategy for the sector consisting of the following five main elements: the need for an international perspective based on the strategies of multinational companies and the need for monitoring of their behaviour; the call for a strategy for the West Midlands and British motor vehicle and component industries based on a publicly owned motor vehicle manufacturer in the UK providing the full range of vehicles; the need to encourage greater co-operation between manufacturers and component suppliers, particularly on the design and development of new and existing vehicles; the need for national investment, training and technology policies for the industries which take full account of their importance to the West Midlands and British economies; and the need to support and build alliances with trade unions, employers, employers' organisations and other interested parties where they share similar policy perspectives to those set out above.

Advocacy work on the sector has taken a variety of forms. The most obvious are providing inputs to conferences and publishing and disseminating research findings in order gradually to build up the WMEB's credibility in offering an authoritative view on the sector and to secure an input for the WMEB to the development of present and future public policies. It has been recognised, however, that the WMEB's role can be more effective if it is joined by other organisations sharing similar perspectives towards the sector. For this reason the WMEB has embarked upon a longer-term campaign to build alliances with other local and regional authorities in the UK and Europe as well as with the trade union movement.

Two Birmingham conferences were organised in October 1985, bringing together, first British local authorities and trade unions and, secondly, British and European authorities. Both conferences led to the establishment of working groups which are presently aiming to convene recall conferences at the end of 1987. The British Motor Industry Local Authority Network (MILAN) is undertaking a programme of seminars, plant visits, industry research, area studies and information exchanges in preparation for the launch of a major policy report. The European working group is directing its energies towards influencing the EEC to improve co-ordination of its regional, social, economic and technological programmes in relation to the motor industry and the specific impact of these programmes on regions dominated by motor vehicle and component manufacture. The group is campaigning for a new form of special EEC programme of assistance to regions suffering employment decline due to technological change and restructuring in the industry. Both working groups aim to articulate a 'fourth interest' representing the views of regions and communities alongside those of management, trade unions and national governments. The WMEB played an active part in the formation of both groups and has taken a leading role in their development.

Alliances with employers and trade unions are more difficult to establish than with other local and regional authorities because the overlap of interests is not always as strong or as permanent and because the different representative organisational structures do not mesh so easily. Employers seldom share all elements of the WMEB's policy perspective as set out above. Alliances with this group therefore tend to be transitory and based around a single issue on which the company or companies' commercial interests coincide with the WMEB's strategic approach to the sector. Alliances with trade unions are less short-lived but inter-union differences and the problem of separating immediate industrial relations issues from a longer-term strategy for the vehicle and component industries require careful negotiation. In pursuing this alliance, the WMEB has devoted considerable time and resources to establishing a West Midlands Auto Industry Trade Union Forum which brings together senior trade union full-time and lay officials with local and regional authority representatives. This is a potentially powerful lobby group capable of minimising the divisions which have hitherto impeded a coherent and unified trade union and community view on the future of the sector.

Investment

One of the prime purposes of the WMEB and former County Council's programme of sector studies is to identify opportunities for WMEB investments. Sector studies on foundries, machine-tools, robotics, pumps and valves, locks and keys, and industrial fasteners have provided a contextual overview of the West Midlands industrial structure and sectoral interlinkages, highlighting areas where public intervention is most needed and can be most effective. For the purposes of evaluating particular company investment proposals, this broad research is supplemented by specific 'Sector Statements' which examine the company's performance and business strategy in the light of its products, production process, markets and competitive pressures.

The aim is to assess both the viability of the company's business plan and the potential strategic contribution of the investment to regional economic regeneration. The WMEB also undertakes a programme of 'Annual Sector Reviews' to monitor changes in economic, industrial and technological trends affecting companies in the WMEB's investment portfolio as well as to identify priorities for further investments and to indicate other ways in which the WMEB can influence the development of a sector, for example through the work of its training and technology transfer subsidiaries.

One of the eventual aims of the WMEB's investment policy is to have one or more investments in key sectors of the economy and to use these investments as the basis for guiding the future direction of the sector as a whole. The way in which this long-term objective relates to the Board's immediate work on investment and sectoral intervention is illustrated by the example of the foundry industry.

The foundry sector faces problems typical of many other West Midlands metal-based industries. Declining demand, overcapacity and a price squeeze are inhibiting profitability and preventing investment in the improved products and production techniques required by the sector to break out of the spiral of decline. In 1981 the West Midlands had 28 per cent of establishments and 37 per cent of employees in the foundry industry of the UK. The sector accounted for 8.8 per cent of all West Midlands manufacturing employment. Between 1978 and 1983, however, employment in West Midlands foundries declined by 52 per cent — but there was still an estimated 50 per cent overcapacity in the industry.

Successive governments have failed to address the fundamental problems of the industry. Non-selective foundry aid schemes, operated between 1975 and 1981, encouraged many firms to invest in new productive technologies and capacity, building up considerable debts at a time of high interest rates and market recession. Paradoxically, therefore, the most modern foundries have often been the most vulnerable to closure. Government-inspired rationalisation programmes, most notably in the steel castings sector , have been designed not to maintain the optimum capacity for future demand but to diminish capacity in the industry further.

This was the state of the industry when the WMEB was being established. It is not surprising, therefore, that four of the first six investments by the WMEB were in non-competing foundry companies. One of these investments failed within a matter of weeks but the other three continue. The sectoral evaluations of these companies, undertaken to guide the investment decisions, formed the basis for a broader report on the West Midlands foundry industry (West Midlands County Council Economic Development Unit 1982). Three hundred copies of this report were circulated to interested parties and a conference held in

May 1983. Arising from the conference, a joint export marketing scheme was established, bringing together two foundries and a machining company in a collaborative project to enter the American export market. Although the WMEB has since considered investments in a number of additional foundries, these have been rejected because they did not appear to have long-term viability or they would not be complementary to the Board's existing portfolio of investments in the sector. None the less, it is probable that the WMEB will undertake further investments in the industry and is currently preparing an updated foundries sector study.

The WMEB's involvement in the foundry industry exemplifies the way in which sector work provides a strategic context for investment. Detailed and authoritative analysis, liaison with interested parties during the course of the research, and subsequent collaboration with these parties in policy development and implementation provide a broad framework for investment in selected companies. A similar approach has been adopted for other sectors, notably robotics, and will be applied to further industries in the future.

In addition to providing a context for investments, sector work has attempted to investigate areas where investment enquiries from companies have *not* been forthcoming and to generate fresh proposals accordingly. This aim has been pursued through three studies grouped under the collective title of the WMEB's 'Pro-active Strategy'. The first study undertook an assessment of investment opportunities in fifty firms in traditional Black Country metal-based industries. In contrast, the second surveyed firms in less traditional activities with growth potential, covering scientific instruments, synthetic resins and plastics, and radio and electronic components. The third study investigated the reasons why relatively few investment enquiries had been received from the Coventry area. The studies are labelled 'pro-active' because they not only reveal a clearer picture of potential WMEB investee firms but also provide a marketing exercise which helps to clarify firms' perception of the WMEB and generate enquiries. The company orientation of these studies complements the more aggregated work at the sectoral level.

The Underlying Rationale for a Sector Approach

Having examined the principles and practice of the sector approach to industrial intervention in the West Midlands, we now go on to discuss the broader characteristics of sector strategy and the reasons why this approach has been adopted by the WMEB in preference to other models for economic intervention. The sector approach is founded on an appreciation of the dynamic interlinkages between firms and industries, sectors being constituted as groups of firms with common inputs, outputs or productive technologies. However, this definition of the term 'sector' is not without complications.

Not all inputs lead to the same outputs while similar outputs may involve different inputs or process technologies. Steel, for example, has multiple end-uses while car window seals can be manufactured from rubber or plastic. Despite these complications, there are generally sufficient commonalities in the competitive environment of a group of firms to permit an explanatory contextual assessment. These commonalities may not, however, coincide with standard industrial classifications for statistical purposes and sectoral assessments must therefore involve both qualitative and quantitative investigations.

A further complication is that plants or establishments and company structures are far from simple and there is not always a direct connection between the production unit and the decision-making focus within a firm. There is no simple way of overcoming this complication but awareness of it is crucial to explaining the dynamics and prospects for sectors and the companies or establishments within them. Notwithstanding these complications, the key characteristic of the sector approach is that sectors are conceptualised as embodying economic relationships which extend beyond the performance of individual enterprises or industries and which transcend geographic boundaries.

A second term which requires some clarification is the often used and much abused word 'strategic'. At its simplest, this label signifies the opposite of 'piecemeal'. A strategic approach to sectoral intervention implies taking into account the rationale for, and combined effect of, a range of interventions. The analysis addresses a set of interrelated problems within and across sectors. 'Strategic', in this sense, does not prescribe that intervention must be founded upon and preceeded by a comprehensive sectoral analysis. Rather, intervention and analysis should proceed simultaneously, the one guiding and informing the other via an iterative process of research, intervention and evaluation within overall policy parameters. It is in this sense that the sector approach to analysis and intervention in the West Midlands is seen as strategic.

In addition to this strategic character, the sector approach has the advantage of *coherence* since it offers the potential for assessing the impact of a combination of co-ordinated policy instruments in related fields such as investment, training and technology transfer. It also provides a basis for *consensus* both on the nature of the problems to be addressed and on the action stemming from that analysis. It is because sectors have real meanings for workers and trade unionists, managers and employers' organisations, training boards and governments that it is possible to mobilise these interests around common policies and projects, as illustrated above by the examples of WMEB work in the clothing, motor vehicle and foundry sectors. In each case the degree of consensus within the sector was limited or latent and was only gradually mobilised as research and intervention developed in tandem.

A final, essentially pragmatic reason for adopting a sector approach to industrial research and intervention is that it offers the most sound basis for consistent *analysis*. Standard statistical data are usually classified on a sector basis. This therefore provides the starting point for industrial analysis. While any classification system is arbitrary to some degree, the limitations of sectoral classification are mitigated by other analytical factors in the WMEB's selection of sectors for investigation. The point has already been made that companies do not always fit easily within a single sector. Moreover, an analysis of each sector individually would not yield an explanation of the workings of the economy as a whole. Hence, the objective of the WMEB's sector research is not to provide comprehensive coverage but incrementally to develop a dynamic picture of interlinkages within the regional economy. Some industries, notably motor vehicles, machine-tools and foundries, have been identified as of crucial strategic significance to the West Midlands economy, not only because of their importance in their own right but also because of the interrelationships between them. Other industrial activities, defined as 'sectors' for the WMEB's purposes, have been prioritised for attention due to their strategic significance to manufacturing as a whole. Robotics and advanced manufacturing technology, for example, have been the subject of several major studies in a five-year programme of research and intervention.

In summary, the sector approach has been adopted as a model for industrial research and intervention in the West Midlands because it is strategic and coherent, provides a basis for building consensus, and is analytically pragmatic. These strengths are illustrated below through the examples of ways in which the sector approach has been applied to an analysis of the case for investing in indigenous industry, rather than promoting inward investment, and to intervention via technology-based initiatives. These two illustrations share a common theme, namely that interventions which address generalised problems such as low investment levels or technological backwardness need to be located in specific industrial contexts. This requires that the generalised problem is confronted in ways which relate to other aspects of firms' behaviour within their particular industrial environment. This is best achieved through a sector approach.

Indigenous Versus Inward Investment

We have described above how the WMEB prioritises investment in indigenous manufacturing industry. The sector approach sets the context for WMEB investments by influencing the investment process prior to, during and after the decision to proceed with an investment. Industry studies and the WMEB's Pro-active Strategy exert an influence on the types of enquiry received from firms seeking investment capital. Partly as a result of these investigations, the WMEB's investment portfolio more or less reflects the sectoral composition of West Midlands manufacturing industry. Sector Statements on specific companies at the time of the investment decision do not make explicit recommendations on whether an investment should or should not proceed. They do, however, complement and inform the financial appraisal of the company and introduce wider economic, social and strategic considerations into the decision-making process. The WMEB's ongoing programme of sector reviews, which monitor sectoral trends affecting companies in its portfolio, provide a sectoral framework for the future strategies of investee firms and for extending its investment coverage. This, in summary, is how the WMEB's sector work relates to investment in indigenous industry. Less obvious, however, is the way in which the sector approach has determined the very low priority attached to attracting inward investment to the region.

The underlying objectives of encouraging inward investment are to substitute domestic production for imports, increase employment and improve the economy's technological infrastructure. This implies that inward investment is not desirable where job displacement effects would exceed the potential employment gains, taking into account technological improvements in competitiveness. From the multinational company's viewpoint, the decision to invest abroad is clearly motivated by a desire to extend and increase its market. The form the investment takes will depend to a large extent on the technology involved with a wide range of options including licensing agreements, collaborative ventures, takeovers, assembly operations or full manufacture. In order to exploit a technological advantage and increase its market it is a necessary, if not sufficient, condition for the company to enjoy a monopolistic or oligopolistic position. This stems from the fact that the company faces additional costs in establishing production in a new geographic area due to relatively poor knowledge of the economic infrastructure, suppliers, skills, local markets, communications, language and culture relative to indigenous competitors. The monopolistic advantages such companies must possess include capital resources, technology, marketing, management, economies of scale and political bargaining power. It is because of these relative advantages that inward investment poses a threat to indigenous manufacturing industry.

Inward investment is most likely in those sectors where multinational companies are dominant, markets are international, and the major companies have a technological lead. The decline of the West Midlands machine-tool industry provides a perfect example of these factors. Over the past few years, restructuring in the sector has led to increasing ownership by Japanese and American multinationals. What remains of the indigenously owned sector has become increasingly dependent on foreign technology through licensing of products in the expanding markets for computer numerically-controlled lathes and machining centres.

Having identified those sectors in which inward investment is most likely, the next stage in the analysis is to establish the sectors where it is most desirable. Even where inward investment may appear to benefit the indigenous industrial structure, however, the actual benefits will be contingent upon the form of the investment and the conditions under which it takes place. There are two main circumstances under which inward investment would appear to be desirable.

The first is in those sectors which do not presently have any indigenous representation. The problem here is that there is no supporting infrastructure of suppliers and hence any new investment is likely to be restricted to assembly of imported parts rather than full local manufacture. This in turn means that there will be few beneficial multiplier effects on indigenous industry, while the permanency of the investment may be questionable.

The second circumstance under which inward investment may be desirable is where it would complement the existing indigenous industrial structure. The most common experience of this is where the indigenous sector is declining because it is technologically retarded. The difficulty here is that there is no reason why the incoming firm should necessarily assist the existing industry since the primary aim is to compete and take over the market.

As a general conclusion, an analysis of international market conditions can indicate those sectors in which inward investment is most likely, while an analysis of the regional industrial structure can identify sectors in which such investment is desirable. The problem is that these two categories are almost invariably mutually exclusive. A sector approach to determining priorities for investment therefore favours support for indigenous manufacturing industry. Measures aimed at attracting inward investment are neither strategic nor coherent in the senses discussed above.

Technology Transfer

The West Midlands Technology Transfer Centre (WMTTC), developed jointly by the WMEB and Aston University at Aston Science Park, is one of a range of complementary technology-orientated interventions by the WMEB and former County Council (Marshall 1985). Others include specific investments in a number of firms producing or introducing advanced manufacturing technology, training courses in new technology skills, provision of computer-aided pattern-making facilities at the WMCRC, and a shareholding in Warwick University Science

Park, as well as research and advocacy activities. While technology transfer is far from the exclusive concern of the specialised centre set up for this purpose, the WMTTC is intended to play a specific role by encouraging the diffusion of new technologies between different users and producers of advanced productive technologies, strengthening linkages between sectors and subsectors of West Midlands industry. The broad objectives of the WMEB's strategy for technology-based intervention are:

(i)   To encourage use of new technology where it enhances competitiveness or develops new linkages and new areas of production in the regional economy.

(ii) To do this in ways which encourage participation by the workforce, build existing and new skills and open up novel areas of employment (West Midlands Enterprise Board 1986b).

This approach is based on a rejection of models for technology transfer applied elsewhere which favour the transfer of technical knowledge and expertise from educational research institutions to private industry. While not discarding the potential contribution from academia, the WMEB's approach prioritises measures to promote technology transfer between firms and sectors. This approach recognises that it is impossible to treat technological aspects of a firm's or sector's activities in isolation from other aspects of their strategies and operation, such as finance, marketing and training, or from the broader economic processes which govern intercompany and intersectoral relationships. The diffusion of computer-aided design in the motor components industry, for example, is motivated more by customer requirements in terms of quality, design and lead times than by any notional technological imperative. Likewise, product development is generally more strongly motivated by a concern with product differentiation or with increasing value added and profit margins than with developing an entirely new product. The simplistic view that there are a large number of new products in large companies' research and development departments or educational research establishments awaiting exploitation ignores the fact that most research is orientated towards defending existing markets rather than developing new ones. The longer a new or improved product is delayed, the longer a company is able to exploit its existing market.

For these reasons the WMTTC has adopted a sector approach to its activities, which aim to promote the inter- and intrasectoral diffusion of existing technologies rather than sponsor new product innovation. Prior to the WMTTC's establishment, a regional innovation campaign was conducted in conjunction with consultants from Bath University through a series of promotional seminars for industrial managers coupled with follow-up surveys. Almost 300 companies expressed varying degrees of interest in using the WMTTC's services. The composition of its data base of potential clients reflects the West Midlands' industrial structure with strong representation of engineering and metal-based industries. Sectoral analysis has selected two initial target sectors for the WMTTC, namely motor components and machine-tools. Both these sectors occupy important strategic positions in the regional economy while both are under pressure to adopt new products and processes in response to changes in markets, customer requirements and competitive conditions. The WMTTC is presently in the process of contacting firms in these sectors, offering information and consultancy services to assess their technological needs and potential in the context of commercial objectives and wider strategic considerations.

Concluding Remarks

This chapter has ranged widely from the origins and roots of the WMEB's sector strategy in the structure of the West Midlands economy and the principles upon which intervention was founded to a description of the approach in practice and its underlying rationale. The intention has been to provide a broad overview while recognising that the concepts discussed and practical examples provided raise as many questions as they answer. In concluding, there are several general points which deserve further emphasis.

First, it should be stressed that sector work is not the be all and end all of local economic intervention. Other local economic objectives, notably measures to tackle poverty and social disadvantage, need to be addressed both within and in addition to a sector-based strategy.

Second, sector strategy needs to be based on clearly defined objectives. The concepts of both 'sector' and 'strategy' are neither uncontroversial nor unambiguous. In situations of controversy and ambiguity — and local economic intervention is almost always beset by such circumstances — clear objectives are essential to prioritising resource allocation, determining future directions and providing a lead for other economic agents to follow.

Third, sector strategy is not just one of a series of alternative approaches to economic intervention. Rather, sector strategy is based on a rationale of coherence, consensus and analysis which provides a more solid base for intervention in the economy than limited, piecemeal approaches.

Fourth, it should be emphasised that sector strategy is not necessarily limited to a particular industry or group of industries. It represents a flexible approach to intervention in individual industries but, equally importantly, can be applied to forms of intervention which are not immediately industry-specific, for example technology-based interventions which span a range of industrial sectors.

Finally and most importantly, the sector approach to intervention is precisely that — an *approach* rather than a blueprint. It represents an approach to research and analysis, to intervention and to advocacy in a way which combines these different areas so that they become mutually reinforcing parts of an overall strategic framework.

This final point relates back to an issue raised in the introductory section regarding the extent to which the West Midlands experience of sectoral intervention can provide a model for other regions and national government. The answer to this question is a qualified 'yes'. As an approach to economic intervention, sector strategy is universally applicable but the precise *form* of that intervention will depend upon the industrial and institutional structures, the resources available and, above all, the degree of consensus and political will needed to pursue the wide-ranging and integrated programme of research and intervention which necessarily stems from a sectoral analysis of problems and potential in the economy.

One of the architects of the Greater London Enterprise Board, Ken Livingstone, has stated that 'the Labour Party has seized on the important but limited success of Labour council Enterprise Boards as the answer to our problems at exactly the same time we have realised the limits of their effectiveness' (*Guardian*, 23 September 1985). In this chapter we have attempted to provide an equally honest assessment of the strengths and limitations of sector strategy and industrial intervention in the West Midlands. The WMEB's experience does not provide a panacea for the long-term, structural problems of the British economy. It does, however, provide a practical demonstration of the contribution which local and regional agencies might make to a more ambitious national strategy for economic and industrial regeneration while avoiding the failed, simplistic formulae applied by previous generations of socialist economic planners.

References

Armstrong, K.M. and J.A.Lewis (1986), 'Skill Shortages and Recruitment Problems in the West Midlands Engineering Industry', *National Westminster Bank Quarterly Review*, November, pp. 45–57

Bessant, J., D. Jones, R. Lamming and A. Pollard (1984), *The West Midlands Automobile Components Industry*, West Midlands County Council Economic Development Unit. *Sector Report No. 4*, Birmingham: WMCC.

Debenham, Tewson and Chinnocks (1983), *Money into Property*, London: Debenham, Tewson and Chinnocks

Edge, G. (1981), *Priorities for Economic Development in the West Midlands*, Birmingham: WMCC

Edge, G. (1986), *Priorities for Economic Regeneration in the West Midlands*, Birmingham: WMEB

Elliott, D. (1984), 'The Limits of Tripartitism', unpublished paper, South Bank Polytechnic, London

Elliott, D. (1986), *The Sector Approach to Industrial Research: Fiddling While Rome Burns?*, West Midlands County Council Economic Development Unit *Economic Review No.4: Research for Economic Development*, Birmingham: WMCC, pp. 6–16

Gaffikin, F. and A. Nickson (1984), *Jobs Crisis and the Multinationals: The Case of the West Midlands*, Birmingham Trade Union Group for World Development/ Birmingham Trade Union Resource Centre

Leigh, R. and D. North (1983), *The Clothing Sector in the West Midlands*, West Midlands County Council Economic Development Unit *Sector Report No.3*, Birmingham: WMCC

Marshall, M. (1985), 'Technological Change and Local Economic Strategy in the West Midlands', *Regional Studies*, 19.6, pp. 570–8

Marshall, M. (1986), 'National Economic Forecasting at Local Level: Applications of the Cambridge Model in the West Midlands', *Local Economy*, 3, pp. 49–60

Marshall, M. (1987), *Long Waves of Regional Development*, London: Macmillan

Marshall, M. and J. Mawson (1987), 'The West Midlands' in P. Damesick and P. Wood, eds, *Regional Problems, Problem Regions and Public Policy in the UK*, London: Oxford University Press, Ch. 5

Metal Working Production (1983), *The Fifth Survey of Machine Tools and Production Equipment in Britain*, London: Metal Working Production

Oakey, R., A. Thwaites and P. Nash (1980), 'The Regional Distribution of Innovative Manufacturing Establishments in Britain', *Regional Studies*, 14.3, pp. 235–53

Spencer, K., A. Taylor, B. Smith, J. Mawson, N. Flynn, and R. Batley (1986), *Crisis in the Industrial Heartland: A Study of the West Midlands*, Oxford: Clarendon Press

West Midlands County Council Economic Development Unit (1982), *The Foundry Industry in the West Midlands*, Sector Report No. 1, Birmingham: WMCC

West Midlands County Council Economic Development Unit (1983), *The Machine Tool Industry in the West Midlands*, Sector Report No. 6, Birmingham: WMCC

West Midlands County Council Economic Development Unit (1986), *Economic Review No. 4: Research for Economic Development*, Birmingham: WMCC

West Midlands Enterprise Board (1986a), *Poverty and Family Income Trends in the West Midlands*, Birmingham: WMEB

West Midlands Enterprise Board (1986b), *Policies andPriorities Towards Technological Change in West Midlands Industry*, Birmingham: WMEB

West Midlands Enterprise Board (1987), *Future Prospects for West Midlands Industry and Employment*, Birmingham: WMEB

9 Macro-economic Management and Industrial Policy

Jim Tomlinson

All advanced capitalist countries pursue both macro-economic management, attempting to regulate aggregate output, employment, prices and
the balance of payments, and industrial policy, attempting to improve
the performance of particular sectors of the economy, broadly or
narrowly defined. This chapter is concerned with the relationship
between these two types of policy. It starts from the proposition that
macro-economic policy has been generally on the retreat relative to
industrial policy over the last fifteen to twenty years. In the first section
this process is looked at in very broad terms, and some explanations
and implications suggested. The second and third sections look at the
macroeconomic/industrial relationship in two very different countries
— France and Sweden — to see what can be drawn from their histories.
The last section looks at the United Kingdom. The focus here is on the
macro-economic implications of any radical departure towards a more
ambitious industrial policy.

The Retreat of Macro-economic Policy

Macro-economic policy has meant very different things in different
advanced capitalist (we are referring specifically to OECD) countries.
Whilst the Anglo-Saxon literature is dominated by the Keynesian–
monetarist controversy, and the assumed demise of Keynesianism, this
kind of framework means rather little outside the UK, the United
States, Austria and, arguably, Sweden. In France and West Germany,
for example, macro policy never had the same prominence, and its
conduct was much less linked to fiscal policy, which is usually seen as
the central feature of Keynesianism. Nevertheless, despite these differences in the meaning and significance of macro-economic policy all
OECD countries have seen a shift towards a greater emphasis on
industrial policy in recent years. (For countries other than the UK,
France and Sweden, see Norton (1986) and Thompson (1987) on the

Table 9.1. Levels of import penetration (imports of goods and services as percentage of GNP)

	1950	1960	1970	1980
USA	4.2	4.6	6.0	12.0
Japan	11.5	11.0	10.0	16.0
Germany	13.0	17.0	20.0	29.0
France	15.0	11.0	15.0	21.0
UK	23.0	21.5	21.5	26.0
Italy	13.0	15.0	18.0	27.0

Source: Piore and Sabel (1984, p. 185).

USA; Donges (1980) and Esseg and Fach (1985) on West Germany; and, more generally, Curzon-Price (1981); Katzenstein (1985); Dyson and Wilks (1983).

A useful starting point in explaining this shift is that for the period from the 1950s through to the early 1970s, and largely irrespective of the macro-economic regime, low unemployment was maintained in nearly all OECD countries. Whilst macro management in this period may have helped maintain investors' confidence, and thereby reinforced the effects of government's commitments to full employment, its direct contribution to full employment was small. Most of the impetus to this full employment came from the expansion of private investment and the expansion of world trade.

The low levels of aggregate unemployment of course obscured regional and sectoral differences in rates. But for the 1950s and 1960s (except in the case of Italy) these differences were small, not only because many governments pursued regional policies, but primarily because the level of import penetration was at a low level (see Table 9.1), which left most industrial sectors in most countries comfortably dominant in their home markets. (British regional policy was notably concerned with the problems of old *export* industries and regions, not of import penetration.)

But a foundation stone of the *Pax Americana* was the commitment to free trade, and this was accepted willingly enough by most European countries (albeit more gradually than the USA would have liked) because of the belief that economic interdependence reduced the likelihood of political and military conflict. The consequent growth of world trade, in combination with high levels of private investment, drove the aggregate economy to unprecedented heights of capacity and capacity utilisation. But it also changed the conditions of competition for individual firms and sectors — increasingly their performance was subject to international competition. So in part, for the same reasons that economic activity generally accelerated, it became less evenly distributed between sectors and regions. This threw into question those policy instruments which precisely focused on the aggregate level of activity rather than the fortunes of any particular sector.

A growing concern with the fortunes of particular sectors was apparent by the late 1960s — that is, before the first oil shock of the early 1970s. Equally, the period from 1968 saw a rise in inflation throughout the OECD world which undermined the politically comfortable tradeoff between inflation and unemployment represented in academic terms by the original Phillips curve. So even in its own terms macro policy was becoming less successful.

Both these problems were exacerbated by the oil shock. This not only imparted a macro-economic deflation to the OECD world. But the slowdown in growth it precipitated threw into relief the problems of particular sectors where demand was growing particularly slowly or even declining and where international competition was intense. Most of this competition, it should be emphasised, was from within the OECD camp, rather than from Third World countries. For example between 1959–60 and 1975 the developing countries' share of British textile imports was stable at 5 per cent, whilst those from developed countries rose from 8 to 25 per cent of the market (Pinder 1982, p. 37). What was occuring was a *reduction* of the relative role of poor countries in OECD trade, as these countries rapidly became more integrated.

The oil crisis also proved a crisis of macro-economic management. Despite their initial agreement to offset the deflationary consequences of the oil price rise by domestic policy, the OECD countries quickly broke ranks and deflated their economies (OECD 1977). Keynesian policies 'failed' in the first serious post-war slump to put them to the test. This 'failure' was not, of course, one of economic theory, but of the provision of the political and institutional conditions of such a policy. In particular, the political concern with inflation, and the leverage available to financial institutions to turn growing budget deficits into a political crisis, undermined the possibility of a Keynesian response.

Despite the pressures to fiscal retrenchment, aid to particular industrial sectors grew in most European countries in the mid- and late 1970s. In particular, iron and steel, coal, shipbuilding and textiles were to a greater or lesser extent supported in most countries. The gathering pace of industrial policy clearly ran against the market-orientated postures both of the economists and the institutions where they were able to make themselves felt. Most notably the OECD came to endorse a stance of 'positive adjustment' which emphasised the need to improve market flexibility and responsiveness when faced with competitive ressures, rather than resorting to industrial subsidy and protection (OECD 1979; 1983; 1984).

These positions are typical of economists' view. Orthodox economists have always looked askance at the discriminatory characteristics of industrial policy, and have preferred macro policies precisely because of their generality (see, for example, Corden 1980). These views find a response in the rhetoric of many politicians, because of the political commitment to an open international economy. In addition, the budgetary consequences of large-scale subvention of loss-making industries in a general climate of fiscal conservatism have reined in the scale of industrial policy in many countries in the early 1980s. Nevertheless, the economists' focus on consumers' welfare as the sole criterion of successful economic policy has never been fully embraced by any government. Industrial policy survives the strictures of the economists because in almost any political calculation the actuality of declining sectors and regions (and balance of payments problems) in a particular national economy appears more compelling than the economists' postulates about the long-run functioning of the capitalist economy in general.

This has been true even for those governments which celebrate the efficacy of market forces. Britain under Mrs Thatcher has continued to have an extensive industrial policy, albeit one notably different in its sectoral emphasis than previous policies (Thompson 1986, Ch. 7). In Reagan's USA a federal industrial policy has continued, albeit heavily dominated as before by defence procurement. The failure of the radical proposals of the early 1980s owed as much to the incapacities of federal government in the USA as to ideological hostility, and at the state level much continues to be done (Thompson 1987).

Untrammelled by any commitment to market forces, the left, though mostly out of power, has enthusiastically embraced industrial policy. In part this has an origin in common with the right's policy prescriptions — an exaggerated emphasis on the incapacities of macro-economic policy. The overselling of Keynesian policies in the 1950s and 1960s has led to a current reaction which oversells the capacity of industrial policy. This is congenial to the left because much of it has never been happy with the inherently *national* character of macro management (Tomlinson 1986). Industrial policy also promises the kind of 'conscious', state-based control or at least influence on capital which fits more readily into the left's general ideological posture.

This chapter is not concerned with any particular kind of industrial policy. But the point of importance here is that industrial policy *per se* lends itself to an inappropriate grandiosity of purpose which needs to be guarded against. As Hayward (1986, p. 230) notes, 'industrial policy is usually a symbolic, unitary fiction to cover a multitude of piecemeal, improvisatory and portentous claims by government to be pursuing a comprehensive and consistent medium- and long-term industrial strategy'.

Nevertheless, industrial policy will remain a focus of concern in all the OECD countries. The reasons are both negative and positive. Negatively, macro management is undoubtedly more constrained than it was, especially because of the scale and fluidity of capital flows, even if these constraints are often exaggerated (Tomlinson 1987; see also discussion of Sweden below). Related to this, the most obvious way to alter international competitiveness, via currency revaluation, is no longer an easy option, if an option at all. Government's capacity to determine the exchange rate of many currencies has been greatly reduced by the scale of the capital flows. At the same time, even when changes in relative prices can be engineered, responsiveness to these price differences has been reduced by the competition on quality characteristics of goods, where deficiencies cannot readily be offset by lower prices (Williams *et al.* 1983).

More positively, industrial policy offers a way of trying to cope with the consequences of the enhanced degree of competition in international markets, where no government dare give up responsibility entirely for the consequences of such competition for both employment and balance of payments reasons.

Sweden

The 'Swedish model' of economic management is rightly famous as the most progressive effort made to reform a capitalist economy. Like all models, it has never functioned as neatly or unproblematically as an outline of its principles of operation might suggest. Nevertheless, for most of the post-war period the Swedish economy has performed very well by the standard criteria of economic performance: growth, inflation, balance of payments equilibrium, and outstandingly well in terms of employment. This section looks in broad terms at the relationship between industrial policy and macro management in Sweden's approach to national economic regulation.

Swedish policy may be called Keynesian in the sense that it puts central emphasis on the achievement of full employment and the use of the full range of budgetary and exchange rate policies to achieve this end. But probably the core of the 'Swedish model' is labour-market policy. The starting point for this is that Sweden will remain an open economy dependent for its high living standards on successful competition in manufacturing activity in international markets. The aim of the Swedish model was to make this compatible with non-inflationary full employment and at the same time to equalise wage incomes across the economy. Labour market policy was thus pivotal because of its three roles (Lundmark 1983, pp. 221–2): to maintain employment by encouraging the mobility of labour and the matching of labour competences to the jobs available; to reduce inflationary pressures in the labour market by making available workers with appropriate skills to the expanding sectors; and to encourage wage equalisation by squeezing the low-wage sectors on the wage front, with the aim of shifting workers to other sectors able to afford high wages.

This, in broad outline, was the core of policy in the 'Swedish model' as advocated by the Swedish trade unions and accepted by the Swedish Social Democratic governments of the 1950s and early 1960s. Industrial policy did not figure in this schema. The presumption was that Swedish private sector firms would continue to be successful in international competition, and policy only directly impinged on this in the provision of appropriately skilled workers. But from the beginning there was a certain ambiguity in the policy concerning profits. The policy was predicated on successful manufacturing activity, therefore high investment, and, given private ownership, on high profits. Yet the policy also emphasised high as well as equal wages, coupled with a continuing ideological hostility to private ownership and private investment decision-making. The issue of how far wage claims could or should be pressed without threatening investment finance was therefore not clearly spelt out (Martin 1984, pp. 206–8, 247). In the long run this problem was crucial to further development of the Swedish model (see below).

Swedish policy in the 1950s and early 1960s was a success without any significant role for industrial policy. But, in the 1960s, pressure for such a policy arose from a number of sources. First, the 'model' emphasised labour mobility as a necessary condition for success. But in the 1960s such mobility was viewed with growing hostility. On the one hand, the costs of labour mobility for individual workers came to be seen as high, and the costs of depopulation of certain areas excessive. Second, the context of international competition became more intense with the lowering of tariff barriers and apprehension over American technological superiority, putting new emphasis on the need for rapid response to technological changes. Third, the Social Democrats seemed to be losing some momentum and were attracted to a greater state role in industrial activity, broadly on the then popular lines of French indicative planning (Ohlin 1974, pp. 126–7).

Between 1966 and 1968 a number of changes in Swedish policy came together to mark a new departure, a new emphasis on industrial policy. The government began to play a larger part in the Swedish capital market, creating a Swedish Investment Bank to channel funds from the ATP (the state supplementary pension scheme) directly into industry, in the form of bond finance. This was done in the name of greater capital market flexibility to aid adaptation. At the same time regional development aids (previously very limited) were extended, though generally the rhetoric of policy continued to emphasise labour mobility and to try and reduce the costs to workers of such movement. There were also some indicative planning exercises, but these amounted basically to exchanges of information and projections of future scenarios.

In 1968 a Ministry of Industry was set up, representing the new emphasis given to industrial policy. But in truth Sweden still had far less of a government role in the private sector than almost any other Western European country. In general, Sweden did not have serious problems of responding to growing competition, and the problems of the 'old staples', shipbuilding, iron and steel, and timber were as yet small. Despite the call of the (first) Meidner Report of 1971 for a 'co-ordinated industrial policy' and a similar call from the Boston Consulting Group five years later, the emphasis continued to be on providing the framework (fiscal, labour and to a lesser extent capital market) within which the private sector made its decisions (Katzenstein 1985, p. 65).

This stance was only reversed in the wake of the first oil shock and the subsequent pressures on shipbuilding and steel. Between 1970 and 1980 industrial support in Sweden grew threefold in real terms, particularly in the form of 'non-permanent industrial grants' (Lundmark 1983, p. 229). This basically meant emergency rescues by the Ministry of Industry, bypassing the traditional tripartite Boards which administered policy, and largely aimed at the shipbuilding and steel industries. These industries gained 46 and 33 per cent respectively of funds spent under this category in 1974–80.

This kind of crisis management industrial policy was accentuated by the unstable parliamentary situation between 1976 and 1982, when the Social Democrats lost office and were replaced by shifting coalitions among the bourgeois parties. To a degree the traditional emphasis on the availability of a job somewhere in the country was replaced by an emphasis on the retention of existing jobs, or at least their only gradual reduction (Henning 1984). Nevertheless, job losses were substantial and employment was only maintained by a continued growth of public sector employment, which absorbed a very large proportion of the growth of labour supply.

With the return of the Social Democrats in 1982 policy took a new strategic direction, significantly developing the Swedish 'model' in a new context. There was acceptance that the industrial sector could not be expected to absorb all those previously employed, but that nevertheless the success of manufacturing was crucial to financing a full employment level of imports. But the key issue was how the investment for such success was to be financed.

As always in policy discussions, several issues were at stake in this question. Partly the question was a straightforward socialist one, of how private sector investment was to be effectively controlled — the issue of economic democracy. But perhaps more important was the fact that it was inherent in the traditional Swedish 'model' that intercompany differences in profits would be accentuated by solidaristic wage bargaining — so the issue of the disposition of the relatively high profits of some firms was unavoidably raised.

In 1982 the Social Democrats accepted that the economy required a substantial shift of resources into industrial investment. This required a shift in the wage-profit share in national income. This was only politically workable if economic democracy were substantially extended. The means to this extension were Wage Earner Funds, by which a share of profits of all companies was transferred to these union-based funds, to be invested in equity (Hashi and Hussain 1985).

The macro-economic complement to this was a 16 per cent devaluation, unaccompanied by large wage increases, which had the effect of reducing real wages and increasing profits. This strategy seems to have worked, with the Swedish balance of payments position sharply improving, and full employment being maintained despite a slightly deflationary fiscal policy aimed at reducing public sector deficits (OECD 1987).

How far can this Swedish experience be seen as vindicating an emphasis on macro-economic policy even in current conditions? First, it must be noted that whilst there has been a decline of *ad hoc* crisis interventions under the Social Democrats, the traditional emphasis on very large-scale retraining of labour has continued. Second, public support for research and development has also increased, to the highest level in Western Europe. So Sweden, whilst allowing great freedom of action to private corporations, has provided highly favourable general conditions.

Swedish macro policy has rested on a centralised bargaining structure which means that political bargains between centralised unions and employers can be 'delivered'. This centralised system has of late been under strain, most especially because of the desire of metal employers (a key sector) both to increase wage differentials and to reduce the state's role in wage setting (Lash 1985). In addition, Swedish wage bargaining has been increasingly influenced by the switch of employment into the public sector, where employment grew from 20.6 per cent to 29.8 per cent between 1970 and 1979, as manufacturing and mining shed workers (Scharpf 1983, p. 266).

However, the strains of decentralisation are nothing new (the demise of Swedish corporatism is periodically, and prematurely, announced), and it is far from clear that the 'neo-corporatist' arrangements which sustain the Swedish policy regime are yet severely threatened. Equally, whilst the decline of manufacturing employment is a very important feature of Sweden (and other countries) it is a process which has ceased in the mid-1980s, with small increases in employment in the last three years (OECD 1987, p. 16).

Nevertheless, the Swedish case does indicate the continued viability of macro-economic policies — but under highly specific conditions. These conditions of course include the continuing capacity of Swedish firms to compete internationally, and to use prices as a competitive weapon. This is in contrast to the UK, where there is substantial evidence that price is relatively unimportant to competitive success (NEDO 1977). The lesson may be that whilst low prices cannot compensate for poor design, quality, after-sales service, and so on, *given* a high reputation in these areas, price reductions can expand market share.

Whether generated within private firms or under pressure from government industrial policy, such successful industrial activity implies a shift of resources into investment. In Sweden such a shift required a new twist to the 'model' but one which was not out of line with the tradition of 'corporatist' policies and the politics that made such policies possible (cf. Lundmark 1983). A considerable socialisation of investment was the key, not for the classic Keynesian reason, to offset the psychological instability of the investor, but to obtain agreement on a shift of output into profits to finance investment. On this basis successful industrial activity could be combined with the continued use of macro-economic instruments.

France

If Sweden might be seen as the paradigm case of successful macro-economic policies, France is often seen as the home of dirigistic policies towards industry. Certainly there has never been the same obsession with limiting the role of the state as in the Anglo-Saxon countries. But much of France's reputation rests on the regime of economic planning in the post-war period which was by no means synonymous with what is usually understood by industrial policy.

French planning has meant radically different things in the years since 1946 (Estrin and Holmes 1983; Michaelet 1974). Initially the focus was on reconstruction of the basic industries, and until the early 1950s planning was 'central' rather than 'indicative'. The heyday of indicative planning was between 1953 and 1965, when Modernisation Commissions sought to promote innovation and growth across industrial sectors, but targets became less like objectives, and more like forecasts. Intersectoral 'coherence' was aimed at, but in fact growth was highly uneven, and in particular rapid growth eventually caused serious balance of payments problems.

Macro policy in this period was dominated by the traditional instruments of monetary policy, fiscal policy being subordinate (Hayward 1986, p. 220). There was poor co-ordination between macro policy and planning, devaluations and deflations interrupting the growth encouraged by the planning process. In the 1960s the rise of inflation led to more focus on macro policy, but this did not really come into the sustained prominence accorded it in other countries until after the oil shock of the early 1970s — rather a reversal of the pattern in many countries.

In the 1960s the goal of competitiveness became the focus of policy, rather than that of growth as in the 1950s. This policy was particularly manifest in the promotion of 'national champions' to fight the international competition — especially the Americans. But unlike many countries' industrial policies, this was not a policy selective between sectors, but one which tried to raise corporate competitiveness in most sectors of the national economy. Central to this policy was the state's role in credit allocation. France was characterised by industry's high dependence on bank lending (rather than the stock market). In turn these loans were guided by the Bank of France and behind it the Ministry of Finance, the central bank offering both approval and partial guarantee to the lending banks. Thus industrial strategy in France had a capacity for action much greater than in the British case because of the largely pre-existing relationship between finance and industry (Zysman 1977; 1983).

After the oil crisis French policy came closer to the norms of the rest of Western Europe. On the one hand, there was a growth of *ad hoc* crisis-based interventions in specific sectors and firms. At the same time a new emphasis was put on a (deflationary) macro policy, aimed primarily at containing inflation and reducing the balance of payments deficit. The Barre government after 1976 exposed 'positive adjustment' *à la* OECD, but intervened to slow the decline of traditional sectors like coal and steel (Green 1983, pp. 173–4). After the second oil crisis there was again a shift towards a more aggressive planning stance, with the emphasis on the development of new high technology sectors.

Like Sweden, France was in the 1960s faced with the growth of competitiveness, but with a much less clear strategy of response. Corporatist arrangements were notably weak, with a fragmented trade union movement and governments of the right. Planning was in this period especially insulated from political pressures and largely 'technocratic' rather than tripartite like the various boards regulating public policy in Sweden. The crisis of the 1970s in both countries forced an industrial restructuring which was willy-nilly defensive in character, given the employment significance of the basic industries like steel, coal and textiles.

The Mitterrand government of 1981 inherited, like the Social Democrats in Sweden in 1982, a mixture of industrial interventions with which to cope with an adverse international environment, but without the same economic or political capacity to link industrial strategy to macro policy (on the Mitterrand government generally, see Machin and

Wright 1985). Economically, the exchange rate was much more of a problematic weapon in France than in Sweden. Up to 37 per cent of French imports were paid for in dollars, so a dollar devaluation was likely to have adverse consequences for the balance of payments. Politically, a devaluation was considered impolitic given the traditional French attachment to the strength of the franc. In any event, if the aim was to raise profits via devaluation, there was little likelihood of the acquiescence of the newly buoyant left in France in such a process.

One way of posing the French socialist' strategic dilemma is put by Hall (1985, p. 82; see also Hall 1986). Given the central concern to reduce unemployment and promote industrial growth, an expansion of investment was central. Given the continuing dominance of private firms (despite extensive nationalisation) this implied a need to raise profits. This could be done directly, for example by incomes policy, but this was politically unpalatable. Alternatively, it could be done indirectly by raising domestic demand, but with the danger that this would cause balance of payments problems before investment increased substantially. Of course, this strategic choice never occurred in such a stark form. Nevertheless, what was done largely conformed to the second approach, with the hope that world output would pick up to help exports over the 'hump'.

The macro-economic policies of the Mitterrand government aimed at reducing unemployment especially by increased social welfare expenditure and direct employment creation in the public sector. Such a strategy raised two immediate problems. First, given the government's decision not to devalue the franc, there was the problem of both the economic effects (inflation) and financial effects (loss of confidence) brought about by forced reductions in the franc's value as the balance of payments deteriorated. Second, the policy involved large additions to employment costs, via higher minimum wages and increased employer welfare contributions. This could not but offset to some degree the employment creating effects of the increased demand. In addition, the rise in employment costs obviously mitigated the hopes of raising profits and hence private investment as part of the industrial policy.

The industrial policy pursued after 1981 is much less easy to summarise than the macro-economic policy. Part of the policy consisted of a radical policy of nationalisation, both of banks and major industrial firms. These nationalisations were seen (amongst other objectives) as means of bringing about a rise in industrial investment, especially in 'high-technology' areas, an emphasis which the Socialists continued from the previous government (Hayward 1986, p. 227). But whatever the efficacy of nationalisation as a means of pursuing industrial policy, plainly it cannot evade the macro-economic implications of trying to raise the level of industrial investment, but only transfers the financing from the private to the public sector. By 1983, half of all French investment was state-financed (Hall 1985, p. 90).

A substantial part of the political argument *within* the Socialist government was over the degree and nature of the control to be exercised over the newly nationalised sector. The results of this argument were substantial changes of policy, but the overall impact of the nationalisation was to widen the sphere of direct state responsibility for industrial investment precisely when many industries were running into sharp financial difficulties as a result of the world slump. In some areas, such as chemicals, nationalisation was vigorously pursued, but generally finance was made available on a large scale to both 'old' industries, such as steel and coal, and 'national champions' in industries such as computers, chemicals, and motor cars.

As Hall (1985, p. 90) suggests, the scale of nationalisation helped the French government 'to overcome one of the classic structural constraints of capitalism — the dependence of investment on business confidence'. But this, of course, only applied in the public sector. More generally, it did not solve the incompatibility of trying to expand investment in general via a policy which sharply boosted consumption (public and private).

The policy reversals of the Mitterrand government are most apparent in the macro-economic area. Fiscal expansion was reigned back from 1982 and the macro-economic environment became increasingly austere. In part the reasons were 'macro-economic' — the fall in the franc, the sharp rise in the public deficit and the loss of confidence these engendered.

But the pressure on the public budget also forced a change in industrial policy, this became less ambitious, less grandiose and much more selective in its objectives. Increasingly, the focus shifted from infrastructural and sectoral policies to those based on firms, with management quality of the firm an important criterion. Whatever the industrial logic of this, it was compelled by the 'macro-economic' pressure to reduce budget expenditure (Hall 1985, p. 96).

More broadly, the policy reversals aimed at trying to restore investment in the private sector, and this involved an ending, and in some cases a reversal, of welfare reform. Hayward (1986, p. 235) goes so far as to argue that the desire to raise industrial profitability and the capacity to invest was the central reason for the reversal of French policy. Of course, this strategy raised its own problems, as the slowdown in demand expansion itself hindered profitability.

This chapter is not concerned with the appropriateness of French industrial policy to the French economy. Rather, the purpose here is to highlight the relations between industrial policy and macro-economic policy and the problems of these relations. In France under the Socialist government after 1981 there were clearly very compelling political reasons for increasing current public expenditure both for enhanced transfer payments and direct employment creation. This, in combination with increased public investment in the newly enlarged nationalised sector, meant either higher taxes or higher borrowing. Given the commitment to an expansionary macro-economic policy most of the effect fell on borrowing. This had the hardly surprising consequence of stimulating capital flight. So while a large proportion of investment was not *directly* in private hands, it could not escape being affected by the state of business confidence, reacting as this did to the conditions of public finance. So widespread nationalisation may aid an industrial policy by giving a direct role in certain industrial sectors, but it cannot in this way be insulated from pressures arising from the vagaries of financial confidence.

Equally a policy which focuses on the reflation of demand is not easily made compatible with an industrial policy which requires a sharp switch of resources into investment. This compatibility is especially problematic where the government is also keen to redistribute resources down the income scale.

Ultimately, France lacked the political mechanisms to make possible an agreement on combining the reflation with resource switching into investment. Once the initial 'redistributive Keynesian' policy began to founder, investment was encouraged by conventional deflationary policies, a policy not only problematic in economic terms, but politically disastrous for the Socialists, as it reversed previous policies without any consensual alternative.

The United Kingdom

The British academic emphasis on the monetarist — Keynesian controversy mirrors the dominace of macro management in Britain's overall economic policy stance. But this macro-economic focus has been much 'narrower' than in Sweden, as well as notably less successful — narrower in the sense that it has relied on a small range of instruments within fiscal and monetary policy, without either integrating these *economically* with a labour market policy, or being linked *politically* to a consensual 'corporatist' framework. Thus post-war governments have notably lacked a policy in any strong sense on the labour market, and their main activity (apart from continual exhortation to 'responsible behaviour') has been periodic and crisis-stimulated incomes policies, resting for the little success they have attained on a strained claim to trade union loyalty, rather than a systematic pattern of negotiation with the 'social partners'.

Two issues arise from Britain's emphasis on macro policy; why has it existed, and why has it failed? On the first point a key factor at crucial times has been the external orientation of the UK's economic policies, relating to the role of sterling as a reserve currency (particularly important up to the 1960s), and then the role of the City of London as financial centre for international dealing in all currencies. This has led to a concern with the exchange rate, and more generally the retention of international financial confidence, out of all proportion to any conceivable benefits of such a posture for the national economy. In consequence of this posture, the exchange rate has been denied the role of an instrument of economic management, a role it as played in both France and Sweden. Changes in the sterling exchange rate have been the *consequence* of failures in policy, not part of the policy reportoire.

The fetish of macro policies also relates to the capacity of the key state agencies in economic policy-making. By far the most important agency since 1919 has been the Treasury, whose role has been akin to a continental European Ministry of Finance, coupled in the 1950s and 1960s with a concern with the *level* of unemployment. The great battles of the Treasury of the 1940s converted it to the use of the budget for adjusting the level of demand and output in the economy (within a generally buoyant economic framework), but imparted no interest or capacity in the area of the *composition* of output.

Industrial policy in the UK has, then, been pursued against the grain of the UK's dominant economic (and political) posture as an international power. It has consistently run up against the overarching powers and narrowness of concern of the Treasury. In addition, the state has lacked the leverage over the investment behaviour of firms given either by a direct leverage over a large industrial and banking sector (as in France), or informal leverage over a largely non-state but industrially orientated banking sector (as in West Germany).

Thus post-war economic policy in the UK has been dominated by a strategy in which international financial calculations have predominated, made fortuitously compatible with a full employment policy in the 1950s and 1960s by the buoyancy of world demand. In those decades the decline in relative living standards in Britain received increasing attention but did not create the basis for a crisis in policy-making as long as employment remained buoyant and inflation low.

In the 1970s and 1980s Britain shared an exaggerated version of the 'stagflation' of the advanced capitalist world. The focus on financial status in a crisis-ridden world economy, coupled with the continued weakness of the manufacturing economy, laid it uniquely open to speculative movements of capital which alternatively led to panic domestic inflation (in the mid-1970s) and grotesque losses of international competitiveness (in the early 1980s). In the face of such speculative movements, and in the absence of any consensual basis for a reorientation of policy, the traditional macro-economic instruments lost much of their effectiveness. Even mild fiscal expansion could unleash capital movements compelling reversals of policy.

Table 9.2. Fixed investment in manufacturing in the UK, 1965–85
(£ million at 1980 prices)

1965	1966	1967	1968	1969	1970	1971	1972	1973	1974
6637	6674	6332	6798	7412	7990	7292	6345	6786	7431

1975	1976	1977	1978	1979	1980	1981	1982	1983	1984	1985
6778	6470	6774	7220	7496	6479	4865	4705	4778	5755	5850

Source: Economic Trends, Annual Supplement, 1987.

Across the political spectrum in the 1970s there was a loss of faith in the traditional nostrums of macro policy, a widespread concern with increasing the efficiency of production. But under Mrs. Thatcher the commitment to free capital flows and the role of the City left the industrial economy subject to forces which no industrial policy could have easily dealt with, and which the Conservatives' own incoherent version could do little to alleviate.

There is a wide consensus of opinion on the importance of a 'new departure' in economic policy towards an emphasis on industrial re-generation, if little agreement on how this is to be done. The question here is what would be the macro-economic implications of such a new departure, if, in whatever precise form, it were to come about. Any such radical departure, to be effective, must involve a sharp increase in the level of industrial investment. Plainly the starting level of such an investment boost will vary according to, among other things, the phase of the economic cycle. Investment levels are highly cyclical, as is illustrated by the figures in Table 9.2. As is clear from these figures, however, although there has been a cyclical recovery from the very low levels of manufacturing investment after the collapse of 1979–81, the level remains substantially below the last peak in 1979, and well below that of 1970.

The overall role of low investment in Britain's decline in manufacturing competitiveness is not straightforward (see Smith 1984, pp. 193–9). The comparative data in Table 9.3 show that gross investment of all types is only slightly below that of most other countries in recent years. However, this has been a shortfall sustained over a number of years, with cumulative effects of a substantial kind. Hence data on the amount of capital per worker show a substantial gap between the UK and competitors, whether one looks at the whole economy or just manufacturing (Smith 1984, pp. 195–6). Also, because of the low level of British GDP the absolute levels of investment would be lower in the UK even if the share of GDP were similar, which also helps to explain the low per capita capital stock.

Table 9.3. Gross fixed capital formation (as a percentage of GDP)

	1980	1981	1982	1983	1984	1985	1985*
USA	19.1	18.6	17.2	17.2	18.1	18.6	8.6
Japan	31.6	30.7	29.7	28.3	27.8	27.5	N/A
West Germany	22.7	21.8	20.5	20.5	20.2	19.5	6.6
France	21.9	21.4	20.8	19.8	19.0	18.9	N/A
UK	18.2	16.4	16.2	16.3	17.4	17.2	8.7
Italy	19.8	20.2	19.9	17.9	18.2	18.2	8.9
Canada	27.8	23.5	21.5	19.2	18.1	18.6	6.5

* Investment in machinery and equipment as a percentage GDP.
Source: OECD *Main Economic Indicators*.

The reasons for this low level of investment, or how it should be tackled, are not discussed here. It may be argued that to focus on the global total of investment, as the left traditionally has done, is to start at the wrong place (Smith 1984; Tomlinson 1986). But clearly, a consequence of a radical industrial policy would be to raise that investment, with inescapable macro-economic implications.

Assuming that a persistent current balance of payments deficit (investment inflow) is not plausible, as a simple matter of arithmetic higher industrial investment must involve a lower level of (rate of growth of) some combination of public (mainly non-industrial) investment, and public and private consumption. Such is always the case, but the conflicts inherent in such arithmetic are likely to be compounded in the UK in the near future.

Apart from the absolutely low levels of industrial investment from which the UK starts, there will also be especially strong pressures under a reformist government to expand public investment and public consumption. The first of these will arise from the prolonged (since the early 1970s — see Table 9.4) decline in this sector, where most of the cuts in public expenditure have fallen. This has precipitated a major crisis in housing, and has also limited expenditure on other infrastructural projects. So expansion in this area will be pressed strongly both by those emphasising the social policy implications of the current rundown, but also because of the widespread political agreement on the focus on public non-industrial investment (that is, construction and maintenance) as a form of employment creation. As so often in the past, public works form a kind of lowest denominator of agreed reflationary instruments, a consensus which any reformist government would ignore at its peril.

But employment policy also raises the issue of current government expenditure. Any plausible employment policy which has regard both

Table 9.4. Share of investment in government expenditure on goods and services (per cent, excluding consideration of transfer payments)

1970	1971	1972	1973	1974	1975	1976	1977
21.3	20.1	19.0	21.6	20.8	17.7	15.8	14.2
1978	1979	1980	1981	1982	1983	1984	1985
12.3	11.6	10.2	7.5	6.7	8.3	8.4	8.8

Source: Calculated from Economic Trends, Annual Supplement, 1987.

to the quality and quantity of jobs, must envisage a major expansion in the public sector. Even the most successful industrial policy is not going to re-employ directly the 2 million workers who have lost jobs in manufacturing since 1979. Equally, expansion of private services sector jobs is simply too slow to absorb the currently unemployed rapidly (Metcalf 1985), even if one could ignore the quality of most of the jobs created there (Cutler et al. 1986).

In sum, any plausible scenario for a future reformist government, embarking on industrial policy, is likly to require a parallel squeeze on private consumption. This consequence would follow independently of whether the industrial investment was in the public or private sector: if in the private sector the mechanism would have to be higher profit or lower wage shares; if in the public, higher taxes, given the constraint on a major expansion of borrowing imposed by financial institutions.

So, put at its simplest, a successful industrial policy would require a squeeze on the main source of consumption demand, real wages. As noted above, such a squeeze was successfully pursued in Sweden after 1982. But the conditions of success for such a policy are plainly not easily reproducible in the British context. First, the logic of trying to expand the economy via export growth fed by devaluation is much less plausible in the British than in the Swedish case. In the UK price competitiveness appears much less significant, given the long-standing problems of quality, design, reliability, and so on, which do not seem to be easily offset by price changes (NEDO 1977; Schott and Pick 1984; Design Council 1983). This means all the more that the stimulus must come from the public sector (tax cuts would raise private consumption, as well as imports, very rapidly).

Second, the policy was part and parcel of the long-standing 'corporatist' arrangements in Sweden, which have meant an agreement on policy between the government and the main trade union confederation the Landsorganisationen i Sverige (LO), which has itself initiated many post-war policies. In the UK, such corporatist arrangements have been bedevilled both by the ideology of free collective bargaining with unions, a peculiar form of 'parliamentary cretinism' (Hirst 1981) and a trade union confederation which is neither organised for nor has the resources for initiation or co-ordination of trade union policy.

In Sweden a deal which traded lower real wages for higher investment was only acceptable to the unions because of the parallel movement towards a significant degree of socialisation of investment via wage earner funds.[1] Again the conditions of such a socialisation seem far removed from anything conceivable in the UK. Collective union control over substantial investment resources appears to be at odds not only with the unions' perception of their own role, but in conflict with the much stronger private financial institutions (insurance companies and pension funds) in the UK, in comparison with Sweden. Of course there are other paths to the socialisation of investment, but to succeed as part of a 'new social contract' any path would seem to require a substantial role for unions, raising precisely the same problems as the general lack of 'corporatist' institutions noted above.

The key macro-economic problem for the implementation of a radical industrial policy is, then, the requirement it would impose for an incomes policy. The context of such a policy might well not be to 'share out growth', as most Left advocates seem to hope, but to manage a reallocation of resources which would inevitably leave significant numbers of people worse-off. This, it should be noted, would set a much harder task for incomes policy than in its recent relatively successful period, 1974–8. Then real wages were rising strongly, and fear of inflation could be mobilised in support of the policy. The first of these is not a possible correlate of the kind of industrial policy envisaged here, and the second element is at best an unreliable ally for such policies.

This section has focused on the macro-economic consequences of industrial policy. But, of course, the link also runs the other way. Ignoring the political conditions, the most likely cause of a change of industrial policy stance is a renewed balance of payments crisis, within which a depreciation of the exchange rate was held to be unacceptable because of its inflationary consequences, or ineffectual because of the quality characteristics of British goods. Such a scenario would arise if the deterioration in the UK's manufacturing trade balance were no longer offset by a positive trade balance on oil, and the previously most reliable earner of invisible receipts, banking and finance, continued to lose market share as it has in recent years.

It is this scenario which is most likely to put industrial policy on the agenda, as the only alternative to domestic deflation; though the immediacy of such a crisis is likely to make such deflation unavoidable in at least the short run. In turn that deflation would exacerbate the management of the crisis on a consensual basis.

Overall, the clear danger in the British context is of a cycle of policy and policy reversal similar to that in France, arising from ignoring the macro-economic correlates of a radical industrial policy. The point to be emphasised by way of conclusion is that industrial policy cannot be seen as an alternative to macro-economic policy, but these two must be seen as complementary. Above all industrial policy does not avoid the need to examine the traditional set of problems for an expansionary macro-economic policy — problems of the path of real wages, the problem and possibilities of conventional economic management and some kind of income policy. Industrial policy must be inserted into this nexus of concerns, not detached from it.

Note

1. My colleague Deborah Mabbett has suggested that the squeeze of real wages in manufacturing in Sweden has also been made more tolerable by the parallel increase in well-paid public sector jobs for women, thus offsetting the squeeze on male earnings in manufaturing as far as dual-earner households are concerned.

References

Corden, W.M. (1980), 'Relations between Macroeconomic and Industrial Policies', World Economy, 3.2

Cutler, T. et al. (1986), Keynes, Beveridge and Beyond, London: Routledge and Kegan Paul

Curzon-Price, V. (1981), Industrial Policies in the European Community, London: Macmillan

Design Council (1983), Design and the Economy, London: Design Council

Donges, J.B. (1980), 'Industrial Policies in West Germany's not so Market Economy', World Economy, 3.2

Dyson, K. and Wilks, S., eds (1983), Industrial Crisis, Oxford: Blackwell

Esseg, J. and W. Fach (1983), '"Social Market" and Modernisation Policy: West Germany', in Dyson and Wilks (1983)

Estrin, S. and P. Holmes (1983), French Planning in Theory and Practice, London: Allen & Unwin

Green, D. (1983), 'Strategic Management and the State: France', in Dyson and Wilks (1983)

Hall, P. (1985), 'Socialism in one Country: Mitterrand and the Struggle to Define a New Economic Policy for France' in P.G. Cerny and M.A. Schain, eds, Socialism, the State and Public Policy in France, London: Frances Pinter

Hall, P. (1986), *Governing the Economy*, Cambridge: Polity Press

Hashi, I. and A. Hussain (1986). 'The Employee Investment Funds in Sweden', *National Westminster Bank Quarterly Review*, May

Hayward, J. (1986), *The State and the Market Economy*, Brighton: Harvester Press

Henning R. (1984), 'Industrial Policy or Employment Policy? Sweden's Response to Unemployment' in R. Henning and J. Richardson, eds *Unemployment: Policy Responses of Western Democracies*, London: Sage

Hirst, P. (1981), 'On Struggle in the Enterprise', in M. Prior, ed., *The Popular and the Political* London: Routledge and Kegan Paul

Katzenstein, P.J. (1985), *Small States in World Markets*, Ithaca, NY: Cornell University Press

Lash, S. (1985), 'The End of Neo-Corporatism?: The Breakdown of Centralised Bargaining in Sweden', *British Journal of Industrial Relations*, 33.2

Lundmark, K. (1983), 'Welfare State and Employment Policy: Sweden' in Dyson and Wilks (1983)

Machin, H. and V. Wright (1985), *Economic Policy and Policy-Making under the Mitterrand Presidency 1981–84* London: Frances Pinter

Martin, A. (1984), 'Trade Unions in Sweden: Strategic Responses to Change and Crisis', in P. Gourevitch, A. Martin *et al* eds, *Unions and Economic Crisis*, London: Allen & Unwin

Metcalf, D. (1985), 'Employment in the Second Half of the 1980s', paper delivered to the Socialist Economic Review Conference

Michaelet, C.-A. (1974), 'France' in R. Vernon, ed, *Big Business and the State*, London: Macmillan

Morvan, Y. (1985). 'Industrial Policy' in Machin and Wright (1985)

NEDO (1977), *International Price Competitiveness, Non-Price Factors and Export Performance*, London: NEDO

Norton, R. (1986), 'Industrial Policy and American Renewal', *Journal of Economic Literature*, 24.1

OECD (1977), *Towards Full Employment and Price Stability*, Paris OECD (the McCracken Report)

OECD (1979), *The Case for Positive Adjustment*, Paris: OECD

OECD (1983), *Postwar Adjustment Policies: Managing Structural Change*, Paris: OECD

OECD (1984), *Positive Adjustment: Manpower and Social Policies*, Paris: OECD

OECD (1987), *Economic Survey: Sweden*, Paris: OECD

Ohlin, G. (1974), 'Sweden' in R. Vernon, ed, *Big Business and the State* London: Macmillan

Pinder, J. ed, (1982), *National Industrial Strategies and the World Economy*, London: Croom Helm

Piore, M., & Sabel, C. (1984), *The Second Industrial Divide*, New York: Basic Books

Scharpf, F.W. (1983), 'Economic and Industrial Constraints of Full Employment Strategies: Sweden, Austria and West Germany 1945–1973' in J. Goldthorpe, *Order and Conflict in Contemporary Capitalism*, Oxford: Oxford University Press

Schott, K. and K. Pick (1984), 'The Effect of Price and Non-Price Factors on U.K. Export Performance and Import Penetration', University College London, Discussion Paper 84–01

Smith, K. (1984), *The British Economic Crisis*. Harmondsworth: Penguin

Thompson, G. (1986), *The Conservative's Economic Policy*. London: Croom Helm

Thompson, G. (1987), 'The American Industrial Policy Debate: Any Lessons for Britain?', *Economy and Society*, 16.1

Tomlinson, J. (1986), *Monetarism: Is There An Alternative?* Oxford: Blackwell

Tomlinson, J. (1987), 'The Decline of National Economic Management?', mimeo

Williams, K. *et al* (1983), *Why are the British Bad at Manufacturing?* London: Routledge and Kegan Paul

Zysman, J. (1977), *Political Strategies for Industrial Order* Berkeley: University of California Press

Zysman, J. (1983), *Governments, Markets and Growth*. Ithaca NY: Cornell University Press.

10 The Politics of Industrial Policy

Paul Hirst

Inevitably the discussion in this chapter is slanted in its concerns towards the United Kingdom and towards future policies. It is slanted towards the UK because that country is now one of the least successful of the major industrial nations on a number of crucial indicators, such as balance of trade in manufactured goods and stock of capital per worker. The UK has suffered most fully from 'deindustrialisation' and the policies of successive governments since the early 1970s have failed to reverse this trend. As Williams *et al*. point out in chapter 2 manufacturing output is no higher in 1987 than it was in 1979, and this despite five years of recovery from the 1982 trough of the depression. The UK is the prime case of industrial failure and of the need for policies to revitalise manufacturing performance. It is slanted toward the future because the Conservative government, now in its third term in office, has foresworn an active industrial policy or attempts to direct investment toward manufacturing. On the contrary, the Conservatives have dismantled exchange controls and liberated markets in equities and financial services, have entered into an exhaustive programme of privatisation of state-owned utilities and manufacturing enterprises, and have stressed the right of company managements to manage, weakening the power of organised labour by legislation. Conservative policy envisages economic recovery through the effects of freeing markets and promoting competition, the most efficient firms will survive and make such investments as market conditions dictate. Conservative policy for economic recovery places particular emphasis on small firms, on the marketed services and financial services sectors, and gives a low priority to the maintenance of output and employment in 'traditional' manufacturing industry. In these circumstances an active policy of industrial recovery and industrial investment will have to await a government with different economic policies and attitudes, whatever its party-political colour. British industrial policy is, therefore, inevitably a matter for the future.

Does Manufacturing Matter?

Our discussion so far contains an unargued presupposition, that the manufacturing sector and its continued healthy growth is a central part of a major developed capitalist economy. Is this so? Many economists, sociologists and politicians, by no means all of them Conservatives, dispute the centrality of manufacturing industry. Derogatory references to 'obsolete smokestack industries' or to 'metal-bashing' are a sign of the times, unthinkable in the 1950s and 1960s when public discussion was dominated by the logic of industrialism and sustained economic growth. We now know that there is no 'logic' of industrialism. Industrial development and change is a complex socio-political process with many non-economic conditions and constraints. Technologies do not impose inevitable decisions but a 'menu' of choices in an organisational and economic environment that influences what is chosen but does not rigidly determine it. We also know that sustained economic growth was not merely a matter of specific techniques of macro-economic management, but also of the institutions which underpinned a full-employment economy at both the national and international level. With the collapse of these regulatory mechanisms, forecasting techniques and demand management policies became insufficient.

That experience should teach us to question the inevitability of a 'logic of post-industrialism', the move to an economy based on information and services, in which the manufaturing sectors' contribution to GNP will decline steadily and manufacturing output will shift to less developed economies. In this vision marketed and financial services become the central sectors, both dependent on information processing, and less developed economies exchange goods with the information-rich developed economies that control forecasting, marketing, product development and new high-technology knowledge-based commodities. Information banks and science parks are the central sites of this new post-industrial economy, not factories or mines. Bell (1974) and Nora and Minc (1980) are among the more thoughtful examples of such a futurological vision.

Other more pragmatic views accept the decline in the saliency of manufacturing but envisage a 'high-tech–no-tech' mix of science-based industries, information-based financial services, and a service sector with mostly low-wage and low-skill jobs. The corresponding fact is a radical differentation of the labour force between a well-qualified and well-paid sector of executives, professionals and skilled specialists and the unqualified and unskilled mass, many of whom are unemployed or semi-employed. Social policy has to recognise this divide, to accept quite different forms and levels of provision of education, housing, health care, and so on: on the one hand, a market- and insurance-based high-quality system for the well-to-do; and on the other, a minimum safety net to prevent mass social disorder for the rest. This radical divide and the divisive social policies that follow from it are almost inevitable if one abandons the goal of a full-employment economy with high and uniform standards of services for all. It rests on pessimistic assumptions about employment patterns and economic growth that presuppose the decline of manufacturing employment no less certainly than the full 'logic of post-industrialiasm' argument that hopes for a high-technology and high-skill society at the favoured end of the international division of labour.

It is difficult to talk of manufacturing and its place in the economy without envisaging the network of social relations of which it forms a part. But it is essential to avoid the deterministic and schematic think- ing which either writes off the manufacturing sector or specifies its future composition in a necessitarian way. Manufacturing remains a major source of employment in all advanced industrial economies, representing some 44 per cent of the employed labour force in West Germany, 34 per cent in Japan, and 38 per cent in the UK (World Bank 1987). But the importance of the manufacturing sector is not confined to the numbers employed in it, it has a place in the structure of a major capitalist economy in an open international trading system that is difficult to supplant. Even if employment in manufacturing were to fall to a level comparable to that of employment in agriculture in the UK (3 per cent of the labour force) that would not necessarily alter its salience to the British economy. The crucial questions are industrial *output* and the balance of trade in manufactures. Falling employment in manufac- turing can have various causes, depression, deindustrialisation or growth in productivity. For deindustrialisation not to have deleterious consequences for the economy as a whole, other sectors must make a correspondingly larger contribution to employment, to GNP and to meeting the trade coming into the country with balancing exports of commodities and services. A major capitalist economy would, there- fore, have to be able to export primary products, financial or marketed services in sufficient quantity to balance industrial decline.

At one time some economists envisaged oil fulfilling this role in the UK. Indeed, Sir Alec Cairncross was sanguine enough to attribute deindustrialisation to the side-effects of becoming a major oil producer (Blackaby 1978). Few would do so today. As Williams *et al*. demonstrate in chapter 2, it is now less a question of 'when the oil runs out' than how to prevent a series of disastrous balance of trade deficits even at the peak of oil production. The balance of trade in manufactures is so unfavourable that it threatens the balance of payments, despite the contributions of oil production, tourism and financial services.

It is unlikely that the UK can do more than hold its present position as an international financial centre given stiff foreign competition, and it will be even more difficult to do so if the manufacturing and trading base of the economy is eroded. The growth of world trade in manufactures remains faster than that in services and the advanced industrial economies continue to trade overwhelmingly manufactured goods with one another. This pattern is likely to continue for the reason, demonstrated by Williams *et al.* in Chapter 2 that a very large part of the marketed services sector is not internationally tradable. Such services are most efficiently provided locally and the rate of growth of marketed services in particular national economies is closely linked to the rate of growth in national income. Manufacturing is still a crucial component in sustaining high rates of growth in GDP.

Manufacturing failure thus exposes a major capitalist economy, like that of the UK, heavily dependent on imports, to a serious balance of payments constraint. The unfavourable balance of trade in manufactures drives the balance of payments into a chronic tendency towards deficit. The readily available policies of national economic management, in the absence of a determined drive towards industrial renewal, are the driving-up of interest rates to attract foreign lenders, and consequent policies of 'sound finance' to maintain the value of the currency and keep inflation low. Economic management is dictated by the needs of a foreign-orientated *rentier* economy. The failure of manufacturing then creates conditions inimical to manufacturing investment and to growth in demand for national manufacturers' goods: higher than average interest rates, an overvalued currency, a restrictive policy on public expenditure. The result is an economy in which borrowing for manufacturing investment costs more than in the more successful competitor countries, and in which firms will only invest to sustain a given market share or in low-risk projects. Manufacturing failure is then self-reproducing and if there are no other sectors that can plausibly counteract the effects on the balance of payments the decline in manufacturing constrains the performance of the whole economy.

As the contribution of oil to the UK's balance of trade trails off in the 1990s and the UK becomes a major oil importer once again so the problem moves into a new dimension. It is then no longer a matter of containing manufacturing import penetration at current levels or of maintaining the UK's current share of world trade in manufactures but of increasing exports to pay for oil. The relative decline of the British economy will have to be reversed, a tough prospect in an economy in which many manufacturing sectors have been in a condition of absolute decline, of steady contraction in employment *and* output.

Conditions an Industrial Policy Must Meet

To show the structural importance of the manufacturing sector in the British economy and to demonstrate the macro-economic necessity for its revitalisation and expansion is not to demonstrate the need for an industrial policy. It might be argued that the constraints are macro-economic and need, therefore, be addressed only by appropriate macro-economic policies. If the sources of manufacturing failure are underinvestment due to the high cost of borrowing and a lack of business confidence in the prospects of growth in domestic markets then the answers are policies to reduce interest rates and increase domestic demand, assuming foreign willingness to support the resulting short-run balance of payments deficit in the interests of growth in international trade. But high interest rates are as much a consequence as a cause of manufacturing failure. Deindustrialisation is not a simple function of relative underinvestment due to macro-economic constraints. In the two areas of most dramatic import penetration in the UK, motor cars and consumer electronics, non-price factors, such as quality of the product and after-sales service, delivery times and marketing strategy, have been crucial, and in the specific case of video-cassette recorders (VCRs) there was no British competitor but a very large British market with strong demand. An *industrial* policy is needed because British industry has failed in product development, production organisation, marketing and export strategy in sector after sector, a degree of failure that indicates industry will not simply recover by itself in the right economic climate. An industrial *policy* is needed because it is clear that British industrial management is primarily responsible for these failures in decision-making and that, without an external stimulus and assistance from appropriate public bodies, firms will respond with caution born of failure, a response that locks them into a risk-averse defence of given market shares. Industrial decision-making has to be a central public policy concern, not merely aggregate levels of demand or investment.

Any strategy of industrial development must, therefore, pursue micro- and macro-economic policy objectives as a co-ordinated package. Such a strategy implies distinct but co-ordinated mechanisms of regulation at both levels. An industrial policy cannot by itself substitute for an appropriate macro-economic regime, one cannot hope to unlock national constraints by a strategy of 'picking winners' which then transform their own national and export markets. A successful industrial policy implies raising the level of investment as a component of national income *vis-à-vis* consumption; limited localised investments in safe 'winners' simply do not address the scale of the problem. To do this implies policy initiatives only central governments can provide: creating tax incentives to invest in manufacturing, controls on the export of capital, and attempts to lower interest rates and/or to create 'privileged' sources of industrial investment finance at low rates of interest underwritten by the state or by a levy on the financial sector. An industrial policy also implies continuity in macro-economic policy, ensuring that public agencies and companies follow through policies until completion of the investment cycle. It also implies control of incomes of workers in firms undertaking major investments or supplying them so that earnings do not outstrip productivity at industry level, and it implies policies for retraining workers to prevent skill shortages in the areas covered by new investment.

An industrial policy therefore implies the stabilisation not only of particular industrial sectors but also as far as possible, the whole national economy on a course of planned growth. This is useless if the resulting investments result overwhelmingly in products that are substandard on many of the significant parameters of international competition in manufacturing. The difficulty here is straightforward: what products to make, how to make them, how to sell them, and how to keep customers who have bought them happy. These questions are difficult to answer in a period of rapidly changing technologies, fragmented national markets and uncertain prospects for international trade. If the state has a large part in creating a macro-economic environment conducive to manufacturing investment through central government policies it is not true that central government should have an equally large part in directing and determining investments themselves. The aggregate level of investment is irrelevant, except to the scale of the disaster, if decision-making at firm and industry level leads to a failure to utilise it effectively. Here any advocate of an British industrial strategy has to face two very sobering facts. First, that British central government is ill-adapted to industry-level investment planning, having a record of bad investment decisions for (example, the decision in the early 1970s to extend basic blast furnace capacity as a result of very optimistic assumptions about the demand for steel based on equally optimistic estimates of economic growth — on which see Williams *et al.* 1983). Second, state-sponsored British management at firm level has an equally disastrous track record of investment decisions (for example, the BL management's decision to create a highly automated and dedicated production line for Metros at Longbridge based on output levels never justified by markets — on which see Williams *et al.* 1987). Neither civil servants nor state-sponsored managers have records that would justify giving them direction of an investment-led industrial policy.

This indicates the danger of any strategy that relies on high-quality decision-making and concentrates investment funds on a limited number of major projects. There can be little doubt that trying to create the British equivalent of the Japanese Ministry of International Trade and Industry (MITI) and set it the task of 'picking winners' would lead to a balance sheet in which costly failures outweighed successes. For example, Smith (1984) correctly demonstrates the catastrophic failure of the UK to make adequate provision for private research and development, and also the diversion of central government research and development effort toward defence and nuclear energy. He then rather paradoxically advocates a British MITI and assigns the task to the state. This is not to say that central government should abdicate concern for British involvement in research and development policy or leave investment wholly to private firms.

Central government should create funds to sponsor research on product development, industrial organisation and market trends and agencies to promote the diffusion of such research among investment and production decision-makers. It should, by specifically targeted education and training policies, try to raise the quality of British industrial management personnel. It should create a system of tax allowances that favours *successful* manufacturing investment. This would be difficult to achieve. Such allowances would have to be discretionary, to be applied for and to be carefully investigated. Firms genuinely expanding investment in manufacturing and boosting output would need to be distinguished from those diversifying through investment in other sectors, or growing through acquisitions and mergers or importing most of their designs and more than a certain portion of components. An additional depreciation allowance for successful firms would be a possibility. Central government should encourage co-operation between firms in pooling knowledge and solving problems. It should dramatically increase the level of public support for exporters both through consular services in target countries and export guarantees.

The state is also a major orchestrator of infrastructure investment both through direct central government initiatives and controls on local authorities' spending on capital projects. As Tomlinson shows in Chapter 9, Table 9.4, the share of investment in government expenditure on goods and services fell from a high of 21.6 per cent in 1973 to a low of 6.7 per cent in 1982, and in 1985 it stood at 8.8 per cent. Infrastructure investment as a share of GNP is much lower in the UK than other advanced industrial economies. Investment in buildings and general construction has substantial effects on employment because it is relatively labour-intensive and it relies on manufactured inputs sourced mainly from British suppliers. At the low-technology end it would benefit the building materials industry, whilst at the high-technology end it could create the market base for major initiatives with strong export potential, for example, laying networks of fibre optic cable in major population centres. The central and local governments still have the personnel and the project management capacities to put higher levels of infrastructure investment into effect — indeed, many local authority planning and architect's departments are now distinctly underemployed.

One should eschew the idea that an 'industrial policy' must inevitably concentrate on certain types of industry or certain sizes of firm. The danger of having a small number of 'target' industries is that it will usually rest on what are little better than hunches about trends in industrial structure. These hunches then have an unhappy tendency of being self-fulfilling, as Piore and Sabel (1984) and Sabel and Zeitlin (1985) show in the case of the state-sponsored rationalisation of the complex and diffuse specialist textile industry of the Lyons area in France during the 1960s. On the contrary, the aim of an industrial policy should be to encourage investment across as many sectors and types of firm as possible. 'Traditional' industries, such as textiles and clothing, can be encouraged and developed in advanced industrial economies as Zeitlin and Totterdill show in Chapter 6. They are not to be automatically written off as inevitably falling to competition from NICs, since non-price competition is crucial in fashion-dominated markets and labour costs are a small percentage of price for all but rock-bottom-priced clothes in discount stores. Investment choices need to depend on knowledgeable and unprejudiced assessment of specific projects and therefore on a less than rigid conception of which industries represent the future.

This sort of 'intimate knowledge' is seldom found among central government officials or financial analysts in banks or merchant banks. Once one passes below the level of the large firm, other networks of assessment become essential. At every level assessment needs to bring to bear knowledge that is not found on a balance sheet or summed up in standard forms of financial assessment and reporting. Knowledge of industrial processes, markets, even the character of key personnel is often qualitative and hard to acquire unless one is 'in' the industry and often also in the locality where the firm operates. For medium-sized and small firms, this qualitative knowledge becomes crucial.

If investment is to be directed toward the small and medium-sized firm then good local networks in which local councillors and local government officials, local economic policy specialists, business people and representatives of labour can fruitfully interact are crucial. The aim of preserving a local industrial base and building upon existing firms is perhaps superficially less ambitious than the British government's regional development policies of the 1950s and 1960s. It implies complex forms of co-operation between the public and private sectors in which local government may provide specialist services to firms, like market forecasting, exhibition centres, promotion and public relations, shared capital facilities (like CAD equipment) or hire services for equipment. It may involve direct investment and/or encouraging co-operative development agencies, or perhaps building networks of mutual assistance like credit unions. It implies local economy research by the councils' economic development agencies and education and training for business people and workers in market opportunities and relevant skills.

As several contributors to this volume point out, following Piore and Sabel (1984) and Sabel and Zeitlin (1985), the aim of such local strategies ought to be to sustain or re-create thriving ' regional economies' based on manufacturing districts with networks of small and medium firms in a mutually supporting but diversified cluster of industrial lines. Good examples are the pattern of co-operation among companies in the Lyons area in France, discussed by Lorenz in Chapter 4, and the complex patterns of division of labour and mutual support between firms in the 'Third Italy' discussed, in the case of textiles, by Zeitlin and Totterdill in Chapter 6, and in the case of furniture, by Best in Chapter 7. Without such districts and without the patterns of mutual support and collaboration between firms and between public and private agencies they stimulate, the life of the small firm in manufacturing is often nasty and brutish, and frequently short. An economic policy that stresses dog eat dog competition, that views the firm as an isolated entity, that limits relations between companies to market transactions, simply ignores the necessities of industrial ecology and the benefits to efficiency and survival of mutual support. The isolated firm cannot draw on the same resources as the firm in a competitive but also collaborative industrial district.

If local authorities want to support the remnants of such districts and build them up, they need to shed a good deal of economic dogma, both Conservative- and Labour-inspired. Local authority interventions should put industrial success first, and other policy goals should be adapted to whatever interventions that primary goal requires. Worker-orientated strategies directing public investment to preserve employment in existing unionised firms are a local version of the 'rescue' workers' co-operatives of the 1974–9 Labour government inspired by Tony Benn. As such they tend to start from and to reinforce failure.

An 'industrial policy' should, therefore, be viewed as broadly and undogmatically as possible. It should not be counterposed to policies of macro-economic management. It should take account of what government agencies are likely to be able to deliver. It should not automatically prioritise one model of the firm, or one model of production organisation. This would all be no more than rather negative and worthy advice, the pronouncements of an economic Polonius, if one did not specify the kind of mechanisms whereby investment decisions at the appropriate level are made with sufficient knowledge to succeed and the kind of mechanisms whereby macro-economic policies receive a sufficient degree of assent to persist for the time required by a strategy of industrial recovery. We have already given one example at the regional and local authority level: the building of robust networks of consultation and collaboration between the different parties in-

volved, combining public services for firms, knowledge-sharing between firms and with public officials, and so on.

Political Obstacles to Industrial Recovery

As will be clear from contributions above, some local authorities have
begun to see the need for such networks and it is here that the most
immediate and likely success for industrial policy in the UK may come
about. Paradoxically, the Conservatives' severe limits on local authority
spending and their abolition of the major metropolitan councils may
favour effective change. Local councils have to collaborate with one
another on a regional basis and they have to try to use information and
consultation to promote economic development because they are unable to throw lots of money at the problem. The other scenario, had
Labour come to power in the early 1980s, is of large authorities controlled by the Labour left, heavily dependent on the unions and
possessing large investment funds. Such authorities would probably
have taken existing firms into quasi-public ownership without changing patterns of work except to impose union norms and without
changing the relation between firms and between them and public
bodies implied above. This would have resulted in investment to
preserve existing patterns rather than to build networks which promote
change.

It is when we turn from the few hopeful local straws in the wind to
the national level that things become bleaker. It must be emphasised
that this is not merely because a Conservative government is in power.
Mrs Thatcher's government has used the existing system of party
government decisively; she has certainly enhanced its tendencies toward
authoritarianism and centralism but she did not invent them. The
problems with devising consistent and effective economic policies and
pursuing them over a long period are primarily *political* in the UK.
Effective economic change implies a change in political style and the
building of new practices to supplant existing forms of government.

British politicians have always reached, in trying to solve economic
problems, for a neutral 'economic technique'. They have perceived
economic policies as devices of management to be imposed by political
authority, rather than as strategies dependent for their success on
being embedded in society and on receiving vital non-economic inputs
such as consent and willing collaboration. This is no less true of
Labour, right and left, than it is of Mrs Thatcher. George Brown's
National Plan implied building up viable apparatuses of corporatist
consultation, generating objectives from them and getting the partners
to such agreements to stick with them. Labour simply lacked the
political commitment to build these apparatuses and the 'Plan' re-

mained a (disastrous) public relations exercise. The post-1973 Alternative Economic Strategy simply ignored the need to control incomes effectively in an investment led boom; it refused to tackle the (political) problem of an incomes policy. It sought one-sided 'planning agreements' to be imposed on firms by state power under threat of nationalisation.

A viable industrial policy needs to be followed across the lifetime of at least three Parliaments. It implies a consistent government policy and one committed to stabilising and securing investments against economic fluctuations. This involves public spending to support firms even if there have to be austerity measures elsewhere, otherwise the investment cycle will slow or fail to mature. That demands a widespread public recognition that industrial recovery is the first priority in public policy. The UK's economic policies have fluctuated wildly since 1945 and, even since 1979, policy has been inconsistent in the extreme. Mrs Thatcher's consistency is more a matter of style than policy: monetarism was quietly abandoned and the PSBR reduced to one indicator among others; twice, in 1983 and 1987, mini-booms have been fuelled by loosening credit in a kind of electoral Keynesianism. In giving prominence to public expenditure cuts and making the Treasury dominant, Mrs Thatcher has simply confirmed in an extreme form a long-running British economic vice. Public sector capital spending has been used as a mechanism of economic adjustment since 1945, only the aims of such adjustment have changed. The Treasury has shown a consistent failure to assess the investment needs of the public sector on their own time-scales. It represents a triumph of fiscal over operational management, the dominance of the short term. If the Conservatives' privatisation schemes have any merit it is to free large parts of British industry from short-term constraints in investment planning. An industrial policy implies a longer view and the institutions and practices of insulation and stabilisation to support it. This implies both radical attitudinal and institutional change in British government.

Such stability and consistency in policy imply broad political and social consensus. The aim of industrial policy must command strong support in Parliament and across more than one political party; the specifics of industrial policy need to be both formulated and willingly implemented by the major interests involved. Such consensus politics implies 'corporatism', both formal and informal, as a major mechanism of policy-making. Policy must emerge from broadly representative bodies in which the major interests consult and bargain. Consultation and bargaining among major interests rather than party manifestos as a source of policy is commonplace among the successful industrial countries, particularly small and open ones like Sweden or Austria. It is derided in the UK by left and right.

Such processes have never been a strong part of the British political culture. The UK is a very centralised state and institutions of corporatist consultation, let alone effective policy-making, have been weak and half-hearted measures. They are weaker than ever now. Mrs Thatcher has drawn the lesson that centralised state authority and the private management of the firm are the only two possible centres of effective decision-making, and that consultation and corporatism produce evasion and fudge. In a sense she is quite right — the Labour governments of 1964–70 and 1974–79 lacked the capacity to insist that corporatist bargains stick. They allowed the TUC to play at bargains it could not deliver. Labour lacked the capacity to get effective national economic policy agreements out the of unions and paid the price. Corporatist consultation and bargaining is not a substitute for political authority, it is another form of authority and it depends on the capacity of participating interests to have such internal authority that they can deliver on the bargains they strike.

Why this pecularity of the British? Because both the major British political parties have been committed to the idea of authoritative party government. A majority in Parliament gives a party legislative sovereignty and sole control of the executive, so that it is in theory able to impose its lawful will. This conception of Parliament as a source of desired social and political changes imposed by a centralised and highly concentrated administrative machine has been shared from left to right. Mrs Thatcher is often condemned for exploiting the British constitution's tendencies toward elective despotism, but what else did Hartley Shawcross wish to do in 1945 when he is alleged to have said 'we are the masters now' and what was Tony Benn's vision of Parliament and government but a machine for a Labour Party of the left to drive through social change without check? This conception of party government and centralism has been reinforced by the absence of regional governments and the limited autonomy of local government.

Organised labour and business are both weakly federated and are dominated by short-term considerations in assessing policy. Neither the CBI nor the TUC has had the capacity to impose policy on member firms or unions. For the unions, autonomy to bargain at whatever level they find appropriate, from industry to shop, and with a minimum of legal constraints, has been regarded as 'normal' industrial relations. Incomes policies have always been regarded as short-term emergency makeshifts, to be 'followed' by a return to normal collective bargaining. Incomes policies imply a centralisation of wage determination that undermines the primary aims of the unions. Unions are, therefore, willing in effect to forgo certain economic policy objectives highly advantageous to workers as a whole to preserve forms of bargaining which reinforce existing union structures. Industrialists are no more able to combine and agree on policy for the long term. British managements have operated in a financial system geared to the short term, to international financial services and to consumer credit. External finance for firms has been costly and risky in the form of share issues or costly and short-term in the form of bank loans. The structure of governance of companies and the openess of the stock exchange to merger activity has meant that since the 1960s at least managers have had to adopt risk-adverse strategies that produce acceptable annual statements and dividend levels that appease existing shareholders. Managements operate in a competitive and defensive culture where dialogue between firms at industry level or making commitments to collective action at national level seems remote.

Changes since 1979 have further reinforced this defensive and short-term outlook on industrialists. The liberalisation of financial markets has exposed British industry to extreme short-term fluctuations. The abolition of exchange controls has led to a heavy flow of investment abroad. The internationalisation of financial markets and the floating of exchange rates has led to rapid and violent currency fluctuations. The internationalisation of equity markets and the liberalisation of the City has further exposed firms to mergers and takeovers. The City takes an ever shorter-term view of performance; from a (short-term) annual accounting and reporting cycle analysts are turning to quarterly estimates of performance. All this short-term fluctuation might be tolerable were it not for extreme uncertainty about long-term prospects for the world economy.

Most major British firms are multi-industry multi-product groups of companies controlled by a non-specialist senior management with predominantly financial skills. Industry-specific knowledge and commitment to manufacturing are, therefore, generally to be found much lower down the managerial chain and with less impact on policy. Moreover, the current climate is in many ways inimical to growth through in-house investment. A slowly growing world 'real' economy means large funds of internationalised 'loose' credit. This can be used to borrow to acquire other firms rather than to invest internally. A takeover is an 'investment' to the acquiring firm just as surely as buying a second hand machine-tool rather than a new one is. Such extentions to capacity by acquisition are a sound strategy for risk-averse firms in uncertain times. What can be considered from a financial reporting perspective as 'investment' by the firm has no impact on the total level of investment in the national economy, however.

The internationalisation of financial markets favours this trend but the outlook is not a new one in British management. It stems back at least to the merger boom of the 1960s. Most British 'industrial' firms actually have managements which share the financial services sectors' outlook. Many major 'industrial' companies are as much financial companies and siphon off internally generated funds for lucrative non-industrial and foreign investments. Many major groups' senior managements adopt a 'portfolio' attitude to the specific manufacturing subsidiaries and industrial operations under their control.

The upshot is a management structurally and attitudinally led away from seeking or believing in major extensions to capacity in pursuit of a larger share of home or export markets. A management culture which is dominated by defensive attitudes, by competition to the exclusion of co-operation and by the obsession with short-term results is hardly likely to give rise to a long-term plan for industrial recovery. The unions, marginalised and driven into pragmatism as they are by Conservative legislation and mass unemployment, will still present great resistance to an incomes policy.

It appears, then, that the sort of collaborative political culture necessary to sustain a long-term policy of industrial recovery simply is not there. Management, the unions and political parties operate an exclusionist and anti-dialogue policy and are reinforced in it by the economic, industrial and political environment: it just does not pay to talk or to offer concessions. Mrs Thatcher is often challenged as an anti-consensus politician, indifferent to dialogue and compromise. But those who criticise her are often no better in practice. The Labour Party is almost uniformly opposed to dialogue and compromise with other parties — to propose *talking* to the Alliance about policy without specific commitments is still considered daring. Dr David Owen, the former leader of the SDP, has shown himself as intransigent and as much an anti-consensus politician as Mrs Thatcher, particularly on the issue of merger talks with the partner party in the Alliance, the Liberals. Weakly solidaristic and poorly organised interests, and antagonistic political parties, appear to offer little hope of a programme of building a stable policy consensus through collaboration and bargaining.

The opposition parties are divided but the dispute is mainly over slogans and symbols. In fact the three opposition parties have a great deal in common, chief among which is a paralysing failure to offer a credible policy alternative to Conservatism. None of the three parties has a viable strategy for industrial recovery and none has a policy of macro-economic management that is more than a liberalised version of current Conservative practice. Even if Labour were able to form a majority government in 1991 it is unlikely on present form to have either the policies, the political will or the support of sufficient social interests to tackle the UK's economic problems. A weak government buffeted by the City and the international financial markets and forced to make policy concession after policy concession to the facts of economic crisis is the most likely prospect. A coalition government is likely to be just as weak and aimless, if not more so, if it fails to prepare its ground carefully in advance.

Prospects for a Coalition for Recovery

The usual assumption in politics is that coalition governments make for compromise and therefore for moderation. It is difficult to get across that a coalition representing a large majority of the electorate (say 60 per cent) is in a position to do things that no one party dare do for fear of loss of electoral advantage. It is difficult to get across that taking policy from inter-party bargaining rather than from manifestos does not mean a bland compromise, if the bargaining is open and exploratory. To give an example: no one party dare tackle the structure of subsidies that has created a 'middle-class' welfare state: mortgage interest relief, occupational pensions, company cars, and so on. To bite into this mass of tax concessions has a dual advantage — it creates funds for investment and it trims the consumption of the affluent, who have the greatest propensity to consume foreign manufactures. Most politicians, many Conservatives included, regard this massive but ramshackle structure of subsidies, which grew without plan, as an unjustified and economically damaging liability, but no party would dare make it the central plank of an election manifesto. A coalition, taking its policy from post-electoral bargaining, could afford to do so, but only if it were part of a determined effort to remedy industrial decline.

Without a strong coalition government it will be impossible to engineer a significant shift in national income from consumption to investment. Without a government that seems set to last and that can claim overwhelming electoral legitimacy it will be difficult to bargain with powerful vested interests in the City and with management. Without such a government, broadly based and yet determined to take radical measures, it will be difficult to reasssure the major money and equity markets.

But such a coalition cannot be created unless it is prepared. The realities of policy requirements for industrial recovery and the realities of electoral politics, which make a single party's victory against the Conservatives extremely difficult, both push in this direction. Party histories and politicians' attitudes stand in the way of recognising that and of preparing not only for coalition government, but preparing to operate in a different way in government. Parties adapt slowly because they can withstand prolonged periods of defeat and absence from office. Labour faced thirteen years in the wilderness between 1951 and 1964, the Liberals several decades before the Lib-Lab pact of 1974. This encourages politicians to cling to party symbols and styles; even if policies change it is within a definite and exclusive party identity. Such resistance to political evolution is acceptable if the economic and social framework is relatively stable, if one's opponents pursue policies not completely outside one's own political spectrum. That is no longer the case and the prolonged failure of Labour, in particular, to adapt to confront and compete with a governing party whose acts violate its basic expectations and principles shows how internally paralysed it has become. Labour has been slow enough to adapt and if it takes much longer it may find itself marginalised as a party of resistance to the dominant socio-economic trends, a party of permanent opposition in permanent decline like the French Communist Party.

Labour has been trapped without a viable economic programme since the failure of its attempts in the 1960s at economic modernisation. Labour embraced the liberal collectivism of Keynes and Beveridge in the post-war period and found its most eloquent ideologist in Crosland (1956), who mapped a programme for social democracy in a full-employment economy with a strong and successful privately owned and managed industrial sector. Crosland's egalitarian and redistributionist vision supposed that private industry could be left to manage itself, given a stable macro-economic climate provided by Keynesian regulation. The failure of British manufacturing industry gradually undermined Labour's position and by the early 1970s had fatally weakened it. Wilson entered power in 1964 with the promise of economic modernisation and industrial rejuvenation. The UK's failure was then perceived as relatively slower growth than our EEC neighbours and a steadily decreasing percentage share of world trade. The Wilson programme failed, on the one hand, because of lack of political will. Labour failed to harness effectively both unions and industrialists and allowed economic policy to be reduced to plans, discussion forums and White Papers. It failed, on the other hand, because manufacturing's problems were hidden in the assumption that large-scale mass production in expanding markets would continue for the foreseeable future. Where the Wilson government was relatively decisive was in promoting through the Industrial Reorganisation Corporation (IRC) mergers that, it hoped, would create corporate 'national champions'. These 'champions' proved incapable of resisting import penetration when markets for manufactures became internationalised among the major industrial nations during the late 1960s and 1970s.

Britain's failure then shifted from relative failure in world markets to a loss of domestic market share, with the corresponding phenomenon of 'deindustrialisation'. British industries were now faced with the threat of absolute decline with the corresponding losses in productive capacity and employment. Industries like motorcycle or TV tube manufacture were virtually eliminated. Labour's response to this new crisis was broken-backed. The Labour right and centre had at best a pragmatic commitment to muddling through, rescuing firms with handouts or taking them into public ownership. The Labour left had a comprehensive programme, the 'Alternative Economic Strategy' (AES). The first version of this was unveiled in Labour's 1973 programme. This viewed industrial policy simply as a matter of coercing a higher level of investment from recalcitrant firms through selective nationalisations and planning agreements. It envisaged radically strengthening the powers of organised labour whilst doing almost nothing about the problems of design, production organisation and marketing which were at the root of the UK's industrial failure. It strengthened worker's capacities to resist technical change and had no effective proposals to control incomes in what it hoped would be a full-employment economy. In fact the Labour right and centre were able to impose a set of incomes policies as a simple condition of economic survival, but had no industrial policy. Resisted by the left and by rank-and-file union pressure, Labour's incomes policy collapsed in the 1978–9 'Winter of Discontent', proving conclusively that Labour, despite its link with the unions, could not enforce effective corporatist policies of income regulation. That had been Labour's prime claim to office in 1974, following the 1972 miners' strike, and given its eventual bankruptcy there is little to surprise us in Labour's defeat in May 1979.

Labour has lacked credible policies of macro-economic regulation and industrial recovery since then. It has found no substitute for Crosland's social democracy. A regime of protectionist and autarchic state socialism, in which producers are given captive markets and consumers are stuck with whatever they make, which is what the most radical variants of the AES amounted to, is quite simply electorally impossible. Policies still have to pass a plebiscite and even many of the poorest of the plebs would reject that. A Labour Party of the left of the type the Bennites tried to create in the early 1980s was an electoral liability and despite the failure of such policies to capture the whole party, they contributed significantly to Labour's crushing 1983 defeat. The Labour Party is trapped looking for a strategy that is both electable and radical. It is trapped because it looks for a substitute to Crosland in the form of a package of policies for a party government. But the UK's economic problems are beyond the solutions conventional party governments can offer. Shifting national income from consumption to investment, cutting the tax handouts and subsidies to the affluent, are policies no one party can carry out alone. Building viable networks of corporatist consultation and bargaining, taking policy from such processes, are moves no one party has the authority to introduce. Effective institutions of regulation for an industrial policy have to be built by collaborative work, they cannot be promulgated in the Queen's Speech.

An industrial policy will take time. Time to work out its composition and to build networks to sustain it. Time for the investment cycles to bear fruit. Time is one thing a conventional political party government does not have. An industrial policy withdraws substantial resources for investment and such a programme takes many years to come off. In the meantime, a government must maintain and service the ancillary programmes of retraining, income support for the unemployed, and so on. The four-year effective life of a single party government is too short to offer convincing proof of recovery, indeed at this period the policy may have barely begun to show benefits while the macro-economic policy constraints necessary to support it are still in full operation. Reduction in tax subsidies, control of consumer credit, income controls, will all involve constraints on consumers and the household sector. Any government will then face an impossible electoral test if it has not sought to build up policies through bargaining and educate the public in doing so. A single party government using conventional administrative means will simply lack the capacity to create this legitimacy.

No policy can hope to be robust enough to survive which is brainstormed by party advisers, filtered though party politicians and then handed over to civil servants. It will be picked to pieces and implemented at best in part. British central government lacks the means for high-quality decision-making in complex areas such as industrial policy. It can make a mess of manpower planning, the supply of schoolteachers or predicting traffic flows. The construction of corporatist institutions, collaborative networks, and 'public/private' agencies outside conventional administration bypasses the need to try to turn ministries into things they can never be.

British party politicians find it difficult to see that a party may be most effective as a organ of social leadership rather than as an exclusively party government relying on state authority to get things done. Social leadership means both mobilising the capacities of civil society and drawing from it the commitments and resources necessary to solve problems of social organisation. If the Labour Party were to see itself in this role as an orchestrator of wider processes of collaboration and bargaining, if it dared to experiment with developing policy through discussion with other parties and organised interests, then it might find the strategy it is looking for.

References

Bell, D. (1974), *The Coming of Post Industrial Society*, London: Heinemann

Blackaby, F., ed. (1978), *De-Industrialisation*, London: Heinemann.

Crosland, C.A.R. (1956), *The Future of Socialism*, London: Cape

Nora, S. and A. Minc (1980), *The Computerisation of Society*, Cambridge, MA: MIT Press.

Piore, M. and C. Sabel (1984), *The Second Industrial Divide: Possibilities for Prosperity*, New York: Basic Books

Sabel, C. and J. Zeitlin (1985), 'Historical Alternatives to Mass Production', *Past and Present*, 108.

Smith, K. (1984), *The British Economic Crisis*, Harmondsworth: Penguin

Williams, K., J. Williams and D. Thomas (1983), *Why Are the British Bad at Manufacturing?*, London: Routledge and Kegan Paul.

Williams, K., J. Williams and C. Haslam (1987), *The Breakdown of Austin Rover*, Leamington Spa: Berg

World Bank (1987), *World Development Report*, Oxford: Oxford University Press

Index

aerospace, industry, 85, 103, 125, 225
Aikin Seiki, 175
Alliance (Liberals, Social Democrats, UK), 86, 282
Alternative Economic Strategy, 279, 284–5
Amalgamated Engineering Union (AEU), 145
Ancona, 22
Aoki, Masahiko, 39
Arna, F.K., 185
ASDA, 161
Asian Traders' Association (UK), 237
Association of Scientific, Technical and Managerial Staff (ASTMS), 146
Atkinson, J., 98
Austin-Rover, 7, 78, 80–1, 82, 86, 88, 89–90, 127, 227, 274
Austria, 14, 18, 44, 52, 57, 248, 279
Automated Sewing System project (Japan), 175–6
Automated Small-Batch Production Committee (ASP, UK), 116–17

Baden-Württemberg, 22, 24, 27, 29, 39, 46, 48, 50
Bagnasco, Arnaldo, 24, 25
Baird Group, 172
Bank of France, 257
banking and finance, 1, 7, 17, 22, 23, 26, 29, 45, 54–5, 60–9, 78–9, 85, 180, 195, 210–11, 214–21, 253–4, 257, 258–9, 269, 272–4, 276, 280–2
Barcelona, 23
Bari, 22
Barre, Raymond, 257
Basic Research in Industrial Technologies For Europe (BRITE), 175
Bassett's, 180
Belgium, 196
Benetton, 27, 163–4, 165
Benn, Tony, 277, 280, 284
Benton, Lauren, 27
Berufbildungsgesetz, 135
Beveridge, William, 284
Birmingham, 17, 48, 125, 181, 224, 227
Black and Decker, 38
Black Country, 224, 239
Boch, Rudolf, 48

Boeing Company, 211
Bologna, 22, 115
Borken, 24, 44
Bosch, 37, 39, 53
Boston, 23
Boston Consulting Group, 254
Bradshaw, J., 91
Brazil, 52
Bremen, 40, 42
British Home Stores, 163, 167
British Leyland, see Austin-Rover
British Steel Corporation (BSC), 79–80
Brown, George, 278
Brusco, Sebastiano, 23, 97, 111, 112, 211
BSR, 227
Burton Group, 163
Butcher Report, 148–9

C & A, 163, 165
Cadbury, 227
CAD/CAM Scheme (UK), 179
Cairncross, Sir Alec, 271
Cambridge Econometrics, 233
Canavese, 22
Capecchii Vittorio, 48
Carpi, 22, 25, 181
Centro Informaziano Tessile Emilia Romagna (CITER), 181
chemical industry, 36, 50, 259
'CLOFT' scheme, 178
clothing industry, 7–8, 9, 22, 27, 44, 155–90, 216, 229, 234, 241, 276
coal industry, 79, 224, 257, 259, 285
Christopherson, Susan, 62
Clothing and Allied Products Industry Training Board (UK), 234
Clothing Industry Scheme 1975 (UK), 178
Coats-Viyella, 157
Comau, 112
Como, 22
competition
    international, 1–8, 11, 40, 71–7, 86–93, 155–61, 167–8, 191–211, 225–6, 249–50, 253, 257, 261, 284
    non-price, 5, 72, 167, 191–4, 196, 199, 201, 210, 252, 264, 273, 276
    price, 7–8, 111, 155, 157–61, 177, 196, 199, 201, 202, 210, 256, 264

289

computer industry, 22, 36–7, 39, 60 *n*9, 259
computerisation
  Computer-Aided Design (CAD), 9, 99, 110, 112, 117, 138, 143–7, 150, 170–2, 173, 228, 235, 237, 243, 244, 276
  Computer-Aided Manufacturing (CAM), 99, 110, 112, 117, 138, 143, 146, 150, 172–3
  Computer-Integrated Manufacturing (CIM), 96
  Electronic Point of Sale (EPOS) Systems, 165
  Flexible Manufacturing Systems (FMS), 28, 96–7, 99, 101–19
  management information and production control, 173
  Numerically-Controlled Machine Tools (NC, CNC), 23, 25, 83, 99, 101, 112, 113, 123–30, 140–3, 146, 150, 172–3, 174–5, 228, 243
  robots, 99, 229, 236, 239, 241
Confederation of British Industry (CBI), 281
Conference of Socialist Planners, 230
Conran, Terence, 163, 204
Conservative Party (UK), 11, 13, 71, 74, 116, 184, 223, 229, 230, 262, 269, 277, 27, 279, 282, 283
Consorzi Fidi, 210–11
Consorzio Poggibonsi, 209–10
Contarino, Michael, 25, 50
Cook, Nathaniel, 103
co-operation, *see* flexibility, flexible, specialisation
Co-operative Regional Industrial Laboratories (USA), 44, 67 *n*95
Copenhagen, 22
corporatism, 14, 20–1, 255–6, 257, 260, 264–5, 279–81, 285
Council of State Planning Agencies (USA), 41–2
Courtaulds, 157, 161, 178
Coventry, 125, 127, 181, 224, 239
Cowley, 81, 88
Credit Co-operative of Modena (Italy), 210–11
Crosland, Anthony, 284, 285

Dagenham, 88, 90
Daly, A., 83
Day, Graham, 81
Debenhams, 163
de-industrialisation, 1–8, 71–7, 134, 191, 224–8, 269, 271, 273
Delta, 277
Demag, 39
Denmark
  industrial districts in, 18, 22, 46, 48–9
  labour market policy in, 43, 55
  labour relations in, 48–9, 50, 57

  local government in, 45
Department of Trade and Industry (DTI, UK), 72, 86, 116, 178–9, 183, 184
Design Advisory Service Funded Consultancy Scheme (UK), 179
Detroit, 42
developing countries/NIC's, 7–8, 40–1, 72, 155, 156, 161, 167–8, 177, 194, 204, 250, 276
Dortmund, 42
Dunlop, 227

East Elbia, 46
Eastern Europe, 89, 204
East London Leather Clothing Association, 186 *n*15
East Midlands, 155
Edge, Geoff, 230
Edwardes, Sir Michael, 80–1
electrical and electronics industries, 13, 27, 39, 47, 63 *n*52, 84, 87–90, 93, 227, 239, 273, 284
Emilia-Romagna, 5, 48, 111–15, 210
employers' associations, 20, 26, 49–50, 55–8, 182, 186, *n*15, 235, 236–7, 240, 255–6
engineering industry, 22–3, 39, 44, 50, 56, 83, 100, 103–15, 122–32, 133, 212, 224–5, 226, 235, 239, 245, 255
Engineering Industry Training Board (UK), 136
entertainment industry, 23, 47, 217, 235
European Economic Community (EEC), 4, 12–13, 81, 92, 167, 175, 178, 237, 284

Fall River, MA, 44
Falster, 46
Federation of Clothing Designers and Executives (UK), 234
Ferranti, 87
Fiat, 112
Finniston Report, 134
flexibility
  automation and, 5, 80, 95–121, 140–3, 165, 170–6, 176–7
  markets and, 1, 11, 18, 32, 98, 122–3, 156, 162–7, 201
  skills and, 2, 5, 7, 32–4, 37, 49–51, 95–101, 142–3, 171, 172, 174–6, 181, 219
  within mass production, 11, 37, 65, *n*73, 95–101, 102, 106–7, 108–9, 113, 115, 118–19
Flexible Manufacturing Systems (FMS), *see* computerisation
flexible specialisation
  and economic success, 3, 6, 14, 19–20, 201, 205
  co-operation and competition in, 2–3, 17, 25–31, 33–40, 45–52, 123, 131, 164–7, 177, 192, 201–2, 212–13, 219

defined, 2–3, 17–22, 53, 96, 98–101, 115, 122–3, 156, 213
macro-economic regulation and, 2, 19–20
role of trust in, 46–52, 96, 99, 127–9, 182–3
sub-contracting and, 6–8, 18–19, 26–31, 34–5, 53, 111–12, 113, 122–32, 164–7
technology and, 2, 17, 25, 33, 96–101, 102, 103, 105–6, 112, 118–19, 156, 170–6
see also: flexibility, industrial districts, multinational corporations
Flextronics, 37
Florence, 22
Ford, Henry, 219
Ford Motor Co., 20, 36, 80, 88, 89
Fordism, *see* mass production
foundry industry, 226–7, 237, 238–9, 240
France
compared with UK, 4, 20, 78, 85, 122–32, 139–40, 157, 257, 261, 265
decentralisation in, 43, 45
economic performance in, 4
industrial districts in, 18, 23, 46, 123
industrial policy in, 85, 86, 253, 256–60, 276
macro-economic policy in, 256–60
organisation of production in, 122–32, 139–41
Franchi, Maura, 115
Freemont, C.A., 50–1
French Communist Party, 284
Friedman, David, 29
furniture industry, 8, 9, 14, 22, 23, 46, 192, 196–211, 217

GEC, 79, 81, 82, 227
General Agreement on Tariffs and Trade (GATT), 4, 12
General Electric, 38
General Motors, 20, 38, 50–1, 80, 88
Genoa, 22
Gerber Garment Technology, 172–3
Gerhard Schüler, 205
Gildermeister, 39
GKN, 227
Glasgow, 181
Glynwed, 227
Granoretter, Mark S., 64 *n*67
Great Universal Stores, 163
Greater London Council (GLC), 9–10, 186, *n*14, 214, 217, 220
Greater London Enterprise Board (GLEB), 9–10, 180, 186 *n*13, 214–21, 246

Habitat-Mothercare, 163, 204
Hackney, 181, 185–6 *n*12
Hackney Fashion Centre, 182, 186 *n*14
Halewood, 88
Hall, Peter A., 258

Hamburg, 40, 42
Handsworth Technical College, 234
Handy, C., 84
Haringey, 186 *n*12
Harris Queensway, 203–4
Hayes, Robert H., 79
Hayward, Jack, 259
Herrigel, Gary, 28, 29
Hildebrandt, Eckart, 25, 50
Honda, 89–90
Hong Kong, 161, 167, 194
House of Lords Select Committee on Overseas Trade, 75
Hull Kristensen, Peer, 24, 50
Hyman, Richard, 98, 100

IKEA, 202–4
Ikeda, Masayoshi, 38
Ilongot Headhunters, 68–9 *n*110
IMI, 227
incomes policy, 13, 20, 252–3, 258, 264–6, 274, 279, 282, 285
industrial districts
banking in, 17, 26, 29, 56, 210–11
collective services in, 17, 26, 36, 48, 56, 168, 209–11, 277
conditions for the emergence of, 45–52, 182–3, 202, 217, 277
co-operation between firms in, 3, 6–8, 17, 25–9, 201–2, 209–11, 277
historical examples of, 17, 46, 48
labour relations in, 24–5, 48–51
regulation in, 17, 24–5, 48–51, 111, 123, 182
revival of, 2–3, 22–9, 45–52
see also: flexible specialisation
industrial policy, 8–15, 250–2
and high tech, 42–3
and macro-economic management, 11–13, 224, 229, 248–68, 271–4
'intimate knowledge' and, 183, 276
limitations of, 85–6
necessity of, 12–13, 177, 194–5, 250–2, 270–4
political preconditions for, 13–15, 278–86
'public sphere' and, 7, 14, 131, 182–3, 220, 240–1, 276–7, 286
sector strategy and, 193–6, 214–21, 223–4, 230–46
see also: local government, planning
Industrial Reorganisation Corporation (IRC, UK), 84, 214, 229, 284
Industrial Training Act 1964 (UK), 136
Ingersoll Engineers, 117
injection moulding industry, 23
Institute for Employment Research, 233
Institute of Manpower Studies, 98
investment
and consumption, 13–15, 263–4, 273, 285
financial calculations and, 79–80, 102, 108, 110, 116–7, 143–4, 146

level of, 5–6, 13, 59, 155, 157, 177, 214–15, 225, 238, 249, 256, 258, 262–3, 265, 273–4, 285
public, 253, 258–60, 263, 274–5, 279
utilisation of, 5–6, 85–6
Italy
compared with UK, 5, 8, 14, 157
economic performance in, 1, 4, 168, 205–6, 249
exports, 167–8, 196, 199
industrial districts in, 2–3, 22–8, 46, 168, 182, 205–11
labour relations in, 24–6, 50, 111–16
macro-economic policy in, 20
organisation of production in, 5, 13, 97, 111–16, 157, 168–70, 185 *n*3, 205–11
productive decentralisation in, 97–8, 111, 167–8, 205–9
International Monetary Fund (IMF), 54, 75
Islington, 186 *n*12

Japan
compared with UK, 4, 5, 81, 83, 84, 89, 118, 142–3, 271
economic performance in, 1, 4, 83
exports, 87–93
industrial districts in, 2–3, 18, 23, 24
industrial policy in, 85, 86, 192–4
labour relations in, 107–10, 123
organisation of production in, 5, 31, 37–9, 51, 83, 98, 107–10, 142, 211
training in, 109
Job Training Partnership Act (USA), 43
Johanson, Jan, 63
Johnson and Johnson, 36
Jutland, 22, 24, 46

Katz, Harry C., 50
Keynes, John Maynard, 91, 284
Keynesianism, 1, 11–12, 14, 18, 42, 53, 54–5, 56, 58, 59 *n*3, 84, 248, 250, 251, 252, 279, 284
kibbutzim, 55, 70 *n*128
Kochan, Thomas, 50
Kodak, 38
Koike, K., 107
Krupp, 39
Kurt Salmon Associates, 166

Labour Party (UK), 11, 41, 79, 84, 85, 86, 116, 179, 229, 230, 246, 277, 278, 280, 282, 283–6
Lambeth, 181, 186 *n*12
Lancashire, 17, 155, 180
Landsorganisationen i Sverige (LO), 264
Leeds, 179, 181
Liberal Party (UK), 283
Little Neddies, *see* National Economic Development Council
Littlewoods, 163, 167
Livingstone, Ken, 246

Local Action for Textiles and Clothing (LATC), 10, 183–4, 235
local government
collective services, 10, 22, 26, 36, 44–5, 179, 181–3, 211, 217, 219, 220, 221, 235, 276–7
direct investment, 9, 179, 180, 185–6 *n*12, 195, 214–21, 231–3, 237–9, 240, 241–3, 246
industrial policy, 8–10, 21, 40–5, 179–84, 192, 194–6, 214–21, 223–47, 277–8
see also: industrial districts
Locke, Richard M., 50
Loi Deferre, 43
London, 8–10, 42, 43, 155, 176–7, 179, 185 *n*4, 196–200, 210, 214–21
London Clothing Association, 186 *n*15
Longbridge, 80, 81, 88, 274
Los Angeles, 23, 27, 28, 47
Lucas, 227
Lyons, 7–8, 17, 23, 25, 122–32, 276, 278

Machine Action Project, 67 *n*95
machine-tool industry, 5, 22, 28, 29, 39, 50, 103, 205, 225, 227–8, 237, 241, 242–3, 245
macro-economic regulation, 1, 2, 9, 11–12, 14–15, 18, 20, 53–9, 73–7, 84–5, 131, 248–68, 270, 271–4, 279, 284–6
Madrid, 27
Magna, 36
Marches, 46
Manpower Services Commission (MSC), 152, 183, 184, 234
markets
de-regulation of, 191, 269
fragmentation of, 1, 3, 6, 11, 18, 35, 80–1, 82, 122, 156, 162–4, 274
Marks and Spencer, 157, 163, 164, 165, 166, 167, 173, 177
Marseilles, 42
Marshall, Alfred, 17
Massachusetts, 27, 42, 43
mass production, 1–3, 11, 18, 20, 30, 31–2, 37, 40–1, 49, 51, 52, 53, 59 *n*3, 96–101, 102, 106–7, 112, 116–17, 122, 133–4, 135, 156–61, 202–5, 213, 219, 226
see also: Flexible specialisation, flexibility, multinational corporations, neo-Fordism
Mattson, Lars, 31
Meager, N., 98, 134–5
Meidner Report, 254
MFI, 203–4
Milan, 22
Ministry of Finance (France), 257
Ministry of Industry (Sweden), 254
Ministry of International Trade and Industry (MITI, Japan), 26, 108, 175, 192–4, 220, 274–5
Mississippi, 41–2

Mitsubishi, 176
Mitterand, Francois, 257–60
Modena, 22, 23, 26, 27, 112–15, 210
Molins Co., 116
monetarism, 84–5, 191–2, 260, 279
Montedison, 36
Morgan, J., 91
Morgan, J.P., 219
motor-cycle industry, 5, 81, 284
motor vehicle industry, 13, 20, 30, 31, 37,
   38, 39, 40, 42, 50–1, 78, 79, 80–1, 87–90,
   93, 98, 101, 103, 107, 112, 113, 119 n2,
   155, 225, 226–7, 235–7, 240, 241, 244,
   245, 259, 273
Motor Industry Local Authority Network
   (MILAN), 10, 236
Multi-Fibre Arrangement (MFA), 167, 178
multinational corporations,
   decentralisation of, 2–3, 18–19, 31–40, 64
   n65
Murray, Robin, 100, 102
Mürzuschlag, 51
Myers, A., 83–4

Nathan, B & I, 196
nationalisation/nationalised industry,
   79–81, 229, 236, 258–60, 274
National Confederation of Artisans (Italy),
   210–11
National Economic Development
   Council/Office (NEDC/NEDO, UK) 84–5,
   107, 178, 214, 224, 229
National Enterprise Board (UK), 214, 224,
   229
National Governors' Association (USA),
   41–2
National Investment Bank (UK), 85
National Plan (UK), 214, 224–5, 278–9
National Union of Tailors and
   Government Workers, 234
Needle Trades Action Project, 67 n95
neo-Fordism, 40, 46, 95–7, 99–100, 112
   see also: mass production, flexibility,
   Flexible specialisation
Netherlands, 196
New, C.C., 83–4
New United Motors Company, 50–1
New York City, 23
Newcastle, 181
Next, 163, 164, 167
Nicholson, Bryan, 152
Nishiguchi, Toshiro, 38
Nissan, 89
Nottingham, 161, 179, 181
Nottingham City Council, 10
numerical control (NC, CNC), *see*
   computerisation

oil industry, 73–5, 250, 254, 257, 265, 271
Olivetti, 64–5 n72
Organization for Economic Co-operation

and Development (OECD), 250, 252
Ouchi, William G., 30
outworking, 161–2, 176–7, 185 n4, 234
Owen, Dr David, 282
Oyonnax, 23

Paine, Thomas, 28
Penrose, Edith, 212–13, 218
Perrow, Charles, 57
Philippines, 68–9 n110, 161
Phillips, 89
Piore, Michael J., 96, 115, 122, 276
planning, 10–11, 14, 192–4, 214–21, 223–4,
   246, 253, 256, 257, 285
Plessey Engineering, 127
Poggenpohl, 204–5
Portugal, 167
Prais, S.J., 84
Prato, 22, 25, 27, 49, 53
Principles, 163, 167
printing industry, 23, 217
Private Industry Councils (USA), 43
protectionism, 2, 4, 12–13, 71, 86–93, 155,
   250, 253
Proudhon, Pierre-Joseph, 28

Reagan, Ronald, 251
Reggio Emilia, 22
Regional Aid and National Selective
   Assistance Schemes (UK), 178–9
Reiser, Vittorio, 115
Reiss, 165
Renault, 31
retailing and distribution, 100, 156–7, 161,
   162–7, 176–7, 184–5 n2, 185 n6, 202–4
Rhone-Alpes, 126
Richard Shops, 163
Richardson, G., 211–12
Rolls Royce, 125
Rosenheim Woodworking School, 205
Rousseau, Jean-Jacques, 29
Route 128, 23, 27, 42, 47

Saglio, Jean, 23, 25
St Etienne, 17
Sakaki, 23, 25, 29
Sassuolo, 22
Say's Law, 57
Scott, Allan, 28
Sector Working Parties, *see* National
   Economic Development Council
service sector, 1, 21, 144–5, 229, 269, 271–2
Seste San Giovanni, 51
Shawcross, Hartley, 280
Sheffield, 17, 48
shipbuilding industry, 250, 254
shoe industry, 22, 27
Sicily, 46
Silicon Valley, 23, 27, 42, 47
Singapore, 52, 194
Singh, Ajit, 74

skills, *see*: flexibility, training
Smaland, 22
small firms, *see* industrial districts
Smith, Keith, 274–5
Social Democratic Party (SAP, Sweden), 253, 254–5
Social Democratic Party (SDP, UK), 282
socialism, 1, 11, 93
Socialist Party (France), 257–60
Solingen, 17, 48
Sony, 90
South East Economic Development Strategy (SEEDS), 10
South Korea, 52, 161, 194
Spain, 167, 196
Springfield, MA., 44
steel industry, 39, 44, 79–80, 224, 226, 229, 238, 239, 250, 254, 257, 274
Stinchcombe, Arthur L., 69 *n*121
Stonehill, 196
Storper, Michael, 28, 68 *n*102
Sienunu, John H., 42
sub-contracting, 2–3, 6–8, 18–19, 26–31, 34–5, 37–40, 44–5, 53, 64 *n*67, 97–8, 111–12, 114, 122–32, 150, 164–7, 176–7, 181, 201–4, 211, 227–8, 236, 243
    see also: flexible specialisation, industrial districts, multinational corporations
Sweden, 14, 15, 22, 202
    compared with UK, 260–1, 264–5
    corporatism in, 255–6, 257, 264–5, 279
    economic performance in, 253–6
    industrial policy in, 253–6, 257
    labour market policy in, 20, 55, 252–3
    macro-economic policy in, 248, 252–6, 257, 260, 261, 264–5
    training, 20, 255
Swedish Investment Bank, 253

Taiwan, 52, 161, 194
Takamiya, M., 141
Taylorism, *see* mass production
Technology,
    see: computerisation, flexibility, flexible specialisation, mass production, industrial policy
Technical and Supervisory Staff Union (TASS), 145
Tesco, 161
textile industry, 14, 17, 22, 24, 44, 46, 48, 49, 50, 53, 130–1, 155, 179, 183–4, 235, 250, 257, 276, 277
Textile/Clothing Technology Corporation (TC), 2, 175
Thatcher, Margaret, 43, 74, 76, 85, 86, 99, 251, 262, 278, 280, 282
'Third Italy', 22, 23, 24, 25, 39, 46, 217, 277
Thorn-EMI, 89
Tolliday, Steven, 98
Tootal, 157
Tower Hamlets, 181, 186 *n*12, 186 *n*15

Tower Hamlets Clothing Centre, 182
Toyota, 38, 50–1, 130, 175–6
trade unions, 19–20, 21, 25, 32, 33, 36, 44, 48–51, 55–8, 86, 95–6, 104–6, 110, 113, 117, 145, 175, 179, 180, 181, 182–3, 216, 234–5, 236–7, 240, 253, 255–6, 257, 260, 264–6, 277, 278, 280–1, 284, 285
Trades Union Congress (TUC, UK), 280
training, 6–8, 17, 26, 42–4, 49, 50–1, 55–8, 84, 85, 95–6, 117–18, 131, 133–54, 176, 177, 181–2, 205, 216, 228, 232, 236, 238, 240, 255, 274, 275, 277, 286
Treasury (UK), 261, 279
Treaty of Rome, 92
Triglia, Carlo, 25, 27, 49
Trumpf, 54
trust relationships between firms, *see* flexible specialisation
Tube Investments, 227
Turin, 22, 47
Tuscany, 47

unemployment, 20, 24, 41, 49, 56, 71, 75–6, 91, 92–3, 123, 133, 142, 161, 177, 179, 191, 194, 196, 227–8, 250, 254, 255, 258, 261, 264, 270–1, 286
United Automobile Workers Union (USA), 50
United Electrical Workers (USA), 105
United Kingdom
    balance of payments/trade, 73–7, 85, 86–93, 265, 269, 271–2, 273
    de-industrialisation of, 1–8, 71–7, 134, 191, 224–8, 269, 271, 273, 284
    economic performance in, 1, 3–4, 6, 71–7, 84–5, 134–5, 260–2
    financial sector in, 7, 77–9, 85, 186, 214–21, 260–2, 265, 280–2, 283
    import penetration in, 72–4, 86–93, 155–61, 167–8, 177, 185 *n*7, 198–9, 205, 256, 284
    industrial policy in, 8–15, 84–93, 97, 155, 177–84, 214–21, 223–47, 251, 261–6, 269–86
    labour relations in, 5, 77–8, 80–1, 82, 117–18, 260, 264–5, 280–1, 285
    local government in, 9–10, 43, 45, 179–84, 214–21, 223–47, 277–8, 280
    macro-economic policy in, 1, 12–15, 20, 73–7, 84–93, 224, 229, 248, 257, 260–6, 272–4, 279, 284–6
    management problems in, 5–7, 80–6, 273, 284
    multinationals in, 84, 89–90, 228, 236–7, 241–3
    organisation of production in, 5–8, 77–84, 116–19, 139–52, 156–62
    regional policy in, 41, 178–9, 229, 249, 276
    training in, 6–7, 84–5, 117–18, 133–54, 228, 232, 236, 238, 240

weakness of corporatism in, 14, 264–5, 279–81
Urban Partnership/Programme Schemes (UK), 183, 230
USA
   compared with UK, 1, 20, 84, 118, 152, 156–7
   de-industrialisation of, 1, 191
   economic performance in, 1
   industrial districts in, 2–3, 18, 22, 24
   labour relations in, 50–1, 103–7
   macro-economic policy in, 1, 248, 249, 251
   organisation of production in, 31, 37–8, 50–1, 102, 103–7, 156–7
   training in, 152

Vauxhall, *see* General Motors

Weiner, Martin, 77
Weinstock, Lord, 79
welfare state/welfare policies, 9, 18, 19, 20, 40, 41, 45, 52–9, 75, 92, 249, 258, 270–1, 283, 285, 286
West Germany
   compared with UK, 4, 6–7, 14, 78, 83, 132–54, 271
   economic performance in, 1, 4
   exports, 87–93, 196, 205
   industrial districts in, 2–3, 18, 22, 46
   local government in, 44, 45

   macro-economic policy in, 20
   organisation of production in, 31, 39–40, 53, 83, 139–43
   training in, 6–7, 20, 26, 43, 57, 135–8, 205
West Midlands, 7, 122–32, 155, 161, 179, 223–47
West Midlands Auto Industry Trade Union Forum, 237
West Midlands Clothing Resource Centre Ltd, 231, 235
West Midlands Co-operative Finance Ltd, 231
West Midlands County Council (WMCC), 10, 127, 180, 223–47
West Midlands Enterprise Board (WMEB), 10, 223–4, 230–42
West Midlands Low Pay Unit, 234
West Midlands Technology Transfer Ltd, 231, 234, 243–5
West Midlands (Tyseley) Training Ltd, 231
Wiener-Neustadt, 51
Williamson, Oliver, 29–30
Wilson, Harold, 214, 284
Wolfsburg, 90
Woolworth, 163, 165

Xerox, 3

Yorkshire, 155, 180